Mama Rose's Turn

MAMA ROSE'S TURN

*The True Story of America's Most
Notorious Stage Mother*

Carolyn Quinn

UNIVERSITY PRESS OF MISSISSIPPI ❧ JACKSON

www.upress.state.ms.us

Designed by Peter D. Halverson

The University Press of Mississippi is a member of the Association
of American University Presses.

Photograph on page ii: Rose Hovick and her daughter Rose Louise (ca. 1917). Courtesy of
the Gypsy Rose Lee Archive.

First printing 2013

∞

Library of Congress Cataloging-in-Publication Data

Quinn, Carolyn.
Mama Rose's turn : the true story of America's most notorious stage mother /
Carolyn Quinn.
p. cm.
Includes index.
ISBN 978-1-61703-853-2 (hardback) — ISBN 978-1-61703-854-9 (ebook) 1. Lee, Gypsy
Rose, 1914–1970. 2. Entertainers—United States—Biography. 3. Hovick, Rose Thompson,
1892–1954. 4. Havoc, June. 5. Mothers of entertainers—United States—Biography.
6. Mothers and daughters—United States. 7. Actors—United States—Biography. I. Title.
PN2287.L29Q56 2013
792.02'8092—dc23
[B]   2013015120

British Library Cataloging-in-Publication Data available

This book is dedicated to the memory of another indomitable woman, the grandmother who had such a fabulous hand in raising me, Margaret Ford Yoerger. Regally impervious to peer pressure, she was a lifelong member of a temperance organization, a blackout warden for the Civilian Defense Patrol in World War II, and one major-league terrific lady.

CONTENTS

AUTHOR'S NOTE

THIS BOOK UNOFFICIALLY BEGAN ON BROADWAY OUTSIDE THE WINTER Garden Theater on the day after Christmas in 1974. I had just been lucky enough to see my very first Broadway show. It was as fabulous an introduction to the theater as any child interested in Broadway could ever have hoped for: a last-minute opportunity to see musical comedy genius Angela Lansbury star as Gypsy Rose Lee's mother, Rose, in the first revival of *Gypsy*, one week before it closed.

I had been playing Lansbury's London cast recording of the musical for three months straight. I adored the story of stage mother Rose described in the liner notes, the story of a woman determined to make her two daughters into stars, taking them on a performance tour of the country on the old vaudeville circuits in the 1920s and in burlesque in the 1930s. The day before we saw the show, Mom and Dad had surprised me with *Gypsy* tickets under our Christmas tree.

After the phenomenal show was over I spotted a sign outside the theater and noticed, for the first time, that the full name of the show was *Gypsy: A Musical Fable*. "Fable? Why are they calling that show a fable?" I asked my parents, who were both teachers. "Gypsy and June and their mother were real people, not a fairy tale."

"Sure, but they probably had to change a lot of the story," my mother said. "It was probably a lot different than the version we just saw on the stage. Can you imagine? A mother who let her child work for Minsky's Burlesque, of all places? They probably had to clean the whole tale up for public consumption."

I was thirteen, and it was the first I'd heard of such a thing. "Can they really do that, though—change the details in a show that's about actual people?"

"Oh, sure! They do that with movies and shows all the time," my dad said.

Well, this didn't seem right to me, but I was hooked. I had gone to see what I thought would be a true Broadway story and found a mystery. What,

I wondered, might have really happened to Rose, June, and Gypsy that was different from the story I had just seen?

Back home in the suburbs of Jersey, I examined the *Gypsy* record album and saw that the show was "suggested by the memoirs of Gypsy Rose Lee." Not "based on" but "suggested by." What an intriguing way to put it! I tried, over that Christmas vacation, to find Gypsy's book at the public library, but the book wasn't in the collection. Neither did the old Scotch Plains Bookstore stock it. It was out of print. I attempted to locate a copy for months, even asking friends' parents if they had the memoir on their bookshelves, but no one did.

Finally I called my grandmother. I knew if anybody could find that book for me—out of print or not—she would. And she did. Mom Mom was delighted to be the one to locate it, and I was thrilled to receive it.

Gypsy Rose Lee's book was filled with period details about vaudeville and burlesque that I loved, but it was also different in a lot of ways from the show. Then I heard that her sister, June Havoc, had also written a book about her life. It was called *Early Havoc*. My grandmother managed to find a copy of that for me, too.

Then the mystery deepened. Gypsy's book had been a predominantly fun, light-hearted, pleasant read; June's contained one melodramatic, somber vignette after another, reading like a minor horror story. The books were not just light-years but entire galaxies apart. It was hard to believe these two authors had ever been anywhere near one another, let alone that they were sisters describing the same childhood events experienced with the same mother. Due to the differences in the two books, I discovered that many people believed June's darker one contained "the real truth," while Gypsy's was "the whitewashed version," but I had a hunch this evaluation wasn't exactly accurate.

Fast-forward six years. I was in college when June's second book, *More Havoc*, was released, and remembering my childhood interest in Gypsy Rose Lee en famille, I bought the book the moment I saw it was for sale. There was another surprise. This memoir was, for the most part, lighter in tone and different in style from her previous one. Not only did her first book differ from Gypsy's and from the musical, it also differed from her second book. The changes in June's account didn't make sense at first, but then I realized the books might have been written with the assistance of two different ghostwriters or editors.

Fast-forward again, this time to about the year 2000. When I first obtained Internet access and found I could search for anything I liked by simply pressing a few buttons, I remembered all of the stories about Rose Thompson Hovick. She was one of the first people I ever "Googled." That's when I discovered that Rose was believed to have committed a murder. I tried to find information about this speculation for days, but I located absolutely nothing. I even wrote an email to the police in charge of the locality in question. My mail came bouncing back bearing the message, "Sender doesn't like recipient." It struck me as highly unusual that, if this woman had indeed ever been a murder suspect, no information about the crime seemed to be readily available. I was also taken aback that the cops were "saluting" people who asked about an alleged murder with such a response.

Fast-forward one more time. When I heard Patti LuPone was going to play Rose in a revival of *Gypsy* in New York City, I tried running "Rose Hovick" through Google again. This time I got an intriguing surprise: a link indicating Gypsy Rose Lee's archive of personal papers, including letters from her mother, Rose, were housed in a library right in my new hometown. Letters from Rose! So many people had so much to say about Rose, I thought, and there were so many versions of who she was, but she had never written her own book or had a chance to speak for herself. Would her letters provide this posthumous theatrical legend with that chance? I had to find out.

I went to the library that very night, but I was told the special collections room was already closed for the evening. On the next available Saturday, I went back. I had initially planned to read Rose's letters for about an hour, then go to a movie. I went in for an hour and stayed for five, until the library closed.

The story I found in the correspondence files of Rose, Gypsy, June, Rose's mother, Anna, and sister Belle went in a whole different direction from everything that had been previously published, and this account was better than any movie. I concentrated on what I found, not on various versions or legends claimed about Rose after the fact. The letters mostly dated from 1938. Gypsy's book ended in 1937. I could usually only hit the library on Saturdays, so during the week I proceeded to fact check everything I thought I knew about the whole group, using historical societies and records, and going through newspaper archives available online.

My hunch about June's take on the family's story turned out to be right on target. Gypsy Rose Lee, and not June, had been the more truthful of the two sisters. In her autobiography, Gypsy tweaked her version of events a bit to make them funnier, but for the most part she had stuck to the facts, and her stories checked out. June, I realized with a growing sense of mild horror, had published one fabrication after another about her family. She even made up wild stories about how her grandfather and her Aunt Mina, Rose's other sister, had died. June claimed she was four years old when she sat by Mina's deathbed as her aunt died of an overdose of multicolored pills. Actually, Mina died in California of a contagious illness in 1923 when June, age nine, was appearing in vaudeville in Corning, New York. I have the vaudeville ads and the family telegram about Mina's death—and multicolored pills weren't on the market in 1923.

Perhaps the biggest surprise of all came on the day I found, in the library archive, a letter dated November 2, 1944, from a very upset Rose Thompson Hovick to her daughters, who had been telling the media that they'd never been to school a day in their lives. Actually, Rose had hired a tutor for them, and Gypsy had attended "schools." In Rose's bold handwriting, the letter read: "Some day the public will know the truth about your mother and they I am sure will not condemn me like you girls have done. I have a clear conscience thank God for the way I raised you both and I know I did all I could for you with what I had to do with." I realized, with a start, that Rose had foreseen the day when someone would think to take a closer look at her story and set the record straight—and that the someone in question was me. It gave me chills.

The results of all I've found are in the book you are about to read.

One final note: Rose Thompson Hovick's story predominantly concerns seven women—her grandmother, mother, sisters, and daughters—who altogether had at least twenty-one surnames, possibly more. These include maiden names, married names, and her two daughters' stage names. Three women usually went by their middle names rather than their given names. One, Belle, used her first name in letters to family and a nickname with everyone else, and she and Rose seemed to have fun swapping their middle names. This exchange may not have been much of an issue in the grand scheme of their lives, but it made for a researcher's nightmare. Don't believe me? Try finding one of these individuals in the census. I have made an attempt to explain the various "name games" that went on with the whole group but for the sake of consistency, I tried throughout to use just one name per person—with the exception of Rose's daughter, Gypsy Rose Lee. She was born Rose Louise Hovick, but she was called Louise as a child and Gypsy Rose Lee later. I refer to her variously as Louise and as Gypsy, as the most well-known part of the family legend is that Louise morphed into Gypsy.

Anyway, *here's Rose!*

Mama Rose's Turn

THE ALL-AMERICAN ORIGINAL

THE CREATIVE TEAM THAT HAD ASSEMBLED, ALONG WITH THE OPENING night audience, at New York City's Broadway Theater on the pleasant spring evening of May 21, 1959, had every reason to be nervous. The team was about to make theatrical history, but certainly didn't know so yet—where Broadway shows are concerned, nothing is ever certain anyway. All the creative team knew at the moment was that this show, *Gypsy*—so loosely based on the memoirs of performer Gypsy Rose Lee that it had to be billed as *Gypsy, A Musical Fable*—had been beleaguered with difficulties during its creation, rehearsals, and out-of-town run in Philadelphia.

Gypsy Rose Lee, born Rose Louise Hovick and initially called Louise, had written a book that was a charming, and sometimes uproarious, account of her Jazz Age childhood, spent traveling with a vaudeville act starring her adorable and talented little sister, child star Baby June. The act was managed by the girls' enchanting, slightly amoral rogue of a mother, Rose Thompson Hovick. When June reaches her teens, she outgrows her babyish act, realizes that vaudeville is dying out as a form of entertainment, and elopes with one of the act's backup dancers. Mother Rose creates a new act around Louise, no easy feat. By her own admission, Louise has no talent whatsoever. The duo prevails. Burlesque is the only form of vaudeville still thriving. But in the late 1920s, burlesque was about the lowest entertainment genre of all. Louise enters the burlesque scene out of financial necessity, and she becomes Gypsy Rose Lee, comic burlesque star extraordinaire. June, on her own, eventually becomes the respected actress June Havoc. The book ends as Gypsy Rose Lee temporarily leaves the stage, the only home she's ever known, to appear in Hollywood movies.

Readers were delighted with the story, and the book landed on the *New York Times* bestseller list. Arthur Laurents, a gifted playwright and the author of theatrical hits *Home of the Brave*, *The Time of the Cuckoo*, and most recently the book of the musical *West Side Story*, was hired by producer David Merrick to write the script. Initially Laurents was not intrigued by Lee's story. Then he spoke with an acquaintance at a party.

The woman, dark-haired, funny Selma Lynch, had known the real Rose. She described Rose as charming and charismatic—and also a ball-buster. Laurents had found his main character: She would not be Gypsy Rose Lee, but her mother, Rose. He left out most of the real Rose's delicate charm and concentrated on creating, instead, a more dramatic character, an issue-laden human steamroller.

Tough Broadway belter Ethel Merman was signed to play Rose. Once Laurents knew the identity of the actress for whom he was writing the part, he shaped the character of his fictional Rose to match Merman's boisterous personality. Laurents developed a brilliant script about a take-no-prisoners stage mother. The focus of Lee's story was shifted from the two performing children and onto Rose, presenting her as their driven, fame-obsessed mother from hell, who wanted her children to become stars to fulfill her own exaggerated need for recognition. Laurents came up with script conflicts that add considerable spice to the storyline. In the show's penultimate mea culpa number, "Rose's Turn," Rose breaks down and admits that she chased after onstage fame for her children simply because she had been starved for attention. Then she declares she's going to start dreaming for herself, yelling—five times in a row with increasing volume—"For me!" This number ends with Rose letting out a long, frustrated scream. The relatively relaxing read Gypsy Rose Lee had put together was transformed into a riveting, but almost entirely fictionalized, script.

Jule Styne, who had composed the hit shows *Gentlemen Prefer Blondes*, *Bells are Ringing*, and *High Button Shoes*, was hired to write the music for *Gypsy*. Styne had once played the piano in a burlesque orchestra, so he knew exactly how to capture the percussive flavor of the joyfully brash burlesque numbers and incorporate it into his score. Styne was also a compulsive gambler. He owed so much money to his bookies that at one point Arthur Laurents was shocked to see enforcers chasing Styne down the street, threatening to break his legs. Styne outran them. His participation in the show was off to a flying start—literally.

A relatively new songwriter named Stephen Sondheim was brought on board to write the lyrics. He'd recently been the lyricist for another hit, *West Side Story*, and initially wanted to write both the music and lyrics for *Gypsy*, but both producer David Merrick and Ethel Merman wouldn't allow him to. Sondheim was too inexperienced to be trusted with both tasks. Sondheim was disappointed about having to work with a collaborator, yet he genially went along with the plan. Styne and Sondheim worked well together, coming up with so many song numbers that the show was judged too long.

Director/choreographer Jerome Robbins, on the other hand, did not work well with anybody. His disagreeable nature was notorious in the New York theatrical community. In one almost incredible incident, Jule Styne got fed up with Robbins for not authorizing the building of a platform he'd requested to raise the height of the orchestra members. The pit in the theater was so low that Styne's music could not be heard properly. Styne asked for this platform many times, but it never appeared. Styne himself was not exactly a model of restraint. He threatened to pick Robbins up and throw him into the orchestra pit, where no one would hear the choreographer's screams. It's a wonder the volatile Robbins survived directing *Gypsy* without getting himself murdered.

Then the real June, actress June Havoc, decided to create disruptions. She dodged Arthur Laurents and producer Leland Hayward when they asked her to sign a legal release so that they could use her name in the musical. She also threw a rather astonishing fit, directed at Arthur Laurents, for adapting Gypsy's "vulgar" memoir into a musical. Laurents stated that he found the book "touching," which set June off again. The encounter culminated with June's pronouncement that *she* was touching, not her sister. She ranted further that Gypsy was so cheap she "ate out of tin cans."

June made sure to check out the show during an out-of-town preview performance in Philadelphia. She walked out at intermission in outraged, white-faced—but almost certainly feigned—shock. June claimed to be "upset" that the story created by Laurents was *not* the story of her childhood at all. So much had been changed around for dramatic effect that about the only remaining truths were the names of the three main characters and the fact that June had once starred in vaudeville. The real story, she hotly proclaimed, had not been anything like what was taking place on that stage.

In actuality, June did not like the way she was being portrayed in the show: as a brat without talent. It did not bother June that her mother's life story was being distorted almost beyond all recognition, or that her sister was not exactly being shown in a true light, either. Gypsy Rose Lee had been born with abundant confidence, yet the character Laurents created for her in his script was that of an unsure shrinking violet. None of these distortions concerned June one whit. She was focused on the facts about her that had been altered. This fictionalized plotline would not make Baby June look as glorious as she remembered.

June, primed for warfare, contacted her attorney when she got home. Thus began what can only be described as a sabotage campaign against the show's plotline. June insisted that the entire list of changes that she wanted be made in the script. Some of them were justifiable; others were outrageous. Fortunately the producer, David Merrick, was a former attorney. He had no problem with the idea of a battle with June Havoc or anybody else. He had heard that Gypsy Rose Lee had another sister named Beth (actually a half-sister named Betty Hovick), who had once visited Gypsy in New York City in the 1930s. Betty was one of Gypsy's father's children by his second wife, Elizabeth, not one of her mother Rose's children (there had only been Gypsy and June), but recalling the half-sister gave the gleeful Merrick an idea. He reckoned that if there had been one additional sister, there could have been more. And if there had been more, they'd have been in the vaudeville act. Merrick suavely proceeded to change the name of June's character from "Baby June" to "Baby Claire."

June was infuriated, and rendered powerless, by this development. She had been raised to be a diva. She thrived on attention. The last thing she wanted was to get written out of the script completely, but that's what Merrick proposed to do. This tactic—plus the offer of a royalty percentage—silenced her.

June finally cut the crap, caved in, and signed the release. "Baby June" was reinstated as the name of her character. The title of the show was altered to appease her; it became *Gypsy: A Musical Fable*, the subtitle a subtle, usually overlooked signal to the world that this story was not exactly the full truth.

Ethel Merman had never suffered from stage fright in her life, and this opening night was no exception. She was the one island of calm among the creative team of stressed professionals, all hoping for a successful show while steeling themselves for a possible disaster. Gypsy Rose Lee noted in the appointment calendar that also did double-duty as her diary that she didn't know if they were "coming in as a hit."

Yet come in as a hit they did. The reviews were great, in large part because of the character Laurents had created for Rose. Walter Kerr called her "the mastodon of all stage mothers." The *Newark Star-Journal* pronounced her "a boiler room in full operation." Laurents's larger-than-life version of Rose became the stuff of legend from the moment she came up the aisle and barreled through the theater. She entered carrying a dog and a huge purse, wearing an absurdly big bow in her hair, interrupting Baby June and Baby Louise as they went into their song and dance routine. Rose called out stage directions to her eldest daughter, beginning with the now immortal line, "Sing out, Louise!"

The prestige of everyone involved was elevated, and *Gypsy* became a gloriously prestigious entry on its creators' resumes. Royalties from the show would largely support Gypsy Rose Lee for the rest of her life. June would make a bundle from it, too. Jule Styne's legs weren't broken by his bookies, and his rousing musical compositions have gone down in musical history as among the very best; in particular, no musical's overture has ever surpassed the one he created for *Gypsy*. No one ever failed to take Stephen Sondheim's work seriously again. The script by Arthur Laurents is still considered one of the best books of a musical ever written. As for Jerome Robbins, his choreography survived, replicated in later productions, and so did he.

Gypsy was revived on Broadway not just once, but, as of this writing, four additional times, with Angela Lansbury, Tyne Daly, Bernadette Peters, and Patti LuPone each getting their chance to shine as Mama Rose. All were nominated for the Tony Award, Broadway's ultimate acting honor. Three of them—Lansbury, Daly, and LuPone—won.

All but lost in the ongoing *Gypsy* hoopla that has thus far lasted for over half a century is the true story of Rose Thompson Hovick. She was a child born on the North Dakota prairie who grew up to become the mother of two entrancing daughters she took on the road and put on the stage. She beat the odds, making both of the girls into theatrical successes, in and of itself a stunning accomplishment. But who *was* Rose, this woman whose justifiable belief in her children's talent first carried them from Seattle, Washington, to Hollywood, California, then onward to the stages of the old vaudeville touring circuits? What was the real story behind this little trio? How did Rose get from the prairie to vaudeville, burlesque, and immortalization on Broadway?

Her story, it turned out, did not begin anywhere near a theater. It began two generations before Rose was born, when her forbears, astute hospitality workers, arrived in America.

PART ONE

HOSPITALITY

When friends are at your hearthside met,
Sweet courtesy has done its most
If you have made each guest forget
That he himself is not the host.

—THOMAS ALDRICH BAILEY

CHAPTER 1

RESILIENCE ON THE PRAIRIE

THEY WERE A FAMILY BLESSED WITH AN INHERENTLY WELCOMING SPIRIT. Their bright outlook was their main talent, and they would take it all the way to the bank in America. The family members that reached American shores first set a precedent that would influence Rose's mother, Anna Egle Thompson, Rose herself, and, much later, Rose's daughters: Rose Louise, the one who would become Gypsy Rose Lee, and Ellen June, who would be known to the world as June Havoc.

Carl and Rosina Egle already had a bit of a nest egg when they arrived in America on July 7, 1851, with their six children. Born into a Catholic family, Carl had been a farmer in Baden-Wurttemberg, Germany, which had been beset by a local radicalist revolution in 1848–49, which spread like a contagion when the populace received news of another revolution taking place nearby in France. The populace demanded government and social reforms, demands that led to armed military insurrections. Carl and Rosina already wanted to settle elsewhere, and the insurrection spurred them to action. They wanted to raise their six children in a more peaceful environment, and to expose them to better opportunities than existed in Baden-Wurttemberg at the time. Carl saved until he was able to bring the entire family over at once. None had to be left behind and sent for later, as poorer immigrants often were obliged to do. When they boarded the *Emblem*, a ship that left the Old World for the New from the port of Antwerp, Belgium, the fares for all of the Egles were fully paid.

Carl was forty-seven and his wife, the former Rosina Huttenger, was forty-two. Christina, the oldest of their children, was nineteen when the family disembarked from the ship at Castle Harbor in the New York City Battery. Jordan, the eldest boy, was seventeen. Sophie was eleven. Their school days in Germany may have ended early, because the immigration records of all three older children listed "Farmer" as their occupation. The remaining three children, Johanna, seven, Lorenze, six (and destined to be Rose Thompson's grandfather), and the baby, Simon, five, were all listed on the manifest as "Child, Youngster."

Carl and Rosina may have had German contacts that had already immigrated to the United States and told them about the plethora of opportunities awaiting there. Such prospects may have made it easier for them to uproot all of their children, which couldn't have been easy for a couple in their forties. Emigration was always a gamble, but it paid off handsomely for the Egle family. While it isn't clear where they lived directly after their arrival in New York, by the end of the next decade most of the family had resettled in Farmington, Minnesota Territory, a small town in rural Dakota County. Farmington was located about twenty miles south of the growing cities of Minneapolis and St. Paul and near the Wisconsin border. Minnesota was admitted to the union on May 11, 1858, and the Egles had positioned themselves well. Dakota County grew at an astonishing rate, leaping from a tiny population of 583 people in 1850 to a whopping total of 16,312 residents by 1870.

The Egles prospered in the growing town. By 1868, the family that had arrived as German farmers, presumably not knowing much English, had assimilated. They had a new and profitable American farm and later owned stores and buildings in the business center. If the new world of America had been rumored to have streets that were paved with gold, they had certainly struck some.

Lorenze and his brother Simon—"L. Egle & Bro.," as they billed themselves—went into the hospitality business. They owned a rollicking tavern called the Farmington Billiard Room on the corner of Oak and Third Streets, in the business district near the train tracks. The tavern was advertised in the *Farmington Telegraph* as having a room that was "large and commodious, with two first class tables, a constant supply of the choicest wines and liquors" and "ale, beer and cigars." Chances are good there was even a piano to provide music and entertainment along with the libations. Lorenze and Simon didn't stop with selling drinks and refreshments. The brothers also sold ice in the summertime for use in iceboxes, the forerunners of refrigerators. Then L. Egle & Bro. made sure they were the local agents for a new invention known as D. L. Jacques' Combined Hydraulic Pumps. Plumbing in the form of indoor water pumps had just arrived in Farmington, and the Egles positioned themselves to profit from it.

Lorenze, who by now sometimes used the more common Americanized spelling of his name, *Lawrence*, married Mary Louise Herber, a woman from another close-knit immigrant family hailing from Luxembourg. The newlyweds were well suited. The Herbers were fellow hospitality merchants who also owned buildings in Dakota County, including the Luxembourger Hof, a local hotel. A photograph still exists of that hotel, with several members of the populace posing in front of the large edifice, which featured four ladies positioned in four of the upper story windows. Possibly they were the Herber daughters, or perhaps, as was later rumored among area historians, they were members of the world's oldest profession. That hotel may have been their headquarters.

For most of the Farmington portion of her life, Lorenze's wife, Mary Louise, was called Louisa, possibly because one of her sisters was also named Mary. Such duplicate naming wasn't uncommon in Catholic families. Often all of the daughters would be named after the Virgin Mary, then given a middle name that they were called by. Mary Louise/Louisa usually simply signed herself M. L. Later in Seattle, far removed from her sister Mary, she reverted to being Mary Louise.

Mary Louise and Lorenze's first child, Anna, who would grow up to be Rose Thompson's mother and the grandmother of Gypsy Rose Lee and June Havoc, arrived on July 21, 1868. Anna was named after Mary Louise's mother, Anna Herber. Mary Louise's second daughter, Rose, who was named after Lorenze's mother Rosina, came along in 1871, the first of the American-born Roses and one of quite a few children who would be named Rose in honor of Rosina over the next few generations. Rose Egle was a sweetheart of a child and well regarded. Another little girl called Lula followed in 1874, with a boy, Carl, Lorenze's father's namesake, arriving on the scene in 1875. For a happy period of time that would prove to be achingly short, Lorenze and Mary Louise Egle had a lively family of four children. A fifth child, George, named for one of Mary Louise's brothers, was born in 1878.

Popular Lorenze became a member and "chosen officer" of the volunteer Farmington Hook and Ladder Company in January 1873. The family saloon continued to do a healthy business, although ever since the first murder in Dakota County's history had taken place in a watering hole in 1872, a temperance lobby grew up in the town, longing to shutter the Egles' place. There were six active saloons in the area, and only one murder had occurred in one of them, but those odds hardly impressed the reformers. The character leading the charge of the Farmington temperance movement was John Emery, a transplant from Maine. He was also the outrageously blunt editor of the *Farmington Press*, unafraid to present his biased opinions on a whole variety of topics as printed facts. The Egle saloon continued, but only at the temperance crowd's sufferance. On July 9, 1874, the *Farmington Press*, with a wink and a grin, reported, "Several crusaders visited Egle's saloon on the evening of the 3d, and prayed—that he would fix them up some cool lemonade: which he did."

A year later Simon Egle bought a second building and had it moved close to the saloon, preparing for expansion. Like almost all of Farmington's buildings in the business district—save for C. R. Griebie's handsome brick general store—it was made of wood.

The thriving Egle saloon was successful to the degree it drove many of the more respectable—that is to say, sober—members of the Farmington community half crazy. Those that lived near the place, in particular, were not happy with the nightly fracases at the boisterous establishment. John Emery loved blasting the Egles in his newspaper. Concern for propriety may have motivated the temperance crowd, but such was evidently not constraining Lorenze, Simon, and their wives. Their corner of town was swiftly becoming infamous, as they allowed their customers to enjoy themselves to the hilt.

Lorenze and Simon figured that any customers' money would do. The proprietors ran into trouble and got hauled into court after getting caught selling liquor to minors. Together, the two defendants were fined twenty dollars and costs. This was a huge punitive fee for the 1870s, yet the brothers paid it and returned to their bar.

On October 28, 1875, Rosina Egle passed away at Lorenze's home. Hers was the beginning of a spate of family deaths. Lorenze may have taken the loss of his mother particularly badly because he landed back in court six months later. He got fined again, paying ten dollars this time for disorderly conduct. Perhaps he was imbibing his own libations a little too liberally by this point. John Emery made cracks in the paper that Lorenze was a drunk, but John Emery's great joy in life came from lambasting anybody who didn't resemble his own aggrandized, sober self. He may have been the editor of the local newspaper, but he was hardly a reliable source.

In March of 1876, Simon Egle's wife passed away, far too young at age twenty-three. Within seven months of Simon's wife's death, the firm of "L. Egle & Bro." was dissolved for reasons unknown. Simon may have simply wanted a fresh start. Possibly the pressure put on the saloon by the temperance group made the Egles realize it would be wiser to close it on their own terms than wait until it was shut down by some future decree. Lorenze's business-savvy wife Mary Louise, the financial brains behind the operation, placed an advertisement in the paper requesting that anyone who remained indebted to the firm "make immediate payment to or to settle account with Mrs. Mary L. Egle."

The Egles were an adaptable lot. On August 25, 1877, the *Farmington Press* reported that the Egle Saloon was closed, but that it "will be fitted up as a boarding house or second-class hotel." Over and over again, Lorenze and his descendants would exhibit a talent for always finding ways to create a nice, steady income. The whole group would be forever open to new avenues for making money. It didn't matter whether funds came from the clientele of a boisterous saloon or the guests of a comparatively quiet hotel. It mattered only that the money came in—and they already owned the building. The place was remodeled and put to a whole new use.

The editor of the *Farmington Press* had a bit of fun at Lorenze and Simon's expense on May 23, 1877: "The old saloon corner looks a little lonesome, now, but it isn't half so noisy as it was at times—which indeed is an improvement that those who live and move nearby can well appreciate. There can be little doubt that nearly every saloon in the place could have been closed up, more than once, under the laws we had for years, had they been thoroughly enforced." He later added, "We hope to see a good and clean hotel or restaurant on the old corner; but we may well fear that the old sore will break out worse in some new and more dangerous spot." This assessment came from John Emery, so it was over the top, but it raises the question of just what exactly might have transpired in that rowdy saloon.

Little Anna Egle was growing up within a lively family business involving billiard rooms, hotels possibly frequented by good time girls, taverns, transient travelers, and tipplers. Farmington was a small Midwestern town, not exactly Minneapolis, St. Paul, New York, or New Orleans, but Anna's daily exposure to a wide variety of different types of people put her at ease with them all. This child was happy among itinerants. Much later, while she was married, her early socialization might explain why Anna experienced no problem and no fear of turning a hefty profit by sewing and selling attention-grabbing outfits for mining camp hookers, despite living during a time when most married women stayed home. Her early years may also have influenced her middle daughter, Rose, who didn't hesitate to take her children on the road in a traveling vaudeville act. Anna, Rose, and later Gypsy Rose Lee and June Havoc, were all comfortable with the idea of staying in hotels, often choosing them over other available accommodations. Most saloons offered music in the form of piano players, and some even featured performances by dancing girls, making the local tavern the unofficial entertainment center of its day in many small towns. Taverns were forerunners of the vaudeville theaters that would come into vogue a generation later, and in light of this evolution, the family's trajectory from the tavern to the hotel to traveling on the theatrical circuits would be a natural one.

At the end of the summer of 1877, tiny Lula Egle, aged four, contracted scarlet fever. The little girl passed away on a miserable Saturday night. Lula had adored horses. The white headstone that her parents chose for her, still visible today at Highland Cemetery in Farmington, was lovingly inscribed to "Our Little Lula." Underneath these words there is an engraving of a pony.

The rest of the Egle children, Anna, Rose, and two-year-old Carl (George had yet to be born) fortunately managed to remain untouched by the contagious disease that had robbed them of Lula, but that wasn't much consolation. The entire family was clearly devastated when they lost their little girl.

Pretty nine-year-old Anna, known by the nickname Annie, was adored by the people of Farmington, as was her sister Rose, called Rosie. Fortunately for Mary Louise, Annie was a strong and healthy child. She was also bright and, with two parents who spoke German, probably bilingual. Possibly while helping her mother raise her siblings, Annie realized she had a knack for sewing, which she pursued. In Anna, Lorenze and Mary Louise were raising an emotionally strong little girl.

The family moved forward after Lula died, as they always would when an unpleasant event befell them. They proceeded to open their new hotel where the bar had been. They named it not the Egle Hotel, but the *Eagle* Hotel, Anglicizing their surname—which people probably mispronounced anyway—and honoring the American eagle, a symbol that adorned the great seal of their adopted country.

Anna's father, Lorenze, may have begun drinking a bit more heavily than usual after Lula died, which would not have been an unusual reaction for a father who had lost a child. It would also not have been the first time that a tavern owner became a bit too enamored of his own wares. Lorenze was a fun-loving guy with a bubbly sense of humor that would be passed down to many of his descendants, especially Gypsy Rose Lee. The following May, Lorenze, who may or may not have had a few too many drinks, created a bit of amusement with a gentleman named Mr. Martin Niskern, owner of the Niskern Hotel and a business rival. Mr. Niskern had strolled past the Eagle Hotel carrying a sack of flour. The *Farmington Press* reported gleefully in a news item titled "A Fall and a Rise" that Lorenze "was tempted to the little pleasantry of knocking the sack off Niskern's back from behind; this created a fall in flour; whereupon mine host, who wears a good-sized boot, immediately returned the compliment by a *rise a posterio* of his funning assailant. The result was considered a draw game, well played." Indeed!

A month later, in June 1878, one last child, little Georgie, was born to Mary Louise and Lorenze. Georgie's arrival brought joy to his parents and siblings, who were still grieving for Lula.

Lorenze's brother Jordan, a widower, remarried in his 40s, wedding a sturdy-looking divorced woman named Clara Day. Originally from the town of Machias, Maine, the Day family had gone west to Minneapolis. Clara had two children from her previous marriage to William Alonzo Moor, but the marriage was miserable because William drank. Irascible Clara would soon prove to be a less than positive addition to the Egle family, so it's also possible she might just have driven Moor to drink.

Back at the hotel, Mary Louise and Lorenze were attracting additional customers by hosting, for several days, two dentists and an eye and ear specialist, who also sold "Brilliant Alaska Crystal Spectacles." Naturally, these guests brought additional revenue into the hotel. Then a spell of ferociously hot, unrelenting weather hit the area in October of 1879. The *Farmington Press* noted, "The hot south wind steadily depressed and prostrated human vitality, and many persons suffered severely from bilious and nervous complaints."

The heat spell may have caused Lorenze to try to cool himself down by drinking more alcohol than usual. On October 8, 1879, the *Farmington Press* reported that Lorenze had become sick and almost died. Unfortunately, the newspaper spoke too soon. In the next issue, it was reported that Lorenze had died sometime later that same day. John Emery egregiously added, "His death is no doubt attributable to his habits of excessive drink." John Emery often received hate mail due to his inability to refrain from printing unflattering judgments of the populace in his paper. The official cause of Lorenze's death was listed as "softening of the brain," hardly a medical assessment. A few days later the heat wave broke. A welcome breeze finally brought milder air into Farmington while Mary Louise and the children buried their Lorenze.

More trouble was to come, and the second tragedy hit only a month and a half later. This one was huge, disastrous, and affected the entire business center of the town of Farmington. Afterward, the event would always be referred to as the great Farmington fire of 1879. For the grieving Egle family, the timing of the fire could hardly have been worse. It started on Saturday night, November 22, 1879. The wind that had been tearing through the area was described as "very violent," contributing to the worst possible scenario for what was about to happen. A fire that began in the barn of the Niskern Hotel. Several stalks of corn had been piled against Niskern's wooden barn, and sparks from the engine of a passing train caused them to ignite. Niskern was a tough man who had once witnessed an Indian massacre. He would later file suit against the railroad.

At half-past nine in the evening, the sharp-eyed engineer of a subsequent train, a Chicago, Milwaukee, and St. Paul freight that was passing through Farmington, spotted the fire in the pile of cornstalks. He blew his train's whistle frantically to alert the populace. Townspeople saw that the barn near the wheat elevator was on fire, and in turn they sounded the alarm. By then the barn had gone up in flames, far too quickly for anyone to remove the animals trapped inside. Two fine horses, four cows, and several pigs did not survive the blaze, and neither did Mr. Niskern's platform carriage. Animals in an adjoining barn, fortunately, were rescued before it was destroyed, a small victory on what must have been a terrifying night. Unfortunately the burning barn was attached to the Niskern Hotel. The wind made matters worse, prompting the fire to burn through the hotel swiftly, then igniting the store behind it. The valiant water brigade of townspeople that went into action outside these structures wasn't any match for this fire. It furiously devoured one building after another. Other people attempted to remove items from the hotel, hurling them out into the street, salvaging a few things.

Chaos reigned in Farmington that night, yet no incident could have better conveyed the spirit of this courageous little town and its people than their response to the widespread, disastrous fire. A spirit of "all hands on deck" arose, with everybody pitching in to try and stop the fire's progress, including many of the town's young boys, who would be singled out for rare praise by John Emery for their bravery later in his report about the event.

The Egle family was active in the midst of the inferno. Many pieces of their furniture were successfully removed from the Eagle Hotel. But it's enough to make one's blood run cold to think that a newly-widowed woman and three of her four remaining children, who ranged in age from four to twelve, attempted to assist in battling such a fire. Annie, age ten and a half, and Rosie, seven, were certainly old enough to help, and little Carl, age four, may even have been pressed into service. Only the fourth child, baby Georgie, was too tiny to assist in fighting the fire. At the age of one year and five months, Georgie alone was probably entrusted to the care of a friend while the madness continued.

Owing to their quick-wittedness, several of Lorenze Egle's brothers were later credited with starting a branch of the Farmington fire department that night. They improvised an Egle Brothers bucket brigade and are still remembered in Farmington for this action over a hundred and thirty years later. Their efforts clearly helped to bring the fire under some semblance of control.

One place after another went up in flames as the fire spread along the rooftops. It engulfed five more buildings, including Ben's Barbershop, proudly run by former slave Ben Richardson. It next engulfed a private home, and then, heartbreakingly for Mary Louise and her fatherless children, the fire destroyed the Eagle Hotel. The entire north side of Oak Street was in ashes. Then the buildings on the south side of Oak Street caught fire, but the townspeople didn't give up. They kept tossing little buckets of water onto the buildings. The horses were saved from a livery stable before that went up. Even the large brick general store owned by the Griebie family, the one edifice in the center of the town that the populace had hoped would be able to withstand the flames, did not make it. The flames from the nearest burning wooden buildings were blown into the store through the roof and took the store down from the top.

The fire reached the point where it was about to burn out, with little left to annihilate. Then, almost as a last hurrah, it ignited the wheat elevator. This was the largest structure in the town, and it contained approximately fifty-four thousand bushels of wheat. Much of the wheat was lost, and so was the elevator. The children's uncle Jordan Egle had had two hundred sacks of barley stored there, but luckily he had moved quickly. He and several others managed to remove all of their grain before the elevator was consumed.

The way this little town had pulled together during the fire was fabulous, with almost everybody helping out—save for some looters, who were nothing less than a disgrace. Amazingly, considering that more than twenty-five buildings were lost in the fire, nobody was killed or injured. The Eagle Hotel, valued at $2,000, was gone, but at least Mary Louise had $500 in insurance, and the family had managed to get several of their pieces of furniture out safely. Their losses were not as bad as they might have been. Many owners of neighboring buildings that were destroyed had no insurance. Still, Lorenze had left Mary Louise the hotel, which had helped to provide his family with a livelihood. Now it was gone, literally turned to ashes.

Mary Louise and her four remaining children were not alone in the now devastated town. They were surrounded by a large, loving extended family and kindly taken in by Mary Louise's younger brother, Peter Herber, and his young wife. The Egles temporarily moved to Peter Herber's farm in nearby Castle Rock. The farm was large enough to require the assistance of a live-in farmhand and another resident servant from Germany. There were two baby cousins for the children to love, and little Anna's namesake, her grandmother, lived there.

The situation in Farmington on the morning after the fire was bleak. The center of town was annihilated. The odor from the fire, in particular that emanating from the ruins of the wheat elevator, made the townspeople gag. But the merchants of Farmington maintained a positive attitude. The trustees issued a new ordinance banning the construction of any additional wooden buildings in the business district. Rebuilding was about to begin—with bricks, this time around. Within a week, cheeky John Emery of the *Farmington Press* could not restrain himself from publishing the quip, "Thanksgiving was very generally observed by the closing of the shops and stores—on the burnt spot."

Likewise, Mary Louise rallied. She promptly opened a restaurant in the newly rebuilt center of Farmington. But the resilient woman's troubles were far from over. Her youngest, little Georgie, passed away a few weeks before his second birthday in June of 1880. Within seven months, Lorenze had died, the great Farmington fire had destroyed their hotel and forced the family to move, and now the baby was gone. The situation got worse on February 12, 1881. Mary Louise's other son, Carl, age five and a half, also died. The family's strong Catholic faith helped to sustain them through all of these miserable events. Somehow, Mary Louise was still standing.

Annie and Rosie Egle were now the only surviving children in the family. Both were vibrant, beloved girls and had a large circle of friends. They bonded, as they missed Lula, Georgie, Carley, and their father terribly.

Their uncle Jordan Egle, soon to be a purveyor of Jordan Egle's Condition Powders—advertised as a cure for, among other things, pinkeye in horses—may have hoped for marital bliss with his divorcée bride, Clara Day Egle. He may even have found it, if only temporarily. Yet in June, 1881, the two of them stood before Justice Judson. Clara had wanted to attend a local event called the Masonic Ball and got dressed up and ready to go. Jordan had not been amenable to this outing. Clara claimed that in the ensuing argument, which must have been considerable, Jordan had ripped her clothing. Examination of the items in question indicated that this was not the case. The damage was too minimal for the battle royal Clara described to have actually happened; the lady was a confabulator. Justice Judson suggested a settlement amount for the slightly torn clothing to end the matter, but Jordan would not agree to pay. The judge placed him "under bonds to keep the peace." The marriage collapsed in earnest within another month and a half. Jordan placed a notice in the *Farmington Press* informing the entire town that he would not pay any of Clara's outstanding bills. The divorce papers had yet to be signed, but their union was over (though Clara would remain in the business district and cause additional trouble later).

Popular young Annie Egle, meanwhile, had become a statuesque teenager. She caught the eye of a new arrival in town, a blue-eyed, pleasant-faced, highly responsible young man by the name of Charles J. Thompson. Charlie, as he was known, was six years Annie's senior and had come from Monona Township, Iowa, around 1882 to run the train depot. His parents, Stephen Hurd Thompson and Elizabeth Bowles Thompson, were of Scottish and Irish extraction, but they weren't immigrants. Like Annie, Charlie had grown up in a big family, where he was one of nine children living on a prosperous farm. Eight of the nine Thompson children survived.

The Thompson family's lives revolved around neither hotels nor taverns, but the Presbyterian Church. Charlie's father had been involved in the choir, taught in the Sunday school, and joined the Masonic fraternal organization, as Charlie would. Their family home was no-frills but happy, usually decorated with fresh flowers and filled with the sounds of music. Young Charlie played the piano by ear in the local Farmington band, a sideline to working for the railroad. He had already proved himself to be a responsible and competent railroad employee, a status that led to his transfer to Farmington.

Charlie and Anna began a courtship; it led to a proposal. On Tuesday, October 6, 1885, the two were married by the local Catholic priest, almost certainly at Mary Louise's insistence. She was not about to let her daughter get married in the church of any other denomination. Rosie Egle, Annie's beloved little sister, was one of her witnesses. Charlie's best friend, Henry Vollimer, was another.

Annie's mother, Mary Louise, was overjoyed. At last they had a reason to celebrate, after so many years of heartache. Mary Louise held an enormous six-hour long reception at her home. The residents of Farmington turned out in force, two hundred strong, to congratulate the young couple. They brought gifts (silverware, rugs, silver serving dishes, chairs, a wine set, towels, glasses pitchers, and more) to help furnish Charlie and Anna's new apartment, which would be over the rooms of D. J. Johnson's tailor shop. It was an impressive collection of presents and a testament to the high regard in which the people of Farmington held Annie and Charlie. Uncle Jordan Egle bought them an entire bolt of new cloth. Two of the nicest gifts came from Mary Louise and Rosie. Mary Louise gave the newlyweds a ten dollar gold piece. Rosie gave her sister and her new husband a rocking chair. Charlie and Annie boarded the seven o'clock evening train to the nearby town of Hastings, and from there went on a weeklong honeymoon trip to Iowa to visit Charlie's family. The marriage was off to a positive start.

Rosie Egle came down with what would later be called a strep throat infection. Prior to the advent of antibiotics, that condition alone would have been miserable enough, but the lively teenager's symptoms became worse. Her strep throat infection turned into rheumatic fever. Rheumatic fever can inflame the heart and joints, causing chest pains, heart palpitations, joint pain, fever, and even a rash. The sweet teenage girl was ailing for several weeks.

Nine months and two weeks after Charlie and Annie were married, on July 28, 1886, their first child, a daughter, was born. They named her Mina Louise. The baby's middle name was chosen to honor Annie's mother, Mary Louise. The birth should have been a joyous event for the family—especially for Mary Louise who, with this birth, became a proud grandmother. But the birth was tempered with anxiety because young Rosie's condition was getting worse.

Try as she might, the lovely girl wasn't able to rally. Only ten short days after becoming Mina's aunt, on Saturday, August 7, 1886, Rose Egle died. Irving Todd, the kind editor of an area newspaper, the *Dakota County Tribune*, was among many people clearly grieving Rose's loss. He wrote a beautiful tribute:

> It is seldom that a death occurs which casts a deeper and more widespread feeling of sadness over a community. Young, bright and vivacious, she was known by almost every one in the village, and known only to be regarded with the kindliest friendship. Among her schoolmates she was an especial favorite and her untimely death is deeply deplored by all who knew her. The sad occurrence preaches a sermon more eloquent than words of the uncertainty of human life and the wisdom of so living that when called suddenly hence there shall be left behind no enmities or strife—naught but friendship and good will, to be cherished with pleasant memories.

A standing-room-only funeral was held at the Catholic church for the child whose short life had brightened that of so many others.

Rose's sister Anna suddenly became the sole surviving child of Lorenze and Mary Louise Egle. For the rest of her life, in letters to family members that she'd send around the time of her July 21 birthday, Anna would remark on how she'd "made it" to another "milestone," as if hitting another birthday were no less than a miracle. To a young girl who had seen her entire family, save for her mother, wiped out, it was.

Within a month, Mary Louise sold her restaurant and moved for a time, along with her brother, Peter Herber, to Clearwater, Wisconsin. She needed a change of scenery and a project after Rosie's death, and her brother helped her find one. Peter needed to get a new family hotel up and running, and who better to assist him than his former hotelier sister? It may have been in Clearwater that Mary Louise met a veterinarian from St. Paul, Dr. Carl A. Stein. Stein was often summoned from St. Paul to evaluate animals before they were purchased and would stay in various towns for days at a time to examine ailing animals. Mary Louise returned to Farmington for a month, took over her old restaurant again, then managed to marry Dr. Stein in a ceremony they apparently kept secret from all of her Farmington friends. "Not even the birds had whispered anything about the event," Irving Todd, the editor of the *Dakota County Tribune* reported. Mary Louise Stein, as she would henceforth be known, came back to town a month later to help Anna nurse little Mina Louise. The baby had taken sick when she was just over a year old. Fortunately, the ministrations worked.

A year after Mary Louise married Carl, trouble in the form of the termagant Clara Day Egle found Charlie and Anna Thompson, landing the otherwise affable Charlie in court. All of the details of the case were purposely not fully recorded by the *Dakota County Tribune*. In contrast to the *Farmington Press*, which had featured John Emery's blunt diatribes and would have announced the case details, the classier *Dakota County Tribune* only report obliquely, "For some time a state of unpleasantness has existed between Mrs. Clara D. Egle and the family of Chas. J. Thompson, the particulars of which it is not necessary to enter into at this time." The unpleasantness that couldn't be named must have had the vastness of a Midwestern sky. What the paper did allow to be reported was that Charlie and the little band in which he played were scheduled to perform at the 1888 Fourth of July ball, yet he refused to countenance the idea of playing music "for his whilom enemy to dance to."

Neither did the rest of the band. Clara Day Egle , somehow, some way, had managed to unanimously alienate every single one of the band members, not just Charlie. What Charlie said to Clara is not precisely known, but the gist of it was that he most emphatically did not want her attending any dance where she would be in proximity to his wife, Anna. Clara was far too low-class to be at the same ball with Anna in Charlie's opinion. Clara tried to have him placed under arrest because of what she regarded as a threat. The paper only reported that his statement would have provoked "a breach of the peace." This matter actually went to trial before a jury a week later.

Clara claimed her son-in-law Fred Griebie, the general store owner, was a witness to Charlie's alleged threats. Griebie may not have been any more enamored with his mother-in-law than the Thompson family was. He would not corroborate Clara's version of events when he was placed on the witness stand, despite her claim that he was present when Charlie Thompson threatened her. Other witnesses were sworn in. They could not back Clara's allegations up, either. The judge dismissed the case.

Jordan Egle, who had the misfortune to be Clara's husband, was still unhappily married to the virago. He was also Anna's uncle. He may have considered this needless trial to be the last act in his domestic melodrama. His divorce lawyer proceeded to get Clara out of his life several months later, thus restoring Jordan's peace—if not Farmington's. She purchased a building in town and later opened a candy store.

A second child was born to Charlie and Anna Thompson on July 16, 1889. They named him Stephen Hurd Thompson after Charlie's father, but he was to be called Hurd throughout his short life. Following Hurd's birth, Charlie and his growing family relocated. Perhaps he was still feeling either embarrassed or furious by Clara Day Egle's false charges against him. His railroad bosses were always impressed by his work ethic and transferred him to another small town. Located about fifty miles southeast of Fargo, North Dakota, their temporary new home was Wahpeton. It was named after its original residents, the Wakhpetonwan band of the Dakota tribe. The local founding fathers wisely shortened Wakhpetonwan to Wahpeton, which was easier to spell and pronounce.

Wahpeton's twin city was Breckenridge, Minnesota. The two were separated by the Red River, which served as a state border. A branch of the St. Paul and Pacific Railway—to later become part of the Great Northern Railroad, Charlie's ultimate employer—was located in Breckenridge, but the family preferred Wahpeton as a home base. It was there that Charlie and Anna Thompson's third child, another baby girl with violet-blue eyes, was born.

They named this second daughter Rose.

CHAPTER 2

WILD PRAIRIE ROSE

THE NEWBORN ROSE ELIZABETH THOMPSON WAS GIVEN HER FIRST name in honor of Rose Egle, Anna's beloved sister who recently had died from rheumatic fever. The name also honored Rosina Egle, Lorenze's mother, who had been Rose Egle's namesake—but perhaps by the time this new Rose came along, Rosina was but a faded memory. Her middle name was a salute to Charlie's mother, Elizabeth Bowles Thompson.

North Dakota had been admitted to the union on November 2, 1889. The students at the newly formed University of North Dakota voted to make green and pink, the colors of a pretty and popular North Dakota flower, the wild prairie rose, their school colors. Legend has it that the students picked those colors because they were "suggestive of our green prairies and rosy prospects." The colors evoked both the majesty of the new state and the optimism of the students. The wild prairie rose would later be adopted as the official state flower of North Dakota.

Charlie and Anna Thompson's new daughter, who would spend the first two years of her life on the North Dakota prairie, qualified, in a way, to be called a wild prairie rose. She was born on the last day of August in 1891. The Wahpeton *Richland County Gazette* reported that Charlie "look[ed] very happy" at the birth of this third child and second daughter. Mary Louise Stein, whom life had dealt one blow after another, could only have been thrilled to hear that Anna's new baby was named after her late, lovely daughter, Rose. Mary Louise was to be close to this new grandchild for the rest of her life, and little Rose Thompson would cherish her.

A photograph that still exists of Rose and her brother, Hurd, taken when Rose is about a year and a half old by Powell's Art Studio in Wahpeton. Hurd wears a dark tunic with light trim that resembled a dress, apparently the height of fashion for little boys in the early 1890s. Rose sits on a low chair beside him in what looks like a child's version of a long evening gown, with a large lace collar that must have been at least four inches wide. If Anna made the clothes, it's plain she was already talented with a needle.

The two children are both blonde, with pale eyes. Rose's eyes were later described as violet, similar to a deep Wedgwood blue with a slight purple tinge. The expression in the eyes of the children informs the viewer about their characters. Hurd's is calm and rather complacent—although both children look bored, so the photo session may have gone on a bit too long. As she looks out from under wisps of unruly, curling thin hair, Rose has a more intense gaze than Hurd, but her boredom is quite evident. She's looking slightly away from the camera, and her lips are pursed as if she's fed up with the photo shoot, not to mention wearing that particular outfit, and wants to get outside and play. The children are not smiling; it was not the custom in those days for a photographer to ask his subjects to smile. It took too long for the photograph to be shot, as exposures could take up to ten minutes.

Close in age, Rose and Hurd were companions throughout the time they spent in North Dakota. It was probably Hurd who started calling Rose by the nickname "Rony" (it rhymes with "pony"), which she was to go by for the rest of her life. Morton Minsky, meeting her for the first time in the early 1930s, even thought Rony was her given name. Hurd, age three when she was born, might not have been able to pronounce Rosie. It may have come out Rony. Rony she was to remain.

Later, Rose was said to remember the lilacs that grew in Wahpeton, but she may have confused the town with Farmington. By the time she was nearly two and a half years old, the whole Thompson family was back in Farmington again, living with Mary Louise Stein, who had also returned there—and, just like Clara Day Egle, had opened a candy store. She and Clara were now business rivals. Charlie's new job assignment was as the day operator of the Farmington train depot. Dr. Carl A. Stein, Mary Louise's second husband, may have passed away by then. He isn't mentioned in any later articles concerning the family's life in Farmington. Mina, Hurd, and Rose found themselves living right over Mary Louise's confectionery store, with easy access to the best treats in town.

Then on a cold Minnesota winter's night, January 29, 1894, another fire broke out in the business section of Farmington, and this one started right in Mary Louise Stein's candy store. This time the disaster started when a lamp that was hanging in the confectionery store on the first floor of Mary Louise's new, brick-fronted building fell to the floor, setting it alight. Anna and Charlie weren't at home, but Mary Louise and her grandchildren were.

Probably with the help of eight-year-old Mina, Mary Louise managed to scoop up Hurd, age five, and two-and-a-half-year-old Rose, and get them out of the building alive. Unfortunately this time the fire spread so rapidly that there was only time enough to grab the children and run. The four of them left the building with literally nothing but the clothes on their backs.

The fire department tried but wasn't able to save the building. This fire was ferocious. Crowds of people came out to help, and the firemen instructed them to try to save the adjoining buildings. Another fire in Farmington would have recalled the worst of the last one for members of the populace who had been there, but they had learned from it. The adjoining buildings were saved.

Mary Louise, though, lost everything she had once again. Her building was destroyed. Her stock of candy and confectionery items was gone. And the household goods, including the nice collection of wedding gifts that had been given to Anna and Charlie, were gone as well. It isn't known how much Rose saw that night, or what, if anything, she was able to remember of the incident. The fire had broken out at eight o'clock in the evening, and she may even have been asleep when it started. It was an unsettling and scary night, but Rose may have become bolder for having survived.

Mary Louise had insurance again, thankfully: $800 on the building and $200 more on the contents of her store. Charlie also had $200 worth of insurance. Most of their losses could be replaced. Within a week, the *Dakota County Tribune* reported, "Mrs. Stein will rebuild." History had repeated itself. In short order Mary Louise's rebuilt edifice was almost ready for occupancy, but Charlie, Anna, Mina, Hurd, and Rose didn't stick around and wait for it to open. The Great Northern Railroad had a position they wanted Charlie to fill in Seattle, the newly selected western terminus, and the whole group was moving there. Mary Louise would join them within the year, even though she would still retain ownership of the building back in Farmington.

Seattle was a lively little city, still in the process of growing. It had an abundance of pine trees, with a mist that blew gently inland from the Pacific Ocean. The weather was usually temperate but exceedingly damp, with cloud cover that rarely dissipated. The snow-capped peaks of Mount Rainier rose elegantly over the town, lending a picture-postcard ambience to the area even when it rained—and it rained more often than not. Seattle residents learned to carry their umbrellas every day and to take the rain in stride.

Several areas of the town were so hilly that in 1891 the city engineer took steps to level the inclines to make navigation between neighborhoods easier. This project began shortly before the Thompsons arrived, as did an enormous rebuilding boom following the great Seattle fire of 1889, which destroyed twenty-five of the city's blocks. If the Thompsons arrived in the midst of continuous construction, they surely must have felt right at home.

Their fourth and final child was born on December 19, 1895, in Minnesota. Anna and Mary Louise probably took advantage of the free travel allowed Great Northern Railroad employees and their families to return to Farmington often, in part to check on Mary Louise's building. Maybe Anna went back in order to have access to a specific doctor or midwife during this last baby's birth.

The baby was another little girl. They named her Belle Evangeline. The Catholic Church in Wahpeton had been St. John the Evangelist and may have inspired Charlie and Anna to choose Evangeline as Belle's middle name. Later, Rose Elizabeth would sometimes call herself Rose Evangeline, and Belle Evangeline, who favored the nickname Betty, would call herself Belle Elizabeth. Their names were like toys; they could be played with.

In Seattle, the family rented a place on 7th Street, then moved to Roy Street, and finally, when Belle was almost a year and a half old, to 10th Avenue North (later renamed Nagle Place), to a house occupying land where Seattle Central Community College now stands. A block away, a Seattle street called Broadway had a trolley car line.

Mary Louise Stein made a return trip to Germany with her brother, George Herber, and sister Mary Buschen. The trip back to the old country began with a stay in New York City in June 1897. Then the trio boarded the Red Star Line's steamer *Northwestern*, sailed across the Atlantic, and arrived in Antwerp, Belgium. From there they made their way to Luxemburg. Old friends and family members met them. Later, they all went home to the town of Diekirch. George would tell the *Dakota County Tribune* that the prices in their old European stomping grounds were so low, compared to those in America, that he could have lived "cheaper and better" in Belgium; he could "enjoy himself better there than here." They must have been having one of the best times of their entire lives on that trip. While there, George even found a wife. Charlotte Tremont of Luxemburg returned with the three siblings to the United States to marry George in Farmington.

In one unexpected way, though, the timing of their trip to Germany could not have been worse. Mary Louise had helped Anna with the children while in Seattle, but August 23, 1897 she wasn't there. The day was hot. The house on 10th Avenue North was about two miles from Lake Union, and young Hurd, age nine, and other neighborhood children made a habit of trekking to the lake to go swimming or at least wading in the summertime in the shallow end of the cold waters. Hurd was not much of a swimmer.

Hurd was playing in the back yard of the house when an eerie episode began to unfold. Anna was lying down at ten o'clock that morning, probably due to the heat. She proceeded to have a terrifyingly vivid nightmare in which Hurd had drowned in Lake Union. Anna awakened from this hideous dream, panicked. But when she looked out the window, she was relieved to see Hurd in the yard, playing outside with toddler Belle. Anna went back to sleep. It was an unwise move, one that may well have haunted her for the rest of her life. While asleep, Anna had the same nightmare once again. Hurd, though, was alive and well. It was almost a two-mile walk to Lake Union, so getting there would have taken Hurd at least forty-five minutes and on a hot day, probably longer.

The second time Anna had the dream, she got up again and took another look out the window, hoping to see her son. At that point Hurd wasn't in the back yard any longer. Anna went down the stairs, saw one of Hurd's friends outside and asked where her son was. The child told her that Hurd had gone off somewhere. Anna reportedly did not feel alarmed when she heard this report, despite just having had two clear and disturbing dreams about her little boy drowning in Lake Union. She didn't head off in that direction, determined to prevent the child from swimming in the lake, as many a mother might have done. Perhaps she thought she'd be going off half-cocked. The woman was living in a time period when women's intuition was often written off as women's hysteria. Anna simply reasoned that Hurd went off with neighborhood children all the time and basically dismissed the matter! This reasoning is especially strange, considering that she had gone down the stairs trying to find the boy twice.

Hurd did go off in the direction of Lake Union. It isn't known precisely whom he went off with, but if that person was an adult, this incident may have had darker implications than the sensibilities of the 1890s could have imagined. Anna, whose dreams had begun at ten o'clock in the morning, did not become alarmed until that evening, when Hurd did not return to the house on Tenth Avenue North for dinner. At that point, she began to question the neighbors as to whether they had seen her little boy. Nobody had.

Charlie came home later in the evening. Anna told him that Hurd had been unaccounted for since that morning, but reportedly she still did not feel anxious about the child. Charlie and E. L. Winslow, a friend who was boarding at the Thompson house, and Mr. Miller, one of the neighbors, immediately went out to search the neighborhood. There was no sign of

Hurd—the boy with the light, complacent eyes—anywhere. Charlie and his two friends continued to look for the child for hours before they finally reluctantly gave up the search for the night, hoping against hope that the boy had decided to sleep over at one of his friend's houses and that there was nothing more to the episode.

Yet the child still did not turn up the next morning. Another search was begun, with Winslow leading two other men. Once again, they did not find Hurd, but they found the little boy's clothes. His blue cap, matching shirt, knee pants, shoes, and stockings were all located on the western shore of Lake Union. The three men knew immediately what had probably happened. They borrowed a canoe from one of Seattle's many Native American residents and boarded it, paddling around the lake, searching for the boy's body. It didn't take them long to spot it. The little one was found in the lake, drowned and trapped by a submerged log. He looked like he had been doubled up with cramp, which beset many people who tried to swim in Seattle's icy cold waters. The body was brought straight to a local undertaker. A neighbor went to give Anna the terrible news that her son was dead and that he had drowned in Lake Union. Her worst nightmare had literally come true.

Seattle's deputy coroner Butterworth headed the investigation into the child's death, during which a suspicious development came to light. The *Seattle Post-Intelligencer* reported, "All efforts to find out who the boy went out with were unavailing, as the children in the neighborhood seemed too frightened to give out any information." What could possibly have been going on with the neighborhood children? Why wouldn't they tell the coroner in whose company Hurd had been seen going to that lake? And why were all of the children who were questioned afraid to speak up? Hurd may very well not have been seen heading for the lake with another child. Was he with an adult, possibly even a pedophile? The way the body was found raises questions as well. The body was found trapped under a log, but no further information about the log and its position was recorded. If Hurd had not gotten entangled in underwater growth, it's hard to imagine him pulling a log over himself as he was drowning. It's easier to think that he may have wound up under the log because an adult strong enough to lift it—and none of his fellow nine-year-olds—had managed to confine the boy under it deliberately.

At the time, no one picked up on questions that would seem glaring a century later, when children's deaths at the hands of pedophiles would become widely publicized. But a child who had not been a good swimmer whose naked body was found dead under a log in a lake, after having gone off with a person whose identity every child in the neighborhood was afraid to reveal when questioned, may well have met with foul play. This child's death might not have been the accidental drowning that it was declared. Had a predator who wasn't a stranger targeted Hurd, perhaps Anna had picked up on an odd feeling that something was wrong from an adult who knew both her and the child. Charlie and Anna, for their part, believed that children in the neighborhood who had gone swimming with Hurd were too terrified by seeing him drown to speak up.

We don't know if Rose was one of the children who was questioned. Neither do we know if Rose was in the house when her mother was told that Hurd was dead. Rose was a few days short of her sixth birthday when Hurd died. The turmoil of those days, when he was first discovered to be missing and then found dead, followed by seeing his body laid out for a wake (held inside the house, as was customary at the time), must have been horrific for the bright little girl. She may also have temporarily gotten lost in the shuffle of adult activity and sorrow that played out around her. Rose's intact family had been shattered, and her only brother was gone.

CHAPTER 3

THE UNVANQUISHED SEATTLE SCHOOLGIRL

GRANDMOTHER MARY LOUISE STEIN RETURNED FROM EUROPE THAT OC-
tober and stayed for a while back in Farmington, visiting all of her friends
and family members and shrewdly checking on her building, which she was
still renting out. She was the one who, unsubstantiated family legend would
have it, urged Anna to put little Rose, her own daughter's namesake, into a
convent school.

There is no evidence to support the claim that Rose went to a Catholic
school. Seattle's oldest Catholic boarding and day school was Holy Names
School, but the only possible match for Rose in their attendance archives is
an intriguing listing for an "R. Thompson," who was enrolled from August
to December of 1898. If that particular R. Thompson was Rose, she would
have been seven years old. Perhaps she kicked up enough of a fuss to avoid
having to go back after a few months. It's doubtful that any Catholic school
could have contained her for long.

There's also the possibility that if Rose was sent to board in a convent
school, she may have been sent to one in the Farmington or the greater
Minneapolis/St. Paul area, rather than to a school in Seattle. The family's
ties to Minnesota remained strong. Yet the trail leading back to Rose's alleged Catholic school remains cold. Later, Rose would use her alleged stay
at a convent school as a plot device, telling her daughters fabrications about
running away from such a place to elope with their father—even though
Rose and their father didn't elope.

Mary Louise moved to Seattle permanently to reside with the Thompson
family. She held on to her building in Farmington for a few more years
before she ultimately sold it to one of her tenants. On June 11, 1900, the
Thompson family moved again, this time to a house Charlie had astutely
bought at 323 4th Avenue North, near Harrison Street, for $1,300. The house

was located about six blocks from the one where they resided when Rose's brother Hurd died. This move was all to the good, removing the family from a home where they had experienced so much misery. Built in 1896 and situated on a small hill, the two-story, seven-room house had a bay window in front and an outer finish of fir siding. It also featured a front and back porch.

In a move the would have made any one of the members of the Egle and Herber families back in Minnesota proud, in 1905 Charlie proceeded to build a second house on the property while still living in the first one. Mary Louise had once made a living renting out rooms at the Egle Hotel back in Farmington, and her wealth of rental experience would positively affect the rest of the family. Not only would Anna and Charlie make a habit of renting out whatever space they had available, they made a nice profit from it. Later Rose would follow suit, and later still, Gypsy Rose Lee and June Havoc did the same. Now, Rose's family rented out one of their two new 4th Avenue North houses and spare rooms in the other house, while also residing there themselves. Such rentals helped defray the costs of building the new house and brought in additional money for minor luxuries.

They hired two servants to live with them, according to the 1900 Census. Servants Hilda Troast and Rita Kuppe had moved in with the family. They may have been either relatives or friends from back in the Midwest. A Trost family had lived in Wahpeton. Two servants in the Thompson home would have precluded the need to board the children at a school—even if Anna had already begun putting her sewing skills to work, regularly leaving home on sales trips to hawk her loud creations to good-time girls.

By 1907—and probably before—Rose was attending Warren Avenue School, a beautiful public school on Warren Avenue and Harrison Street in the Lower Queen Anne Hill neighborhood of Seattle. It was an impressive Greek Revival style school with four columns flanking a front archway that supported a railed balcony. The school opened in 1903, mainly due to overcrowding at two nearby public schools, Mercer and Denny. If Rose went to public school from the beginning and was never in a convent after all, she would have attended Mercer, housed in a smaller, boxier building. Going from Mercer to the new Warren Avenue School must have seemed like transferring to a palace.

But a palace it wasn't, at least not for Rose. It was a school, a place with mindless rules and regulations where children were sent during most days of the year because the law forced them to go—not a place the majority of them would have willingly sought out. The high-spirited, astute young girl felt stifled by it. Rose was a pretty, wholesome-looking girl who dressed in popular demure children's fashions, such as prim blouses with high collars and puffed sleeves. She tried to tame her curly, unruly long hair by wearing it in braided plaits tied at the ends with large silk bows. She had entered her teens and was eager to get on with her life.

The Thompson family's musical talent had been passed along to the girl, and Rose found it supremely easy to pick up and learn to play various instruments. But merely sitting back and playing music was too staid for this vibrant teen. She toyed with the idea of becoming an actress, but that was only going to happen over Charlie Thompson's dead body. Charlie felt that acting was not a respectable profession for a woman, and there is ample evidence that—especially in Seattle in the early 1900s—he was right. One of the biggest vaudeville promoters in Seattle, John Considine, was notorious for not only presenting girls onstage in his variety shows but also worked a lucrative sideline as their pimp. Overtly pimping the ladies may not have been the norm with most promoters, but up to that point the American theater had an informal tradition of allowing the gentlemen in the audience to zero in on whatever lady on stage took their fancy. Often the men would make arrangements for sexual liaisons afterwards. Theater audience members were predominantly male until the mid-nineteenth century, and while Rose may not have been fully cognizant of what was unofficially taking place at variety shows, Charlie certainly was. Charlie, like any good father who loved his daughter, believed this sort of environment was simply not good enough for his Rose.

Rose nevertheless managed to get into a summertime theater troupe when she was somewhere between twelve and fourteen years old. The naturally musical teen played the mandolin and enjoyed herself so much that she would welcome the chance to provide a show business lifestyle for her own children just a few years later. If she returned to school after that summer, it could only have been under duress. She apparently ran away at one point to join another popular children's act known as the Juvenile Bostonians, a company that featured excellent, well-received child performers who performed dramas to packed houses and got terrific notices. Ernest A. Wolff and Emma Lang from Victoria, British Columbia, ran it and surely had perfected the art of managing their little troupe. Emma was wonderful and loving with the child performers; they even called her Mother Lang. Rose loved the theater, and she must have thoroughly enjoyed her stay with the Juvenile Bostonians, however brief. But Charlie found out about Rose's adventure, and that was the end of Rose's participation. She was forced to return home, chafing under the family's constraints and apparently also feeling stifled by her school.

Rose wasn't alone in feeling constricted. Her mother was of a similar turn of mind. Anna was a talented seamstress and created strikingly outlandish hats, clothing, and lingerie that she realized could be sold for magnificent sums of money to the flashy women who peopled the world's oldest profession—women similar to the very types Charlie was attempting to shield Rose from in the theater. Anna would make an informal career of going from one gold rush or silver mine discovery camp to another, following in the wake of the miners and selling her wares to the ladies who serviced them.

By 1906, Anna was living apart from the family, working and staying in the nearby town of Everett, Washington, and running a millinery shop. She may have temporarily separated from Charlie. In divorce papers filed in 1929, he would claim that she had abandoned him in 1905. It's more probable that when the opportunity to run the Everett shop presented itself, Anna simply took up the chance to make some additional money, the entire family's favorite thing. She was to remain with Charlie for the rest of his life, staying with him even after he divorced her.

Whatever the circumstances were that led to Anna's temporary move to Everett, the example it set for her three daughters was clear: Marriage vows did not exactly have to be kept. If there is a reason to pursue another option, grab it and go. The girls may have absorbed this unconventional concept a little too well. Mina, Rose, and Belle were to have at least eight known marriages between them, possibly more. It's clear that altogether they walked away from seven.

Rose remained with her father and grandmother in Seattle. Sometime prior to 1906, her family moved from 323 4th Avenue North to the new house they had built next door, number 321. Both were nice, spacious yet unadorned wooden structures. Mary Louise knew how to make a profit from unused space, so the whole of 323 was rented out for twenty dollars per month. Extra rooms in 321 were also rented out, a one-room rental bringing in two dollars a week, and two rooms plus a bath netting three dollars more.

On Valentine's Day, 1906, Rose was fourteen years old, in sixth grade, and fed up with school when she made the Seattle papers for the first time. "Three Runaway Girls Enjoy Brief Liberty" read the headline, and the delicious notoriety must have pleased Rose. A little girl originally from Iowa named Hazel Stringer, age twelve, along with her parents and older sister, were boarders at the house at 321 4th Avenue North. It was a great arrangement for Rose, who now had a live-in best friend to have fun with and corrupt. On February 13, 1906, Rose and Hazel met their other school friend, Ethel Boyce, age thirteen, on the way to Warren Avenue School, and innocently feigned that they were heading to the school. They actually had already made other plans.

Rose was the ringleader of this AWOL episode. Her powers of persuasion had already been fully activated, and she was already capable of coming up with elaborate schemes. She wasn't afraid of going against the established grain. She never would be. The merry threesome had decided they would all play hooky from school and have a day to themselves full of wonderful freedom. Rather than heading for school, the girls went visiting. And the plan didn't stop there. The next day, the trio planned to go over to Everett, Washington. Rose wanted to see her mother, bringing her friends along.

When it was time for Rose, Hazel, and Ethel to return home after class, the three went instead to the Felt Hotel, where they took a room and stayed overnight. Somehow the unaccompanied girls were allowed to check in. How they obtained the money to pay for the room is unknown; perhaps the next morning they all sneaked out without checking out. If so, Rose was setting a precedent that she was to follow many years later, when she would find ways to avoid paying hotel bills in full when traveling with her daughters' vaudeville act. Rose was hotelier Mary Louise Stein's granddaughter, so even as a kid she probably knew how to handle herself in a hotel, including how to talk her way in and out.

Naturally, by evening, the three girls' poor parents were frantic and summoned the cops. The police took the report that the three lasses were on the lam and broadcast the girls' descriptions all over the general Seattle area—and, for good measure, to the surrounding communities as well—issuing the equivalent of a runaway schoolgirl all-points bulletin. Their liberty ended the next morning. The three were apprehended at the train station in Ballard, Washington, when they tried to board a train to Everett trip to see Anna. By noon on Valentine's Day, all of the parents had shown up at the Ballard police station and retrieved their daughters. It was fortunate that their girls had been returned to them unharmed—this time.

It's interesting that the reason the girls gave for taking off was simply be relieved of the burdens of school. Rose longed to bust loose and had acted on this desire by running away from school this time and also, allegedly, on a few other occasions. The later runaway Rose stories that were handed down in family lore all involved Rose escaping from school to join chorus lines or otherwise becoming involved with shows that were passing through dark and rainy Seattle, where the lights and apparent glamour of the costumes, musical numbers, and various storylines probably were an even more welcome respite to Rose than they might have been had she lived in, say, sunny St. Augustine, Florida. Shows staged in Seattle vaudeville theatres must have been attractive to this intelligent, stifled child, who seemed to long for their light.

This isn't to say that Rose was a bad student at school. Far from it. The *Seattle Times* included a children's section in the Sunday edition, which ran a weekly series of writing contests. These were open to any grammar school students in the state. The stories had to be original kid's compositions, but could be fiction or nonfiction. They couldn't be shorter than one hundred words or longer than three hundred. Entrants had to write their stories in ink, count and list the number of words used, and also list their names, addresses, schools, grades, and ages. A different story topic was chosen each week. First prize was three dollars, second prize two dollars, and third prize one dollar—impressive sums for a child in 1907. Rose decided to enter the contests.

Her first story, "Frogs Haunted Him," appeared in the paper on May 5, 1907. Rose wrote about a fictitious character called Tommy Jones, who plays hooky from school to catch, tease, and liberate a few frogs, two of which he holds captive in the cellar of his house. Then he dreams that the frogs' relatives are all furious at him for stealing their family members. Thousands of the frogs then invade Tommy's bedroom. The boy gets up and takes the frogs back where they belong, and all's right in the frog world. The moral of the little story came in Tommy's declaration that he'd never play hooky or pester frogs again.

It's a cute little story and a clear rewriting of Rose's caper the year before, complete with the relatives of the two missing "frogs" clamoring for their return. "Frogs Haunted Him" was clearly the work of a child who'd been lectured repeatedly about not playing hooky. She may have even chosen the subject matter thinking that it contained the sort of platitudes that judges at the paper, if they were anything like her parents and teachers, probably wanted to hear. Unfortunately for Rose, this first entry didn't win a prize.

Rose was undaunted. She submitted her second story entry, and this next one was to be a winner. Her subject was "the vagabond." Rose won second place, and therefore the two-dollar prize, for her well-written story, which appeared in the Children's Times section of the *Seattle Sunday Times* on May 19, 1907:

Dad Not So Slow

"I wonder if dad really is as brave as he pretends to be. I'm going to test him and find out," said little Billy Jones one afternoon to his little friend Teddy Michaels.

"I'll tell you what we'll do. I'm going to get some old clothes; yes, old vagabond's clothes, paint my nose and go to the back window and yell 'Hands up!' Won't that scare him, though?"

Both boys laughed heartily and both thought it was a very fine idea.

The stars were just beginning to shine when two little plotters appeared around the fence, each carrying a large bundle of clothes. They crept quickly into the cellar and in a few minutes Billy's toilet was completed. He was certainly a sight. He crept quietly forth, Teddy being left to keep watch. Now for the window, thought Billy. He climbed up very cautiously, peering behind now and then to see if anyone was watching him. Now to open the window. This was not a very easy thing—it was such a squeaky old thing. He was just halfway in the window when, alas. Tips the dog, heard his little master and gave a loud bark. This scared Billy and he fell full length across his father's bed.

Like a flash his father awoke, took the vagabond by the neck and threw him out the window.

Billy did not have far to fall, as it was just a couple of feet from the ground, but. Oh my! The scare he will never forget. He arose quickly from the ground and made his way to the cellar to find it vacant. Teddy had received as much scare as poor Bill and ran home. Billy rubbed the paint from his face, changed his clothing and crept quietly into the house, feeling quite guilty and feeling proud at the same time, not of himself, but of dad. Dad was the hero.

ROSE THOMPSON
Seventh Grade, Warren School, Class A
321 4th Avenue North, Seattle

It's a creative take on the idea of the vague story assignment of "the Vagabond," with a child testing the response of his father to the sight of a holdup man, and winding up thrown out a window in the bargain. Chances are Rose had never met a real vagabond in her life, even though Charlie worked in a train station near Seattle's infamous Skid Road. This was a street so jam-packed with saloons, houses of prostitution, and other nefarious establishments that it inspired the slang term skid row. Plenty of genuine vagabonds hung out on Skid Road. Rose had accepted the worst vagabond stereotype, the criminal stick-up man. But she describes the fine art of sneaking around—including the sound of the bedroom window squeaking when opened—so well she could only have been speaking from direct personal experience in that regard.

❧

By 1907, Rose's delicate-looking older sister Mina had met a stout young man with gray eyes and brown hair. He bore the unusual name of Stetson Gerdon Harlan. Called Stet, he had been born in Indiana to American-born parents. The Harlan family lived about six blocks from the Thompsons on 4th Avenue. Mina was the first of the Thompson sisters to marry, and grandmother Mary Louise happily served as one of her witnesses. Mina married Stet in a church wedding in 1907, when she was twenty-one, on September 24, a doubly special day to the bride and groom because it was also Stetson's birthday.

At this point in its history, Seattle served as a gateway to the Alaska gold rush, a final civilized stop for prospectors before they went into the wild. The city attracted prospectors from all over the world. It had its own red light district in the neighborhood of Skid Road. Anna, raised in hotels amongst an itinerant population and possessing an adaptability her daughter Rose later shared, accepted many different types of people and was comfortable selling her attention-grabbing wares to the Skid Road gals. Anna charged up to fifty dollars per hat, the 2012 equivalent of over a thousand dollars, a fact that might explain her ability to afford the two servants at home.

By this time Anna was also hitting the road periodically, going from one mining town to another to sell to the prostitutes that followed the prospectors every time a new mother lode was discovered. Anna traveled as far as the silver strike in the desert of Tonopah, Nevada, and the gold rush in the tundra of Juneau, Alaska. These locales were so far off the beaten path that they were largely unpopulated until their respective mineral veins were discovered.

A 1908 Juneau photograph of Anna, looking as statuesque as a reigning monarch, shows her sporting one of the hats that she sold in Alaska. It's quite fabulous, with what looks like at least two feet of plumes rising upwards, with a few additional ones cascading downward to frame Anna's face. It has a half-brim on the right side. Yes, that hat would have definitely gotten the fancy ladies' attention! The responsible girl raised in Farmington had become a minor entrepreneur, enterprising and bold. Anna's sales trips into the tough mining territories took place during a time when most married women only left the house to go shopping, attend teas with neighborhood ladies, or to go to formal dances or worship services. As far as we know, Anna went off on those trips unaccompanied, staying in hastily constructed boomtown hotels that reminded her of the one in which she'd been raised.

Charlie did not join Anna. She took off on her own, while he continued to work for the Great Northern Railroad. Rose had one parent who was tied down and another who consistently busted loose, but both of her parents were busy with work. Had she been allowed to become an actress, seventeen-year-old Rose would have been working, too. Since that wasn't possible, she started casting about for a way to obtain additional freedom. And then she thought she found one: His name was Johann Olaf Hovick.

PART TWO

ROSE: THE WOMAN

*If you had a mother like mine, you wouldn't go
handing her out to everyone. She's one of the
wonders of the world, like the Hanging Gardens
of Babylon or the Colossus of Rhodes.*

—GYPSY ROSE LEE

CHAPTER 4

HOVICH V. HOVICH

TALL OLAF JOHANN HOVICK WENT BY THE AMERICANIZED NICKNAME
Jack. He was born on August 6, 1886, in the town of Crookston, Minnesota,
located on the opposite side of the state from Farmington, near the North
Dakota border and close to Rose's birthplace of Wahpeton. Both Jack and
Rose had moved to Seattle when they were young children. Their Minnesota and North Dakota origins immediately gave them something in common when they met.

Jack's family situation had been rather unhappy. His parents, Sven and
Marit, with their daughters Hilma and Mattie, had emigrated from Norway
and settled first in Minnesota, a move that was fine for most of the family
but proved disruptive to Jack's already emotionally fragile mother. Another
baby boy named Ole J Hovick was born two years before Jack's arrival but
didn't survive. Jack's descendants believed his name was chosen as a way to
honor the lost child.

Losing the baby only added to Jack's mother's misery. Most immigrants
adjusted to America easily because they had chosen to relocate there; some,
like Marit, who may have been swept up in her husband's desire to live elsewhere, didn't. Marit didn't speak English well and longed to return to her
beloved home in Norway. By the time Jack came along two years later, her
level of melancholy had increased exponentially.

Sven had made his living in Norway from the sea, most likely as a fish-
erman. Minnesota, where a large proportion of Norwegian immigrants
settled, while a nice enough location, was simply the last place for a seafar-
ing man to resettle, attempt to earn a living, and raise a family. Sven didn't
like staying in a landlocked location. He wanted, even needed, to live by
the sea. Baby Jack was still tiny when Sven decided they would relocate to
Seattle, where he could get a job working on a boat again. Besides, the state

of Washington, with its pine trees, mountains, sea, waterways, and inlets, reminded the Norwegian family of home.

Unfortunately, their move to the more familiar-looking location didn't help the homesick Marit Hovick. She felt ever more isolated and became worse. As a result, little Jack was not well supervised. The boy pretty much raised himself on the city streets—but those streets were exciting and fun for him. Seattle was the last bastion of American civilization for the get-rich-quick prospectors who were heading north to Alaska for the gold rush.

Jack was seven years Rose's senior and had been working as an ad man for one of Seattle's newspapers when he met the vibrant young girl. Sometime during the winter of 1910, as the old saying goes, one thing led to another. Somehow, somewhere, Jack and Rose arranged to meet for a romantic tryst—or maybe they didn't plan a tryst at all, and one accidentally happened. In any event, when Jack and Rose were married on May 28, 1910, Rose was already pregnant with the daughter who would become Rose Louise Hovick, later known to the world as Gypsy Rose Lee.

There may very well have been an outcry when Charlie and Anna Thompson realized their teenage daughter Rose was with child—and initially without a husband. In any event, the young couple rushed to marry, and whether the marriage came about because of parental pressure or by their own choice is not known, though Jack was reportedly a very decent young man and would have wanted to do "the right thing." Rose would later tell her children a riveting tale in which she had sneaked away from a convent school to elope with Jack, but this doesn't exactly seem to have been the case. Factuality was nonessential to lots of the entertaining tall tales Rose loved to spin. The truth about this one was that Rose's mother, Anna, and beloved grandmother, Mary Louise, signed as witnesses on her marriage certificate, so the marriage took place not only with their blessing but also their participation.

Jack and Rose's union may not have been a true love match. It may have been conducted simply to ensure that Rose Louise was born while her parents were in wedlock rather than out of it, though Rose and Jack initially tried to make a go of this marriage. Jack attempted to build a little house in the Fauntleroy neighborhood of Seattle and settled there with Rose. The house was still unfinished, with a roof wide open to the sky, when not quite seven and a half months later, on January 9, 1911, their daughter Rose Louise was born during a snowstorm.

The storm was a major and debilitating one and had raged for several days. It involved thirty-seven-mile-per-hour gale force winds, rain, snow, and sleet. The blizzard conditions sent ships in nearby Port Townsend and other coastal localities scrambling to find safe harbors and even caused a Great Northern Railroad train, headed for points east, to return to Seattle, mail bags, passengers and all, when it reached Whitefish, Montana. The baby came in the midst of all this, and in a house without a full and completed roof.

It was bound to be an uncomfortable birth, given these conditions, but it was a hard birth, too—hard on Rose. Rose was a petite woman, and Jack was a very large man. Rose's first baby took after Jack and perhaps Anna, who was soon to be rechristened Big Lady by her granddaughter. The child Rose Louise was to prove to be a gigantic baby, weighing in at over twelve pounds, and Rose was trying to give birth to her under primitive conditions: fully conscious, at home, with gale-force winds outside, snow coming in through the exposed sections of the roof, while lying on the dining room table. There was no doctor. The only attendants at the birth were neighborhood women, probably Anna Thompson, almost certainly grandmother Mary Louise Stein, whom Rose Louise would soon start referring to as Doddie, and a woman later described as a black midwife.

This midwife was clearly a good one, since the gigantic baby was delivered alive and in good condition. Legend has it that the big baby was taken outside and washed in the snow. Legend also has it that baby Louise, as she was to be called, was born with what looked like two veils, meaning with the amniotic sac still intact when the child entered the world, and the sacs had to be punctured. One had been over the baby's face, and the other over her body.

Part of the personality that would become Gypsy Rose Lee began at that moment. Babies born with veils were said, in those days, to enter the world with psychic abilities. The veil of the amniotic sac was a sign. Several years later, baby Louise's childhood nickname would reflect her having been born with veils, when Rose started calling the dark-haired, dark-eyed child— who had a passion for reading tea leaves, dream analysis books, and astrology tomes—Gypsy.

Rose adored her grandmother Mary Louise so much that while she named this firstborn daughter Rose, after herself, she also selected Louise, after her grandmother, as the child's middle name. Louise was the name Rose Louise would usually be called, so as to avoid confusion stemming from having two Roses residing in the same home. This child was the third Rose in a direct line from the original one, Rosina Huttenger Egle, who was followed by Rose Egle and then Rose Thompson. With the snowstorm still raging after the large baby's birth, the family didn't register it or obtain a birth certificate for the newborn, procedures that probably were not mandatory at the time.

But poor Rose had suffered through what must have been a long, rough, and excruciating birth. She should have been in a hospital, with direct access to medical doctors and whatever kind of painkillers were available in 1911, not on a dining room table with snow coming in through the roof. The teenager needed more than just the midwife to help her through this horrific birth. The baby was far too large for little Rose to deliver easily and in a safe manner. Rose was, in effect, torn to shreds. The delivery caused the young girl to suffer painful lacerations that reportedly never quite healed properly. The birth was painful to the point that Rose would never want to have another child. But having just one baby was not in the cards.

In the wider world beyond the Hovick house in Everett, the first feature film was released in 1911, the same year that Rose Louise Hovick was born. *Enoch Arden* was a two-reel movie made by D. W. Griffith and concerned a man's return home after having been stranded on an island. The movies had arrived, and they were soon to capture Rose's imagination.

By the time little Louise was a year old, Rose was sufficiently recovered from the birth to have taken an appraising look at her daughter, realizing just how beautiful this baby of hers happened to be. Rose would always adore having pictures taken of herself and her children and submitted a photo of Louise to a healthy baby contest. Baby Louise won.

And then another baby was due in the Hovick household, even though Rose emphatically did not want another one. Sources vary as to when her next child was born, with 1913 being the best guess. The child herself was to believe she was born in 1912. Rose would later say in an article that she ostensibly wrote in the 1940s that her second child was nineteen months younger than Louise, which would have put the second child's birth in August of 1912, rather than in November. Then Rose clouded the issue of the child's birth. When the family had a vaudeville act, Rose carried five different birth certificates for her in order to get around the child labor law. These including a faked birth certificate registered in the 1920s, where she listed Rose Louise's birth date with this second child's name.

The child, of course, was to be named Ellen June Hovick, called June, and within a few years she would become known professionally as Baby June. While Rose was pregnant with her, Jack Hovick kept calling the baby Olaf, hoping she would be a boy that he could name after himself, and perhaps also wanting to honor the little boy his parents had lost. This baby's full name was going to be Olaf John.

Rose had other ideas. She emphatically did not want to go through another birth after surviving the nightmare that had been Louise's painful entrance into the world. Rose was still only a teen herself when she had Louise. The idea of having a second baby was appalling to her. Not being the passive type, she tried to end the pregnancy. Rose tried punching herself in the stomach. She took pratfalls. She even tried to stop eating in the hope that doing so would result in the miscarriage of Olaf John. Nothing worked. Rose had a feeling the child was a little girl, not a little boy. And the baby was a tough little thing. Rose may have tried all sorts of ways to lose it, but this baby was proving to be indestructible.

The baby was born a bit early during a brief trip that Jack and Rose made to Vancouver, British Columbia, making the baby a Canadian citizen rather than an American. Fortunately for Rose, this time the birth took place in a hospital. Owing to Rose's near hunger strike during the pregnancy, it was said, the child's head could have been fit into a teacup. Accordingly, the birth was probably a lot easier on Rose than her first childbirth, but after Rose's many attempts to lose the child, it's a wonder the baby was normal.

If this child truly was born on November 8, 1913, in a Vancouver hospital, Rose certainly made a fast recovery. Her older sister Mina had divorced Stetson Harlan, her first husband, and married a mine assayer from Minnesota named Harry A. Briggs, on November 14, 1913. One of her two witnesses was Rose.

Olaf John wouldn't do as a name for Rose's second tough but fragile-looking baby girl, of course, so the name was feminized into Ellen June. From the first, Rose and Jack seem to have called the child June rather than Ellen. Later, Rose may have told June that her birth name was Ellen Evangeline, and that she had given her daughter her sister Belle's middle name. But the child would be listed as Ellen June on her parents' divorce papers when they were filed in court a year later.

Where Louise was brown-haired and dark-eyed and would always be tall for her age, with almost a sturdy build, June was a blonde, blue-eyed, delicate cutie right from the start. She bore a bit more of a resemblance to Rose than did Louise, who looked more like Jack. Even before the children were in show business, photos reveal that both girls were adorable children. Louise was gorgeous from the day she was born, and ultra-thin, graceful June, while not a traditional beauty like her sister, nevertheless had the bearing of a little fairy princess.

Rose, still just a teenager herself, now had two babies to look after, and two babies, she felt, were enough. The fact that she had been injured during the ordeal of giving birth to Louise may have colored her views on childbirth—not to mention men—for the rest of her life. Having the second baby so soon after the first surely had done nothing but terrify the young woman further, despite the fact that the second birth turned out to be easier. But Rose would seek out additional children to back up both of her daughters' vaudeville acts and would be a magnet for children throughout her entire life. Children always seemed to adore her, but still, for Rose, two of her own were more than enough. If being married meant taking the risk of having more giant-sized babies, it may have been right after Louise's birth that Rose started looking for a way out of her marriage.

Life within the home she shared with Jack, Louise, and June was not exactly going smoothly, either, prompting Rose to find a way out. Jack, who craved stability, wanted to be a good husband and a decent provider for his children. Outside forces intervened when he lost his job sometime during 1913, putting more strain on what was probably already a marriage built on the shakiest possible foundation. It would be a year before he managed to find another job. The duo was already on the road to divorce, and getting there wasn't going to be the easiest trip.

It isn't known when or why the little family moved from the house in the Fauntleroy section of Seattle, where Louise had been born, but in all probability, the move resulted from Jack's joblessness. He borrowed money from friends and relatives in order to pay for his wife and children's expenses and even to build another little house, this time on Rainier Beach, an area of mist-covered mountains, water, sand, and majestic pine trees that was rustic and unspoiled—and desolate. Very few people were living there at the time, although the area was served by a streetcar line, had electric street lights, and featured a neighborhood school that Jack hoped Louise and June would one day attend.

But Rose hated the new house on Rainier Beach. She thought it was "barn-like, damp and full of knot-holes," as she would later state in one of the affidavits filed during her divorce proceedings. The dampness was aggravated by the house's proximity to an inlet of the Pacific Ocean, and this was not an ideal situation for Rose. She was already suffering from the asthma and lung problems that would plague her for the rest of her life. According to Rose, the conditions in that beach house gave her the grippe. That assessment may not have been accurate. It may actually have brought on one of her frequent and debilitating asthma attacks. Either way, she got sick and blamed the house.

Jack had a whole different version of Rose's grippe attack. He claimed that she had faked the case of grippe. He had gone out and obtained a doctor, who gave her a prescription, but that rather than taking the medicine,

Jack said, Rose drank a quart of whisky, polishing it off within twenty-four hours. Two days later, perhaps after awakening from a whisky-induced hangover, Rose decided she was fed up with living in the "barn" and ran back to her parents' house. Jack believed that this flight back home to Charlie and Anna took place mainly because Rose enjoyed living closer to the bustling center of Seattle. Thus the unhappy marriage segued into a more chaotic phase. Rose began a series of moves back and forth, in and out of Jack's place. Their toddlers were dragged along for the whole messy ride.

Rose and Jack separated for the last two months of 1913, perhaps immediately after June's birth, if November 1913, and not 1912, was actually the month and year when June was born. But her parents got together again at the beginning of 1914, moving first into the West Apartments, where the monthly rent was only fourteen dollars. Later, after Jack was finally employed by the *Seattle Sun* newspaper in February, he decided to move his floundering little family into a newly built, lovely, red-brick colonial-style building known as the Orinoco Apartments on Stewart Street, near Seattle's central business district. He figured that Rose, who adored being around a lot of people and action, might just like the place. The rent there was twenty-one dollars a month, but the place was so nice that he felt it was well worth the price.

Rose was much happier living at the Orinoco Apartments, if not within the marriage, though she and Jack must have had something as a couple since she returned to him every time she left. Rose wanted to stay at the Orinoco, but Jack's long spell without work made additional economizing imperative. Rose arranged for the family to move into a smaller apartment within the same building for a lower rent.

Unfortunately, the reduction in rent of $2.50 per month was still not enough to get the struggling family back on its feet, even though Jack was now earning a monthly salary of one hundred dollars. Jack was still paying back the funds he'd borrowed while unemployed. He realized that in order to clear up his debts once and for all, the family would need to move to another building a little over a mile away. He found a new flat at the Zindorf Apartments, with an easier to maintain monthly rent of fourteen dollars.

The stucco Zindorf Apartments were in a perfectly adequate, but much less elaborate, building than the tonier Orinoco Apartments. Rose couldn't stand the place on first sight. She did not want to live there. Besides, since the rent was lower, the individuals already residing there were considerably less prosperous, so Rose said that the Zindorf was filled with questionable characters. It was not, in her opinion, a fit place for her and the children to reside.

According to Hovick family legend, one of the last straws for Jack came after he brought a cute kitten home to give to Louise and June as a pet. Rose may have been drinking when she saw the tiny creature, because her otherwise lifelong love of animals would have had to temporarily desert her in order for her to do what she allegedly did next: Rose destroyed the kitten. The killing wasn't done in a merciful manner, either. The story goes that Rose killed the helpless kitten with an axe. If the story was true, this act was intended as a way of getting even with Jack. Whatever Rose's motivation for such an act, Jack's family reported he was never to wipe the sight of the destroyed little animal from his mind. To Jack, that was it. He was finished. The incident signaled, loud and clear, that it was time for him to end his increasingly nightmarish marriage. Driving Jack to this particular point may have been Rose's strategy in the first place. The killing was a hideous act, but it did make a statement: Rose was fed up with anything that came from Jack.

On June 20, 1914, Rose and Jack must have had the mother of all fights. Rose would charge in her divorce papers that on that date Jack hit her, threatened to murder her, and even choked her, and that he had beaten her on numerous other occasions. She also said that Jack had beaten and threatened to kill the children. It is not known if Jack and Rose temporarily separated yet again after this fight, though if they did, it was probably all to the good for the sake of both parties—not to mention the children, who had already been eyewitnesses to too many horrific parental battles. According to the affidavit that Rose would later file during her divorce proceedings, Little Louise incurred Jack's wrath at least once. Rose claimed Jack became violent with the child before locking her in a closet "on account of some trivial matter." The specifics of this matter were not defined.

The family war had escalated to such an extent that Rose might have been truly terrified that her two girls would be either hurt or—more to the point—spirited away from her so that Jack could raise them himself. She stashed both of the girls away with either a friend or a family member and did not let Jack know the identity of their protector. At a time when women were encouraged to be docile, obedient, and to let their husbands rule the family like minor demigods, Rose nevertheless found the courage to do the right thing by her daughters.

Nine days after this fight, Jack called Rose on the telephone and told her that he would be coming over that afternoon with a dray to move the furniture. At his wits' end with the mess that his marriage had become, Jack also told Rose that she could follow the dray if she wanted, or she could "do the best she could." Jack was fed up and, since at that point he did not tell Rose precisely where the dray would be taking their belongings, Rose figured he was trying to take the furniture and run. Rose knew the Zindorf Apartments only by reputation. She had never been inside, had not seen this new apartment that Jack had managed to secure, and did not know for a certainty where her furniture was about to be taken. Maybe it was destined for the Zindorf. Maybe it wasn't. Jack hadn't specified during the phone call. Rose decided that Jack was not going to take anything whatsoever out of their apartment at the Orinoco. Jack came by and spoke to Rose at that point, but he didn't manage to get the furniture out of the apartment. Somehow, Rose managed to see to it that Jack left empty-handed, and Jack temporarily retreated.

The minute he was gone, Rose swung into action. She barred as many of the doors and windows as she could and fled the place. Then she ran directly to the stately, brick Romanesque style Pioneer Building in Pioneer Square, several blocks away, to visit her attorney, P. V. Davis. Once there, she treated him to an earful about Jack.

Jack's temporary retreat may have been only as far as the Orinoco apartment house gardens. Once he saw Rose leaving the premises, he figured out a way to get back into his old apartment, going in through a window that Rose had overlooked and hadn't barred. What happened next depends on whose divorce affidavit one believes. According to Rose, Jack went inside the apartment and tore up the furniture before moving it. Whatever he could get out that window he'd opened went outside and away with him. He even took bedrails through the window and off the premises. When Rose got back, she was forced to sleep on the floor throughout the next month, and she was not amused.

Rose not only filed for the divorce, she petitioned for a restraining order to keep Jack away from her and the children. Then she hit him with a second restraining order, this time to prevent the *Seattle Sun* from handing Jack his weekly twenty-five dollar salary until Rose's fifteen dollar per week support payment had been deducted. Then there was the property dispute. Jack had bought and later sold a piece of property in the Fauntleroy Park section of Seattle, perhaps including the unfinished little house where Louise had been born. Rose was supposed to get a part of that sale but never did, she charged in one of her affidavits, implying that Jack stashed the proceeds away where Rose could not get her hands on it.

The picture Rose and her attorney painted of Jack in the divorce documents was not at all pretty. She claimed Jack had locked Louise in a closet and beaten the child almost insensible, and that he had attempted to choke Rose to death. If these events happened as stated, then they qualified as abuse. If they didn't, Rose's lawyer, P. V. Davis, was a lot savvier than Jack's attorney in knowing how to get and keep the judge's attention focused on his client.

Jack's lawyer, C. J. Smith, was remiss in failing to use the story about Rose killing the kitten. The affidavits do not mention it. If Smith had utilized the episode, it may have supported Jack's claim that Rose was not a fit guardian for the girls. On the other hand, this was a time when wives almost always were awarded custody of children during divorce cases, and animal rights were virtually non-existent. People who didn't want the burden of kittens to feed had no qualms about killing them. It was common to tie kittens up in a cloth bag and drown them. At the time criminal profilers and psychiatrists had not yet discovered that violence toward animals was a symptom of psychopathology. Killing a kitten in 1914 didn't pack the emotional wallop that it did later. These factors may help to explain why the kitten incident was left out of the affidavits.

According to one of Jack's responses to one of Rose's divorce complaint affidavits, the bedrails Rose claimed Jack had allegedly climbed through a window to "liberate" had actually been removed sometime beforehand, and in Rose's presence, so that he could return them to the store from which they'd been purchased. There would be no need for beds at the family's proposed new digs at the Zindorf Apartments, which came complete with Murphy beds that could be pulled down from the walls in the evenings and raised during the day to provide more floor space for the occupants. Jack denied having any property other than the furnishings of the apartment at the Orinoco. Most importantly, Jack denied that he had an "ungovernable temper" and denied that he'd ever hurt Rose or had done anything violent to little three-year-old Louise, explaining he had been trying to "correct her in her mis deeds [sic]." Jack added that Rose was "harassing" him with garnishments to his salary that had been filed and served on his bosses at the *Seattle Sun*. If the garnishments didn't stop, he'd lose his job. Nevertheless, Rose's lawyer filed another application to continue the restraining order.

Jack brought character witnesses in to sign affidavits on his behalf, and these documents tell a whole different story. His sister Hilma's husband, J. Fred Braid, advertising manager at the *Seattle Times*, had never seen any evidence indicating that Jack was violent; neither had he ever seen Jack threaten Rose or beat the girls. Fred indicated that he saw a caring husband and father whenever he saw Jack with his family. Jack's friend Owen Rowe, who had loaned Jack fifty dollars to pay his family's expenses while he was unemployed, also filed an affidavit testifying to Jack's decent character and love for his daughters. The business manager of the *Seattle Sun*, A. J. Copeland, who also stated in an affidavit that Jack was a terrific man who loved his family, added an intriguing line concerning Rose's statements in her affidavit about Jack allegedly threatening to kill her and the children. Copeland said plainly that he thought these allegations "can have no foundation in fact and must be wholly imaginary on her part."

Both of Jack's friends' statements seem to imply that Jack may have wanted custody of Louise and June. In an answer to Rose's complaints, Jack's lawyer wrote that his client did not believe Rose was fit to have permanent custody.

There was only one slight problem with the accounts given by Jack and by his two friends and brother-in-law: The judge, Boyd J. Tallman, had not been present when the death threats attributed to Jack had allegedly been made against Rose, a fact that placed the jurist in a legal dilemma. Judge Tallman had been born in Pennsylvania, relocated to Walla Walla, Washington, and worked as both a teacher and a lawyer before being appointed in 1900 to the bench of the superior court of the state of Washington for King County. Tallman was considered a competent judge of high caliber. He had presided over hundreds of legal cases, most of which were never overturned by a higher court.

Judge Tallman considered the case before him now and decided the best course of action would be to play it safe. If Rose's accounts were true and accurate, he could not allow Jack continued contact with her and the children. It was better to rule on the safe side and keep Rose, Louise, and June away from Jack's potentially explosive physical presence than to risk a disaster. The judge had several opportunities to view both Jack and Rose in court and get a feel for their characters. Both were reportedly highly charismatic people, but Judge Tallman was in a position where he had to believe, and favor, one litigant's word over the other. Did he see a more ingenuous quality in one that made him predisposed to rule against the other, or did he simply err on the side of reason?

Whatever Tallman may have seen or sensed, his rulings were to break Jack Hovick's heart. First, the preliminary order decreed that Jack was restrained from contacting Rose or the children. He was restrained from removing the children from Rose's custody. He was restrained from taking any more furniture out of the Orinoco apartment. And the *Sun* was going to continue to be obliged to hand over a portion of Jack's salary to Rose's attorney every Saturday. That was only the preliminary order, but Jack Hovick's cause was already lost.

A little over a month later, on August 19, 1914, Judge Tallman issued his findings of fact and conclusion of law regarding *Hovick v. Hovick*. And the respected Judge Tallman sided with Rose completely. She was granted the divorce. Tallman ruled that Jack had been negligent in his support of his family, "notwithstanding the fact that the said defendant was a strong and able-bodied competent man"—a cruel determination, since during one whole year of this marriage, Jack had been unemployed, but actively looking for work. The judge ruled that Jack had threatened and choked Rose. He ruled that Rose was a fit and proper person to have permanent custody of the two small children. Tallman also ruled, on an additional but minor issue, that Jack had to pay the balance remaining on the furniture that would remain in Rose's possession. He ruled that Rose should be paid thirty dollars alimony monthly, double what she had originally asked for. He even ruled that Jack had to pay for Rose's divorce costs.

It wasn't lost on the judge that Rose and Jack were polar opposites. One of his conclusions was that "on account of the great differences in the nature and disposition of the said parties, their objects and aims in life, their method of living, it is impossible for the said parties to continue to live together and that it is for the best interest of both of said parties and the society in general that the said parties be divorced." If Jack's side of the story was veracious but ignored, the scandal of this ruling must have been an unbearable burden—added as it was to Jack's losing custody of his two beloved children. He was inconsolable at losing the children, yet delighted to have freed himself of Rose. Jack hit the road for a brief period, jumping trains and riding the rails from place to place, hobo-style. It was a financially struggling young man's idea of a much-needed vacation, one that allowed him to put some distance between himself and his ex-wife. Eventually he met a lovely young woman named Elizabeth on the beach in Santa Monica, California, while working as a promotions man for the movie studios. Elizabeth came from a German family from Colorado and was interested in becoming a nice, old-fashioned hausfrau. This was the kind of bride he'd hoped to find in Rose. For Jack, this sweet lady was a perfect match. He married her three weeks after they met. The couple settled in the Los Angeles area. They had two children, Jack and Betty.

Elizabeth later told Gypsy Rose Lee how much Jack had missed her and June after divorcing Rose, and how he'd initially hoped Jack, his firstborn, would be another little girl, filling the gap the absence of Louise and June had left in his life. He had to wait for the second child, Betty, to make her appearance before he finally felt better about losing his first two girls.

June was to have virtually no memories of her life with Jack. The divorce papers stated she was only one year old when *Hovick v. Hovick* was raging in the King County courtroom. But Louise remembered her father fondly and would resume contact with him later.

After all that fuss about her desire to remain in the Orinoco Apartments during the divorce proceedings, Rose ultimately didn't stay there. It's probable that when Jack left Seattle, the alimony payments stopped for a while, prompting her to move. Or maybe Rose was simply homesick for Charlie and Anna Thompson. She returned to her parents' two-story wooden home at 323 4th Avenue North with the two children, likely to the delight of her adoring father, who was still employed by the Great Northern Railroad and had to stick close to home while Anna went off on her sales jaunts. And Rose might have remained on 4th Avenue North but for the intervention of fate in the form of her toddler June, which gave Rose quite another idea.

CHAPTER 5

TH£ BABY STANDS ON HER TOES

PARENTS WHO ENROLL THEIR CHILDREN IN SPECIALIZED ARTS CLASSES they wish they had taken themselves believe they are giving their offspring a gift. In 1914, Rose was only twenty-three years old. She was a young-minded twenty-three, still a bit too interested in theater and films, and she had enrolled gorgeous yet pudgy little Louise—the child who had won the healthy baby contest when she was only a year old—in a ballet class in West Seattle at the Douglas Dancing Academy. The owner of the dancing school taught the class, held in the spacious Oddfellows Hall lodge building. He was professionally known as Professor Harold Douglas. Rose actually need not have bothered enrolling her oldest daughter in the "professor's" dance emporium. If ever a child had two left feet and no interest whatsoever in the performing arts, it was Louise. Louise was four years old by then. She was adorable but a bit too chubby. Still, dancing lessons for little girls were in vogue at the moment, and Rose was always very much attuned to the times, especially when it came to anything theatrical.

It's possible, yet highly unlikely, that Louise first entered the dancing school while Rose was still married to Jack Hovick, who would still have been trying to recover financially from his bout of unemployment. He would have been justified in rejecting this new expense. Indeed, anyone would have been justified in believing it was frivolous, especially for a child as disinterested in dance as Louise. But it is more probable that it was actually Grandpa Charlie Thompson who paid for the lessons after Rose and the children had returned to his home, although he vociferously disapproved of the idea. Charlie still considered theatrical people to be the scum of the earth.

Louise went through the motions of participating in her ballet class, probably longing from the start for the moment when it would end. Rose may have enjoyed it more than her daughter did. She would sit in the back of the room with the other mothers, watching the proceedings. One day she had little June by her side when something rather extraordinary happened. June was a silent two-year-old. She did not speak yet. Her muteness may have been the result of a developmental delay brought on by Rose's attempt to miscarry June by not eating enough during her pregnancy, causing June's birth weight to be abnormally low. Then there was the turmoil of June's early months, spent living in different locations with embattled parents. The toddler might very well have felt it was safer to make herself as inconspicuous as possible. Moving in with Rose's parents stabilized the family situation, at least for the children.

But one fine day, when her big sister Louise was galumphing around the studio with the rest of her classmates to tunes played on the dancing school piano, June realized that in this venue it was perfectly all right for toddlers to get up and be seen. Something stirred within the heart of two-year-old June.

The baby rose from her place beside her mother. She made her way onto the dance floor with the rest of the children, all of whom were older than she. Then she began to dance alongside them. Family legend held that the baby even got up that day and attempted to dance *on her toes.*

As a non-speaking baby, June definitely knew how to make her wishes known via the grand gesture. Rose was beside herself with delight. Here, finally, was a child who wanted to dance, and who would take to the performing arts that Rose had loved since the happy days when she had run off and joined the Juvenile Bostonians. June would embrace all the fun Rose had before her marriage, her pregnancy with Louise, and everything else that had happened in recent years—all of which had conspired to make Rose thoroughly miserable. At that moment, when June got up to join the action in that little West Seattle dance class, Rose probably felt as if the sun had come out from behind all those dark clouds.

Rose insisted that the baby deserved private lessons with Louise's dancing teacher, who initially did not want June as a pupil because she was far too young. Rose persisted, Professor Douglas finally agreed, and the lessons were arranged. Rose paid for them with Charlie's money, if not his blessing. He was soon to soften on that score. June, a naturally lithe and graceful little girl who was able to take direction, loved her dancing lessons and was also exceedingly talented.

Rose's faith in June was soon rewarded. Two-and-a-half-year-old Baby June made her debut at one of Charlie Thompson's lodge halls, with Charlie himself roped in to serve as her piano accompanist. He did not approve of any endeavor that was even remotely theatrical until he saw his grandchild dance and witnessed how beautifully her performance went over. The little one's act was even covered by a Seattle newspaper. Charlie was sufficiently proud of her to purchase ten copies, one for himself and the rest to send to family members and friends—including Anna, now known, due to her stately height and bearing, to her grandchildren as Big Lady, who was off somewhere selling creations to fancy ladies and missed her granddaughters' debut. Young Louise also appeared in that first little lodge show. She wore a tough girl comedy costume with a feathered hat, a bright red sweater, and a slit skirt. She also attempted to talk-sing a song, probably a popular number called "When Francis Dances With Me." Charlie was impressed with June's performance, and he finally admitted to Rose that she might have a valid point about show business being a career path for June. But he hastily added that he didn't think performing was a good idea for Louise.

The performing arts momentum grew for the baby. Intensive dance lessons for June—and probably a class or two for Louise—continued apace. The baby continued to excel in her classes and progressed at a rate that can only be described as phenomenal. Rose was probably shocked that she had an honest-to-goodness dancing prodigy on her hands. Rose had always had a healthy interest in the theater, but now she realized her tiny daughter was a gifted dancer. This awareness was enough to catapult Rose's interest in the performing arts to a new level. There wasn't a doubt in Rose's mind that this child wanted—even needed—to be trained as a performer. Many decades later, June was to say, "Mother was never stage-struck. That's all part of the fable. Her dreams were never for herself." Her hopes had been, instead, for June. It didn't seem to occur to anyone involved with the child—not Rose, not Charlie or Anna, and certainly not Professor Douglas who was profiting from providing the Hovick kids with dancing lessons—that the two-year-old had not exactly chosen the theater as a career. This child could not yet declare anything. She could perform in lodge halls with her mother's prompting and direction, but she still was not talking. The child, however, seemed to adore learning to dance.

It might have been natural for Rose's interest in a career of her own to arise again at this time, in tandem with her children's lessons, but by this point there was a complication. Rose's severe and debilitating asthma was untreatable and incurable. Often she could barely draw a breath, especially when she was under strain or duress. She was known to cough piteously and without let-up. The smoldering fumes from a powder that could be set alight gave her minimal relief, but this treatment didn't halt or reverse the asthma. There were days when Rose's airways were so constricted she could barely function. This condition was not compatible with an onstage career. If it had been, Rose might have been in the dancing school alongside the children, perhaps joining one of Professor Douglas's classes for older girls

A candid photo of the children, taken around this time in a leafy glen on a sunny day—presumably in the Seattle area—shows two striking, though contrasting children, who look almost like two little fairies in the woods. Louise is a bit sturdier than her sister, with short dark hair cut in the straight, sleek bob like that was soon to be made famous by actress Louise Brooks. June is more ethereal, small-boned, delicate, and with hair so blonde that even in a black and white photograph it looks as if Rose had already started bleaching it (she later did so regularly). The girls are sitting casually on the grass and seem very small. They're caught in a relaxed moment simply being kids, but there is something special, already, about them both.

Rose, meanwhile, wasn't done with men. She tried marriage for a second time, marrying Judson Brenneman on May 27, 1916, at the First Unitarian Church in Seattle. Getting married in a Catholic church, with its prohibition against divorce, was no longer possible for her. Judson was a traveling grocery salesman initially from Columbia City, Indiana.

But it was June, not the newlyweds, who appeared in the Seattle Times the day following the wedding, in an article about the fifty-six students scheduled to appear in the Douglas Academy Dancing School recital, otherwise known as "Ballet 1916," to be presented at the Moore Theatre a few evenings later. The story features a photograph of three-year-old June Hovick in toe shoes and a tutu. June had begun her private lessons at age two-and-a-half and had already risen to the status of featured performer just a few months later. One can't help but feel impressed by the little one's accomplishments. Thirty high school girls were also appearing in this recital, but it was wee June, the newcomer, who was highlighted as the dancing school standout. She would be "appearing as Pavlova in a solo toe dance." Rose was later accused of pushing this child ahead, but Professor Douglas might have been the initial force behind June's advancement. June could not have been profiled in the paper without the approval and promotion of Douglas.

June's dancing ability may have been exceptional, but a growing child of three should not have been wearing toe shoes. Doing so was almost as harmful as Chinese foot binding. Today it is believed that children should not wear pointe shoes until they are at least twelve years old. Back in 1916, no one really thought about such dangers, let alone realized that putting little June in toe shoes this early would lead to deformed feet in adulthood.

At the moment, the child loved to dance, her mother made it possible for her to study with the best teacher in Seattle, she was excelling beyond all possible expectations, and the recital, of course, went on.

So did more appearances at lodge halls and charitable benefits in and around Seattle. Rose's baby may have been three, but she was already getting professional bookings. Again, it would later be said that Rose pushed June into show business, but as the situation with Louise had already demonstrated, a child can only be pushed so far into a discipline like ballet dancing. A baby who hates dancing class need only sit on the floor and refuse to participate, but June never did. She wanted to be among the dancers. Young Louise misunderstood and felt shunted aside by the attention her sister was able to command through her dancing talent, yet it's to Rose's credit that the child she concentrated on advancing now was the one who loved dancing, not the one that didn't take to it. And it's to Rose's credit that she did not hold June back.

One evening June's name was on the same performance roster as the premier ballerina of the day, Anna Pavlova. June may have been only three, and she may not have talked yet, but could she ever deliver! "Baby's Twinkling Little Feet Delight Big Crowd at Ad Show," announced a September 9, 1916, *Seattle Times* headline above a photo of June. She was pictured perched on a stool and clad in a tutu with her hair—which was too short to be curled yet—cut in the same Dutch boy bob style Louise wore, covered with a cute knitted skull cap. She's also in beribboned knee socks and pointe shoes. The photo caption reads:

> Baby June, 3-year-old dancer who delighted a large crowd at the Ad Club Show at The Arena last night, is called a Second Pavlova. Her little legs and feet spoke poetry of motion that is equaled only by few professional dancers said those who saw her. She practically charmed the crowd with her interpretation of the difficult dance, "The Magic Fairy."

The Ad Show was an extravaganza, put on for the first time that year by the Seattle Ad Club. It featured a masquerade ball and a pageant, with coronations of both a masque queen and a juvenile queen of hearts, both of whom had her own royal court. The pageant included floats. It was not a small affair by any means, and Rose's little June had been hired to be part of the entertainment. The baby was doing a grand job, and she was on her way.

※

Rose's marriage to Judson didn't work out. Judson was probably the "Bubs" that both June and Louise would recall, however vaguely, in their memoirs.

Bubs believed the two children belonged in public school and could also benefit from a Sunday school education. An initial attempt to send Louise and June to Sunday school didn't work—at least not for June, who was hysterical on and off and for three days after hearing about baby Moses being abandoned in the bulrushes. Little June was talking by then and prone to spectacular meltdowns worthy of grown divas. In this instance, she had become upset at the thought of the infant Moses possibly drowning, an insight that may have lead to grand-scale hysterics, yet also revealed the child's developing big-heartedness. Judson wasn't impressed. He called her a spoiled brat and a heathen. Rose was livid that June had been subjected to the terrifying Moses story, a reaction that must not have gone over well with Judson. But Rose had a valid point: If the story frightened and upset her child so much, then why should June have to listen to it? She may have already been knocking her audiences dead with her mesmerizing dancing, but June was too young to be hearing about child endangerment.

But Judson didn't stop wanting to educate the children. According to June, Judson also wanted the unattainable: to have more children with Rose, the last thing that Rose wanted. She had suffered enough with the first child and hadn't wanted the second. A third was out of the question. Judson had initially fed Rose a line that, when married, they would just be platonic friends, and that he would support her two children—or so he said in order to get Rose to agree to marry him. He was in for an unpleasant surprise when, on their wedding night, he expected more from Rose than she was willing to deliver. For her part, Rose felt she'd been lied to and betrayed.

The marriage lasted little more than a year on paper and probably ended much sooner, since within ten months Rose, June, and possibly Louise had left the dampness and constant rain of Seattle and were firmly established in Hollywood, California. Movies were the latest trend in the entertainment world, and Rose saw no reason June shouldn't have a chance to appear in them. Besides, Rose had never been enamored of Seattle's wet climate. Asthmatics loved Southern California; the warm and dry weather there helped their condition, or at least didn't make it worse. Charlie pitched in to finance the family's move, and off Rose and June went.

Louise may initially have been left with either Charlie or another family member or friend; reports about this matter vary. It's possible she stayed with a friend of Rose's who was interested in Christian Science, a new faith primarily based on positive thinking. Christian Science was in vogue, and Rose had become an adherent. Rose signed Louise up for school and enrolled her in kindergarten in Seattle, where she attended John Hay School. It's possible that a child who loved to learn as much as Louise could have gone on to college to become a doctor or a professor, had she been allowed to stay in school. But show business beckoned this family, and, with the exception of a bit of traditional schooling and lessons later from a tutor, Louise was a self-taught child, reading books on her own about whatever subjects caught her fancy.

Louise was soon reunited with her mother and sister in Hollywood, and they all began making the rounds of casting agents' offices in an attempt to get into the movies. Louise was the more photogenic of the two sisters. For the most part, although June did manage to get a few small parts, both girls got cast as extras in crowd scenes.

Louise may have been enrolled in another public school in California. No evidence has surfaced indicating that the child went to school there, but Rose would later claim Louise briefly attended "public schools." June was still far too young to attend school. Rose may have seen no point in subjecting her children to school in a state that they were just visiting, especially when she had not enjoyed school herself. She had another education in mind for both of her daughters, the one offered at the Celeste School of Dance run by Ernest Belcher, a London-trained dancing teacher considered the father of ballet in California. Ernest Belcher's students were consistently hired to appear in the movies, and among them were Mary Pickford, Pola Negri, Ramon Navarro, and much later, even the phenomenal child movie star Shirley Temple, who was discovered by motion picture talent scouts while taking one of Belcher's dance classes. Between dancing school, making the rounds of casting offices with the children, and living in hotels catering to theatrical performers, Rose picked up a lot of information about opportunities available to child performers. One of the tidbits she heard and acted upon led to the next opportunity for her youngest daughter, when June was selected to be the child queen of an event called The Allied Carnival.

It was February 1917. America's entrance into World War I was still two months off, but a group of kind society matrons in Los Angeles had banded together to hold a major fundraiser for the British Red Cross. The war was still Europe's exclusive problem, but the Angelenos had decided to get involved and help the people who were affected. They came up with an elegant carnival event program. The Shrine Auditorium was taken over by an event that was priced reasonably so that people of all ages and social classes could enjoy it.

Pageantry and spectacle were the order of the day. A Mrs. W. A. Clark Jr., who was the president of the carnival, also served as its adult queen, and the event began when she entered the Shrine in a pale blue French colonial gown, attended to by her courtiers. Mrs. Clark had a contingent of costumed "vice queens"—a term that was not as hilarious at the time as it would sound later—attending her. The vice queens represented England, France, and Belgium, and many more cultures and countries were represented at the fête, which included a Gypsy wedding, a Native American fortune-teller, opera singers, Japanese sumo wrestlers, and a bagpipe band. There was even a grand formal dance. Cannons fired flowers into the crowd while people were dancing. The flowers were numbered. A wheel of fortune was spun, and the owner of the flower with the winning number received a jeweled prize. There were also little cakes served with jewels hidden within them, which must have given a whole new meaning to the idea of raiding the dessert table.

The carnival was to include a Saturday matinee for children, with a grand march of Mother Goose characters to be held in honor of England. After a search for an appropriate child to act as a tiny monarch, the committee selected little June as queen of the frolic. June lead the grand march of children, dressed as characters from Mother Goose stories and fairy tales. She would also be making her toe-dancing debut for the Los Angeles public at the matinee performance to follow. At one point during the festivities, the woman portraying Mother Goose laid a golden egg, and a tiny fairy dancer popped out of it. Articles concerning the event don't name the child, but this fairy dancer was almost certainly June.

June was said to be three years old in a February 12, 1917, *Los Angeles Times* article about the frolic, even though she had been declared to be three in print a whole year earlier in Seattle. She was at least four years old by this time, possibly five. Rose's assertion that June was three may have been intended to make the child look like even more of a prodigy than she was already. That was the trick of stage mothers everywhere: The younger a child performer was made to appear, the longer she could be considered for kiddie roles. The line about June being three may also have been one of Rose's strategies for keeping June and Louise away from the clutches of the Hollywood truant officer.

The *Los Angeles Times* article states that June was not a child performer in the movies, without mentioning that the main reason the family was in

Hollywood was to help her become one. As publicity, it was a brilliant ploy to announce the child toe dancer's participation as the queen of the children's portion of an extravagant event in a movie town, only to casually throw in the fact that the child *didn't* work in the movie industry. June had probably already been to countless film role auditions, and if she hadn't already appeared in movies, she soon would.

June played more benefit engagements. Her genius for dance was becoming apparent. Rose realized June could watch another performer's act a few times and then replicate it perfectly. There were adult performers who could not match the little girl's gift for learning dance routines—a sign of both the child's near-total immersion in dance and show business culture, as well as her own precocious talent for dance and mimicry. Her ability to learn by watching was also to prove useful. The little dancing doll could pick up routines that other child performers used to bring down the house. It was much easier to coach this type of child, who could learn routines by osmosis, than it would have been to try and make a professional out of another whose learning curve wasn't as steep. June had a ball with all of this, since she was performing dances that she loved and getting positive reinforcement for doing so. Louise seemed to sit back and watch it all, not quite sure what, if anything, she should have to do with entertaining.

Around the time Rose was married to Judson Brenneman, she had at last zeroed in on a way to get June to talk—or at least sing. She taught the child a little four-line song to perform on command at auditions. June delivered again, learning the short ditty and singing it whenever Rose instructed her to do so.

Except for taking the girls to auditions and bringing them to and from their dance classes, Rose probably had no other job beyond acting as her children's unofficial manager. Several times, Rose had to return to Seattle to obtain money to keep the Hollywood adventure going. There were also periods when her purse held only a single coin. During one such time, June landed a performance at a private party. Rose made her play the gig even though the child had the chicken pox, because after payment they would have money to pay for food. Rose put plenty of greasepaint on the little girl's face to cover up evidence of her condition.

It was around this time that Rose began putting ideas into operation that had been in her head since 1907, when she won a writing competition with "Dad Not So Slow," about dressing up as a phony vagabond. She didn't dress as a vagabond or a bum, but at times, when in need of money, she put on a costume that would have done any actress proud. When visiting towns where the children were booked for engagements, Rose would target the men running various lodge halls. She would try to convince them to book an extra performance for the children, either at the hall itself or at a theater owned by a lodge member, so they could earn a little more cash. Rose delivered such performances with props: lodge pins she had collected from her father (who was a member of eight different lodges), from Judson Brenneman, and from anyplace else she could find them. Carting Louise and June along with her, Rose would don the appropriate pin before knocking on the door of whatever lodge hall looked prosperous and therefore promising. She would tell the mogul of the lodge that her husband—a member, she'd casually mention, of the very lodge they happened to be in—had deserted her, leaving her "alone in the world with two babies to support," to quote one of her favorite lines, almost her unofficial motto. Rose was a delicately pretty woman with a lot of charm, a Gibson girl hairstyle, and a fragile face that, in one photo, looks worthy of immortalization on a cameo. Her good looks, along with her soft, convincing voice, enhanced her credibility. She usually didn't wear makeup; she didn't need to.

But during these forays to see lodge brothers, she'd make her fair complexion look paler than normal with deliberately applied light powder. She would pretend to be hungry and weak, and require the children to feign the same. June could usually cry or whine alongside her mother on cue; Louise had a much rougher time participating in her mother's con game. Rose would ask the lodge's grand master for "a little hot soup" before getting down to the business of what she really wanted. Initially, this was a chance to have the children booked for an engagement. Rose refined this scam over the years, and the details would sometimes be changed, but the basics of the routine were always there.

This routine was an original way for Rose to get cash she wanted. By this point in her life, she had surrounded herself with entertainers and actors. Actors pretended to be characters other than themselves, earning their livings feigning emotions they didn't truly feel and reciting lines that other people wrote. It wasn't exactly the worst crime for Rose to recite a few lines herself. Louise was not comfortable with this routine, but she was nonetheless impressed by Rose's excellent acting ability!

And the more Rose got over on people like the lodge members who could help her, the more she realized she thoroughly enjoyed scamming them. The world of show business was filled with so many nearly broke, small-time rogues that she had company, and her new milieu certainly beat the heck out of her old existence as a housewife living in near isolation in

Rainier Beach. Composer Irving Berlin would write lyrics to "There's No Business Like Show Business" extolling actors who stole the linen at theatrical hotels and were then driven out of town by the sheriff. It was far easier for many of these hopefuls, living in temporary theatrical hotels, to make off with a few of the hotel's items than it would have been for them to pull the same stunts at home. The show business atmosphere lent itself to lax morals.

Rose did have to struggle constantly for money in California, where she and the girls continued to live hand-to-mouth. If Rose's methods were unorthodox, at least they succeeded in bringing in money for her to support them all as they went in search of that elusive big break for June. And there were possibilities in Hollywood for Louise as well. She was a gorgeous little girl who photographed like a dream—at least until her baby teeth fell out and her permanent ones came in crooked. Rose tried to navigate their way through the slightly bizarre show business culture. Hollywood in 1917 was a tough place for the little trio, but it was still sunnier and warmer than Seattle, and it did offer more opportunities. Unfortunately it also attracted hundreds upon hundreds of other people, all seeking the same few breaks. Rose, June, and Louise didn't manage to strike Hollywood gold on this, their first foray.

Judson Brenneman filed for divorce on September 5, 1917. Back in Seattle, Rose obtained the services of a new lawyer, Robert B. Walkinshaw, who would also become a beloved local conservationist (a peak in the Olympic Mountains, Mount Walkinshaw, would be named in his honor.) The marriage was officially dissolved by October 19, with Judson claiming cruelty as his reason for wanting his freedom back. There is a dearth of information in the divorce documents, perhaps because this marriage was so brief that there wasn't too much to recount—save for Judson's claim that his marriage to Rose had "rendered his life burdensome" and Rose's hot denial of same. When Judson Brenneman's second divorce was filed, years later, so that he could reclaim his freedom from his next wife, Mildred, cruelty was the charge he made in an attempt to get out of that marriage, too. Two subsequent claims of cruelty may reveal considerably more about Judson Brenneman's inability to get along with either of his wives than about either one of them. On the other hand, Rose might have made his life impossible.

She stayed in town long enough to secure her liberation from Judson, and then, with Louise and June, she went back to California. They were in time for June to appear with Mary Pickford and Fatty Arbuckle at the US naval training base on Thanksgiving Day. June did her bit for the war effort by entertaining the troops.

Charlie Thompson often joined Rose and the children for vacations. In an old photo, he could be seen with June, holding a pet dog, and Louise in front of a roller coaster at an amusement pier, probably in Venice Beach. Rose's little sister Belle, meanwhile, had married an entrepreneurial man named Reginald Rankin and was also living in California, in Sacramento. Reginald and Belle, who now went by the nickname Betty, had a baby boy, Norman Kimber Rankin, in January 1917. Little Norman, named for Reginald's father, was to be Anna and Charles Thompson's third and final grandchild.

Reginald Rankin might actually have been a better match for Rose. The two were similar: They followed their own paths and weren't concerned about playing by anybody else's rules. Belle was more conventional than Rose. Belle had sustained a permanent knee injury when she twelve years old, which left her with a stiff leg. She would have to rest it by stretching it sideways on a bench or couch. The injury made the otherwise vivacious young woman, who had the same curly golden brown hair and light blue eyes Rose had, stand out in an unfortunate way. Her disability may have made her more interested in fitting in than her sister would ever would be. Belle's knee injury caused her to limp, and it may also have caused a considerable amount of physical pain. At some point, perhaps during her first marriage, she developed a drinking problem. Alcohol may have eased her physical pain, but it also began to play havoc with her mind. Perhaps as a result of Belle's drinking, Reginald's union with her began to unravel.

Occasionally Belle would join Rose and her children in Hollywood or on one of the threesome's early performance jaunts. In one photograph Belle is shown reclining next to Rose, little June on her lap in a deck chair at what looks like a theatrical hotel. To Rose hotels were comfortable places, perhaps because her mother had been raised in one. The children are both dressed in striking attire. Big Lady may have been responsible for how well turned-out Louise and June consistently were. Louise, in particular, looked stunning in just about any ensemble she wore.

Although no evidence substantiates Rose's alleged third marriage, both daughters remembered that there was a third husband. June specifically recalled that this marriage was to a chiropodist named Daddy Jay. The trio moved into Daddy Jay's house, and he promptly regretted it. Whether Rose and Jay were indeed married or simply living together, the children certainly put a heavy strain on this relationship with two memorable mishaps they created in his backyard. First June and Louise accidentally burned Daddy Jay's garage to the ground. Then they messed around with his nice outdoor pond filled with expensive, imported fish. The duo accidentally killed all the fish when they played a game that involved removing them from the pond with a pin.

Daddy Jay's backyard would never be the same again. He decided, perhaps in his own self-defense, that the girls should be shipped away to a school posthaste, but Rose became frantic over the idea. Worse, he also wanted Rose to have more children. In her eyes he was as bad as Judson Brenneman. It was hardly a radical idea for a man to want to have his own children—to everyone but Rose. She was done with childbearing and, after this relationship, finished with the idea of domesticity, too. She and the children returned to show business after their stay with Jay. Rose never looked back. If her bridges to a traditional home life had been burned, Rose's response after this last disaster was not a lament but a hallelujah!

June, meanwhile, finally made it into the movies. A surviving film clip of her carries subtitles written in Czechoslovakian, proving it was distributed much farther than simply within the United States. It was a Rolin Films movie called *On the Jump*, starring the bespectacled comedian Harold Lloyd. Lloyd plays a bellhop in a hotel where he is beset by one slapstick mishap after another. June is onscreen for only a few seconds, but the child's dancing talent is amazing. When the bellhop is not looking, the little fair-haired girl comes bounding down the hallway to the registration desk and hides by getting into a box. Harold Lloyd has to carry it—without realizing June's in there—along with two gigantic stacks of china, to the room of a guest. It's hard to balance the two china stacks plus the overloaded box with the child in it, so after he accidentally closes a metal gate on the extremely long beard of an older man who might just be the hotel manager, he drops the box in the hallway.

June, with her platinum blonde hair in curls, looks adorable in a pretty ruffled dress that seems to be made of organdy. Painfully thin, the tiny girl extends her skinny arms for balance after she emerges from the box with an air that indicates she's got every right in the world to be dancing in the hallway of a hotel. She goes into a quick, well-executed toe dance. She also does a turn around one of the guest rooms. Harold Lloyd watches her routine, then does an imitation of her attitude, pose, and dance steps, though he can't pull them off as well as June does. Then June exits the room and is gone.

On the Jump is a slapstick silent film. The remaining copy is slightly grainy and unclear, but it's funny and professionally done. Every actor nails his part, and young though she is, June equal to the rest of the ensemble. She was beautifully trained. The movie puts to rest any idea that Rose may have been out of line for encouraging her child to develop her dancing skills. To have stifled the high energy and dancing ability of this incredible child could have been worse than to have encouraged her. The film also confirms that June's talent was genuine. A child without any natural ability to dance would not have been able to pull off the cameo performance June gives here.

Harold Lloyd's *On the Jump* and another movie June appeared in, *Hey There!*, were shot on overlapping film schedules between December 1917 and January 1918. Those were the days when a silent feature film or two could be shot in a month, even simultaneously. *Hey There!* concerns film studio shenanigans. There are crowd scenes, but no obvious signs of June or Louise. Both children were said to have also appeared as angels in a dream sequence in a Mary Pickford movie.

These jobs were small and the pay wasn't enough to support the little family. Their longed-for break wasn't forthcoming. Hollywood was becoming a horribly frustrating existence, especially in light of June's talents. She was often overlooked at movie auditions, an illogical state of affairs that later reduced Rose to tears when she relayed it to her father. Too many children were competing for too few movie jobs in cutthroat early Hollywood. It was evident to Rose that some of the other little girls were selected for roles simply because their mothers had no problem lying on the casting couch. Doing so was out of the question for Rose. Legend may later have had it that Rose had been an obsessed, out of control stage mother who would do anything to help her children get ahead, but in reality Rose had limits. She wouldn't allow the opportunistic men in charge of movie casting in Hollywood into her bloomers in order to get her toddler a movie part.

One of the few auditions the children were taken on turned out positively for June—but with a twist. It came about because the rail-thin child was hired to play a hungry urchin. This was not what Rose had had in mind for her pint-sized ballerina when she brought the girls to Hollywood. Something else would have to be done. Rose's wonderful grandmother, Mary Louise Herber Egle Stein, who had always had such a positive influence on her, passed away on January 9, 1919, while they were still in California. The day also happened to be Louise's eighth birthday. Mary Louise was buried in Los Angeles, according to Catholic tradition, in the consecrated ground of Calvary Cemetery, as had been her wish. As Anna, who was home at the time of her mother's death, cabled to Charlie when asking for funds to cover the burial, "Catholics don't cremate." In the memoirs they were to write much later, Louise and June did not seem to have known much about their family's Farmington past, despite having lived with Mary Louise, Charlie, and Anna after the girls' parents divorced. It's possible that Mary Louise never spoke of the painful loss of her first husband and four of her five children to her two great-granddaughters.

Maybe it was when June was playing a five-week dancing engagement at the Hotel Alexandria in Los Angeles—perhaps the family's last stand in LA—that Rose hit upon a better idea than getting her child into the movies, which weren't showcasing June's dancing ability anyway. Rose had picked up a thing or two from the other performers she met while living in theatrical hotels. She concentrated on the fact that June was a fabulous dancer. Dancers needed a stage. Rose decided to build a little act around June. The family would try its luck in vaudeville, which was not simply a style of entertainment. It was an entire way of life, a subculture unto itself the little family was destined to embrace wholeheartedly.

CHAPTER 6

MADAM HOVICK: THE DEVELOPER OF CHILDREN

IT WAS OCTOBER 1919 WHEN THE FAMILY RETURNED TO THEIR HOME base once again. Back to Seattle, June "Hovig," as she was erroneously listed in the program, was cast to play a boy, Little Billy, in a show called *The Net* at the Wilkes Theater. The plot centered on artists and a doctor at the Detention Hospital for Criminals in London; where June's role fit in isn't clear. A reviewer nevertheless praised the child's "well-modulated voice" and "bearing" and said that she "carried the honors splendidly." By this point, June was at least six years old.

By September 1920, Rose had paired the girls up professionally with the Diehl Sisters, two sisters raised in vaudeville by a woman who was probably far more of a star struck stage mother than the character that Rose would later inspire. Mrs. Diehl's first name was also Rose. Her father had been born in Chile. Rose Diehl had seven children—three girls and four boys—a husband, and a house on Bartlett Street in San Francisco, but she went on the road regularly with the two talented middle girls. Mrs. Diehl and her girls already had an established act and knew the ropes of vaudeville. Rose was lucky to get Louise and June into this act, where they could all learn more about vaudeville firsthand. "Lenore Diehl and Her Three Clever Kiddies Featuring Baby June Hovich" [*sic*] was the name of the act. It was surely Rose Diehl's doing that her Lenore's name came first, but June's name got into the title, too, despite its misspelling. Neither Louise nor the other Diehl sister, Rena (known professionally as Sweetsie) was singled out in either the title or the act itself. These two, along with June, served as Lenore's back up. The double sister act was scheduled to appear at the Loew's Palace Hip Theater in Seattle, which advertised "continuous shows from 1 to 11." It was Rose, Louise, and June's first foray into vaudeville. The hours the children were required to work were already excessive, but the gig looked like a positive step. Rose did not seem to realize it was harmful for children to keep such hours.

It was during this act that June began to sing a song that apparently was considered to be a hilarious number at the time, when sung by a little girl. It was called "Won't You Be My Husband?" The chorus went as follows:

Won't you be my husband?
My number two?
Please do!
Number one has gone, gone, gone,
But what I did for him I'll do for you!
So won't you pop the question
And I'll love you all your life?
If you don't want to be my husband,
Will you let me be your wife?

Tame stuff, if an adult was singing it, but hilarious when it came from tiny Baby June, who was up on stage singing as if she had the emotional desires of a grown woman.

But that number, or others like it, may have brought a few dark and unwanted situations into June's life. She reported later that there were pedophiles who took an interest in her, gaining access to June by feigning an interest in Rose, a classic tactic used by the kinds of men attracted to young children. June stated that these monsters didn't succeed in their mission to deflower her, but the fact that a few of them tried to do exactly that is monstrous. It may have been following these incidents that tiny June developed the ice cold, drop-dead dirty look she would employ whenever she wanted to stop anyone she did not particularly like in his tracks—whether it was a pesky reporter, a truant officer, or any other adult. Louise claimed that June's mastery of that dirty look worked.

All was not well within this little double Diehl sister act. The collaboration with the Diehls, which might have gone on indefinitely, was undermined by Mrs. Diehl's blatant jealousy of June. Her children were older than June and Louise and, like most children everywhere, were not as skilled dancers as the ethereal and accomplished June. Dancing on her toes and looking exquisite in the process was, by now, second nature for June, but more problematic for Lenore and Rena-Sweetsie. They were huskier specimens and, try though they might, neither one could emulate the more talented younger child. As Mrs. Diehl watched June from the wings, she knew

Lenore and Rena could never measure up. June's talent was also problematic for Louise. She couldn't replicate her sister's dancing either, but by this point she was accustomed to that fact. The Diehl girls weren't. Louise was also proud of her kid sister's artistry, but the Diehl girls perceived June as an onstage threat.

June had been on the stage so often by then that she had learned ways to connect with the adults in her audience. She even had divined ways to dazzle them with histrionic moves. Looking as stricken as any adult facing death, she would open a flap of the bodice of her white tutu when performing Pavlova's dying swan number, revealing a red piece of cloth that was supposed to represent a bloodstain. The "bloodstain" brought down the house. June didn't simply dance. She could already act and incorporated sophisticated bits of business into her routines.

The situation enraged the irrational Mrs. Diehl, who had a temper. The better June did, the more jealous the grown woman became of the child star, and this resentfulness inevitably caused a rift between Rose Diehl and Rose Hovick. Rose would catch Mrs. Diehl watching June from the wings, becoming increasingly infuriated over the talented tyke's performance and the positive way the audience reacted to her. Rose Hovick stood back there in the wings, too, keeping Mrs. Diehl under surveillance. Rose wasn't certain what, if anything, the other woman might be planning to do to her child if the other woman's jealousy got the better of her. Somehow the show went on, even if the association between these two families was already poisoned by Mrs. Diehl's resentment. The joint sister act may have only begun but it was already doomed.

Rose Diehl and Rose Hovick's displeasure with one another could only have been further exacerbated on the night in Seattle when members of the Maccabbees, one of Charlie Thompson's many lodges, came en masse to a performance of the Diehl and Hovick act, and honored June, and June alone, with a gift after her performance. Maybe it was after this incident that Rose decided it would be better to put little boys in the next act with June and Louise. There would be no jealousy over June's toe dancing. She found a child from Long Beach, California, who was billed as Laddie Kenneth. Kenneth, June, and Louise formed a new act, "Baby June and Her Pals," subtitled "The Maid of the Movies," a salute to June's bit parts during the silent era. Kenneth was to remain in the act for several years. At first the new act showcased only June, Louise, and Laddie Kenneth. Rose formulated it in the autumn of 1920 and soon arranged for the three children to audition for the owner of the Pantages circuit.

Vaudeville performers were booked by the season onto circuits, chains of affiliated theaters. The managers of the circuits were responsible for booking acts and would proceed to send the performers on a tour of their theaters, sometimes playing only one night in any given town. The owner of the Pantages circuit's real name was Pericles Pantages. An immigrant born on the Greek island of Andros, he renamed himself Alexander Pantages after he heard about the conquests of the warrior king Alexander the Great. He sailed to North America as a ship's cabin boy at the age of nine, prospected for gold in Alaska during the Klondike Gold Rush, and then worked as a bartender. In this last occupation, he came to the conclusion that the way to attract customers to a bar was to provide excellent entertainment. Pantages became interested in building theaters. He opened a successful little theater in Nome, Alaska, called the Pantages Orpheum, with money fronted by actors, whose investments quickly paid off. He traversed south to Seattle, where he opened three more small theaters, all featuring vaudeville acts and the new medium, motion pictures. Those three outposts led to the establishment of more theaters up and down the West Coast, and later, across western Canada and the western United States, finally stopping just past Chicago. Ultimately, like his hero Alexander the Great, he was to preside over an impressive empire.

To his credit, Alexander Pantages was not the sort of man to delegate responsibility for his circuit to underlings. He made a point of auditioning every act himself and judging it on its own merits; he wouldn't book an act on the basis of an established star's name alone. Pantages had a genius for tapping into what the general public would like. His own immigrant experience living among the general populace made it easier for Pantages to gauge popular American tastes. When he auditioned the Baby June act and saw how well the little blonde girl was able to dance and sing, he had a hunch the attraction would go over well with the public. And he was right.

The Pantages circuit was not quite the big time, but it was a close second to the most prestigious circuit of them all, the Orpheum circuit. When Rose brought June and Louise to audition for the Pantages circuit she knew as much, but Pantages was still a step in the right direction. After the audition, Rose and the girls went home to await the verdict. Three agonizing weeks later, Rose was notified by letter that, at long last, her act had been accepted by the Pantages circuit. The dreamed-for break had happened: "Baby June and Her Pals" was to debut on the road at the end of January 1921.

Charlie Thompson came through with money for the costumes and other incidentals Rose needed for the enterprise, and off to the Pan Time—as the Pantages circuit was called—they went. Rose, in her twenties, was still young enough to welcome and enjoy the itinerant aspects of this lifestyle—especially since her own children were being showcased. Managing the act almost required a general's organizational ability, attention to detail, and ability to invade and conquer new territory. Every few days Rose had to move the act from one town and theater to another and take along grammar school age, often cranky or recalcitrant children. The circuit provided performers with their itinerary, but that was it. Vaudeville wasn't like the circus, where the whole show, tents and all, got transported to every venue on the owner's private train. Getting this troupe from one location to the next was entirely up to Rose. Once they got to a new town she also had to find boarding houses or hotels and settle the children, however temporarily. Finding lodging could prove to be a colossal challenge. Most hotels did not welcome theatrical folk. In the theaters themselves, she was in charge of setting everything up for the act: rehearsals, music, costumes, and makeup. Days later, the act would move on to the next theater, and it all began again.

Rose loved animals, so the troupe didn't travel alone. They brought along two dogs, a poodle and a Pomeranian, which Rose would disguise in baby clothes and pass off as infants on trains in order to keep them out of the baggage car. There were also smaller animals that the children could easily carry in their pockets, like June's beloved guinea pig. Louise even acquired a pet monkey that joined them on the road. She would sew cute outfits for him in her spare time. Big Lady may have shown her the basics of how to put a little outfit together for a doll. Louise proved to be as talented as her grandmother with a needle and thread. Creating clothes for her pet monkey led to her nascent ability to sew costumes for the whole troupe.

Mother, daughters, Kenneth, and the pet menagerie thus entered the world of vaudeville, which was full of talent, glitz, glamour, and startling contradictions. Most vaudeville performers could only get hired by being fabulous at whatever they did. They were among the best performers—singers, dancers, jugglers, clowns, magicians, acrobats, musicians—that the period produced. Some gimmicky acts—such as the Seven Little Foys, a family troupe of seven children dressed in matching outfits, led by Eddie Foy, their comedian dad—got by on charm. Most of the seven were talented, though not the entire brood. Their gimmick was that they all looked adorable on the stage. Another act, the Cherry Sisters, was famous for being terrible. It featured five singing sisters from Iowa. Not a one could carry a tune. Their performances were so ghastly that when they were onstage at the Olympia Theatre in New York City, owned by impresario Oscar Hammerstein I (grandfather of Broadway lyricist Oscar Hammerstein II), he actively encouraged audience members to have some fun by throwing vegetables at the act.

Most of the vaudevillians, including quite a few of the immigrant performers, came from rather dire financial circumstances. Many got their start in show business singing for pennies on the street, which was where Rose later found additional boys to join June's act. The impoverished adults who performed on the streets were desperate people. Quite a few of these performers were, to put it mildly, not exactly the most morally enlightened of humans. Some would steal whatever wasn't nailed down, which was why they were usually kept away from the general population in theatrical hotels in big cities, or on the theatrical floors of hotels in smaller towns. In other words, the performers were deliberately segregated from the civilians, as the vaudevillians called non-performers. Rose came to consider vaudeville a jungle and referred to herself as "a jungle mother," but she still enjoyed it so much that she never wanted their time in vaudeville to end.

The troupers may have been kept away from the mainstream public, but on the stage a whole other set of demanding rules governing decency and morality was enforced. A backstage sign at Pantages theaters read:

NO PROFANITY! (HELL, DAMN, ETC.) ALL FEMALE PERFORMERS MUST WEAR FULL LENGTH OPERA HOSE. NO POLITICAL JOKES! NO REFERENCE TO ANY LOCAL RESTAURANT, HOTEL, PEOPLE OR PLACES! NO SMOKING! ANY PERFORMER VIOLATING THE ABOVE RULES WILL BE SUBJECT TO IMMEDIATE CANCELLATION!

(SIGNED) MANAGEMENT PANTAGES THEATER

Libertine performers who were infamous for their shenanigans back at their hotels were unable to say so much as hell or damn on stage. Another sign urged: "Keep it dainty!" Since that sentiment was a theatrical edict, Rose would happily lift the term and incorporate it into June's act once the child—who was probably already seven when "Baby June and Her Pals" premiered on the Pantages circuit—became too big to continue being billed as Baby June. Dainty June worked just as well. June was petite, small-boned, and could reasonably be called dainty well into adulthood, and the word was already wonderfully acceptable to the theater owners. Rose learned to give those in charge whatever they wanted, whenever possible, and if it was daintiness they liked, then daintiness is what they would get.

We don't know if Rose, who reportedly had sticky fingers, became comfortable with shoplifting before or after she and the children went to work on the vaudeville circuits, but if she wasn't proficient at it before, she might have become so while on the road. So many people in their business had no problem with unofficial appropriation of objects they did not own; why should she? Rose was skilled at pilfering, and her children don't seem to have been taught that doing so was wrong. Rose may even have given them a few less-than-ethical tutorials on how best to pull off petty theft. Stealing was a fine sport to Louise and June. During one memorable outing the girls even managed to get over a dozen phonograph records out of a music store by stashing them in their bloomers. They had deliberately dressed that morning in baggy clothes with the phonograph record heist in mind. The girls left the store with their underwear loaded. The record store manager was furious. He came after the children, whom he recognized as part of the show playing in his town. He stormed backstage, screaming accusations. Rose knew that the best defense was a good offense. She threatened the storeowner with a lawsuit over his "false accusations" so loudly that the man fled the theater. These types of stunts may have seemed outrageous, over-the-top, unethical, and wrong in the tamer, stay-at-home world of law-abiding civilians, and indeed they were all of the above. Yet in the rather lawless world of vaudeville, Rose's protestations about the innocence of her guilty children was almost normal.

More serious than shoplifting in the subculture of vaudeville was the crime of stealing another performer's act or material. To vaudevillians, their acts were their entire world, their creative outlet, their raison d'être, their identity and livelihood. So stealing another performer's act was simply not done. To steal another performer's act was the taboo of all taboos, the vaudeville equivalent of committing cold-blooded, premeditated murder. Nevertheless, such theft took place all the time. Milton Berle was so notorious for stealing other comedian's jokes that Walter Winchell referred to him as "The Thief of Bad Gags." Dance routines, original songs, signature costumes, and everything else done on vaudeville stages could be stolen, and often was.

Rose could not have cared less about this taboo. There was a profound fearlessness about her, dangerously combined with the lack of an internal brake, a combination that allowed her to shrug off convention. She had no problem lifting numbers from other acts and letting June perform them. One piece of Sweetsie Diehl's sheet music wound up in Gypsy Rose Lee's archive seventy-five years after Rose initially liberated it. Since June was such a quick study and could emulate another performer's act after watching it two or three times, Rose would watch the little girl's mimicry to see what material worked best for her. Then she allowed it to be incorporated into June's act. So what if the material had been lifted?

Vaudeville people were moved around constantly, which helped Rose get away with such theft. If June saw someone's song and dance routine in, say, Buffalo, New York, one week, it was included in her act a week later. By then, she was already off to another town and so was the performer whose material she had copied. There was little chance that news of the material theft would ever catch up with the family. Rose wasn't going to worry about, or abide by, an arbitrary rule she hadn't created herself.

But Rose failed to appreciate that while it did not matter *to her* if she let her children perform stolen material, such amorality did affect June and Louise. The values of vaudeville were the only ones they were raised with, and to the girls, those rules were sacrosanct. June was mortified when another performer, female impersonator Francis Renault, realized she was wearing a replica of his finale gown in her finale, too. He called for a meeting to discuss the impropriety, embarrassing June. Incidents like this one were to lead, slowly but inevitably, to June's emotional distancing from her mother.

Debuting on the Pantages circuit, June, Louise, and Kenneth did a stunning job on the stage. "While all three performers possess a great degree of talent, Baby June, the youngest of the three, won the hearts of the big audience," according to one undated early review preserved in Charlie Thompson's scrapbook. There were a total of nine numbers in June's act, and the little girl was featured in seven numbers out of the nine. Some theaters had four shows scheduled on weekdays and five per day on Saturdays and Sundays, which meant that on a continuous basis, June was performing either twenty-eight or thirty-five song and dance numbers daily. Several of her dances, like her adagio dance, were better calorie-burners than a modern aerobic workout. Just thinking about a child enduring such a constant daily grind is tiring, and June would later be felled at the age of about twelve with a case of what would currently be termed clinical exhaustion. For about six years prior to that collapse, the tiny girl, who may never have realized exactly how incredible—not to mention gutsy—she was, beautifully carried out every performance assignment.

The act grew increasingly prosperous and would require, at its peak, seven different scenery changes. After the first year with only Louise, June, and Kenneth, the act included anywhere from seven to ten children as Rose began to build up the cast. Another child called Freddie Richards was among those brought on board. Freddie performed acrobatic contortions. Rose managed to locate several talented boys and took them on the road. They usually hailed from impoverished families that welcomed the opportunity to be relieved of extra mouths to feed. One family even handed over a pair of brothers. In 1922, a year and a half after the steadily booked "Baby June and Her Pals" act began, Rose changed its name to "Dainty June & Company." By October 1923, the name was altered again, this time to "Dainty June & Her Newsboy Songsters."

From the beginning, June's responsibilities in the act were sizable. It opened with the popular song "The Bowery" and closed with a military gun-drill finale. June sang two solos and a duet, performed a ballet dance, a tap dance, and the aforementioned adagio dance. Then there was a full dramatic sketch in which she sang a sad ballad about losing her pet dog when he saved her life, giving his to protect hers. Later, another number was added in which June sang a song about a cow, while two of the other children donned a large cow costume with a papier-mâché head. This number was one of those additions that brought down the house. It also proved fortuitous. The cow number was such fun for the audience to watch that the esteemed Orpheum circuit decided to book June's act.

The Orpheum circuit controlled classier theaters across the United States and Canada and booked more prestigious acts than the ones that had played on the Pantages circuit. Consequently, the Orpheum circuit paid higher salaries. Little June's act now paid in four figures per week. The kids had entered the big time. Once the act was booked on the Orpheum circuit, Rose became even more proud of her magical youngest daughter. She sent several articles about how well June's act went over to Charlie Thompson, who preserved them in his scrapbook. "Orpheum Time," Rose happily wrote in the edges of the articles, to show how far up the show business ladder they had risen. "Stopped show 8 curtain calls," another notation proclaimed. Charlie was proud of the little girl as well.

Along with "Won't You Be My Husband?," June's numbers included "Mary," "Nobody's Darling," "Oh! You Bowery Gal," and "Powder Puff Vamp." Later, "I Want to Be a Janitor's Child," celebrating the joys of being messy, was added. This small child also had to sing without the benefit of a microphone to amplify her voice, and she was obliged to project well enough to be heard at the rear of the balcony. She pulled it all off, every time, performing up to thirty-five numbers a day.

On the down side, the child was the star of her own act and, therefore, the ruler of her own universe. For the good of the act, it was absolutely imperative that young June not become upset for any reason. Because her performance could be affected by her mood, the whole troupe would often go to great lengths to make sure that June was happy. On one occasion, one of the boys in the act even handed a present he'd received over to June because the little girl cried that she wanted one, too. The boy couldn't bear her tears, but there was more: He knew they were bad for the show. If this child had been crying, it could cause her face to appear swollen. She wouldn't look as good as she should in front of the audience, and she would not be able to perform as well as she ought.

When the family was planning to celebrate Christmas following a performance, June, age eight, insisted that the rest of the troupe of kids remain in the wings while she took her bows. She wanted to be able to see that they hadn't run back to the hotel to open their Christmas presents ahead of her. Rose's boyfriend, Gordon, was with the act by that time and saw no problem with going along with Rose's wishes; their star attraction had to be kept happy. He corralled the rest of the children in the wings for her to see as she took her bows. Once offstage, they all went back together to the hotel, where Rose had trimmed the tree and was waiting for them with piles of wonderful presents.

At such times June was permitted to behave imperiously. Hers was an unconventional situation for a child, especially one who wasn't a reigning monarch. One of the last things most parents would ever want is to have raised a daughter in such a way that she issued commands or threw tantrums until she got whatever she desired. But the childrearing practices of civilian families simply could not be applied to June. June was the principal player in the act, the act was their livelihood, and the show always had to go on. June had to be appeased at all costs. Had June lived in one place and gone to school, her imperiousness would not have had much chance to emerge among peers. In vaudeville, though, June and Louise had no peers aside from each other and the boys in the act.

Rose, as manager of the act, properly insisted that June be prevented from getting upset before performances. For a mother, however, this attitude was a disastrous parenting strategy. This child was led to believe that she could get her own way in all circumstances. If matters weren't going the way June wanted, all she had to do was howl and her world would be righted for her at once. Louise believed the few adults in their lives did not help matters by constantly telling June she was high strung. She believed that the grown ups talked her little sister into a more outwardly anxious state than June would otherwise have attained had they left their assessment unsaid. Rose was providing June with a solid theatrical background, but she did so at the expense of her daughter's character development. The child shuttled between an onstage overload of hard work consistently rewarded with applause, and a backstage situation where all she had to do was kick up a fuss to get just about anything she desired. June's love for animals may have been what ultimately saved her from embracing the narcissistic fate that was being all but forced on her. Her attitude towards pets and any additional strays that crossed her path remained empathetic. Whenever she and Louise found strays, they would either adopt the animals, or try to beautify them before attempting to find homes for them.

Louise was initially rather disdainful of the vaudeville lifestyle in which she found herself, but Rose worked her into the show. Louise appeared in the opening, during the finale, of course, and in at least one musical number. At first her song was "I'm a Hard-Boiled Rose," a popular number of the day that was also a play on her real first name. Louise was by no means a natural performer like her little sister, but Rose kept trying to find material that would work for her older daughter and finally hit on something that did. A comedy sketch was added where Louise sang "Holy Yumping Yiminy," in which the child spoofed her own Scandinavian heritage. Louise earned stellar reviews for her delivery of the routine, complete with an exaggerated Swedish accent, and for her excellent sense of timing. It was good training for Louise, whose own act, years later, would be more comedy than straight striptease.

Little June was busted at one theater for not wearing the Pantages circuit's regulation "full-length opera hose," thigh-high opaque stockings, during one of her dance numbers. It was a Russian ballet that was probably one of her recycled Pavlova numbers from Seattle. The manager didn't care about June's youth; she was a female performer and had to comply with the circuit's edict. Rose had no choice but to ensure that her daughter complied. She modified a pair of women's opera stockings for her, even though wearing the bulky garment under her toe shoes hurt the child's feet. Another theater vetoed June's "Won't You Be My Husband?" number, which was considered offensive because it was delivered by a child. A third stopped Louise's "Holy Yumping Yiminy" routine. This censure happened in Minneapolis, which included an abundance of Swedish Americans. The theater manager didn't care that Louise was part Norwegian; that routine had to be removed from the act in Minneapolis. It was also removed in St. Paul for the same reason.

The lineup of acts at each particular theater was subject to changes decreed by the theatre manager. Certain spots on the bill were prime. Other assignments were considered no less than a disgrace. The first and last spots on the bill were worst, with the last spot considered the "chaser," the act so bad it would chase the audience out the door before the next show started. Jugglers, acrobats, and animal acts were usually performed first. The second spot was usually reserved for new acts. The third, fourth, and fifth acts all built in momentum, with the headliner in the fifth position to keep people coming back for more after Intermission. The sixth and seventh spots on the bill were similar to the second, intended to keep people in their seats. The eighth position was reserved for the biggest star or act of the show. Then came the chaser act, which was often so bad that the audience would start to leave early. It was usually either the worst or most boring act—or a movie.

Nobody wanted to be the chaser, and it wasn't too impressive to be first, second, or sixth, either. Sophie Tucker was one of the biggest stars in vaudeville. She wielded the clout of a reigning vaudeville empress and didn't relish appearing on bills that included kiddie acts. Tucker demanded that June's spot on the bill be changed during every day of the week they both played at the same theater. Sophie was in an uproar because little June could consistently stop the show no matter where she appeared on the bill. Tucker tried to undermine June's performance as much as possible by moving the girl's act to the first, second, or last positions. Sophie softened a bit towards the child and showed her some kindness when the little girl blurted out her admiration for the older star at the end of the week and asked for her autograph, which Sophie gave her.

These billing wars did not enhance backstage civility. They bred a backstage culture of survival of the fittest. Rose found that rather than shrinking from this savage environment, she thrived amidst its mad challenge. If she'd had a competitive spirit forced by circumstances into dormancy, it could be unleashed in all its glory now. Unleash it she did, although in as ladylike—and therefore camouflaged—a manner as possible. It certainly helped her cause that her act had a cute little prodigy as its star, one who had even given Sophie Tucker a run for her money.

Rose's hidden talents came to the fore when her little troupe played at a theater that had also booked another children's act on the bill. Rose managed June's act with its nine musical numbers, usually watching it from the wings without performing in it herself—save for being onstage in a wig when one of the boys sang "M-O-T-H-E-R" to her. She had a lot of free time backstage. Any rival acts that she targeted left their things in their dressing room when they were on the stage, usually also watched over from the wings by a parent or guardian if it was a children's act. This got the rival parent or parents out of Rose's way.

That's when some of their props or costumes would just seem to disappear. Standing out by coming across as a genteel lady in the backstage rough and tumble world, Rose, who had a warm speaking voice, would give the rival actors whose things had gone missing plenty of sympathy. Too bad her sympathies were faked. It was a pity that she didn't get a chance to act on a stage herself, given her knack for pulling off these performances. She picked up plenty of knowledge of acting in her new environment, and though she didn't use it to perform, she could cheerfully use it in her personal life—especially when she needed to get out of a scrape of her own devising.

On another occasion (according to June, who wasn't always a reliable witness), Rose "liberated" the wig of a female impersonator. She turned on the police investigator looking into the theft after he made snide remarks about the impersonator's presumed lack of manliness. She told the cop he was lucky to be "virile," leading him to feel guilty about mocking the impersonator. The policeman proclaimed it wrong to search the Baby June troupe's dressing room, as the group was led by such a "noble and decent mother." Then, evading him, Rose went into the ladies' room with June in tow and promptly flushed the wig, which she had hidden in her bloomers. She expressed remorse about having to flush it, but only because it was so expensive. No wonder June and Louise later thought their bloomers made great hiding places for stolen records.

These sabotage tactics were depraved, yet they were hardly considered unusual in vaudeville. Carrying forged birth certificates that increased the ages of child performers to get around child labor laws was unlawful but a necessity. The same was true of allowing children to perform even when they had temperatures. When not pulling stunts that might have attracted the burglary squad, Rose was usually quite beloved among the other performers and often acted as their leader. It was Rose who would steer the others to a restaurant after the final performance, usually to a cafeteria or one of the many Italian or Chinese eateries that were popular after Prohibition. Both ethnic cookery traditions had been adapted to American tastes. Italian restaurants added meatballs to spaghetti, and some even continued to serve wine despite the Volstead Act, which prohibited the sale of liquor. Chinese restaurants served chop suey and chow mein, neither of which was Chinese food. June recalled that the most important qualifications for Rose when choosing restaurants was that they be cheap and in close proximity to the theater. Rose had a whole troupe of children to feed, and the Chinese establishments offered the largest quantities of food for the lowest prices.

Rose was a confident and positive woman, one who did not doubt herself, and people loved her for it. Men, in particular, were attracted to her.

She was still a refreshingly unpainted lady in the 1920s. One day at a theater in Detroit, she caught the eye of yet another man. Fortunately, this one was destined to stick around for a few years. His name was Murray Gordon Edelston, and he was about to change the family's fortunes for the better.

Gordon was a black-haired, brown-eyed, tall, and handsome man. His good looks helped to get him past Rose's reluctance to become involved with any more gentlemen. Contrary to the myths that were created about her later—including the belief that she was an older mother who had missed the chance to become a performer herself—Rose was still a very young woman when she put the children into vaudeville. She was about twenty-nine when she first met the dazzling Edelston. A little additional romance in her life was more than overdue.

Murray Gordon Edelston was three years Rose's senior, having been born in 1888 in Minnesota to Jewish parents who had emigrated from Romania. Gordon, as he called himself, was incredibly bright and usually self-employed, and he'd developed a talent for self-promotion. At the start of World War I, his draft card revealed he was working for himself as a booker and living in Columbus, Ohio. He had a wife, Martha, and a little daughter born in New York, on whom they had bestowed the trendy French name Cecille. By the time of the 1920 census, all three were residing in Detroit and living on Woodward Avenue. Gordon was selling stocks. The Edelstons were the picture of a young and prosperous family. But something went wrong. Perhaps Gordon simply felt constricted in his marriage. There surely were problems between him and Martha. He may already have divorced her by the time he met Rose. Gordon may also have had a legal problem stemming from the sale of stocks. When Gordon met Rose, she attracted him more powerfully than anyone ever had. When Rose and the vaudeville troupe left Detroit a few days later, Murray Gordon Edelston, whatever his reasons, left everything behind and went with them.

Edelston had only known Rose and her girls for a few days before making this major leap. But Rose loved him; June, if not Louise, instantly adored him. Gordon's knowledge of publicity and salesmanship were to prove a godsend to the act, which was now called Dainty June and Her Newsboy Songsters. "Reg. U.S. Patt. Off." was added to program notices about the act, even though no such registration existed. Rose had done very well managing June's act, especially since she had neither sprung from a theatrical family nor had any specialized training in the theatrical arts. She had created an act almost exclusively from the know-how she'd absorbed from watching other acts. She'd gotten her little girl into a handful of Hollywood movies, and had even managed the vaudeville act straight onto the Pantages circuit. Gordon was determined to see June get on the more prestigious Orpheum circuit. His business background had given him marketing strategies that were not yet part of Rose's experience of the world.

Gordon felt the whole group needed to put on a more prosperous front. That meant purchasing striking new clothes for everybody. June was outfitted in a white rabbit fur coat with a tam o'shanter hat and even given a few diamond rings to flash, especially on opening days. (The rest of the time Rose usually wore them.) June was also provided with a stunning shiny gown, covered in rhinestones, to wear in the finale—the one that was to cause the child distress later when it was discovered that the gimmick was stolen from the act of Francis Renault, female impersonator. Despite this costume controversy, June kept wearing the finale dress. Beaver coats were all the rage in the early 1920s, so a beaver coat was ordered for Rose, and she and Gordon personally picked all of the skins that were used to create it. Louise and the other children all got flashier street clothes to wear, too, with knickers for the boys, which Louise would also sometimes wear.

Later, Louise claimed she had been made to wear boy's clothes at Gordon's behest so that she would not deflect any attention from June. In photographs both girls are often pictured wearing boy's clothes, but Louise is more often shown wearing a skirt. A note on the back of a photo sent to relatives in Seattle, dated 1921 and featuring Louise riding in a pony cart while wearing a newsboy cap and boy's shirt, was annotated by Rose. The photo coincided with the approximate time of Gordon's arrival in their lives. The note states, "Louise dresses as a boy most of the time, she looks stunning as a boy." She certainly does look stunning, but the way the note was written seems to indicate the child was choosing to dress like a boy and was not being forced to do so by Gordon.

Then there was the matter of their hotel rooms. To save money, Rose had previously rented two low-priced theatrical hotel rooms for the troupe. Rose and the girls stayed in one and the little boys in the act all shared the other. Gordon convinced Rose that if they wanted to appear as if they truly belonged in the big time, they'd better off behaving as if they already commanded a big time salary. Therefore, they should be staying in suites. Louise missed bunking in the same room with Rose and June, all snuggled cozily together in one bed, after Gordon arrived on the scene. But if she protested his joining their family, she was the only one. And even Louise soon came to adore Gordon, to the point that she tried to fast with him on one of the Jewish holy days.

Rose had bought June a giant-sized doll that the girl loved. Gordon told the papers a deliberate whopper, stating that the doll had been presented to June by General Neville, a hero of World War I, to thank the child for her "untiring assistance in his campaign" of selling Liberty bonds. The story was just barely believable, yet it made great copy. That was Rose's Gordon: big, over-the-top, and with promotional instincts that were as extravagant as they were unerring.

Gordon also auditioned several new boys for the act, bringing in children with more talent while the troupe still retained its first original supporting player, Laddie Kenneth. In New York City, Gordon and Rose found Georgie and Tommy Triano singing for pennies in the streets. When the act passed through a mining town in Pennsylvania, Gordon and Rose were also told about Johnny, a severely impoverished boy who suffered from mental retardation but could sing magnificently. Rose was not given much credit at the time, but it is a testament to her decency that she agreed to take this particular child on, since he required more care than all of the other boys and her two daughters combined, care that often fell to Rose. But her effort was well spent; Johnny added value to the act. For a time during 1922, they also took on a little Italian girl from Genoa named Mildred LaSalle, though what she did in the act isn't clear. The troupe also added a boy named Delorre St. Paul, from St. Paul, Minnesota, and Charles Favis from New Orleans.

Gordon and Rose acquired a tutor for all of the children, a good move because otherwise there was always a chance that their child vaudeville stars could be arrested and removed from their custody owing to child labor laws. These children were all too young to be working. The tutor they found back in Minnesota was named Olive Thompson. She was probably no relation to Rose, but Charlie Thompson was one of nine children, and Olive could have been one of his nieces or cousins. It was not lost on Rose that Olive Thompson's teaching certificate might come in handy, since she and Rose shared a surname. There was always the possibility of using Olive's qualifications after she was gone, with Rose claiming to be Miss Thompson the teacher herself. (Olive's papers ultimately became part of Gypsy Rose Lee's archive.) After Olive left her employment, Rose would don prop glasses and pose for newspaper photographs with the children at school desks stored backstage at a theater.

One of Gordon's best innovations was visits to the dentist for all three of his new girls. He also found a doctor who attempted a belated repair of the gynecological injuries that Rose had sustained when Louise was born. Gordon began to appear in articles about June, including one where he said of June, "She is the most tender-hearted child you ever saw. It distresses her to see anything suffer," then segued into a mention of her love and care for General Neville's doll, deftly dropping the general's name. June and Louise both loved animals, but General Neville's doll made better copy.

Rose began to use the self-proclaimed quasi-French title Madame Hovick. The *Wisconsin State Journal* said the other four child performers' parents had given them over to Rose's tutelage. The paper pronounced her "Madame Hovick, called 'The Developer of Children.'" She'd gone from having zero theatrical training to expert status.

Then the dancing cow with the papier-mâché head and June's new barnyard song and dance were added to the act, and the Orpheum circuit's bookers took notice at last. They hired the children. The developer went along for the ride. Whether her new title had been made up by Rose, Rose and Gordon, or a member of the Midwestern press, the *Wisconsin State Journal* was onto something: Rose's methods with all of these children worked. She had taken a group of children with diverse talents and nurtured their abilities until they wound up vaudeville headliners on the big time Orpheum circuit. June, who believed herself to be seven, though she was actually probably closer to nine, would earn the astonishing sum of $1,250 a week.

CHAPTER 7

THE ACT GETS CURBED

BACK IN SEATTLE, CHARLIE THOMPSON WAS HAVING ONE OF THE MOST miserable months of his life during January 1923. First his eldest daughter, Mina, passed away far too early. Both Mina and Belle had been extremely sick with an illness that was almost certainly contagious, most likely a vicious strain of influenza. Their condition became dire. Anna Thompson proceeded to Venice, California, to nurse her two daughters through it. Mina was thirty-six years old and had been married at least three times and divorced twice. None of her marriages had worked out or produced any children. Belle was divorced from her first husband, Reginald Rankin. Reginald was to retain custody of their only son, Norman Kimber Rankin, but Reg had a rather unusual enterprise to found, as we shall see. Norman's upbringing fell to Reg's mother Daisy in Oregon. Belle improved, but Mina didn't. Anna had the miserable task of breaking the news to her husband via telegram that Mina "passed away peacefully" early on the morning of January 13. Charlie replied that he was "broken up by this sad news." The grieving father arranged for flowers to be sent to his wife and prepared to travel to California. His employers at the railroad provided him with a pass to go to Los Angeles to be with Anna and Belle.

Charlie was no sooner back in Seattle when there was more trouble, this time concerning Rose. She was on the East Coast with the children's act, which advertisements proclaimed featured "Dainty June, Honey Louise and Laddie Kenneth," at the Liberty Theatre in Corning, New York, when her older sister died in California. June would later report having been present at Mina's bedside when her aunt passed away from "a drug overdose," but that version of events was clearly impossible. Perhaps the child had once been at the deathbed of another ailing adult and later confused the two events. June remembered Melba, a friend of her mother's who was often drunk at a theatrical hotel where they stayed when she was a toddler. She might have confused Mina with Melba. Or she might not. June later enjoyed amplifying events from her early life into a horror story.

Whatever pathology was behind June's Mina tale, the truth of the matter was that Dainty June & Company were all appearing on stage in Corning on the East Coast, while Mina passed away in Venice on the West Coast. It would not be possible for Rose and June to have made a fast trip to see Mina before the ailing—and contagious—woman passed away. Short biplane rides often took place during that era, but airline travel was still years away from being fully developed. There was no cross-country plane service yet. Coast-to-coast train travel had been in existence for decades, but it was still achingly slow, taking five days each way. The cars of the 1920s had not yet acquired the speed they would achieve later. Rose was not present either when her sister, whom she had dearly loved, died. She and Gordon never left the troupe.

From Rochester, New York, not one week after Mina's death, Rose sent a firm yet calmly worded telegram to her father. The Rochester child welfare authorities had seized June and Louise. The two girls, plus every one of the boys in the act, had been unceremoniously removed from the stage of the Victoria Theater by investigators from the Society for the Prevention of Cruelty to Children—who had literally blown the whistle on them, coming up the theater aisle tooting. The authorities took the children off the stage during a performance in front of a live audience. The raid was conducted in a manner that must have been frightening for the professional troupe of children. In a matter of minutes they went from presenting their act onstage in costume to being whisked away, then ensconced against their will in a Rochester children's shelter.

The apprehension of the children also could not possibly have transpired at a worse time for Rose, who was in the midst of grieving for Mina and also concerned about Belle's condition. Rose had to put her feelings about her sisters aside to concentrate on regaining custody of her children. Little June was frightened out of her wits when she was subjected at the shelter to a medical examination, which proved she wasn't as old as Rose's collection of forged birth certificates indicated. A doctor performed a blood test on her without providing the child with any explanation of what was about to be done. The girl hadn't had a blood test before and didn't even known such a procedure existed. The child who had the lung power to sing at such volume that she didn't need a microphone for her voice to be heard at the back of large theaters let forth with loud, wild terrified sound effects, screaming with rage when the doctor's needle drew her blood.

Rose and Gordon had followed the children to the shelter. Rose let out a few sizable wails of her own from outside the door of the examination room and demanded, at an earsplitting level, to know what was being done to her baby. Shortly thereafter, Rose was brought before the judge. She immediately noticed that Judge Frederick L. Dutcher was wearing a Mason's pin. That was the moment she realized there was hope. Lodge brothers tend to stick together and help one another, and good old Charlie was a Mason. Rose decided to urge her dad to rally his fellow Masons into action on her behalf. She sent a telegram to her father as soon as she was out of the judge's chambers, instructing her father to go immediately to the head of his lodge in Seattle. It was imperative to let the judge know that she, and also Charlie himself, were decent people and competent guardians of her two performing vaudevillians. "Everything all right excepting am unknown," Rose had the telegraph operator transmit to her dad. Although there was definite urgency, she did not come across as frightfully worried; she could handle this matter with ease and knew it. As the mother of performing children whose careers violated the law, it's probable she had rehearsed just such a scenario in her mind many times.

Charlie was still grieving miserably for Mina, but he put his grief aside to assist Rose. He went to work on the legal fiasco, heading directly to see Samuel A. Cox, the Worshipful Master of Iconic Lodge No. 90 in Seattle. The master reacted as hoped. He sent a wire to a Mr. Oliver, his equivalent in rank at the Rochester temple, as soon as Charlie spoke to him. Worshipful Master Cox assured Mr. Oliver that Charlie and Rose were wonderful people and asked for his assistance. Fortunately for Rose and Charlie, Mr. Oliver was happy to help straighten out their mess. The children were, of course, underage, working with the help of forged birth certificates. Olive Thompson may have already departed from Rose's employ by this time, because both girls recall in their memoirs that the judge had a major problem with their lack of formal education. But education wasn't the main issue, as it turned out. The children's act had been stopped by the authorities owing to inappropriate content.

"Dainty June's Act Is Curbed: Child Can't Sing Suggestive Songs and Sit On Men's Laps Any More," screamed the headline of the Hornell, New York's *Evening Tribune-Times* on Tuesday, January 23, 1923. The act employed a sight gag: June was a child singing numbers appropriate for a fully grown torch singer or flapper twice her age. Rose was accused of improper guardianship because the content of the children's act was deemed improper.

The investigator for the Society for the Prevention of Cruelty to Children, Charles Taylor, had been stricken with the immorality of the songs "I'm Nobody's Darling," "Won't You Be My Husband?," and even "I Want to be a Janitor's Child," a paean to messiness that did not belong on the same objectionable list with the other two numbers. Taylor also took issue with one of June's routines, which would seem objectionable even today. The number involved the child, identified in this article as being age eleven, "going out into the audience, setting [*sic*] on a man's lap and powdering his nose."

Eight years later, Louise, having re-christened herself Gypsy Rose Lee, would describe in her memoir how, during her debut burlesque performance, she performed a number called "Won't You Powder My Back?" She used a powder puff, traversed the aisle of the theater, forayed into the audience, and found a man to play along. She also managed to put the number across well from her first attempt. Louise found it easy to segue into this routine in burlesque in part because she had watched June's powder puff number countless times during the girls' vaudeville days.

In 1923, with underage June having been caught by the child welfare authorities performing that number and singing songs deemed just as bad, the charges against Rose were quite serious. Her outward calm in the face of practically losing custody of her children worked in her favor. Rose was probably struggling to keep a straight face as she disingenuously promised to send the girls to the Gerry Society School in New York City, described in the article as "a school for theatrical children." As far as we know, Rose's children never attended any such school. But Louise, June, and all of the boys were promptly restored to Rose's custody and carried on with their tour, the troupe members' school-free lives returning to the vaudeville version of normal.

Rose was still getting the best out of the entire group of kids in her care. She would say in a newspaper article twenty years later, "Managing a troupe of talented, temperamental kids was more work than fun," yet she knew how to create fun, especially for these children who worked so hard and needed relaxing, enjoyable interludes. She didn't care where they went to play in the cities they visited, so long as they all got to the theater in time for the first show. They were gloriously unsupervised most of the time. Rose also came up with ways to create more mainstream childhood traditions for them, particularly around the holidays. There were a dozen eggs for each of the children to dye at Easter, and walnuts to paint gold and turn into ornaments at Christmas. Rose herself would waylay the kids outside of their hotel rooms on Halloween, wearing a white sheet over her head and making noises like a ghost, pretending to be the spook of the theatrical hotel where they were staying. And Rose certainly excelled as a ghost: She scared one of the Triano boys so much that he had to sleep with a light on.

Rose had a talent for telling the children riveting scary stories, works of pure fiction that she claimed were real. The lady could weave a spellbinding, often spine-chilling, storytelling web. One scary tale she repeated so often that both of her daughters incorrectly believed it to be true involved Rose's forebears and the most notorious case of a pioneer disaster in California history, the Donner Party. The stranded, starving pioneers had resorted to cannibalism in order to stay alive during a viciously cold winter when they were cut off from civilization and supplies by a snowstorm. The details as told by Rose, however, did not follow any of the known facts.

Of all the pioneer stories that Rose could have borrowed, this one had an indirect family precedent. Rose's own relatives were not involved the Donner Party, but a forebear of her sister Belle's first husband, Reginald Rankin, had been a member of the group. Reginald's mother's grandfather, Reverend J. A. Cornwall, was that individual. Even he, however, was not involved in the worst aspects of the crisis, having left the wagon train in Salt Lake City before it wound up in extremis. The only one of the three Thompson grandchildren who could truthfully claim kinship with a member of the Donner Party was Belle's son Norman Rankin, not Louise or June.

Still, the incident was infamous in US history, and therefore too good—to Rose, at least—not to be appropriated, embellished, and recounted in a smashing little horror story. Rose told the fable as if the Donner Party relatives had been her forebears, rather than Reginald's. She even claimed to have named her eldest daughter Rose Louise to honor a male relative, Louis, who had died during the disaster. It's probable that young Rose Louise didn't realize her middle name had actually been chosen in honor of Mary Louise Herber Egle Stein, her great-grandmother. Louise and June had called Mary Louise Doddie. Reg Rankin had connected with Belle, bringing his colorful family history with him, just a few years before Mary Louise passed on, and Rose might have found it easier to talk about her non-existent Donner Party relative "Louis" than to bring up the subject of the grandmother she missed with the children. Rose's exaggerated version of the Rankin family's Donner Party story is nevertheless a highly strange one for her to have been telling the girls. She could simply have claimed to have named Louise after, say, one of the kings of France.

Another of Rose's scary tall tales involved a relative of Charlie Thompson's who was said to have committed infanticide multiple times. This story had it that a woman was riding in a sleigh with her children and a young Charlie. She had literally thrown her children from the sleigh to the wolves. This relative, claimed Rose, was stopped right before she could toss out Charlie.

Ghost stories were another Rose specialty. June recalled Rose seeing a vision of a murdered woman—complete with hunched shoulders because her coffin was too small—float through the room. Louise remembered Rose having dreams featuring Mary Louise Stein.

Since Louise had been born "with two veils," said to indicate a baby with psychic powers, Rose encouraged Louise's interest in dreams, astrology, and telling fortunes by reading the tea leaves left in cups. All of these interests came to the fore when the child was given a book on dreams as a birthday present. That book was fortuitous in that it led to dark-haired Louise being given the nickname Gypsy. Meanwhile, she had a lot of fun learning about the occult and telling fortunes.

Louise and the Triano brothers graduated from the grammar school courses taught by Miss Thompson. Rose went out and bought all three of them golden pen and pencil sets as graduation presents, giving the same generous gift to the boys and to her daughter.

Louise recalled Rose's favorite form of punishment was to require her to write out the Christian Science Scientific Statement of Being over and over again. As punishments go this is rather mild. The faith's main testament began, "There is no life, truth, intelligence, nor substance in matter. All is infinite Mind and its infinite manifestation, for God is All-in-all." Rose would also talk about the statement as a means of building the children's confidence. She considered it proof that God really was on their side and would help when they needed Him.

Rose didn't get angry with June and Louise on the day Miss Thompson caught them shoplifting at Woolworth's. She was, however, furious that the tutor made the girls return their ill-gotten gains, making the children hysterical right before their matinee. There it was again: another point where Rose's parenting skills were sublimated to her position as manager of the act, putting what was right for the show above what was right for the girls. On the other hand, since she shoplifted herself, Rose could hardly lambaste her children for doing the same thing.

Rose nevertheless had a way of bringing out the best in the child performers under her care, if not in terms of their morality then at least with regard to their natural talents. She would tell June, when she was a child star in vaudeville, and later Louise in burlesque, "You have a bright star on your head, Dear. You'll never be satisfied with little successes. You'll always want to be bigger and better than anyone in the whole wide world!" This encouragement pumped the girls up whenever they started to doubt themselves. Both children managed to become successful entertainers, so Rose's strategy of urging them to believe in themselves apparently worked.

When June's guinea pig Samba died unexpectedly, devastating her, the stagehands who heard her non-stop sobs went outside, dug a little grave for the beloved animal, took off their hats, and joined June in mourning at an improvised funeral in back of the theater. Rose and Gordon did not hesitate to try and remedy the situation. They immediately went out and purchased two new guinea pigs at a pet store. Rose bought a miniature vaudevillian's traveling trunk full of tiny clothes for June's guinea pigs and another for Louise's pet monkey's clothes and accessories. When she saw June greatly admiring a gigantic doll carriage that she saw in a toyshop in Flint, Michigan, Rose found a way to ensure it would show up many months and miles later under the Christmas tree.

Rose knew how to throw a splendiferous Christmas. The boys' parents would start sending Christmas parcels for them to Rose several weeks before the holiday, and these presents would be trouped from one theatrical venue to another until Christmas. Packages of presents Rose had specially ordered for June and Louise also piled up. Rose teasingly wouldn't reveal the contents to her children, but she would have a grand time allowing them to guess. She would come up with evasive answers that would have done a propagandist proud. The family usually took a hotel suite at Christmastime. Rose added festive touches like lemon-scented soap in the bathroom, ribbons on the windows, and strings of popcorn and cranberries on the tree, along with the family's collection of Christmas ornaments, which somehow always turned up. The Triano boys' mother sent homemade wine every year, and Rose would pour a small portion of it into a bottle for each child, which she allowed them to take along to the theater. This practice scandalized the other performers, but Rose justified it by saying that the wine hadn't hurt the Trianos—and besides the wine was full of iron and therefore good for children!

Even Louise's pet monkey was allowed to drink a portion of the wine. One year this practice became problematic. The monkey was a tiny Capuchin, so small that he got drunk relatively quickly. The Capuchin bit Rose when she tried to put some bloomers on him. Rose admonished the little guy that it "wasn't proper" for him to be naked on Christmas. She also bit him right back so he could see what it felt like to be on the receiving end of one of his own tactics.

"Merry Christmas to my little stars," Louise recalled Rose saying to the children on Christmas mornings. Under the lavishly decorated tree there were wonderful presents: arts and crafts supplies for the two girls, along with books—particularly for Louise—and dolls. One year there was even a Victrola and records. It was on the morning after the girls received the Victrola that they donned their most capacious pairs of bloomers, entered a music store, and stole several records by stashing them in their pants. Rose and Gordon also purchased quality sports gifts like roller skates and baseball equipment for the little boys. These gifts were in addition to the presents their parents had sent from home. Even the pets got presents. Rose created a tiny pet Christmas tree bedecked with little treats that the dogs and monkey could enjoy. She also trimmed a massive tree with ornaments, lights, and her hand-strung garlands of popcorn and berries for the rest of the troupe.

The events in Rochester, meanwhile, weighed on Rose and Gordon, who didn't want to see anything even remotely similar to that raid happen again. The children's ages continued to be the act's biggest problem. If the girls could appear to be older than they were—at least on paper—the child authorities would leave the troupe alone. A few months after almost losing custody of the girls, Rose contacted a friendly Seattle doctor with the thought of having a bogus affidavit created altering Louise's age to get around the child labor laws once and for all. The doctor signed and had even notarized the affidavit, although the document was a work of pure fiction, if not outright fraud. Louise's birth had taken place at home and was not attended by any doctor. The doctor might have lost his license had his participation in this scam ever come to light, but he signed the affidavit nonetheless. The document changed Louise's 1911 birth year to 1908.

Louise's birth date was easier to change than June's because Louise was born in Seattle. June was born in Canada, and getting around that country's registration system was considerably harder. Even the friendly doctor Rose had found could not create a bogus document for a child born outside the United States. A forged birth certificate for June was ultimately procured from Native American counterfeiters Rose somehow found in Seattle, perhaps with the help of one of her mother's demimonde connections. Rose brought Louise with her to Vancouver as backup and lookout for what amounted to a clandestine operation. After faking a faint in front of a clerk and getting him away from the files by asking him to please get her a glass of water, Rose carried off a successful birth certificate swap in the Vancouver Office of Vital Statistics. The forgery ended up in the files, while the original document was taken from the premises in Rose's purse.

Then on February 4, 1925, while passing through New York City, Gordon and Rose hit on the brilliant idea of obtaining altered passports for the whole family, with Louise and June's bogus info included on Rose's passport. Belle had remarried an actor named Frank Thornton, and since both he and Belle were living in New York City on 104th Street, Belle was drafted to sign off on Rose's passport application as a witness who could vouch for her. Louise was listed as having been born in 1908 and June in 1910, thus changing the ages of the two girls to seventeen and fifteen, respectively, and putting them both beyond the reach of the child labor laws at last. Louise really was fifteen, but Dainty June was only thirteen, below the minimum working age of fourteen. June was still in danger of being removed from Rose's care. To complicate matters further, Louise believed herself to be thirteen, while June thought she was eleven. Rose had lowered the girls' ages while they were in Los Angeles trying to enter the movies, a stunt she'd pulled in hopes that the girls would look more precocious. But the ruse had never been explained to the girls themselves.

The passport application included some whoppers. First, it listed John Hovick as having been born in Spokane, Washington, when he was born in Minnesota, as Rose well knew. Then it claimed his current residence was unknown. Jack, Elizabeth, and their two children, Jack Junior and Betty, were residing in Los Angeles, and Rose and the others all knew as much. But these two Jack Hovick red herrings could only help, Gordon and Rose reasoned, if anyone tried to check out their application. The application goes on to claim that the entire troupe, including the little boys who were also underage and also were issued passports, was about to embark on a theatrical tour of Europe in ten days. The documents therefore had to be processed by the passport authorities as quickly as possible. But of course they never boarded the SS *Olympic* on February 14, 1925, as they had claimed they would. They only wanted to get their hands on a federal document that altered the girls' ages, and once that aim was accomplished, they purposely missed the boat.

Later during that year of the passport caper, Louise had the chance to appear onstage with Fanny Brice, one of the biggest comediennes of the day and a major, beloved star. Rose did not hesitate to volunteer Louise's services when she was told that Fanny needed to find a teenage girl to perform a scene in her act. Louise was such a beautiful child, and here was a chance for Rose to get the kid noticed. Fanny found a glorious orange dress for the young girl to wear, one that made her look even more stunning than usual. But Louise's scene was cut after only two performances, possibly because the gorgeous child upstaged the plainer star, but nothing could remove the experience from Louise's resume. She was able to recount this credit on the Orpheum circuit for years. It would even lead to her biggest break many years later.

Over time, with Gordon's help, the Dainty June act had gotten better and better, to the point that four of June's nine numbers stopped the show. The act continued for so long that it gave the troupe a false sense of security. It was easy—especially for Rose—to believe that their good fortune would continue indefinitely. But then circumstances began to go awry.

First, vaudeville itself had careened into trouble. Radio had been steadily robbing vaudeville theaters of their audiences. People no longer had to leave the house to be entertained; all they had to do was turn on their radios to have comedy shows, dramas, or full orchestras broadcast right into their living rooms. This was a whole new world, the beginning of home entertainment—and one that vaudeville theater owners and performers had never envisioned, let alone prepared for.

Movies were also on the rise, becoming longer and more elaborate. They had expanded from initial films, like the now-iconic one of a man sneezing, which had only lasted for a few seconds, to features that were several reels long. The more sophisticated the movies became, the more customers they were able to steal away from live theater. Many old vaudeville theaters were converted into movie palaces when their audiences disappeared. Vaudeville bills included fewer acts, cut down to three where once there had been nine or ten, and movies were being used more and more frequently as chaser acts. Sometimes a newsreel was the chaser, and then the main act would not even be a live vaudeville attraction. It was, instead, a feature film.

Rose would say that there was no substitute for live performance, but technology had already introduced two that spelled disaster for vaudevillians. The big time was disappearing, leading to an increasingly severe decline in opportunities for the Dainty June Company to obtain the type of high-quality theatrical engagements it had become accustomed to.

People traditionally do not see their role in history as it unfolds. This particular family, with its acclaimed act, had no way of knowing it was being swept up in the progress of time, not purposely swept aside. No one in the family was to blame.

The increasing paucity of vaudeville engagements began to cause financial turmoil for the family, which put a strain on Rose and Gordon's relationship. Louise remembered the couple fighting over both June's act and Rose's inability to say yes to Gordon's frequent and ever more desperate marriage proposals. Gordon had been with Rose for about four years by this time, and he wanted to formalize their union. But Rose being Rose, the strong-willed woman resisted just as strongly as Gordon tried to push the matter. The situation grew more complicated because Rose was from a Christian family and Gordon was Jewish. At the time, what was called a mixed marriage between a Christian and a Jew was considered scandalous. Gordon, faithful to Rose for so long, was not happy. He was becoming fed up.

So was June. She had entered the awkward teenager stage, with all its attendant mood swings and growth spurts. June was miserable over the way she looked. The brave kid had to go onstage daily and become Dainty June in front of a live audience. She felt more like Gawky June. Her nose had become too big, detracting from her cuteness; many years later she would get a nose job, but for the moment her nose was a liability.

And June was no longer comfortable with her act, which worked less and less well as she matured. The comedy arising from the spectacle of a small girl singing adult numbers eroded as June grew bigger and older.

Besides, the child was justifiably burned out. June was bone tired after so many years of steady, hard work. Depending on the number of shows per theater, she was performing up to thirty-five songs and dances per day, sometimes seven days a week. The little girl had been valiant and tireless for years, but finally, one day, she simply could not continue. Dainty June collapsed. A hotel doctor was called in to diagnose the problem and declared that June needed bed rest for two weeks. She was suffering from what would now be termed exhaustion. At the time, her collapse was labeled a nervous breakdown, a term that carried false connotations of mental illness. June needed the rest, but along with it came the disgrace of having failed in her mission to uphold the vaudevillian's unwavering rule that the show must go on.

As needlessly cruel as this may sound today, on the orders of the doctor June was left to her own devices in her hotel bed for two solid weeks. She was almost totally isolated. The act laid off. No one came to visit the girl, to sit with or reassure her. The only people she saw during that period were the hotel maid who brought in her meals and, on occasion, the hotel doctor. But June used the period of her imposed exile wisely, evaluating her situation. She knew that vaudeville was fading and would soon disappear from the public landscape. How this child summoned the fortitude to rally is an enigma, but she was, after all, a resilient vaudevillian. She had always admired the legitimate Broadway actresses who sometimes toured with the circuits more than any of the other acts. She was determined to join their ranks—on Broadway. She had been imitating these actresses since she was about seven or eight years old, at one point startling a reporter by reciting salacious lines from an adult-themed melodrama: "Well Mister, I know your kind. Your God isn't a weal God. He's a God of wevenge . . ." June loved acting. Vaudeville may have been dying, but she knew the theater wasn't, and neither was she. After two weeks, the brave child got up from her bed. She returned to performing in her vaudeville act, but with her mind made up that she would one day be a Broadway actress.

Vaudeville was as exhausted as June had been. It was now an uphill battle to book Dainty June and Company, and that struggle put even more of a strain on Gordon and Rose's relationship. Money became so tight that rather than renting spacious hotel suites to put up a good front, the entire family was now staying all together in one shoddy hotel room, with the two girls sharing a cot set beside Rose and Gordon's bed. Vaudeville, and with it the act, had reached a place where putting up a front was no longer going to help. There were few people left to impress.

The situation was not helped by Rose's strange refusal to see that the material in the act had become yet another problem. Rose had always been able to put her finger on the public pulse and had unerringly led the act in a marketable direction, but now, oddly, her intuition failed her. She claimed that the act itself was fine, even though it wasn't. She could lie about June's age all she wanted, but her baby was looking more like fourteen than four. June tried to will herself not to grow any taller. It didn't work. She became five foot six.

Gordon attempted to remedy the problems inherent in the act, and incredibly, his efforts led to blows, which Rose inflicted on him. Rose irrationally believed the act's failure to get booked was somehow his fault. He was in charge of getting bookings, and they just weren't forthcoming. But the featured attraction was her five foot six baby. Rose went so far as to accuse Gordon of having lived parasitically off the baby for four years.

Everyone, it seemed, was broke, broken, and unhappy—even Louise, who had adopted a Detroit bookstore as her refuge from all this turmoil. Louise, at least, didn't have to carry any guilt about the act's failure, since her role was still minor, unlike her suffering sister's.

Then, finally, the inevitable happened: Gordon imploded. He became completely, totally, and irrevocably fed up with Rose, with vaudeville, with theatrical bookings—with everything. Gordon had walked away from his situation once before when he left his former life to join up with this act. So it wasn't difficult for him to abandon ship again. This time, without bothering to glance backward, Louise watched as he walked away from the act and everyone in it, including the woman he'd wanted to marry.

CHAPTER 8

DAINTY BOLSHEVIK

GORDON HAD LEFT A FEW TIMES BEFORE, BUT HE'D ALWAYS PREVIOUSLY come back. Not this time. After the latest and worst round of fights, Gordon was gone for good. Rose initially remained hopeful that he would return, an indication she had never meant the harsh words that led to his exit. The final argument between Gordon and Rose had taken place in a hotel in Detroit, the same city where he'd been residing before he met Rose and took off with her and the troupe. Maybe he never would have left Rose at all if they hadn't just happened to be in Detroit when that last argument began. Detroit was his former home base and so provided him with opportunities for a temporary bolt hole. He apparently took one, because he vanished that night and did not return.

Rose waited in the hotel for him. The act was on a lay-off. There was no theatrical engagement to play, so the children got to run wild while Rose stayed in her room, crying piteously and awaiting the return of the last man she would ever trust. She waited for ten solid days.

Rose was devastated. The other men in her life, Jack Hovick and Judson Brenneman, had not been compatible partners for her, and she could hardly wait to see them leave. Not this time. Rose wanted Gordon to come back. But too many of the wrong words had been spoken. He was gone. Rose found herself grieving for the end of her relationship. She roused only long enough each morning to hand the children money for food for the day. She remained in her room, alone except for the dogs, which the children would take out and walk. Rose was too miserable even to eat the sandwiches that her children kindly brought to her.

The entire group was, of course, the talk of the hotel. First there'd been all of the loud battles between Rose and Gordon. The snooping, gossipy maid considered their fights a form of entertainment. She loved to listen first, then gossip about what she heard later. Next there was Rose's sobbing withdrawal from the world—not to mention the unsupervised children who kept gallivanting in and out of the building.

When the kids heard a guest complaining to the hotel clerk that no one was looking after them, they became nervous and conferred. The last thing any of them wanted was to be subjected to another trip to a children's shelter. Louise, the oldest and most sensible member of the gang, was going to write a letter to Charlie Thompson in Seattle. This was an inspired idea, since if Charlie were notified about the situation he would not let them remain in distress—not his grandchildren, not the boys, and certainly not his Rose. Sending him a telegram might have been an even better idea. But before Louise could think of this ploy, Rose finally rose up from her bed and took herself in hand. She resumed control of the little troupe.

Rose immediately announced that they were all going to proceed to New York City to start over. She even vowed that she was going to put their act back on the Orpheum circuit, which would show Gordon. That idea, apparently, was the one that provided the catalyst to get Rose up and moving. But even though they would get to New York, the disappearing Orpheum circuit eluded them. Once in Manhattan, Rose sent most of the boys—save for two who presumably had nowhere else to go—back to their families as a temporary measure. The two who stayed settled in with her, June, and Louise at the Langwell Hotel on West 45th Street.

Her daughters' clothes were still the eye-catchers that Gordon had arranged during their better days, ostentatious enough to mark them on the street as theatrical children. Even more eye-catching, to one eagle-eyed New Yorker anyway, was the $4,000 diamond ring Rose was in the habit of wearing. It drew the attention of a female con artist who introduced herself using the mysteriously abbreviated name B. G. Graham. B.G. changed her look on a daily basis, probably to avoid easy identification by her marks. She could be fun to be around, pulling scams like sticking a live cockroach in a desert at an expensive restaurant so that the management would be tricked into giving them all a complimentary dinner. She attached herself to the family, showing up at their hotel and favorite eatery so often she started to frighten them. Rose was right to fear that B. G. was stalking them. Louise became frightened of the look in B. G.'s eyes after she deliberately injured herself, to the point she bled, by walking into a plank of wood at a building demolition site in order to threaten the owner with a bogus lawsuit. It was Louise's first encounter with a sociopath. She could not process what was taking place before her and took off running.

Rose and the girls were in New York City to get their act back on its feet, so they began making the rounds of booking agents' offices, trying to find work. Money was running low. They weren't having much luck. Then, owing to an introduction made by the last person Rose would have thought to have a decent theatrical connection, dead-eyed B. G. Graham, the troupe managed to get an audition before renowned impresario Roxy Rothafel, owner of several theater venues including the famous Roxy Theater. It was the best audition they had managed to land in quite some time. Everyone seemed to rejoice, save for June, who, while thrilled, was also in the throes of still more adolescent angst. June's discontent was perhaps a worse case than most kids her age had to suffer through, as she was put on display while going through the awkward phase.

Yet June's talent caught the eye of Mr. Rothafel. After the audition, Rothafel asked June to sing and dance on the stage, solo and without music. Her routine degenerated into a terrible moment for her. Dancing and singing without orchestral back-up would have been uncomfortable for an adult performer, let alone for this adolescent girl with a collection of insecurities. She felt as though falling through the floor would have been preferable to singing a capella in front of the towering entertainment figure.

June was flabbergasted when Mr. Rothafel asked for her and Rose to see him in his elegant private office, which featured its own soda fountain and player piano. Rothafel made it plain that he had managed to see through June's current lack of polish to the potential that lay beneath. June could become a big star, he proclaimed—with the proper amount of training. Then he offered to provide it.

June had been looking for a solution to the problems with her act and performance. She blamed the elements of the act that were not working on her own head, which hadn't been functioning properly since her enforced seclusion in the Chicago hotel room after she'd collapsed from exhaustion. She was shocked when Roxy Rothafel offered to take her under his professional wing and finance comprehensive acting, singing, and dancing lessons. She had wanted to resume dancing lessons, but when Rose was approached about permitting June to do so, Rose responded that her gifted daughter didn't need them. It was more probable that they couldn't spare the expense.

Rothafel offered June dancing lessons and more. He told Rose she could put an end to the act, which was no longer working effectively anyway. He offered to draw up an agreement. He would financially take care of Rose and Louise, as well as provide June with the best training that money could buy. June was over the moon. She was amazed that solutions to all of her current dilemmas were being handed to her by such a powerful show business impresario. She was still a child and reacted as if Santa had just come down the chimney with every present she'd ever hoped for. Rose reacted altogether differently. She was furious to the point of near detonation. She went straight into battle mode. The idea of giving up the act, after all the years she'd spent building it, did not go over well with her, especially since the suggestion they cast it aside was coming not from her, but out of the blue and from Rothafel. Maybe she also felt there was something untoward about the extremely generous offer that Rothafel was making, coming as it did from a total stranger who didn't really know anything about June beyond what he'd gleaned from her audition. Worse, Rothafel wasn't just any stranger. He was a guy they had met through B. G. Graham, and Rose was already spooked and shaken by B. G.

In Rose's mind, all of these considerations coalesced into a multi-faceted threat. Rose wasn't one to mince words. She reacted to the offer immediately. After she lambasted Rothafel, who fled his office with a look of defeat on his face, she told her daughter that men always wanted something for nothing. Rose didn't realize it yet, but in saying no to Rothafel, she had also alienated her daughter for all time. To overworked, beleaguered June, Rose's rejection of the offer was the last straw. June's loyalty to her mother ended before they left Rothafel's office. June could not, and would not take anymore. She was going to find a way out of everything—the act, every single thing that went with it, and even her family.

Still oblivious to the new problem she took home that night, Rose encountered a more immediate difficulty. Soon after they arrived back at the hotel, two strange young men, posing as dancers hoping to join the act, attempted to rob Rose in the troupe's connected rooms on the twelfth floor of the Langwell Hotel. The ever-present B. G. was there at the time visiting, despite not having been invited over. The robbers tried to pull off a few dance steps to make their audition look legitimate. Then one whipped out a pistol while the other went straight for Rose's hand. She was wearing her flashy $4,000 diamond. The guy holding the gun even had the audacity to whack Rose on the head with the gun butt, hoping to knock her unconscious.

The two thugs hadn't counted on June, Louise, and the boys coming to Rose's aid and attacking them as only four loyal and outraged children could. The kids created a near riot, screaming their professional lungs out and attacking the two idiots who had been stupid enough to take on this whole indomitable bunch.

Other tenants in the hotel came running. Somebody called the cops. B. G., for her part, slipped out during the uproar. It was Louise who really saved the day. The tall young girl executed a wonderfully appropriate stage kick right in the gut of the creep who was holding the gun. He dropped it. Then both robbers fled, leaving the gun on the floor, as well as their light felt hats, which had been knocked off their heads during their battle with the kids.

An ambulance from Bellevue Hospital was called. The doctor who examined Rose found that she was "not seriously injured," though she did have a head wound that required stitches. New York City police from the 47th Street station came to investigate. They found the discarded gun, which turned out to have been unloaded, and the two abandoned hats. Louise received a fabulous write-up in the New York City papers for her well-timed kick.

Rose had been hurt. She was perhaps more shaken up than she was injured. Stitches or not, she had a burning desire to get away from the Langwell Hotel as fast as possible. Rose couldn't shake the feeling that B. G. Graham had set up the attempted robbery, and though her suspicion couldn't be proven, B. G.'s trick of hastily vacating the room while Rose was under attack not only pointed in that direction but clarified her lack of loyalty. B. G. had run to save herself, and Rose felt her instincts regarding the woman were on target. She was getting her girls and the two boys still in her charge out of that accursed hotel without any further delay. They all began packing at once. Incredibly, for the rest of her life, June would consider it nothing less than a form of parental abuse that, even after this criminal attack had played out right in front of her, Rose would not take B. G.'s contact Roxy Rothafel up on his offer.

Rose settled with Louise and June in an apartment building four blocks away from the Langwell Hotel. It was called the Henry Court (originally Henri Court) and located at 312–316 West 48th Street between 8th and 9th Avenues. It wasn't far from the Langwell, but it wasn't a hotel and wide-open to the public. The Henry Court was right in the heart of the theater district and home to many show business types, including a songwriter who found a singer for one of his compositions right in the same building. It became an on-again-off-again unofficial home base for the family for the next few years.

They were soon down on their luck. Rose was serving the children vegetables without meat, meals eaten in those days only by the poor and struggling. She began pawning her diamond ring collection in order to buy food.

They lived for the times when the phone rang and they managed to get an engagement. Then they'd contact the boys and take off.

At this point, perhaps Rose should have tried to put the girls in school and attempted to find another means of support for them all. Perhaps they should have returned to her father's home in Seattle. They'd been in the vaudeville subculture for so long that it such ideas probably didn't dawn on her. Rose should have considered creating a new act for June, with different material that might have been more timely or age-appropriate. It was unfortunate that she didn't, though vaudeville was in such a state that even if she had, chances are the changes would not have helped. The family simply tried to keep going with the same old kiddie act, not altering it, even though it was obvious that June was well past the kiddie stage. June's true age was beginning to show through the lie that she was two years younger. Little girls who are genuinely two years younger do not normally already possess a full bust. There was no way to fix *that*.

Still, the act was booked through the Consolidated Vaudeville Booking Association and made a tour of theaters in coalmining towns in Pennsylvania, in New York, and in New Jersey, never staying more than three or four days in any place, and usually performing for one day only. The troupe was making the same amount of money for twenty-two days of performing that they had once made in two weeks on the Orpheum circuit, but they still had the same number of boys in the act. This wasn't the best business decision. Had the number of boys been reduced, the profits would have been higher. June was teetering on the verge of another collapse, though no one seemed to suspect as much. She was beyond mortified by her adolescent visage. She stuttered. She was even dropping the props used in her act. The child had always been a consummate professional, but the lack of decent venues on a first-class circuit, the death of vaudeville, Rose's rejection of Roxy Rothafel's offer, the unchanging act that no longer worked, and a rotten adolescence were all beyond June's control. The combination of stressors was starting to tear her apart, inside where no one could see.

The original boys in the act, who were like surrogate brothers to June and Louise, were leaving, one by one. They were replaced with new ones who were utter strangers, who were also a bit older than their predecessors. At least Rose was trying to match the new boys' ages to June's. But these boys didn't want to work for onstage experience alone, as the previous boys had; they wanted to be paid. Worst of all, most were only mediocre dancers.

There was one notable exception: a twenty-two-year-old grown man originally from Prineville, Oregon. His name was Weldon Clarendon Hyde, a handle so ponderous he called himself Buddy. Buddy could dance in an airy, effortless fashion. He had a specialty number in the act but constantly changed it. These changes drove Rose wild, but Buddy informed her he was "too creative" to stick to one routine, an astonishing statement. She kept him in the act, since decent talent was increasingly hard to come by. That was her first mistake. She didn't realize that Buddy Hyde was about to alter the course of her life, not to mention June's and Louise's lives.

June was enchanted with Buddy, particularly with his amazing style of dancing and singing. She wanted to learn from him. The teen was still eager to be taught by a decent dancing teacher, and in the absence of an actual one like Professor Douglas in Seattle or Ernest Belcher in Hollywood, she found Buddy. Buddy's ability to focus on June was intoxicating to her. From their first meeting, he seemed to understand what the unhappy girl was feeling, asking where she had obtained her outgrown Dainty June moniker and acknowledging that she was now too old for it. Buddy *saw* her. He realized there was a struggling artist inside the miserable teen, hidden behind her childish outfits and dated onstage material. June was smitten with Buddy.

June was fifteen years old, but she did not know her actual age. She believed herself to be thirteen, looked about eighteen, and was still terribly over-worked, stuck performing an act that was no longer going over with the public. Had she been a civilian, she would have had plenty of opportunities for outright rebellion, such as cutting school, quitting school, boycotting church services, dressing as a flapper or even trying out a milder form of recalcitrance like refusing to do her homework or her chores. Yet June didn't go to school, so protesting via the usual channels was not possible for her, and she didn't attend church services or have a hometown to shock, either. The usual restrictions experienced by a fifteen-year-old girl of that era simply were not hers to fight. Furthermore, refusing to do chores was impossible for June. No vaudevillian worth her salt would refuse to do her show, and June was still the star of the family's failing act. Whether it went over well or not, June would still get out there and work at it. It was a question of dignity.

So the arrival of this new and innovative dancer provided June with a new role model, a suitor, and one of the only forms of rebellion readily available to her. She could carry on a romance with this grown man her mother did not particularly like. Rose's disdain for Buddy only increased his appeal for June. He wasn't really much to look at. He had a plain face and wasn't tall, yet June was intrigued. She wanted to learn all she possibly could—and then some—from Buddy Hyde. He the best of the lot of the new boys, at least in June's opinion.

Louise didn't like Buddy one bit. She felt superior to him. And Buddy neither enchanted nor intrigued Rose. He was twenty-two years of age, nine years older than June, legally a grown man. Rose thought he could have only one thing in mind when seeking out her daughter—and that wasn't dancing.

It wasn't long before June began hanging around with Buddy in order to rehearse new dance routines with him. These were not ones that were going to be used in her act, but improvised new dances the two choreographed together, simply because June wanted to learn new dance steps and be near her young man. One day Rose found June dancing with Buddy in a drafty room and hit the ceiling. She was afraid the girl would overheat herself and become ill. Rose immediately demanded that he stop hanging out with her baby. Rose surely sensed what was happening, and also what was coming. Regrettably for her, prohibiting Buddy and June from dancing together was not the best edict to issue to her rebellious teenager. June's desire to be around Buddy only increased after Rose's decree that they remain apart. An unforeseen consequence of having raised her little star attraction in the unorthodox manner so as to shield June from upset before her performances was now blowing up in Rose's face. June was so accustomed to getting her own way that she was determined to do so again.

Buddy and June resorted to clandestine meetings, which actually lent a sense of intrigue and a bit of danger to the proceedings, ingredients most young people find romantic and irresistible. They set up their meetings by slipping notes to one another while they were both onstage—doing so right in front of the audience, as incredible as that may seem. Their determination to get together and inventiveness in arranging their trysts were daring and admirable. They arranged small liaisons of the tamest variety, like hiding within a backstage curtain called a traveler and kissing. But Rose found them easily, in part because for years June's favorite backstage hiding place had been inside the traveler curtain while watching other performers' acts.

If June had been attending high school rather than employed as a performer in a vaudeville act, she would have had the chance to spend time with any boy away from the prying eyes of her family. But June had virtually never been allowed outside of her immediate family circle. She lived with them, traveled with them, stayed in the same hotel—in fact, the same bed—with her mother and sister, performed with them, had even had some school lessons with them. Getting away from them was not possible, but the iron-willed girl kept trying to find a way.

This time, Rose became enraged. If June's memoir was to be believed, when Rose found June and Buddy together, the fight between Rose and Buddy was played out in front of a live audience, which was watching the chaser act. It was a film with Clara Bow, complete with sound, the latest technological advance intended to enhance the movies. As Clara was bellowing for the police in the film, Rose was shaking and slapping Buddy, blocking the projection of the movie. Who cared what the audience thought? Rose didn't. She slugged Buddy again.

Rose's actions were perhaps more understandable from an adult perspective than from June's. Buddy was twenty-two years old, and June was still being presented to the world as thirteen. Rose was not entirely out of line for being upset at what she found transpiring between a grown man and her teenager.

Rose fired Buddy on the spot, leaving herself with the predicament of not exactly being able to let him leave yet. It was only November. The Dainty June troupe had a tour to finish. It was not going to be over until the end of December. Finding another boy to replace Buddy at this point, while touring the hinterlands, was all but impossible. Rose nevertheless thought she could control the situation and keep the duo separated for that last remaining month. She hadn't reckoned on June's ability to improvise a plan of her own, or on her daughter's steel core, well hidden under her childishly ruffled costumes.

Back in the dressing room where she had dragged June, Rose, all but hysterical, didn't spare her daughter this time. She didn't ask June to copy out the Christian Science scientific statement of being a hundred times. She went berserk and slugged June repeatedly. She accused her daughter of supreme ingratitude and brought up how she'd worked since June was born to make her act a success—and *now this.*

They'd been too closely bound together, Rose and June, too enmeshed. Perhaps formulating a family vaudeville act out of a two-and-a-half-year-old's interest in dance may not have been the brightest idea, but Rose had believed with all her heart that this was what June, her little prodigy, had herself wanted. Up to the point when June collapsed in Chicago, this logic had seemed a plausible sentiment. If June had not been happy with their existence, she had never once said so. But neither the act nor their mother and daughter relationship was working now. It had already been completely derailed by Rose herself back in Roxy Rothafel's office.

Rose was not yet able to see what had happened. During the argument that raged on in the dressing room, Rose broke an ivory hand mirror. Even though Rose had broken it, her big finish to the argument was to declare that seven years of bad luck would befall June, not her. And bad luck—eight years of it—did derail June, who would not get back on a stage until eight years later, in 1936.

⁂

Perceptive Louise was unaccountably distracted. She might have paid much closer attention to June's infatuation with Buddy, except she, too, had become interested in a young man in the act, another dancer named Stanley. Louise enjoyed talking with him. One evening Rose found Louise and Stanley sitting on a bench outside one of the theaters where they were playing. She called her older daughter to come in and get out of the cold. Compared to finding June and Buddy in the curtain, this was tame stuff, maybe even a fluke.

Louise was seventeen and a bit too hefty but still quite stunning. By the end of 1928, Louise had taken on a new behind the scenes role: family diplomat. She consistently tried to patch up the fights between Rose and June, which were escalating, and tried to act as a stabilizing influence. This was a ludicrously tall order for the girl. Louise was still a teen herself, trying valiantly to nurture the others even though no adult was looking after her. The skewed scenario had the eldest child taking on the role of family mediator, attempting to parent both her sister and her mother. At one point, June recalled, Rose called June a Bolshevik, accusing her of "undermining the army." June replied that she *was* a Bolshevik. Louise tried in vain to keep the peace.

June's problems with Rose further fueled the girl's romance with Buddy. Fired or not, Buddy had decided that he and June were not going to be forcibly parted when this interminable tour ended in December. The two young people had come up with an ingenious plan. On November 30, 1928, while playing in North Platte, Nebraska, they sneaked over to the courthouse, bringing two of the boys from the act (Michael Dillon from Los Angeles and Eugene G. Stone, originally from Andalusia, Alabama) along with them to act as witnesses. June listed herself as Ellen E. Hovick, using Rose's middle initial and thinking herself to be sharing her Aunt Belle's middle name, Evangeline, which Rose may have told June was her own real middle name, although it was not. June listed her age on the marriage certificate as twenty-one, a lie made plausible by one of the many birth certificates Rose had obtained as a means of getting around the child labor laws. Louise should have been June's first choice as a witness, but she couldn't be told of June and Buddy's plans for fear she'd leak them to Rose.

The older sister had a keen sense of intuition. Evidence suggests that she sensed there was something amiss. In the collection of family photographs that survive, more photos of the last few months of this 1928 tour were taken than were shot during any other tour. There are photos of June and the various boys in the act; photos of the truck, with the scenery stored on top, that had been driven by one of the boys; photos of a visit from Aunt Belle and her then-husband, Frank; photos of the entire group standing outside various locales. Louise may not have consciously known what her sister was planning, but a part of her seemed to understand that this part of their lives was ending, and she astutely recorded as much of it as she possibly could with her camera. For her part, Rose looks happy in these photos. She seems to have no inkling of what was about to befall her, or that the child prodigy to whom she'd thus far devoted her life was about to mutiny.

The tour continued until the company played at the Jayhawk Theater in Topeka, Kansas, during the last week in December. This engagement was the last one of that particular tour—the end of the road in more ways than one. The Jayhawk was a nearly new venue. It had opened for business only two years earlier and was one of the last grand vaudeville houses that would be constructed. It was possible to stay in the hotel that was connected to the theater complex, but instead the troupe checked into the Throop Hotel, four and a half blocks away, probably because of its cheaper rates.

According to an article in the "Court House Notes and Police Gossip" column of the *Topeka State Journal* that appeared on December 31, the Dainty June Company "blew up" when June and Buddy sneaked away from the Throop Hotel, after the last Dainty June show on Saturday night, December 29. Rose immediately feared the worst when she discovered that June was missing from the hotel room she shared with both of her daughters. She became hysterical, telling the hotel manager, Arch McDavid, that she was afraid June had eloped with Buddy. She was certain that was what they had done. She was half right. Rose didn't yet realize that June and Buddy had already eloped, and that the ceremony was already a done deal, having taken place nearly a month earlier. Buddy had manipulated the schedule well. It would not be possible to annul the marriage one month after the fact.

In any event, when Rose realized that June had vanished, she proceeded to call the cops. Louise would later say that Rose would have liked to call out more agencies, including the merchant marines. Somehow Buddy was rounded up and brought to the police station, although June remained missing. Buddy whipped out his marriage license. It was legal proof that he and June were already married. After seeing the evidence of the month-old marriage, Rose, according to the article, "was more agitated. The police confiscated a small revolver she carried." Buddy would later tell June that Rose had attacked him with the thought of killing him. The safety catch, he said, had jammed when she tried to open fire, serendipitously preventing his murder. Since June wasn't there she had no way of knowing that this was, apparently, a grandiose exaggeration on Buddy's part. The cops had actually removed the gun the minute Rose mentioned it; the only thing Rose had shot off was her mouth!

There were a few more problems with Buddy's account of his alleged near-murder. Rose had been a child of the prairie before winding up in relatively lawless Seattle, unofficial gateway to Alaska during the Yukon gold rush era of the 1890s. If there ever was a woman who knew how to fire a gun, it was Rose. Besides, the gun in her purse belonged to her. Wouldn't she have known how to fire her own gun? Buddy may very well have told June that her mother tried to kill him to push June further away from Rose.

But June would use this story in both of her memoirs. Ever after, people believed that Rose was a wildly out-of-control woman. Had she genuinely tried to shoot Buddy with that gun– right in front of the Topeka cops—she would have been booked on charges of attempted murder. Instead, Rose and Buddy both were allowed to leave the police station, and both of them went back to the Throop Hotel. This was a recipe for disaster if ever there was one. There they both were, returning to the same hotel. They might even have walked back only a few paces apart. June still managed to remain in hiding. Her memoir would later claim that, of all the hideaways in Topeka, she had stayed for a few hours in a whorehouse. The newspaper article makes no mention of where Louise happened to be while these mad events were transpiring. She was waiting in front of a parking lot in the hopes of running into her suitor, Stanley, according to her memoir. But there was no sign of him. Stanley was in the loop with regard to June and Buddy's plans, while poor Louise was not; he'd probably already skipped town to avoid the Dainty June elopement crisis.

Within two hours Rose called the cops again. This time, back at the hotel, she said that Buddy had struck her. Buddy apparently hadn't stolen away to retrieve his bride from the brothel. The cops went to the Throop to answer the call, but once there, they found that Buddy had vanished. They couldn't see any evidence of wounds or bruises on Rose, leading them to doubt the veracity of her story about Buddy's attack. The patrolmen left.

In the final analysis, what preserved June's right to run off with Buddy was her faked birth certificate, which listed her age as twenty-one. After so many years of creating documents to help conceal June's real age from intrusive child welfare authorities and truant officers, Rose had finally gotten her come-uppance. She'd had the choice of either keeping silent about June's actual age, or putting herself in serious legal jeopardy for having allowed June to work since she was two-and-a-half years old. Rose could hardly use the law to get the underage child back when she'd violated it for so long by committing forgery. Rose had never been slow on the uptake. She knew when she was beaten. She also knew she didn't want to be arrested. She kept quiet about June's age, though it nearly killed her.

The *Topeka State Journal* article about the whole fiasco ended with a mention of Louise, unaccountably stating that Rose and "another daughter" had headed towards El Paso, Texas, on Sunday, the morning after June fled. That Texas part wasn't accurate. Rose and Louise weren't able to go anywhere for the moment. Neither of them knew how to drive their car. One of the boys in the act had driven it for them, but he had already taken off with the rest who had deserted. The Dainty June act was officially over. And Rose got stuck paying the hotel bills for some of the boys who'd already skipped out. What an inglorious end to the era!

CHAPTER 9

HALF A DOZEN JUNES

ROSE AND LOUISE WERE STRANDED IN KANSAS. EVERYONE ELSE FROM the act was gone. Rose and Louise were reeling from the rapid-fire events of the last twenty-four hours, but before they could do anything, including think, they needed a driver. They couldn't abandon their car in Kansas and return to the West Coast without it. So Rose sent a cable to a trustworthy boy who had formerly been in their act, Henry Elias of Brooklyn, New York. She probably also wired him train or bus fare. Henry left Brooklyn immediately and found his way west to Topeka.

The boy was literally down at heel when he showed up in Kansas. Rose may have been at one of the lowest points of her life, she may have still been in a miserable state over June's defection, but she was able to rouse herself when she saw the pathetic state of Henry's footwear. His shoes were practically falling apart. Rose couldn't bear the sight. She took the boy directly over to a shoe store and bought him a brand new pair of shoes. Then the three of them got into the car and started heading north and west, aiming for Grandpa Charlie Thompson's house in Seattle.

Rose was devastated and drained. Whether the career she had tried to forge for June had been for better or for worse, whether she should ever have allowed June to go into vaudeville or not, she had believed wholeheartedly in June's talent from the moment the child has risen onto her toes back in Professor Douglas's dancing class at the Oddfellows Hall in Seattle. Rose had spent the previous thirteen years of her life trying to further June's chances in the theater. And while June had every right to grow up, separate herself from her family, run off and create a life of her own, her current situation was in a category all its own. June had not run away from home and gotten married. She'd run away from the family vaudeville act—the family business, really—in which she'd been the star. In the eyes of Rose, who had voluntarily taken on a thirteen-year-long stint as the manager of her child's act, June was seen more as a primary business partner than her daughter. Rose felt June had betrayed her, and her reasons for doing so were vast. June had just turned her back on thirteen years of Rose's best efforts on her behalf. To Rose, the teen's flight into marriage was the mad act of an ungrateful child. Rose's primary emotion was betrayal, and this feeling did not lessen with time.

Rose had always had the ability to face situations and adapt to them immediately, whether she was sneaking dogs onto trains in baby clothes so the pets wouldn't have to ride in the baggage car, or committing an illegal act like ordering forged birth certificates. But now she deliberately closed her heart to her ungrateful younger daughter.

Rose and Louise, with Henry at the wheel, proceeded across the country to Seattle, with Rose keeping up her own spirits by telling horror stories to amuse the two young people. She reportedly burst into tears the minute she arrived home and saw her father, the only person, so far, who'd been reliably faithful to her. Now, Charlie spirited her into the house so that the neighbors wouldn't see Rose's hysteria playing itself out on the front porch. His 4th Avenue North neighborhood was small, cozy, and filled with just enough nosy neighbors that histrionics on the front stoop would have been fodder for gossip—and there was already plenty, what with the teenage June having run off.

Amazingly, Rose rallied in short order, following her family's tradition of resilience. Within three months of June's desertion, Rose put together a new act, one for Louise, and they went back on the road with a new troupe. Henry remained with them. He continued to drive their car and also perform as one of two dancers in the papier-mâché cow costume that had been in June's old act on the Orpheum circuit. The cow routine had always gone over well, so it was recycled. Rose found teenage girls for the new act. She no longer trusted boys. The Orpheum circuit was gone by this point in early 1929, but the girls who joined the new act would not have been Orpheum circuit material anyway. They were basically a cheerful and well-meaning bunch of beginners, teens from Seattle dancing schools Rose had auditioned.

Strangely, they were all approximately the same age as the missing June. There were six of them. Louise, who was told she was sixteen, had fortunately just turned eighteen and was already past the teenage angst stage. But some of these new girls were only fourteen and fifteen years old, right in the worst part of the hormonal hell of adolescence. Maybe Rose had selected underage girls it so that she could get around paying them a decent salary. Was it merely a coincidence that they were the right age to have been June's classmates, had June grown up in Seattle and attended high school there? Only Rose herself could know, but certainly there were additional similarities between these kids and June. Rose's heart may have hardened towards June, but she seemed to be seeking out replacements for her. The very name chosen for the new act makes one wonder. It was called Madam Rose's Dancing Daughters. Rose might have recently been devastated to lose an ungrateful daughter to marriage, but she was, in essence, creating another new act with six replacements. Yet it is odd to think that a seasoned trouper like Rose could consider most of these kids capable of creating a hit act. Louise could, certainly, but these amateurs? Surely Rose realized exactly what they were—unless she had chosen them so as to make Louise appear more sophisticated by comparison.

Louise had become as adept as her grandmother Anna Thompson with a needle, and sewed costumes for the new group. Perhaps at her mother's urging, she first concocted ones that would have been more appropriate for ten-year-old girls: sleeveless dresses with bloomers for one costume, and short dresses with more bloomers, big puffy sleeves, and large ruffled hair bows for another. But in a Dancing Daughters photograph of four of the girls wearing this second outfit and dancing with walking dolls, the outfits do make the kids look younger, which might have been the point. The girls could pass for eleven or twelve. Another shot shows all of the girls, including Louise, wearing the sleeveless floral bloomer dresses she had created. Most of the girls look younger than they are and quite cute in this second shot, but two do not. Louise, at the right end of the line, and the kid standing directly next to her, both appear to be what they probably were: two young women in their late teens posing with a bunch of younger girls.

Rose probably knew what she was doing assembling these girls to back up her daughter. Photos of the whole group casually manage to showcase Louise. It was almost certainly Rose's intention for the younger girls to add to Louise's allure, helping her to appear older, taller, and prettier, if only in contrast. Although she was not the natural-born dancer or performer that June had been, Louise was by now highly experienced in the theater, having been a member of the National Vaudeville Artists union since she was seven years old. The rest of the girls had potential but were not as photogenic as Louise. They were going through the awkward stage, and one of them was downright homely. Only one had any experience, having been in a few dancing school recitals; the rest had none. They were, in effect, high school dropouts. Without trying, Louise stood out like a sophisticated goddess. As strategies went, Rose's was nothing less than brilliant.

Rose found a temporary replacement for June in one of the new children in the act, a cute girl named May Sherwood. May resembled June. She was small-boned and tiny, as June had been before she went through her growth spurt. She also had a lisp, just like June. Emma "Mother" Lang, whose Juvenile Bostonians troupe Rose had joined as a teen, still worked with child performers. She had included May in her Mother Lang and Her Melody Co-Eds act. Rose turned to Lang, desperate to replace June, and Mother Lang recommended the Sherwood girl to Rose, who promptly traveled to Vancouver to meet May and her mother—with Henry Elias acting as their chauffeur, a touch of class that impressed the Sherwoods. May sang June's old vamp number in the new act, and Rose simply adored her. May Sherwood loved Rose in return. May was to consider her various sojourns around the country with Rose, Louise, and the rest of the girls the best time of her life. Until the day she died, May carried photos of the act in her handbag and told stories to any interested person about how she had once performed with the girl who became Gypsy Rose Lee. May used a word to describe Rose that would have stunned those who believe Rose to have been the stage mother from Hell. According to May, Rose Hovick was shy.

At least one of the other girls became jealous of Rose and May's bond, and it also seemed to upset Louise that this little girl, who she thought was nothing like her sister, was being treated like June's reincarnation by Rose. Louise need not have been concerned. Only she was Rose's real daughter. Real daughters were permanent; the rest were destined to be around for only a short time.

The act also included Vanova Richards and her twin, Madeline Richards, Lillian Baxter, Ruby Reed, Lillian Green, and Dorothy Bishop. Rose started with six girls, then added one more for a total of seven. At the end of February 1929, Rose, Louise, and the girls piled into the car, with Henry at the wheel, and proceeded straight down the west coast to Los Angeles. It may have seemed like an odd destination for the new vaudeville troupe, since Hollywood was now almost entirely a movie factory town, but it was closer to Seattle than New York, which was where they were eventually headed. Los Angeles still had plenty of booking agents for acts like theirs, and Rose still had connections with them. She promptly got the new act booked into a theater in Arizona. Their pay would be an insultingly paltry sum of money, but the act was brand new and needed to build up credits and a reputation. It was a start.

On March 3, 1929, they appeared at the Yuma R & N Theater. The *Yuma Morning Sun* published a picture of Louise and June that Rose still used to publicize the act. On the surface, this photograph seems an extremely unusual choice, yet Rose had been struck on first meeting with May Sherwood by the young girl's resemblance to June. She told May and her mother that she would be able to use June's photos for May and that no one would know the difference. The girls' resemblance saved the expense of new photos.

The inexperienced girls were nervous and not yet comfortable appearing onstage. Maybe to show them how easy it was to perform, Rose herself appeared in a number during the debut performance of the act. She stood in the spotlight and sang the mournful song "Mother Machree." The act got off to a shaky start. These girls were overprotected kids, not pros, and they weren't yet sure of how to handle themselves before a live audience—let alone how to roll with the punches of opening day mishaps.

By March 16, 1929, they had performed for three days at an Orpheum theater in Phoenix. It was no longer on the Orpheum circuit, but the establishment had retained the magical old name, which lent an affirming touch of prestige to the engagement. It was a very ornate, pretty theater, with Spanish-style iron grillwork on the upstairs windows and ionic columns out in front. In addition to Madam Rose and Her Dancing Daughters, the bill included the Silver Toned Trio, Linder & Starr, and a movie, John Gilbert and Greta Garbo in *A Woman of Affairs*. It wasn't the old vaudeville bill of nine acts, but for 1929, this was still a decent line-up.

Another gig became available on April 2, 1929, in El Paso. An incongruous *El Paso Times* headline read, "Tonight a Musical Revue Will Be Given Free at Cooking School: 14th Annual Herald & Times Cooking School and Better Homes Exposition 2:30 o'clock this afternoon at Liberty Hall." The revue was to feature Madam Rose and Her Dancing Daughters. An additional article in the same paper identified Louise as "Louise Rose, star of the revue." Rose was Louise's temporary surname. A week later, in Spanish papers advertising another El Paso appearance at a theater for Hispanic speakers, the Teatro Colon, her name was misspelled Loise Rose. Louise Rose, one of the daughters of Madam Rose—it made sense. All of the girls would temporarily adopt the surname Rose. What full name Rose herself was using at the time is unclear. If she didn't also assume a new first name, she would have had to be known as Rose Rose. Her daughters reported that Rose sometimes called herself Jane.

The girls went on at the Teatro Colon with parts of their songs translated into Spanish. It was there that Louise's old standby number, "I'm a

Hard-Boiled Rose," was incorrectly translated into, "*Yo soy una gancha*," the Spanish equivalent of "I'm a hooker." The audience thought it was hilarious. Despite the translation problem, time spent at this theater turned out to be a great experience for the girls. The act went over well with the open-hearted Mexicans, who may never have seen anything like it before. This audience particularly loved the dancing cow routine and the other dances. The American troupe managed to bring down the Hispanic house.

After seeing how the Texas Mexicans appreciated their new act, Rose wanted to let the troupe try its hand in Mexico City, but Henry got lost in the desert on the way there, and the girls started to panic. The plan was promptly abandoned. They headed instead for points east. Rose ultimately settled her troupe back where she had once resided with June and Louise after the attempted Langwell Hotel robbery, the Henry Court Apartments on West 48th Street in New York City. Soon they were accepting engagements in Philadelphia and Canada.

Around this time a new gimmick was added to this act: All of the girls, except for Louise, agreed to allow their hair to be bleached platinum blonde. The girls' bleached hair produced a striking visual effect. Six girls emerging onto a stage with the exact same shade of light blonde hair was the 1929 version of a dazzling visual spectacle. Their new hair color also added to the illusion of sophistication and helped the girls look slightly older, more like young ladies and less like young kids. This illusion was enhanced when the dancing doll routine was cut out of the show.

Rose may have been determined to close her heart to June, but her head continued to seek her lost daughter. June's hair had also been dyed since she was a baby so that she would either photograph better on film, when they were in Hollywood, or look blonder and more youthful from the stage when they were in vaudeville. Lightening June's hair was not considered an unusual thing to do—at least not for a performing family. Now the six girls also had their hair color lightened, becoming in effect June's doppelgangers. Louise was credited with the idea of changing the girls' hair to the pale shade of silvery blonde, and Rose went right along with the plan.

The disaster that happened next was left out of the official version of events. According to May Sherwood, the girls' hair was initially dyed with a lethal chemical mix of pure ammonia and white henna. Their hair promptly began to break off. Rose and Louise had wanted fair-haired girls who would look striking on the stage. They wound up with ones whose hair made them resemble a lineup of scarecrows. Wigs were purchased, and the show went on.

The prettier picture the girls made after their dye jobs led to more bookings and to an inspired new name for the act, with the focus now placed directly on Louise: Rose Louise and Her Hollywood Blondes. And Rose Louise had definitely become the standout. Rose Louise remained the only one left with her untouched natural beauty intact, the single brunette in the group. Louise's stardom, rather than any superficial resemblance the chorus line members may have had to June, surely meant more to showbiz-savvy Rose than anything else. Rose Louise now was the one girl in the act who could truly stand out and command instantaneous attention. The others were indistinguishable.

Back in Seattle, Charlie Thompson had been putting up with his wife's comings and goings for years, and he came to the conclusion that he had had enough. He decided to take action. All of his daughters had been married and divorced repeatedly, so why not Charlie, too? June believed Charlie was enamored with a neighbor woman and wanted to marry her, although he never did. That may well have been his initial plan in August 1929, when he finally obtained the services of a lawyer and filed for divorce. Anna was sent a summons to appear in court within twenty days and answer Charlie's complaint. She did not appear. She may not even have been home to receive the summons. So she was declared in default by the court. On September 26, 1929, Charlie received his divorce. He sold the two houses on 4th Avenue North that he'd owned, cared for, and had rented out since 1900. They would have required too much maintenance for him to continue to perform in his old age, so he bought a new house, a tiny three-room ranch on Rutan Place covered in fir siding. His marriage was dissolved, but Anna still may not yet have known about it.

A year later, Anna was not listed on the 1930 census as a resident of the Rutan Place house (she often lived with Gypsy and Rose during the 1930s). Yet in spite of their divorce, Anna and Charlie seem to have stayed together. Anna repeatedly came back to the man who was now her official ex-husband. June claimed in her memoir that she, Rose, and Louise were staying at Charlie's house "a year after the divorce became final," when Anna found out that she'd been tricked into the divorce. June reported witnessing a contretemps when Anna threw a fit about Charlie's involvement with the neighbor woman. That version of events turned out to be impossible, another of June's tales that were refuted by evidence. June had already fled the act by 1928, Charlie's divorce happened in 1929, and "a year after the divorce became final" would have been 1930. Only Louise could have witnessed the scene.

Additional engagements were arranged for the Hollywood Blondes in locations like Niagara Falls, New York, and Schine, Ohio. By the time they were hired to play in the small town of Schine, the troupe had vastly refined the show. They received a write-up in the *Sandusky Star-Journal* on Saturday, October 19, 1929, a mere ten days before the stock market crashed with a hell of a bang and the world was changed forever. The small article must have done all of the troupers' hearts good:

Do Men Prefer Blondes? Test

Pretty Sextet on Schine's State Bill Will Do Some Local Demonstrating

The age-old problem of feminine beauty is again a matter of discussion. Rose Louise is carrying on where Anita Loos left off. Instead of writing about blondes, however, Miss Louise shows them and permits the evidence to speak for itself. Rose Louise and Her Hollywood Blondes are a sextet of fair-haired beauties, each representing a different type of blonde loveliness. They are also a smart singing, stepping sextet and with the assistance of one lone man they present a miniature musical comedy offering—a combination of songs and dances attractively stated and routined in the musical comedy pattern.

Even Henry Elias had managed to get a mention in this great little review, which raises the question of whether he only performed as the rear end of the cow, or if he'd been incorporated a bit into the act with the rest of the little lovelies.

But it is Rose in particular who, while not mentioned in the article, was due all of the kudos for the way the act had improved. She had taken a group of high school girls and turned them into a respectable attraction, not seven months following the group's taking leave from Seattle. The engagements they were hired to play didn't amount to "playing The Palace," the Rolls-Royce of the vaudeville houses, yet wherever they played, the act was warmly well received. Best of all, these engagements paid.

The group was generally low on funds. There were first six, then seven Hollywood Blondes, plus Louise, Rose, and the driver. Henry continued on as driver until he found a nice girl and left to marry her. Then a good-natured lesbian who had been named Michael and called Mike replaced Henry and endeared herself to the troupe. Mike attempted to do anything Henry had done, only better. Once again, as with the newsboys act, having fewer non-family members on board could have resulted in Rose and Louise enjoying an easier financial time. A chorus of four, not six or seven, Hollywood Blondes would have been more reasonable to manage on the lowered salaries that vaudeville engagements were paying, but either the act—which included a specialty for each girl—could not be restructured with fewer players, or the idea didn't occur to Rose.

Their situation had been improving bit by bit, but it only got worse after Black Tuesday, October 29, 1929, the day the stock market crashed on Wall Street. The crash was the start of the Great Depression. It was Rose and Louise's bad luck that it began right as the skill, if not the salary, of their little act had begun to improve. The stock market crash was such an economic disaster that even *Variety*, the Broadway entertainment trade paper that usually ignored all of the dull reports on finances, covered the catastrophe the following day with an article bearing the infamous headline, "Wall Street Lays an Egg," which borrowed an old theatrical term normally used to describe a flop. If poor ailing vaudeville had already been an invalid, sick, weakening, and on the way out, the new dire financial situation suddenly besetting the entire country finally killed it off. The vagabond culture of traveling entertainers that had enthralled Rose and had been home to June and Louise soon vanished as if it almost had never existed.

Suddenly few theaters showed live acts. It was a lot more profitable for theater owners to rent a film to show than it was for them to pay salaries to performers, musicians, and stagehands. The theater owners couldn't be blamed for choosing to show actors on celluloid, rather than continuing to provide their audiences with the excitement of live performers. Like everyone else in the country, they were doing the best they could, and showing movies was a cheaper option and a way to get by. Now that movies had added sound, they were becoming the most popular new form of mass entertainment. Theater owners could live very well, even during the Depression, by showing movies.

June, meanwhile, finally was in one place long enough to make her first appearance in a federal census. The 1930 census had listed Ellen E. Hyde, whose age was said to be eighteen, with the Hyde family of Portland City, Multnomish County, Oregon. The household also included Buddy's parents and sister.

June and her husband Buddy would soon go on the road, trying their hand at having a dancing act. It did not work out as well as they'd hoped. There simply were not enough decent vaudeville venues left.

Louise, Rose, and their traveling blonde chorus line somehow wound up in Kansas City, and in terrible financial shape. There wasn't any work to be found. No work meant there wasn't any food, and with too many mouths to feed, the situation was becoming untenable. Not only that, all the grand old Kansas vaudeville theaters were showing movies. Finally Sam Middleton, an agent Rose knew from the happy days when she still had June with her, found a theater that would book the new act, but there was a catch: It was a burlesque theater.

Vaudeville performers had a prejudicial attitude towards burlesque, where bawdy jokes prevailed and girls ran around in various states of undress. This was a funny form of prejudice, all things considered. Naked girls were permissible in legitimate Broadway extravaganzas like the *Ziegfeld Follies*, where they were arranged in tableaux to look like paintings or other types of visual spectacles. Unusually for the time, there was no stigma attached to those shows, despite the fact that their girls were just as naked as the burlesque dames were. Naked ladies posed to look like paintings were considered classy, while naked ones bumping to the brash beat of burlesque drums were thought to be low-class. To Rose, just the idea that her young girls would appear in burlesque was a nightmare. Most of them were still underage. Rose became hysterical to the point she was stuttering during her phone call with Sam Middleton. She reminded him of the fact that the girls were still "kiddies." Sam Middleton, who was Caucasian, countered that if those girls were kiddies, then he was "Old Black Joe."

Louise was more practical about Middleton's proposal; the dire situation demanded they consider performing at the burlesque theater. While Rose carried on in a state of near emotional meltdown, Louise stepped forward, took hold of the phone, and accepted the engagement. Once again, she took on the role of the parent, this time not only to Rose, but to the whole troupe. She told her mother and the girls that they could take the job but didn't have to associate with the burlesque performers; in vaudeville, this *was not done*. Louise may have been wise enough to accept the opportunity, but the old anti-burlesque bias was still within her, too. It was another low moment, but at least they'd be paid. The girls and Rose proceeded to the Gayety Theater.

They were in culture shock before they even walked in. The lights and signs outside were a vaudevillian's idea of scandalous, and the display in the lobby left the girls speechless. A fan was being directed at a gigantic photo of a woman with real tassels affixed to her brassiere—or what little there was of one. The fan made the tassels circulate.

These kids should have been back in school in Seattle preparing for geometry tests or chasing volleyballs around a gymnasium as some martinet of a gym teacher blew a whistle. They were about to get a whole other kind of education.

But the job didn't turn out to be as bad as they'd feared. Burlesque may have been bawdy and low class, but it was also upbeat and fun, as was the music. Yes, some of the women were not fully clothed, but the Hollywood Blondes were, and no harm was done to them. The bawdy humor in the show was more suggestive than graphic. The other players were a slightly rougher crowd than Rose and Louise had been used to in vaudeville, but even that aspect of the job didn't prove to be as bad as Rose had initially feared.

Tessie, a performer assigned to share a dressing room with Louise, spoke the words that would inspire her transformation into Gypsy Rose Lee. When Louise told Tessie she didn't feel she had any talent, Tessie told Louise that she did: Her talent was the possession of inherent class. Tessie told Louise that she just had to figure out "how to handle it."

Rose entered the burlesque theater not wanting to speak to the performers and making loud pronouncements that the girls were bound to catch a venereal disease from the backstage toilets. She was pleasantly surprised when the place turned out to be better than she had envisioned. In short order, Rose went from outrage to thrilled when Louise was chosen to participate in a few burlesque comedy scenes. By the end of the four-week engagement, Rose's attitude towards burlesque had made an about face. This change probably happened after she had been around the Gayety for awhile, witnessed how much fun it was, and saw, with her own eyes, how similar it was to vaudeville. Rose came to believe that having a few burlesque credits on Louise's resume would be a plus for her daughter. She told her that lots of stars had jump-started their careers by learning the ropes in burlesque. She soon conveniently forgot the way she'd all but had a nervous collapse when Sam Middleton had first suggested the act play a burlesque venue.

Scandal found them, though—or at least it found the Gayety Theater. The standards for burlesque shows were strict. If a woman appeared completely naked, or even gave the illusion of nakedness, the place could get shut down. One woman in the show, though clothed, presented just such a mirage one night. The theater was raided by the cops and summarily closed. Fortuitously, Louise had left the theater right before the raid. Tessie hadn't. She called to inform Louise that the raid had been caused by one of the other strippers and the "monkey fur" she wore on her onstage panties. So Rose Louise and Her Hollywood Blondes were, once again, out of work. At least they hadn't also been arrested.

It was late autumn and becoming cold in Kansas City. One of the only positive things about being an unemployed act was that the troupe didn't have to stay put anywhere, particularly anywhere that was freezing. Rose decided to take the girls and head south where it was warmer, and got them a two-week engagement at a gambling club in Louisville, Kentucky. Gangsters were said to frequent the place. The troupe's stint there was mainly memorable because when someone in the audience used a new invention, a flash camera, Rose and the girls thought the gangsters had started shooting one another. Rose, shouting, ordered them all to run and hide from the "machine guns." The club owner was amused by the sight of the costumed teens running for cover because of a flash bulb. Rose was certainly letting these girls have an adventure.

Rose settled on Florida as the next place for the troupe to find work. It was a terrific choice, since Florida, with its swaying palm trees and crystalline blue water, was fast becoming one of the biggest resort destinations in the country, despite of the Great Depression. And resorts always needed entertainers. By November 20, 1930, Rose had managed to book the act for twelve weeks at Club Bagdad in Hialeah, Florida, a town close to the vacation hub of Miami. The gang was to get $250 a week until January 1, then $275 a week for the rest of the engagement, wonderful money for that period and an affirmation of how well the act was progressing.

Still, there were seven people in the act, plus Miss Mike the driver and Rose, so Rose figured out a way to save a bit of extra cash by having everyone sneak back into the dressing room at the club every night and sleeping there, not in a hotel. Finessing this plan was quite a feat. The girls stashed pillows and blankets in the car and then had to bring them inside at night to make improvised bedrolls. Blankets were not hard to hide in a dressing room. They could be folded into a pile and easily lost among all the other materials and costumes. Pillows for ten would have been more difficult to conceal. But asthmatic Rose wasn't able to sleep on the floor, so she brought her own army cot. That was also usually kept in the car, and it had to be sneaked in and out of the dressing room too, probably nightly, so that the management would not see it and realize the whole troupe was camping out in the building. Then the cot had to be removed every the morning. Every move they made had to be done under cover of darkness.

Once again, Rose demonstrated her understanding of teenage girls, sanctioning a wacky adventure like this one. Life wouldn't ever have been this exciting had they remained back at their old Seattle high schools. Their hiding place went undetected, and they all had a rather fine view of a papaya grove from the dressing room window. Then a contingent of gentlemen carrying shovels showed up, and Rose and the girls surreptitiously watched the men dig something out of the ground. It was a little metal box. This part of their lives must have seemed to the girls like a chapter out of a Nancy Drew mystery.

Since the club owner kept stalling on paying Rose the agreed-upon salary, she decided to get evidence about his involvement with the strange happenings in the papaya grove. She went digging in the grove herself the next night and was rewarded when she found some packets of white powder. When the club owner failed to pay Rose again, she tried to use the powder as a bargaining chip by taking it to the police. Rose believed it was dope; what else could it possibly be? But the policeman she spoke with was in cahoots with the Club Bagdad owner, and he deliberately misinformed Rose that the packets contained ordinary talcum powder. When the corrupt cop notified the club owner of Rose's find, the latter threatened Rose. Fortunately the troupe was saved by burlesque. The same agent who had booked the girls into the burlesque theater in Kansas City sent the now-terrified group a telegram inviting them to another city to perform. That was all the excuse they needed to hightail it out of the sunshine state.

CHAPTER 10

FRONT AND CENTER

THE EXPERIENCE OF SLEEPING IN THE DRESSING ROOM AT THE CLUB Bagdad sparked new money-saving ideas in Rose and Louise. Rose came to the conclusion that the Hollywood Blondes troupe, which was doing rather well again, could do even better, saving a lot of the money they were shelling out for hotel rooms. It was Louise who came up with the idea of purchasing a tent, an idea pronounced "inspirational." She rose to the occasion and swept the girls along with her. They could carry it along with them and pitch it in or near whatever town they played. A tent, tent stakes, a camping stove, and cooking utensils were purchased. Rose also made sure to swipe some towels and cakes of soap before leaving the last hotel where they stayed. Then the whole group, including the live pig that was used in the barnyard act, moved out into the great outdoors.

The photos that remain from this time in the troupe's life show all of the girls looking as if they're having a fabulous time. They're pictured outside the tent in one photo. That tent was huge, large enough for all of them. The girls and Louise can be seen in one photo reclining on Rose's army cot, all wearing overalls and matching blouses, save for the littlest one, May, who's wearing a dark-colored dress, probably one of the costumes she'd inherited from June. As for Louise, she is easily the most stunning girl in the photo. Louise may not have known it, but by this point she was nineteen. The camping plan was yet another example of Rose's ingenious way of keeping these girls in a happy frame of mind. For the moment, her plan worked. They got to have the sort of exploits that other kids only read about or saw in the movies. The tent provided a sensible way to economize. It is interesting that Louise came up with this financial dodge, not Rose. Louise's business sense was beginning to emerge. She would prove to be adept at economic improvisation for the rest of her life.

One of the events that transpired on one of the troupe's first camping sites was more frightening than dangerous. The tent was pitched in the middle of nowhere beyond the civilized part of Toledo, Ohio. In the middle of the night, Rose heard somebody creeping around the outside of the tent. The noise terrified her. She was responsible for all of the young girls, Louise and their driver, Mike, and, unused to the sounds of the countryside, she panicked. Rose grabbed a gun that she kept handy and threatened to shoot the intruder if he didn't stop in his tracks. Then she fired off a few gunshots only to find that she'd killed a cow in what she had thought was self-defense.

This story made it into Gypsy's memoir. Much later, when rumors about Rose's alleged activities circulated after she was portrayed in a fictitious light in *Gypsy: A Musical Fable*, one of the worst was that Rose had killed not a cow but a man that night outside Toledo. But May Sherwood was to remember sitting, strategically positioned along with the rest of the girls, on a tarpaulin, under which the cow carcass was hidden, when the cow's owner, a local farmer, came looking for it the next morning.

In Toledo Louise's luck was finally to change for the better, and it was a change that would affect the rest of her life. The act had been booked into the Gaiety Theatre in Toledo, as had an act called Girls from the Ziegfeld Follies. The Ziegfeld act had a major problem: Its booze-guzzling star, called Gladys "Youth" Clark, had been arrested shortly after the act's previous engagement had ended. She had assaulted a hotel manager with an inkwell, and he lived to tell the tale. Gladys was stuck in a jail cell, which was probably a good thing. The wild woman had a temper that made her a threat to every community she passed through. Gladys had already been arrested for assault several times. She was now a problem for the jailer of the local hoosegow. Meanwhile, back at the Gaiety Theatre, the Girls from the Ziegfeld Follies were left without a star.

The beleaguered producer of their act was a man by the name of Ed Ryan. He also bore the dubious distinction of being Gladys Clark's husband. His troupe had several more engagements to play on the burlesque circuit, called wheels. The season on the wheels lasted for forty weeks. Ed Ryan's troupe was booked to the end of the season but was without its star, and Ed didn't know what to do about salvaging the rest of the season. But Rose did.

The Hollywood Blondes company had arrived at the Gaiety in the middle of a brouhaha between Ed Ryan and the manager of the theater about how the Girls from the Ziegfeld part of the show would go on without their the volatile star. Rose unhesitatingly waltzed over to the two and volunteered Rose Louise as Gladys's replacement. They needed a girl who could do scenes and strip. Rose volunteered her gorgeous daughter for both jobs. She also made sure to mention Louise's appearance with Fanny Brice, so long ago, on the Orpheum circuit. A credit like that always helped bolster her daughter's rather thin resume, and it managed to get Louise noticed this time. Ed Ryan agreed to give the young woman a chance.

Back in the dressing room, Rose immediately assured Louise that she would not, after all, really and truly have to strip. She told her daughter to strut on the stage to the beat of the music and drop a shoulder strap at the end. This would prove to be one of the most magnificent strategies in the annals of show business: the stripper who didn't take it all off. Carole Lombard had used a similar strategy in California a few years earlier when she showed up for a bathing beauty photo shoot as the only woman wearing a tailored suit. The outfit had been chosen as a means to help Carole stand out among the other girls. Doing the opposite of what is expected not only gets a hopeful noticed, but also allows her to stand out from the crowd. Of all the women in the photo shoot, Carole was the one who became a star.

So would Rose Louise. Her mother dashed from the theater to buy costume material for Rose Louise's non-strip routines, and the confident young woman she left in the dressing room realized her time had come. She was to be the star of this show. It had happened smoothly and easily, but at last, it had happened. Not bad for a girl who'd awakened that morning in a tent, thinking it was going to be just another day as part of an act on a bill in Toledo.

Rose Louise had been around stars for almost all of her life. She saw how imperiously they behaved on the Orpheum circuit, and now she began joyously emulating them. She went outside to watch her name being put up in lights, which must have been one of the best feelings she'd ever had—until she realized that she was to be a star in burlesque, the scourge of vaudevillians. To a child who'd been raised in vaudeville, becoming a burlesque star was a disgrace. Burlesque was considered a trash heap. It was where those who failed in vaudeville traditionally washed up, like the planks of a shipwrecked vessel. There was a societal stigma to playing burlesque, and the bias came from vaudeville and the larger world. There was also the opinion of her straight-laced grandfather, Charlie Thompson, to think about. And there was Louise's unofficial father figure, Gordon, and Stanley, the boy she'd loved during the last year of the Dainty June act. Stanley was out there somewhere in America, hopefully dancing his heart out. Three of these four individuals whose opinions meant so much to Louise were currently absent from her life, but they still were the most important people in the world to her. Louise had arrived at a pinnacle, but her vaudeville upbringing, and its attendant prejudices, prompted her rush to disguise herself.

It was at that moment, or so she would later claim, that Louise decided to put Rose Louise aside and change her name to Gypsy Rose Lee. The spur-of-the-moment choice of Lee" as a surname may have been prompted by the size of the marquee. "Gypsy Rose Louise" might have contained more letters than the marquee could accommodate. Adding Gypsy to her name lent a touch of the exotic to the German-Scottish-Norwegian all-American teenager from Seattle. Her nickname had been Gypsy since the day she was born with two veils during the 1911 snowstorm, and during all those years when the dark-haired, dark-eyed girl would tell fortunes to her troupe. It also sounded much smoother to say "Gypsy Rose Lee" than "Gypsy Rose Louise." When the man who was placing the letters of her name onto the lit marquee protested that he'd been told to put Rose Louise up there, Gypsy immediately pulled rank on him. She was the star. He'd put her name in lights the way she asked for it, and that was that. So it was to be Gypsy Rose Lee who opened that day in Toledo, not Rose Louise Hovick. She had zeroed in on an intriguing, catchy stage name, one that people would remember. This was the first of a series of smart moves she would make over her long career.

The new star went on for the first time only three hours later, wearing a costume she'd hastily sewn backstage herself. Rose, watching from backstage, called out directions, telling her daughter to smile. Louise strutted around on the stage, took pins out of her costume (there hadn't been enough time to sew it together) and tossed them into the tuba. She played around with lowering her shoulder straps, then dropped the dress—but stepped back before the audience could see her without it, letting the curtain cover her. And she pulled off the number to perfection.

The audience loved it, loved her, and went berserk. There was so much applause that the young star thought she should go back out on the stage and take an additional bow. But Rose told her daughter to treat the applause as if it was the audience's typical reaction to her, letting the theater manager and Ed Ryan believe that she always got a terrific ovation. This was unerring advice, illustrative of what a savvy show business pro Rose had become over the years.

Gypsy Rose Lee made her second entrance during the second act. The audience was thrilled to see her back again. She proceeded to do a number called "Powder My Back." The song might not have been the same as the one June had used back in Rochester when the act was arrested for indecency, but the powder puff routine that had caused the child welfare inspector near-apoplexy in 1923 was probably similar, if not identical, to Gypsy's new one. It had just been revised and updated a bit to suit burlesque, and Gypsy knew how to perform it. She'd seen her little sister in action with the same audience-pleasing powder puff prop plenty of times. Gypsy Rose Lee's first magical day as a star concluded with a surprise after the second show that thrilled the romantic young woman's heart. Someone sent her an exquisite basket of flowers during the finale. A note was attached, signed by an admirer.

The audience was pleased with her first day as a star, and so was Ed Ryan. Gypsy was signed to remain with the tour until it concluded in four weeks. Rose negotiated for her daughter like the pro that she was. Gypsy would continue performing her two terrific numbers. She'd also get a better salary than the one originally offered to her. She would even be assigned the star's dressing room. Ed gave the blondes jobs in the chorus. The Hollywood Blondes act itself would be shelved for the rest of the run.

As it would turn out, the Hollywood Blondes act was over for good, but nobody realized it yet. The end of the act had yet to play itself out. Gypsy, having a dressing room all to herself, may have been a mistake, if only because the single room separated Gypsy and Rose from the other girls, giving them the opportunity to discuss their situation away from their leaders. No one was thinking of endings at that moment, only beginnings.

This did not mean that Rose was idle; far from it. Rose had arranged secretly for flowers to be delivered to Gypsy after every performance, during the finale, and in full view of the audience and the rest of the cast. The entire cast assembled on stage during the finale. The resentment of the other cast members was palpable, but the gimmick worked. Rose's gimmicks usually did.

Gypsy was subjected to all manner of harassment from the show's prima donna, a woman named Mary Noel. Mary appeared in an American Indian scene called "Pale Moon." Backstage, Rose was paying particular attention to that scene and to Miss Noel, who had formulated a plot to upstage Gypsy in the finale, in which everyone was in feathers, dressed as birds. Gypsy usually took hold of the two ends of the curtain during the finale and closed them herself as she gaily chatted to the audience. Miss Noel didn't like that bit of stage business one bit; it took attention away from her. So in retaliation for what she perceived as Gypsy's theft of her on-stage thunder, Noel grabbed one of the sides of the curtains before Gypsy could and wouldn't allow the curtain to be closed. But Gypsy was no shrinking violet. She held her own with the woman during the finale. As her great-grandfather Lorenze and Mr. Niskern, his rival hotel owner in Farmington, Minnesota, had once done to each other on the street, Gypsy Rose Lee kneed Mary Noel in the ass. The audience went to burlesque theaters to have a fun time and got more than they bargained for at that show. What an unexpected treat to see two rivals trying to upstage one another! And how deftly Gypsy handled it.

After the great event, both Mary Noel and Rose blamed Ed Ryan. Rose's exhortations proved more persuasive than Mary's. Ed Ryan was inspired to move Miss Noel's placement in the finale away from Gypsy Rose Lee's central position so that Noel could be "better seen" by the audience. Rose had her own ideas about what was important, which for the moment went unexpressed. The next thing the self-aggrandized Miss Noel knew, she was on the receiving end of an anonymous note that compared her singing abilities to that of a frog. The note was signed, "A Well-Wisher." The little missive somehow arrived at the tour's next stop, Cincinnati, on the day that the show moved there from Toledo. Miss Noel screamed over the latest injustice to befall her, accusing Rose of writing the hate letter. Rose simply ignored her. Ed Ryan told Mary Noel she didn't have any proof of who wrote the letter and therefore couldn't accuse anybody. Either to keep the peace or to ensure he didn't get one of Rose's love letters next, Ed assured her that he didn't believe she had written the one that caused Mary Noel's latest meltdown. He must have truly appreciated what Gypsy Rose Lee was bringing to his act, because by then, the circumstantial evidence that Rose or Gypsy was behind the letter was becoming overwhelming.

Flowers from an anonymous admirer arrived again for Gypsy that first evening in Cincinnati. What fun it was for Gypsy to receive such a tribute again and to wonder whom it could possibly be from. She soon found out. The next anonymous note that Mary Noel received from an anonymous well-wisher advised her to "wise up" and find another career, one in which she didn't have to perform for a living. Dressed like a squaw in her "Pale Moon" costume, Mary Noel furiously showed the note to Gypsy and threatened to call the cops on Rose if she received any more demoralizing letters. Gypsy realized the handwriting on her notes and on Noel's notes was the same, evidence that could only point to one person. Gypsy didn't have an actual admirer. This was a devastating development for Gypsy; she had believed with a young girl's hope that the admirer was real. The flower deliveries were nothing more than one of her mother's effective stunts.

When confronted by her daughter, Rose admitted she'd sent the notes and the flowers. Gypsy explained that she could be brought up on charges if the hate mail to Miss Noel didn't stop. Rose's justification was that a mother's love could not be legislated, but she realized this was one of those times when she was beaten. Mary Noel didn't receive any more notes, but Rose wasn't yet finished with her. Rose hired a few local boys to sit in the balcony and start booing whenever Mary Noel came onstage. She even paid for their tickets. This tactic proved even better than writing poison pen letters. It drove Mary Noel nuts and left no direct evidence leading back to Rose. It was a perfect strategy, really. Besides, the Depression was on, so by paying the boys for their services Rose was helping the local Cincinnati economy, giving the boys money that they could put in circulation.

Unorthodox though Rose's methodology may have been, it was effective. Increasingly, Gypsy stood out among Ed Ryan's cast members, looking better and becoming more acclaimed every day. Mary Noel, confronted with booing boys whenever she took the stage, became increasingly shrill and hysterical. Her attitude made her look considerably less professional than Gypsy, just as Rose had planned.

Mary Noel was one problem. There were others. First Mike, the lesbian who had replaced Henry Elias as chauffeur for the troupe, refused to continue to remain with the act when the company proceeded to the next stop, Chicago. She admitted to Rose that she was a lesbian and would not return to Chicago under any circumstances. Mike had been a great driver and had done a wonderful job wearing the cow costume in the Hollywood Blondes act, and Rose wanted her to remain. But Mike would not budge, despite Rose's pleading. Louise didn't have a driver's license, but that was irrelevant; she was going to have to drive the car to Chicago.

Next, the Hollywood Blondes staged a mutiny against Rose, which must have broken her heart all over again, especially if she had taken them on partially to ease the pain of losing June. Rose was the manager of the act, so she had been paid directly for the services of the whole troupe, handling all of their finances and living expenses. She also kept meticulous records of what each girl had earned and spent. While sharing a dressing room with the other chorus girls in the show, the Blondes had been regaled by the chorus members with tales of how much money they could be earning directly. Rose threatened to notify the girls' parents about the way they were behaving and found out that one of the girls already notified hers, and if one girl had contacted her parents, they probably all had. The girls had initially loved and even welcomed the idea of living in the tent, but now they refused to stay in it. They were growing up. The appeal of their adolescent adventure was wearing off. Besides, Louise had turned into the breakout star of the group. May Sherwood, and probably most of the others, did not want to make a career out of burlesque, as Louise was doing. It was a good time for them to begin going their separate ways and looking after themselves. May returned to Seattle with several dollars pinned to her underwear to be used for expenses during the long trip home.

It was painful for Rose and Gypsy to see the girls go. This act, like the initial newsboys act, had created a little family. Now this close-knit group was dispersed. Ed Ryan paid the former Hollywood Blondes for their engagement in the last theater directly, finalizing their break with Rose. And just when matters could not get much worse, Rose and Louise finally heard from June. This postscript to her earlier mutiny must have been the hardest blow to take. Rose had written to June about Louise's rising stardom. She would never be able to forgive June for having run away from their old act, and she could not resist bragging to her about how well she had managed Louise's act. Rose added what she would always add: that she had wanted the same kind of stardom for June.

If she had been hoping that June would send a contrite letter in return, expressing the wish that she'd stuck with her mother and sister—or maybe even begging to come back to them—even that minor satisfaction was not to be. June wrote to Louise not to congratulate her, but to accuse her of lowering herself and her standards by appearing in burlesque. June had written this message on a postcard of herself that was taken by the promoters of a dance marathon she had entered. Dance marathons had begun in the 1920s and were even more in vogue during the 1930s. Only an economic crisis like the Great Depression could have popularized them. As forms of entertainment go, dance marathons can only be described as bizarre, if not downright creepy. This was a bad development; a marathon was no place for June. Contestants would dance for months—literally.

The marathons were usually set up in such a way that couples would dance for part of an hour, then get about ten or fifteen minutes of rest time when they could sleep. At the end of the rest period a bell or a siren would ring, and they had to be back on the dance floor in time for the starting signal of the next hour, or they were disqualified. This went on twenty-four hours a day, for days, weeks, and even months, for whatever couples proved hearty enough to withstand the grueling routine.

And the longer these contests continued, the more exhausted the contestants would become. Most of them arrived in an underweight condition in the first place, near starvation and willing to put up with the demands of the marathon just to get fed. Often, within a few days after it began, dancers would be hallucinating from exhaustion. Or sleepwalking. Or doing all manner of other weird things that the spectators had a great time laughing at. But the spectacle wasn't really funny. It was sadistic and sick.

On the plus side, marathon promoters fed the contestants twelve times a day. Many of these unemployed people might have starved to death otherwise, so the conditions of the marathon did not seem as brutal to them as they do to history. June was one of the ones who believed that getting fed twelve times a day just for staying upright on the dance floor was a rather good deal.

Fate had not been kind to June after she ran away from her family's act. Her marriage had been something of an end in itself, a means of running away. June and Buddy would go their separate ways without rancor, leaving June to support herself as best she could by trying to book her solo dancing act wherever she could get hired. She then hit upon the marathons as a way to earn a little money. Most of the income came from coins thrown by spectators when she got up to sing. At least the marathons gave her a chance to eat regularly.

But marathons were operated by the criminal element. They were dangerous. There were marathon contestants who, after months spent enduring this exhausting schedule of only sleeping a few minutes out of each hour, died when they finally were disqualified, their bodies simply giving out. Undesirables visited the shows during the evening hours. Sometimes girls would be sold off the floor to whoever wanted to have them. Usually these girls were never seen or heard from again. Many of the contestants were so rootless they weren't missed by any family members or friends.

Between marathons, the teenaged June would go to New York City and attempt to audition her way into a legitimate theatrical job on Broadway. She would eat junk food from street vendors and sleep on a bench in the bus station. She'd also sneak into the second acts of various Broadway shows, mingling back with audience members when they returned from intermission and either taking a place in the standing room only section, or stealing an empty seat to watch the stars perform as she longed to perform. June was hungry for knowledge about acting. She wanted to learn all she could from watching established stars in action. So far her attempts to conquer Broadway had not borne fruit.

It seems strange that she apparently never tried to contact Roxy Rothafel, the man who had wanted to finance her professional training when she was younger. Neither did she contact the father in California she barely remembered, who probably would have welcomed her with open arms.

Until the day she died, June wondered if Jack Hovick truly was her natural father. Mistakenly believing he wasn't, June had no use for him or any member of his new family. If she had contacted him, she would have been able to see for herself how clearly she physically resembled the Hovicks, and could have put her mind to rest on the subject of her own paternity. She also would have found a family that wanted very much to reconnect with her. But June didn't bother with any of them. Instead, she remained fixated on her one goal: becoming an actress on Broadway. Meanwhile, she was lost among the criminal element and the lowlife in a marathon, and a picture of her and her dancing partner was on the front of the post card she sent to Louise.

Rose was most devastated by hearing about June's participation in the marathons. That postcard prompted a long crying fit, the kind that could only come from a mother whose heart was broken because her child had gone down the wrong path. It must have felt like a disaster of earth-shattering proportions to Rose to find out that the child prodigy whose talent she had tried to nurture into respectable stardom was embracing a hideous fad just to get food into her stomach. But Rose didn't send for June to join her and Louise. Her trust in the child who had run away was completely destroyed. Taking June back wasn't even an option.

Meanwhile, a review of Gypsy's show appeared in the September 22, 1931, issue of the *Suburbanite Economist* newspaper. The reviewer said of Louise, "Gypsy Rose Lee is a soft voiced crooner, who rather whispers than sings her songs." But the reviewer also said, "You'll like Mary Noel, costumed in black and shimmering silver, playing 'Stardust' and a medley of popular songs on the violin." A critic from Zit's theatrical weekly paper had also come to the show, then provided Gypsy with a glowing review.

Mike the chauffeur may have abandoned the act, the girls may have been leaving, June may have been in an accursed marathon, but the good word was out about Gypsy Rose Lee. Her act was something so different and special that, after it moved, without the Blondes and solo, to a theater in Newark, New Jersey, it attracted the notice of Billy Minsky. He was one of the Minsky Brothers, owners of the biggest and most prestigious chain of burlesque theaters. The Minsky organization wanted Louise booked into their best theater of all, the Republic on Forty-Second Street in New York. It was the best news yet.

But Gypsy's Newark appearance and subsequent New York debut would happen a few months down the road. In the meantime, the Ed Ryan show had yet to wrap up, and, for Rose in full warrior mode, there were still a few loose ends to tie up. There was still a battle going on with regard to Mary Noel—and Ed Ryan now, too. He encouraged the Blondes' defection by paying their salary directly, rather than adhering to the original deal Rose had with them, whereby she was the one who handled the cash. Rose vowed vengeance against both Ed Ryan and Mary Noel. And she had a plan to obtain it.

Rose could have won an Academy Award on the last night of Gypsy's engagement with Ed's act. She was jovial to everyone as she said goodbye. She wished them all the best of luck. She actually had her own barely repressible reasons to be so pleasant. She had liberated Mary Noel's entire "Pale Moon" Indian costume, which Mary wore in the show and Ed Ryan owned, and secreted it in the car. Nothing could put a smile on Rose's face and energize her the way pulling off a successful scam could. And things were finally really and truly looking up, because Gypsy Rose Lee was on the way to an engagement that was to lead to her opening in New York City.

CHAPTER 11

ƁAƬHƬUƁ ƓIN

THOSE WHO REMEMBER GYPSY ROSE LEE, OR KNOW ABOUT HER FROM the legend depicted later in the musical *Gypsy: A Musical Fable*, pretty much know what happened next. She was a hit at Minsky's, of course. But Louise didn't stop there. Louise had become Gypsy Rose Lee, and she would never stop anywhere ever again. Ultimately, she conquered the most significant venue in America, New York City.

She was stately and gorgeous but also uproariously funny. She was well read, the kind of woman who would have been appreciated in New York City whether she worked at Minsky's or not. Even the most celebrated New Yorkers, the ones who made up the literary clique that ate lunch at the Algonquin Hotel, were sophisticated enough to recognize her as one of their own. They didn't look down on her because of her burlesque act; they considered her more interesting because of it.

In many ways, when Louise hit New York, she found her true home. The smart little girl who had traveled all over the country carting a small collection of books with her had landed at last in a place where she could belong. She incorporated intellectual references into her original strip acts. She didn't even strip, just teased, leaving so much to the imagination that her audiences would come back for more, providing repeat business at her performances at Minsky's. The same burlesque scenes and songs were recycled again and again, but the bawdy titles of the shows were changed regularly to bring in new audience members. "Yetta Lostit from Monte Carlo" was one title that survives on a program dated May 11, 1931. "Ada Onion from Bermuda" is another. Gypsy's name was given top billing over the title of the moment, whatever it was, and she did well in all of her Minsky shows.

Rose and Gypsy found a room to share in a unique place called the Cameo Apartments. It was a former supper club that had closed when

Prohibition banned the sale of liquor, and it still resembled a lovely, though faded, restaurant, with silk-lined and mirrored walls. It was located across the street from the Republic Theatre on 42nd Street, which in 1931 was the very heart of New York City's midtown. There were Broadway theaters like the New Amsterdam right across the street from the Republic, movie theaters, a flea circus, a Nedick's hot dog stand—not to mention the never-ending parade of people who came from all over the country and all over the world to settle in cosmopolitan Manhattan.

Rose observed all of Gypsy's performances, watching from the landing on the backstage stairs leading to Gypsy's second floor dressing room, which overlooked the stage, and bolstering her daughter with constant encouragement. Sometimes Rose interfered when she thought a rival act was stealing Gypsy's thunder, as when naked girls dressed in angels' wings were featured in the act following Gypsy's. Rose called the press, pretending to be a churchgoer who objected to the angel act on religious grounds. The act was eliminated, as was another involving a performer who appeared accompanied by white rats. Rose contacted the American Society for the Prevention of Cruelty to Animals about that one, reporting the Minskys for allowing it. She was in top competitive form and delighted in using any means necessary to get perceived rivals out of her daughter's way. It wasn't long before Billy Minsky became less than enamored with Rose. One of his proudest accomplishments came on the day he erected a sign banning Rose from the backstage area of his theater.

Rose wasn't terribly sociable with the Minsky cast members, although performer Mimi Reed got her talking once. Rose was still raw from June's defection and betrayal two and a half years earlier, and all Rose could talk about was June, Mimi reported. In the face of Gypsy's success, which thrilled her, Rose was nevertheless still reeling over what she saw as June's rejection, pouring her heart out to Mimi, a virtual stranger, about her lost daughter, the talented one who was gone.

June was still supporting herself, though just barely, by continuing to participate in dance marathons. She was not yet out of her teens. The environment remained unwholesome, to put it mildly. At one point, or so she claimed, she left the dance floor to accept what she was told was an engagement as a nightclub singer and found herself, instead, duped into a situation where she was kidnapped, drugged, held captive, and subjected to unknown horrors while knocked out. Her captors released her after several days with a bus ticket to New York in her pocket. Somehow, all of this had been arranged with the promoters of that particular marathon. These events reportedly happened during June's second marathon. If the story is indeed true, it doesn't make sense that she would return to such a world and appear in five more of the endurance contests, ultimately participating in seven. She was considered a marathon star, but the disturbing tale doesn't really add up.

Back in New York, the police were raiding Minsky's theater regularly. Their visits were prompted by site inspections from a fanatical, prudish, killjoy, John S. Sumner of the Society for the Prevention of Vice. He would attend as many burlesque shows as possible and report whatever he considered scandalous violations, like showing too much skin, to the cops. The Minsky brothers had actually gone to the trouble of building a custom John Sumner alert system into their theater's infrastructure, putting red lights in the footlight area of the theater that would be switched on—in full and easy view of the performers—whenever Sumner, or anyone suspected of being either one of his mad cronies or a vice cop, happened to be sitting in the audience. If the red lights were lit, the performers knew to tone down their show and wear the least revealing costumes possible so that they would pass inspection. This red light alert system was far from foolproof. It was difficult for the front-of-house staff monitor to every member of the entire audience. There were also times when Sumner or a crony managed to slink into the show, sit down, and remain undetected.

Rose thrilled at being swept up in the raids and getting to ride to the police station in a paddy wagon with her daughter, with the light on the top of the vehicle flashing away, lighting up the night, and the siren wailing. It was exciting and exhilarating for both mother and daughter. It beat the hell out of her former existence as a housewife back in Rainier Beach, Washington.

Gypsy Rose Lee began endearing herself to New Yorkers with her response to her first raid. "I wasn't naked," she innocently insisted to the reporters, "I was *completely* covered by a blue spotlight." One daughter may have been gone, but the other's star was clearly on the rise. Rose could pride herself on how well Gypsy was doing, thanks to her tutelage during the vaudeville years. She continued to observe Gypsy's performances, yet the amount of time she spent backstage, while fascinating, was beginning to wear thin. Rose began looking for something more to do.

Gypsy became friendly with Inez Worth, another Minsky's performer, and Rose befriended Inez's mother, Myrtle. The two backstage ladies developed a potentially profitable and highly timely idea: they would go into business together selling bathtub gin. Prohibition was still in effect, but the demand for alcohol was as great as ever. New York City alone had a hundred thousand speakeasies, but patrons ran the risk of being arrested if they were caught in such places by the cops, so many folks preferred to buy bottles on the sly and drink at home.

The demand for booze steadily increased from the January day in 1920, when Prohibition first went into effect, until the day in December 1933 when it was finally repealed. All manner of home liquor fermenting strategies were put into place, including the outrageous practice of manufacturing gin in bathtubs. Doing so was easy. All anyone needed was a bathtub with a reliable plug, some grain alcohol, which could usually be procured from a bootlegger, juniper berries or other flavoring, and water. These ingredients were thrown together, and after a few days there'd be a tubful of liquor. Bathtub gin usually tasted vile, and there were no regulations in place to make certain that the level of alcohol wasn't lethal. It often caused those who drank it to become sick or go blind, insane, or even die.

Bathtub gin could be sold for wonderfully high prices, and Rose came from a long tradition of people who could be dropped just about anywhere in the world and manage to find a way to turn a healthy profit. Dropping Rose into the middle of New York City during Prohibition had the expected result. Rose and Myrtle put their heads together and came up with a nice bathtub gin recipe. They were all set to start selling their libation and make a nice financial killing. New York, being the most populous city in the country, was a place where they knew they certainly wouldn't lack for customers. But this plan did not last long. Gangsters running bootleg operations in New York City were not about to have these two backstage ladies horn in on their business.

Rose and Myrtle changed their plan. They still went into a business partnership together, but it was to make and sell fudge, not booze. Rose may have harbored memories from the days when she lived above her grandmother's candy store in Farmington. Even so, Rose could not possibly have liked the idea of all of those bootlegging profits that she and Myrtle had to pass up. With her family's background in the hospitality business, she might have been able to create the most palatable bathtub gin in town. Rose didn't lose sight of the idea of selling her own bathtub gin, though. She just shelved that plan for a while.

While Rose and Gypsy were still living at the Cameo Apartments, June and Buddy Hyde, whose marriage was heading for the rocks, paid a few visits. Gypsy was happy to see June, but Rose was rather icy to the couple, and neither offered the pair a place to stay, not even for the night. This reception hurt June deeply. When she had run away from the vaudeville act, she never anticipated that the repercussions would include emotional exile from her family. But Rose never passed up an opportunity to let June know that all of the success Gypsy currently enjoyed could have been June's. June didn't seem to realize just how monumentally her flight from the act that Rose had built around her had hurt her mother. Their relationship had already become a debacle of non-communication, and in the ensuing years it would become even worse.

Gypsy, however, was doing well financially thanks to Minsky's, so Rose located a nice brick attached house in a spanking new residential development in Rego Park, a neighborhood in the borough of Queens. The area had formerly been considered a separate town called Long Island City. Those who lived there in the 1930s still referred to the area as Long Island. The new brick houses in the development had been built by the Meacham Realty Corporation. The homes had striped awnings and a lot of character. Rose's doorbell chimed the beginning notes to the hymn "Ave Maria."

In short order, Anna Thompson arrived from Worcester, Massachusetts, according to a show business periodical called *Greater Show World*. According to the same publication, June and Buddy Hyde also actually stayed in the house for a little while in 1931, during the brief time that their dancing act was booked at Minsky's Republic.

Gypsy managed to extricate herself from Minsky's for a few months by getting a job in a Ziegfeld show, originally called *Laid in Mexico* and later changed to the more socially appropriate title *Hot-Cha!* There was prestige in working for Florenz Ziegfeld, the legendary producer of the classy *Ziegfeld Follies*, and the job did wonders for Gypsy's self-esteem, if not her resume and her bankbook. The low salary she was given made it difficult to pay off the mortgage of the Queens house. She had to return to Minsky's to try to save the little house, but it was no use. The pretty house went into foreclosure by 1933, and Rose and Gypsy lost it. Rose got even for the repossession of the house by uprooting all of the rosebushes on the property before they left.

Gypsy had been wined and dined by several men, and then she met a wonderful guy, Eddie Bruns. He was already married, with a wife he didn't want to divorce for the sake of his children. Eddie's family lived in New Jersey. The time had come for Gypsy to have a place entirely her own where she could entertain Eddie, so she moved into an apartment in a former hotel, which featured dozens of gargoyles among its exterior trim, at 81 Irving Place, near leafy Gramercy Park. She and Eddie would have plenty of privacy.

Gypsy found an enormous ten-room apartment for Rose on the upper west side of Manhattan, several neighborhoods away. Rose did not need ten rooms all to herself, of course, but the possibilities for turning a profit with such a large apartment were inviting. First Rose rented out all of the spare bedrooms. Later she became aware, probably after talking to—or at least eavesdropping on—some of the other performers at Minsky's, that there were plenty of women in New York City who wanted to meet other ladies for romantic purposes and had few rendezvous options. Gay and lesbian relationships were at that time illegal. Undercover police would regularly work gay and lesbian bars in Greenwich Village to entrap them.

Rose swung into action. Not only could the ten-room apartment be utilized as a place where lesbians could meet without fear of a police raid or an undercover bust, Rose could sell her bathtub gin there in peace. She could also throw in easily made, inexpensive spaghetti dinners, then sell them to her guests at a hefty little profit. The soirees were not exactly parties; Rose charged admission. It cost five dollars a head just to get inside the door, more for any ladies who happened to be hungry to gain access to the spaghetti, and still more to get the chance to imbibe Rose's gin. There was also coffee for those who wanted a softer drink than the concoction Rose fermented in the bathtub.

Later it was to be said that Rose was running a lesbian boarding house, and perhaps she did restrict the rooms to lesbians. But it's doubtful she did so, because Rose loved money—anybody's money. Rose would later own two other properties with main houses and cottages that could be rented out, and would even manage an apartment building in the 1940s. Leases associated with the latter reveal that she was a more egalitarian landlord than most Americans would have dared to be in 1940s. Rose's attitude always seemed to be that whoever could pay her was more than welcome to rent from her.

Rose's soirees were open for business twice a week. The lights were turned down low, which was easier on the electric bill, the radio was tuned to a big band program, and the ladies were allowed to have fun in a secure private residence where there wasn't much chance of vice squad interference. There was always a remote, but real, chance the cops could find out about Rose's enterprise, but Rose's parties were arranged by word-of-mouth arrangement, with women referring one another.

It isn't clear what Rose's initial intentions were with regard to the opening of her apartment-based business. She may have simply wanted to cash in on the idea of giving these ladies a place to meet. The Mafia opened gay bars in Greenwich Village for the same purpose. But whether Rose first opened her unofficial establishment out of her usual desire for money or an awareness that she had a personal affinity for the lesbians, or a mixture of both, we do not know. Rose would soon decide, if she hadn't already, that she belonged with the lesbians—and not just as a hostess.

While Gypsy was happily redecorating her apartment on Irving Place, and Rose was busy with her plans for the ten-room apartment, a calamitous family scenario began to unfold back in Seattle. Anna Thompson had returned there after staying with Gypsy and Rose for a time in the Queens house. She had already failed to respond to divorce papers from Charlie in 1929, causing the judge in the case to grant Charlie the divorce. Anna nevertheless went out riding with her ex on the evening of January 3, 1934. They had either reconciled completely or remained on good terms.

That cold night a railroad switch engine was coming down the track at Colorado Avenue and Spokane Street, and Charlie, who had always been the most dependable and responsible of men, somehow missed it. Either he didn't see it coming, or there was a signal failure. The engine crashed into the car while Anna was sitting beside Charlie in the front seat.

Anna came through the accident in a considerably better state than Charlie. His side of the car suffered the brunt of the crash. Both victims were rushed to Harborview Hospital with life-threatening injuries. Charlie hung on at first, but five days later, he died of his injuries. Anna was still in the hospital, though housed in a different room. Doctors decided that she should not immediately be told of her husband's death. Charlie's funeral was held on January 10, 1934. Gypsy was still in arrears for the Queens house and asked to borrow money from the Minsky brothers to pay for his burial. The Minskys complied.

Anna recovered, so Rose did not lose both parents in one fell swoop, but her mother's injuries were extensive. Once-vibrant Anna would live as a virtual shut-in for the rest of her long life. Fortunately Belle, her youngest daughter, had been living with Charlie at his relatively new, tiny Rutan Place ranch house and was able to look after Anna. It was a particularly devastating blow for Anna to find herself impaired, as she had been the most independent and active of women. It was also an unhappy state of affairs for Belle. Caring for a shut-in, she became something of a shut-in herself, unable to leave the house and her mother. Belle, who had a crippled leg of her own, was not able to work; caring for Anna was a full-time, unofficial job. About the only time the two women got out of the house was when they'd attend church services on Sundays. Until she died in the late 1950s, Anna was to praise Belle's infinite patience with her.

June, meanwhile, had met a man who worked with the marathon pro-moters. She refers to him as Jamie Smythe in her second memoir, but this may not have been his real name. June had reported to the site of what would have been her eighth marathon, but instead Jamie took her away with him on a prolonged trip through several western states to scout for a venue for the next show. June was, perhaps for the first time in her life, able to relax and simply enjoy herself, while the syndicate that ran the marathons paid her twelve dollars a day to be Jamie's guide through the majestic west. She had traveled the country so many times as a child that her knowledge of the area was vast. The pair camped out when it was warm. Later, when it became cooler, they stayed at small inns as they traveled from the Midwest to the West Coast. June got the chance to enjoy the Tetons, the Badlands, Yosemite, all of the points in between, and the company of Jamie.

One evening, while gazing into the campfire, June decided that what she wanted to have most in her life was a little girl of her own. She set about ensuring that she got one. It never occurred to June that in this regard she was ahead of her time. Jamie was married to someone else, legally she was still married to Buddy, and the baby would be an illegitimate child. None of that mattered. One benefit of June's lack of a formal education was that she hadn't been boxed in by convention. By the time June knew definitively that she was pregnant, she and Jamie had parted ways, more by accident than by any choice on June's part. Jamie was accused of doing to another girl exactly the same vile thing that had been done to June during her second marathon. This particular girl went missing afterwards and was presumed dead. While Jamie and June visiting another marathon during their location scouting expedition, someone recognized Jamie and accused him of having been involved with the kidnapping and subsequent rape. Jamie was sum-marily beaten, then taken away in a car—presumably to be beaten further, then dumped. That was the end of June's Western respite.

Fortunately the couple was in San Francisco at the time. June was strand-ed, but San Francisco was a big city, and big cities still had booking agents. Through them, she was able to get several dancing engagements in Idaho, Utah, and Kansas since it was close to the Christmas holidays. June landed in St. Louis. Tap-dancing was not conducive to the pregnancy, though, and she came very close to losing the baby after an otherwise pleasant engage-ment at a country club. The hotel doctor ordered a week of bed rest, which saved the unborn child's life. Then, in January 1935, June decided to return to New York City because she wanted to stay with Rose.

It was interesting choice, since June had fled her mother and the act just six years earlier. Rose had not been receptive to June's visits in the years since, either. On the other hand, where else was the girl to go? Her grandfather was gone, her aunt had her hands full with her grandmother, Jamie had been transported beyond state lines, and June didn't really know her father and his new family. June wanted this baby so much, and was so proud of herself for getting pregnant, she actually believed that Rose would be proud of her as well.

Rose was not proud. She opened the door, took one look at June's evident condition, and reacted with shock. She knew enough about her daughter's situation to be highly concerned about all of the ramifications of June's pregnancy. Her daughter was alone, there was no father in sight, so who was going to handle the cost of June's hospital bill when the time came? And this last was about the first thing she said to June, right after asking her just what had happened to her. It was a sign of the times that an illegitimate baby was still such a major scandal that it even shocked the mother of the most famous stripper in America. Next out of Rose's mouth was an exclamation that she didn't know anybody who could "help" June. Perhaps Rose believed that the only reason June would want to come back to her while pregnant was to secure an abortion. But nothing could have been further from June's mind. She wanted this child.

June wasn't happy when Rose told her that Gypsy no longer lived with her but was in another part of town. Rose described herself as a prisoner, lonely in the huge apartment, even though she had tenants and wasn't really alone. Rose arranged for June to stay in one of the spare rooms, provided she paid fifteen dollars a week. Rose insisted that June basically hide in her room on Tuesdays and Fridays, when Rose's contingent of guests came over to mix, mingle, and pay.

June duly remained in her room on the nights when Rose's apartment was officially open for business, until one evening when a noisy fight broke out, and June could not resist taking a peek at it. The only known accounts of Rose's parties come from June's recollections and need to be taken with a grain of salt since June was a prevaricator. If the fight really took place as she reported, it was fortunate that this particular brawl was loud enough to rouse her curiosity to the point she wandered out of her room to make an inspection. If she hadn't, there would be no record of Rose's soirees. On the other hand, the details concerning a fight over grapefruit did not mesh with any known lesbian activities of the 1930s—or, for that matter, any other group's activities in any time period. June described the situation as being tantamount to a riot. Rose's overly strong homemade bathtub gin was obviously too powerful for most mere mortals' systems. It was the only alcoholic beverage on Rose's menu, so it is safe to assume that most of the noise-making revelers were all looped. June could hear Gypsy's voice. She also heard furniture being thrown against walls. Then Rose was calling out above the din to stop a thief, and at that point, June decided to enter the living room, pregnant belly and all.

The fight was taking place in a darkened room, lit only by candlelight, and the scene was bizarre. And the fight was over a grapefruit, an actual piece of fruit that Rose was accusing a gigantic woman—dressed in a man's suit and shorts, worn during the middle of a bitterly cold New York City winter—of stealing from her. Rose railed that the woman had stolen the fruit from her. It's anybody's guess as to what was really going on with that grapefruit, but its ownership was in dispute. Clearly, far too much bathtub gin had been flowing.

June didn't know exactly what was going on, since the ruckus began before she stepped into the room. In the living room she realized at once that this was a lesbian gathering, because many of the women were dressed in men's ensembles, a vision that might have startled a less worldly young woman. But June, used to costumes, remained calm. She didn't particularly care about anything at that moment except keeping the peace and ground-ing the airborne furniture. June turned on the lights and promptly called the cops. She explained what was transpiring in the living room, and that the matter involved someone stealing a grapefruit. The cops didn't miss a beat. Assuming June's deck wasn't too full, they told her she needed to call New York City's infamous mental hospital, Bellevue. That emptied the room. Every one of the lesbians made a mad dash to get out of the apartment. Homosexuality was not just illegal in the 1930s, it was also considered a mental illness. The sounds of the melee that night were masked only by the strains of music. While pandemonium reigned in Rose's living room, Guy Lombardo's band was playing "Lost in a Fog" on the radio. The large lady returned not one but two grapefruit to Rose before she left. So for whatever it was worth, Rose got her grapefruit back.

June became more involved in the running of the unofficial club after that. It was a no-frills establishment, and Rose's members loved it that way. Rose put June to work as the bartender, an easy job since the only booze was bathtub gin. June would pour the drinks into little Dixie cups that Rose appropriated from various New York City ladies' rooms. June would add a cherry to the gin in the cups and sell each one for seventy-five cents, a tidy sum for what amounted to less than half a regular sized drink. This was a time period when a loaf of bread could be had for a dime. Plates of spaghetti sold for seventy-five cents. Coffee, a nickel at lunch counters, went for the princely sum of fifteen cents at Rose's. Rose happily pocketed the profits from everything.

There was one benefit for June in all this: One of Rose's customers worked for an obstetrician and was able to refer her to a compassionate doctor who was to handle her baby's birth.

June's stay with her mother might have continued indefinitely except she discovered Rose's rent scheme. She found out that not only was she paying Rose rent for the room in her mother's flat, so was Gypsy. Gypsy was highly amused by what Rose had tried to get away with; June wasn't. Fortunately Gypsy's generous boyfriend, Eddie, kindly gave June five hundred dollars to help with the baby, and the still pregnant June moved into a tiny room of her own, former servant's quarters on the top floor of another building in a different neighborhood. She wrote later about how she loved her new view of the city lights. June looked out the window of her new room and made herself a promise that she would, one day, return to the stage, which had always been her true home, as an actress. Rose had chosen well for June when she had decided, back when June was a baby dancing on her toes, to direct this child towards the stage.

Rose left New York on a vacation, probably immediately following June's relocation. She went with Gypsy and two of their female friends. They were away from mid-February through March 1935. They were all back in town in time for June's baby's entrance into the world on April 2, 1935. June's choice of a middle name for her little daughter may have been another attempt to reconcile with her mother while also honoring her sister. She named her child, a little blonde with dark brown eyes, April Rose Hyde. Still legally married to Weldon Hyde, June retained his last name, which she was able to bestow on April, thus making her appear to be legitimate. The baby's name, though, may have caused confusion later: April was not Weldon's but Jamie Smythe's offspring.

A whole lot of bathtub gin must have been sold on the night at Rose's place when June finally went into labor; once they heard that June's time had come, the entire lively party moved to the hospital waiting room. Rose, about twenty of the membership, and Gypsy Rose Lee, who was wielding a bottle of brandy, arrived, already in top form thanks to the level of their consumption. The situation was already out of control, and it became steadily worse. It's possible some of the hospital waiting room furniture was even in danger of flying, or actually flew. June's doctor ultimately had to call the cops on the whole noisy, rowdy, uncontrollable group. Then they all got to bear the distinction of having been banned from the waiting room of New York Women's Hospital. Chances are they'd been banned from better places, so none of the merry posse was any the worse for wear.

CHAPTER 12

THE MALEVOLENT CIPHER

A FAMILY CONFERENCE TOOK PLACE IN 1935 IN GYPSY ROSE LEE'S IRVING Place apartment bathroom. Gypsy soaked in the tub, getting ready for a party. Rose sat scrunched up on a little wicker stool. June was situated atop Gypsy's fur-covered toilet seat lid. Rose announced that she wanted to adopt baby April.

June considered this proposal out of the question. She had wanted and even planned for her baby, even if it was only the sort of plan created by a dreamy twenty-one-year-old. June decided not to even acknowledge Rose's offer. It was a mature way of handling her mother; the presence of the baby in her life was causing June to grow up at last. She realized it was kind of her mother to extend an offer to help and was to recall the bathroom meeting as an act of love.

Rose was living in a rented house called Cloudlands in Little Britain, New York, which would have been a nice environment in which to raise a baby. Rose's severe asthma improved slightly when she was in the Catskill Mountains area. Gypsy, meanwhile, was looking for a Catskills property to buy. The rental in Little Britain acted as a temporary base of operations for the duo while on her days off, Gypsy searched the nearby area for just the right house.

That summer Gypsy invited her half-brother Jack and half-sister Betty—her father Jack Hovick's children by his second wife, Elizabeth—to visit New York and stay with her in her apartment in the city. The two California teenagers took a cross-country bus together and were treated to an eye-opening, first-hand look at the everyday horrors of the segregated South. Betty had never before seen the vile "Colored Only" signs on rest rooms and fountains. She was never to forget them. Their arrival in New York came as a breath of fresh air. The teens enjoyed seeing their famous big sister and staying in her elegant apartment. Gypsy showed them a good time and apparently introduced the pair to quite a few theatrical people. More than twenty years later, when her memoir was fictionalized in the musical *Gypsy*, producer David Merrick would say he knew there had been "a third daughter named Beth."

Gypsy found a sprawling fourteen-room house on a hill in Highland Mills, New York, right at the edge of the Catskills. Seattle was surrounded by the Olympic Mountains, and the Highland Mills area may well have reminded Gypsy of her hometown. Her new place was on a vast property that required a live-in caretaker. The property included a barn to house farm animals, small orchards, a built-in swimming pool, and several little cottages. Gypsy loved antiques and gloried in acquiring many new pieces, decorating this splendid house with vivid floral wallpaper and tasteful colonial touches. She installed a practice stage, complete with theatrical lighting, in the basement.

Gypsy named the Highland Mills estate Witchwood Manor. Rose remained there full time, renting out the cottages and the many extra bedrooms at three bucks per person per night. Rose's mother, Anna Thompson, on the mend since the accident that had resulted in Charlie's death, moved in and stayed for awhile, too. Rose got a fierce-looking Great Dane called Jerry as a security measure, added a bunch of smaller dogs, and stocked the place with turkeys and chickens. She sold the eggs, grew beans that rose eight-feet high, and in a move that might have done Tom Sawyer proud, put the tenants and guests to work helping out with the property "for fun." Gypsy was to remember that quite a bit of beer guzzling went on among Rose's tenants. But a toned-down, countrified party atmosphere prevailed, with everyone able to enjoy sitting out of doors with their libations in the milder months. June was to report that many of the people staying with her mother were "lost souls." Perhaps they were, but Rose didn't discriminate. They could pay the rent and were therefore more than welcome. In early 1936, June's daughter, April, stayed at Witchwood Manor with Rose for a while when June, who had been supporting herself and her child as a clothing model, got a gig filling in for a pregnant woman in a dancing act. Rose charged June rent for housing April.

June's career was finally on the upswing. One small break lead to another, and eventually June was cast in *Forbidden Melody* on Broadway. June's years of bad luck were over. She arranged an opening night ticket for Rose to attend the show and see her return to the stage, which Rose promptly sold. The show didn't last a month, but it put June firmly back in the business.

Soon she also married a Harvard educated suitor, Donald Stanley Gibbs, an advertising man from New England.

Good things kept happening for the Hovick sisters, whose vaudeville training was paying off. Gypsy managed to fulfill a dream she had held in her heart for a long time when she landed a supporting role in the *Ziegfeld Follies* alongside her old acquaintance from the Orpheum circuit, Fanny Brice. Gypsy felt like she'd become legitimate, finally landing on a proper Broadway stage as a professional actress. The *Ziegfeld Follies* opened on September 14, 1936. It starred comedian Bobby Clark along with Fanny, with music by Vernon Duke and Ira Gershwin—all in all, an impressive group. Rose may have snubbed June on her opening night, but she made sure she was present for this daughter's triumphal moment. The *Ziegfeld Follies* was a revue that changed yearly. This particular incarnation went over beautifully with the public and was held over at the theater before it went on tour.

Gypsy asked June to reserve one day a week to visit with Rose while she was away and was shocked to find June was reluctant to do so. She felt Rose didn't want to see her. June said outright that her mother had not forgiven her for having run away from the old act and probably never would. She admitted she feared Rose hated her. June was correct on both counts. All the years Rose had put into June's act, which she saw as having been for June's benefit, were rendered meaningless when June ran off.

Rose was probably trying to protect herself now from further upset and grief. It would have been a mistake to trust her youngest child again, since she'd already rejected Rose once, and to Rose's mind, that rejection had been brutal. Gypsy saw Rose use the old cow's head from June's act for kindling in the Highland Mills fireplace. But Gypsy still did not realize just how deep the rift between her mother and sister had become. She had not even known about Rose's animosity towards her sister until June mentioned it.

Gypsy went away on her tour. Whatever conflict was brewing between her mother and sister was left behind. This particular tour turned out to be a stupendous time for Gypsy, despite the fact that it paid a pittance. She appeared in the *Follies* for the prestige that it would add to her name, which she felt had been slightly sullied by all those years spent in burlesque. She roomed with funny, easy-going, down-to-earth Fanny Brice in order to save money. The two became friends, performing onstage and then having fun painting pictures back at the hotel.

While Gypsy was away, a strange and disturbing letter regarding one of Rose's new associates arrived from a woman who signed herself with the almost certainly fake name Kay Ray. A young art teacher by the name of Genevieve Augustine, called Jean or Ginny for short, had begun staying at Witchwood Manor. It's possible that Genevieve may have met Rose back in the Manhattan days when she was charging admission for her spaghetti dinners. Rose would never learn to drive, so Genevieve acted as her chauffeur while staying with her now. According to her father, Genevieve was a young woman who had always been rather troubled, even as a child in Kenosha, Wisconsin. She was one of fifteen children, and her father may not have been the most reliable source concerning her character. A prosperous architect, he had a foul temper and was physically abusive to his brood. Her mother suffered from emotional problems. Photographs reveal that Genevieve and her siblings were all healthy-looking children, but their little faces seem unhappy, guarded, or troubled. Genevieve was the eldest, with long hair and high cheekbones. She could have passed for a somber, downhearted starlet. Her eyes appear to have had no light or joy in them. Perhaps she suffered from depression. Her sister Frances, however, remembered her as "a clown," a child who would attempt to create fun for the rest of her siblings to alleviate the stress of living in an abusive household. Genevieve would be portrayed later as having been a problem child, but Frances remembered her as a rare spark of human sunshine. They had lived in a well-appointed house full of secrets. Genevieve's brother Charles was once beaten so badly that he was moved into the basement while he recovered from wounds their father gave him so the neighbors wouldn't see him. In addition to his demonic temper, Genevieve's father was an inveterate womanizer. He did not always know how to keep his hands to himself and would later be known to have inappropriately touched at least one of his granddaughters. This was a man without any sense of boundaries. It all made for a very disturbing home life for the children.

Genevieve spent part of her high school years at St. Clara's Academy, a boarding school run by nuns in Sinsinawa, Wisconsin. Her grades were adequate. Unfortunately, she returned to public high school in Kenosha for her senior year, landing right back in her unhappy home. She later obtained a scholarship to attend the Chicago Art Institute, getting free of her family again. After attending art school Genevieve escaped from Wisconsin and made her way to New York City to become an art teacher. The details of her love life remain a mystery. A family member would recount that Genevieve was romantically interested in a West Point cadet. In the 1930s, all West Point cadets were male. On the other hand, there was evidence to suggest that Genevieve had become romantically involved with at least one female, an involvement that could have led to her arrest. That prospect alone could have frazzled Genevieve's nerves. Then she learned that her teaching contract with Irving Textile High School was not going to be renewed.

Someone with nerves of steel might have been able to survive these situations, but Genevieve was a gentler soul. She'd had several unsettling years in New York City, moving from one apartment to another, living at three different addresses between 1934 and 1936 alone. She had a steady teaching job until the winter of 1937, so being able to pay the rent, at least, should not have been the problem. Perhaps her menacing friend Kay Ray was behind all the moves.

Kay Ray was said to be a New York City clothing designer, but no record of her has yet surfaced—although not knowing her actual name naturally impedes the search. Kay Ray does not appear in New York City telephone books for the 1930s, and neither does Katherine Ray or Catherine Ray or Kathleen Ray, or any given name beginning with K and combined with the surname Ray.

Kay Ray remains a malevolent cipher. Her true identity is unknown, and she's also faceless, as her image was not captured in any known photographs. What is known is that she invited herself to stay at Genevieve's apartment at some point and the trouble began from there. Ample evidence indicates that Kay was obsessed with Genevieve. A large part of what troubled Genevieve might be attributable to Kay's machinations.

Whatever contributed to Genevieve's melancholy, the young woman slit her wrists on New Year's Day, 1937. This was one story that she wasn't able to keep secret, since it involved a hospital stay. This sad suicide attempt may have been the primary reason that her teaching contract with the high school would not be renewed. Soon after the failed suicide, she went to stay with Rose—and she got there practically over Kay Ray's dead body.

Kay Ray adored writing complaint letters. She wrote several to Gypsy Rose Lee, specifically to sound an alarm about Genevieve. Kay provided Gypsy with the unsolicited advice that she refrain from allowing Genevieve to stay with Rose at Witchwood Manor. It is regrettable that none of the letters Kay wrote to Gypsy survives.

The letters were portents of the chaos that was about to descend. Gypsy, who had been telling fortunes and reading signs since childhood, somehow missed seeing that these notes qualified as ominously bad omens.

Gypsy must have finally contacted her mother after receiving Ray's missives, because Genevieve proceeded to write a stilted and strange reply to Gypsy. The language Genevieve uses is grandiose, almost Victorian, as though she were attempting to sound more formal than she actually was. The note is dated February 21, 1937, a month and a half after her suicide attempt. The young woman had had to contend with all that drove her to slit her wrists in the first place, then a hospital stay, followed by the loss of her job, and finally derogatory letters being sent to the absent daughter who owned the house where she had attempted to take refuge. If Genevieve had thought she was safe from Kay Ray at Witchwood Manor, she was mistaken.

Genevieve wrote to Gypsy to try and fix things at a time when she should have just been resting and trying to regroup. Kay would not allow her to recover; perhaps preventing her from doing so was the whole point. Genevieve's letter to Gypsy begins:

My dear Miss Hovick:

I have been given to understand you have received letters of a nature concerning myself, and that these letters were in every view detrimental to my character, as well as inclusive with false statements.

Consequently, I am taking this time to enclose such proof as will disprove a few of the misinformed statements made to you . . .

Genevieve could simply have written, "Everything you were told about me was a lie." Instead, she uses terms that are so formal they miss the mark. Two sentences in, the letter is already vaguely disturbing.

Not knowing exactly what the statements in the Ray letters *were*, it's impossible to know whether the allegations she made against Genevieve were true or not. Using a revealing choice of words, Genevieve declares she will "disprove a few of the misinformed statements," rather than stating that she will disprove them all. Genevieve continues by writing that Miss Ray had not been "a welcome guest in her home." She doesn't elaborate on how Kay came to be staying with her if she wasn't welcome. She adds that Kay was "ungrateful," not a "good sport" and throws in a major indictment of Ray by adding that she "did not care to be a lady," a euphemism of the time for someone who behaved in a rough-mannered and low-class manner. Then again, in that era if a woman era didn't wear white gloves when she went out, or smoked cigarettes, or used hell or damn in a sentence, she was said not to be a lady. It was a relative term, yet as an insult it packed a punch among those ladies who considered themselves to be among the more refined members of society. Genevieve's choice of "lady" was made as a way of separating herself from whatever Kay Ray had done while freeloading at her apartment, but without revealing what actually transpired there during Kay's visit.

Perhaps Kay had come up with an accusation about why Genevieve wanted to stay at Witchwood, because Genevieve hastens to assure Gypsy that her reasons for staying were to help Rose by chauffeuring her wherever she needed to go, and painting portraits of the other people who were also staying at the manor. She continues:

> <u>Witchwood Manor</u> is all that an artist would want. I find an abundance to paint here; the atmosphere is ideal, and your family very wholesome. They no doubt will be in frames before next Fall.
>
> I am starting a portrait of your mother next week. It will be close to life size. What out fit [sic] would you like her painted in? That is a point of discussion these days. She wishes to wear slacks and a colored smock. I thought of doing a more dignified, or conservative study the first time, since, no doubt, I will do many studies of her. And then there is "Big Lady," and I see her being done in the Monet style. Now, Belle lends herself for a Picasso version. What do you think? John will be used for a character study, and then this Spring all the favorite chickens will be done.
>
> You see, there is a wealth of material here and I shall be very greedy to do it all justice.

She's going to paint Big Lady like Monet, Belle like Picasso, John the handyman as a character study, and then the favorite chickens? The passage seems outré on the surface, but Genevieve wanted to be part of an artist's group back in New York City that required its members to complete fifty paintings before they could join. Given these requirements, anyone and everyone at Witchwood Manor was fair game to sit for at least one portrait, possibly more—including the poultry. The passage speaks volumes about Genevieve's estimation of her own artistic ability. Clearly, if she thought she could paint one portrait in Claude Monet's style and another in Pablo Picasso's, she firmly believed in her own talent and versatility.

Whether or not Gypsy sent Genevieve a reply is not known. She did keep a copy of Genevieve's letter with her legal papers.

Rumors were to circulate later, after both women were gone and could not explain themselves, that Rose and Genevieve were a couple, but they may not have been. The evidence points in another direction. Genevieve was involved with a cadet from West Point. A personal letter that Rose wrote to Gypsy a year later mentioned her relationship with a much younger woman she identified only as Connie. That relationship had been going on for three years, which meant Connie had been Rose's lover as far back as 1935, two years before Genevieve took the chauffeur job.

Meanwhile, Genevieve was in poor physical as well as emotional health and found she needed a surgical procedure. This development only served to depress her further.

June, in her second memoir, claimed Rose made a slew of statements to her about Genevieve after she died. June starts by saying Rose said Genevieve had wanted to stay in Highland Mills permanently, though Rose emphatically did not wish to allow that. She was outraged that Genevieve wanted to stay. She said that the miserable young woman was driving her berserk with constant, unrelenting comments expressing her desire to commit suicide. June claimed her mother also called Genevieve "a tramp" and told her to use "a shotgun" that was in the house if she was so intent on dying. June's wild tale did not stop there. June even said Rose burned Genevieve's diary after she died; it contained information about Gypsy that Rose wanted to suppress. Most outlandishly of all, June, who didn't realize that a photograph of Genevieve's body would one day surface, wrote that Rose said the young woman blew "the whole top" of her head off. In the photo, Genevieve's head is intact.

Revelation of too many details is often the sign of a liar. June's recitation of what she claims Rose said simply does not add up; neither does it match the known facts. Rose was, first and foremost, in charge of Witchwood Manor. If she truly had not wanted Genevieve to stay, all she would have had to do was ask her to leave. Years later, when confronted about the passage by Genevieve's niece Kathy Wagner, June admitted that it was "just something I wrote." If the part about the suicide threats was even slightly accurate, it takes a special brand of fortitude for an individual with no medical or psychological training to listen to suicidal threats on a daily basis and remain calm enough to talk the distressed person out of self-destructive plans. If Rose initially had that kind of patience with Genevieve, she lost it fast. Genevieve needed more help than Rose or anyone at Witchwood Manor could have reasonably been expected to provide for her.

*∿

Gypsy Rose Lee managed to get out of burlesque in the nick of time. In April 1937, just as Gypsy was about to leave the *Follies* to go to Hollywood, where she had secured a movie contract, most of the burlesque theaters in

New York City were unceremoniously closed. Fortunately it didn't matter to Gypsy at that particular moment. Hollywood was calling. Gypsy Rose Lee left the tour of the *Ziegfeld Follies* when Darryl Zanuck of Twentieth Century-Fox Studios bought out her contract. She arrived in California by train with two Dachshunds, a Chihuahua, and what the *Los Angeles Times* reported was a "slight English accent," making a grand entrance at the station.

But whatever optimism Gypsy arrived with was soon quashed. She wasn't in town a day when the *Los Angeles Times* published another article mentioning that studio officials were not going to let her reveal so much as a knee on the screen. A week later, reporter Grace Kingsley wrote a story titled "Gypsy's Strip Act All in Fun," attempting to explain to Angelenos that the burlesque act had been more tease than strip. But the disclaimer didn't work. People all over the country were outraged that a stripper had been allowed to sign a contract to appear in the movies. They believed this was an unacceptable development and a threat to morals. Since most of middle America had never seen Gypsy's burlesque act, they didn't realize that it was mostly a tongue-in-cheek comedy routine. Furious churchgoers launched a letter writing campaign against Gypsy. The studio was bombarded with complaint letters. Literally thousands of missives poured in, stopping her progress within the studio before she ever had any chance to prove herself. This was not the welcome that hard-working Gypsy expected or deserved.

Immediately the studio decided that the name Gypsy Rose Lee had to be buried at once. Her name and her identity had to be changed. Both were too clearly associated with her old stripper image. For the duration of this foray into Hollywood, she returned to using the name Louise Hovick. The studio realized that by allowing Gypsy Rose Lee to sign a contract with them they had taken on a liability. They may have hired her services, but they already knew Louise Hovick wasn't going to work out. They decided that she should be given small, featured—but not starring—roles.

Gypsy tried to settle in nonetheless, working on the first film since she'd worked as an extra in silent movies as a child. She was quick to reconnect with her father, Jack Hovick, and his second wife, Elizabeth. Jack and Elizabeth, along with their children, Jack and Betty, had been in the Los Angeles area for years. They accepted Gypsy into their hearts.

Back in Highland Mills, Genevieve scheduled the surgery she needed. She would not live to go through with it. Already miserable, she was also dreading the surgery. Rose's sister Belle left Highland Mills and returned to Seattle. Belle Thornton married Franklin A. McKenzie, her third husband, there on May 14, 1937. It was another union that was not destined to last. Big Lady may have remained behind with Rose and the rest of her guests and may not have joined Belle. Genevieve's despondency continued. Her inner light went out on June 1, 1937.

Gypsy's new employer, Twentieth Century-Fox Studios, was having its first annual world sales convention in Los Angeles. More than five hundred sales representatives from the United States and foreign countries had congregated at the Spanish-style Ambassador Hotel. Events, including tours of the studio, were to take place from May 31 through June 4, 1937, culminating in a spectacular dance at the Cocoanut Grove night club. The stars were kept in town and on hand during the convention so they could meet the salesmen.

At one convention event, Gypsy Rose Lee was introduced by her new screen name, Louise Hovick. Later there would be rumors that she was in Highland Mills on the early evening of June 1, but that was impossible. Twentieth Century-Fox had a full schedule in place for Gypsy the whole week, between the movie she was making and her convention appearances. Decades later, stripper Georgia Sothern told Gypsy's son Erik that she was in Highland Mills on June 1 and so was Gypsy. She claimed Genevieve was instantly "attracted to Gypsy," even though she was "sleeping with Rose." Georgia's story was that Genevieve made a pass at Gypsy, and Rose shot her dead in a jealous rage.

Yet Gypsy was stuck in Hollywood, making the movie and participating in the convention, as decreed by Twentieth Century-Fox. There's no proof that Georgia Sothern was in Highland Mills. No mention of Georgia's name ever surfaced officially in connection with Genevieve's death. Georgia's autobiography recounts several ways in which she lied during her life, and this story about Genevieve seems to have been yet another.

The actual events that took place were nowhere near as dramatic and sexy as Georgia's fake eyewitness account. Memorial Day 1937 fell on May 31, and at Gypsy's behest, Rose had invited several friends of Gypsy's, described as "showgirls," from New York City to spend the weekend. These showgirls may have been unemployed and between jobs, because they were still there on Tuesday, June 1. They included Pearl Brooks, who lived in Manhattan at the Howard Hotel, Anna Matt, resident of the Hotel Woodward, and Helen Leudhardt of West 59th Street. Two handymen employed at Witchwood Manor, Joseph Bush and John Beck, were also there, and possibly Anna Thompson as well, though Anna's name never made it into the papers. At least seven people were present in the house.

The whole group went to the nearby village of Monroe on Tuesday afternoon. When they returned, the evening was too temperate for them all to go directly back inside the house. They opted to lounge outside on lawn chairs, enjoying the cool Catskill Mountains breezes. Then Genevieve announced that she was going to go inside and bathe. No one found this alarming. No one even thought it was strange that Genevieve would want to leave the party to sit by herself in the bathtub. They were used to her moods, which were usually bad. The relaxed party atmosphere continued outside on the lawn as Genevieve went into the house. The Witchwood Manor property was sizable, and the rest of the group may have been seated quite far from the house. In any event, the group on the lawn did not hear anything disturbing, such as a gunshot. They were talking and laughing, and with Rose acting as hostess of the gathering, liquor would have flowed, raising the decibel level of the talk.

Among the items at the house was a .22 caliber rifle, provenance unknown, perhaps left by one of Rose's previous guests. Alone inside, Genevieve found it. She, who had already tried to kill herself with a razor and had attempted suicide several times before—and threatened it on a regular basis—stumbled upon the last thing she ever should have found.

The unhappy young woman lay down on the braided rug on the floor of her spacious room where she had been staying, propped the butt of the rifle on the floor, and angling the muzzle against her face, managed to pull the trigger. The bullet went into her temple, exited above her ear, hit the ceiling, and then ricocheted onto the fireplace mantle. Genevieve died instantly, her long history of misery finally over.

Out on the lawn, Rose didn't know any of what had just taken place up in Genevieve's bedroom. It wasn't until close to an hour later that Rose and the rest of her guests came back inside the house to find Genevieve lying dead on the floor with the rifle at her side. Everyone was horrified at the sight. Chaos reigned. Since all of the guests went into the room when Genevieve's body was discovered, the crime scene was compromised at once. Someone put in a call, and the local police were summoned. It's probable that the gun did not fall at the angle where it was found when they arrived and photographed the scene.

The cops notified the state troopers, who sent three men to investigate. Troopers, cops, and coroners all hastened to the scene. A photo shows a state trooper and a man in plain clothes, perhaps the coroner, looking shocked and rather sickened while standing over the body of the pretty dead girl. No one found a suicide note. Genevieve's act had been impulsive.

She'd initially gone into the house to take a bath, not kill herself. Finding the rifle had changed the plan.

Rose, her guests, and the handymen were questioned, and their accounts of the evening were consistent. No one among the many people staying in the house that late spring evening came under suspicion for murder. No one was arrested. No one's account of the events was considered even remotely suspicious.

In addition to Coroner Edward Garrison, the Woodbury Township health officer, Dr. Frank M. Bullard, had responded to the call to Witchwood Manor, as had state police troopers W. J. Prange, E. W. Jarvis and Joseph Sayers, for a total of five law enforcement professionals. None of them found any evidence that foul play was involved with this death. Rose was never arrested for murder, tried for murder, or accused of murder. Indeed, the police and coroner's office never believed this was a murder. Those facts, however, have been lost in a maelstrom of malicious rumors and innuendo.

The police had the body moved to Edmund Seaman's funeral parlor and then had the miserable duty of notifying Genevieve's parents back in Wisconsin that their daughter had shot herself in the head. That was when her father told the police that she had been troubled all her life. He was probably devastated, though not entirely surprised, to learn what his daughter had done to herself. He headed on a sad trip east to claim her body.

By the next day, June 2, Coroner Edward Garrison had declared the death a suicide. The evidence was considered open-and-shut, given Genevieve's history of previous suicide attempts. The only fact even remotely unusual about this death was that it had taken place in the home of a star, albeit one who had not been present. The newspapers paid attention to who owned the house, of course. On June 2 and 3, quite a few papers reported the story, and some included photographs of Genevieve. The Associated Press sent the story out on its wire. "Art Student Takes Own Life in Home of Gypsy Rose Lee" was one headline; "Kills Self in Home of Gypsy Rose Lee" was another. Gypsy Rose Lee was the name in the headlines; Genevieve's was buried in the text. Only the New York Times showed restraint, reporting the story under the headline "Woman Art Student a Suicide," though even they put the fact that the death occurred in Gypsy's home in the first line. All of the papers reported that Gypsy Rose Lee had not been present.

On the opposite coast, Gypsy herself made headlines on June 4, 1937 in the Los Angeles Times. Twentieth Century-Fox was still being deluged with complaint letters about Gypsy, so much so that their volume itself became a news item. Four hundred letters had come in at once from one Midwestern town, all opposing the proposed movie career of an ex-stripper. The latest complaint campaign came had been organized by a church.

The article reiterated that the name Gypsy Rose Lee had been changed, or changed back, to Louise Hovick for her entrance into films, but the letters continued to arrive at the studio. Twentieth Century-Fox's Vice President, William Goetz, was besieged. There were too many letters to reply to personally, so he answered each with a form letter. The professional situation for Gypsy Rose Lee was dire, and her first movie hadn't even been released. Her presence at Twentieth Century-Fox was causing untold aggravation for the powerbrokers on the executive floor, the very ones who could have made her into a major star.

Then the situation back in Highland Mills turned in a bizarre direction. Before leaving Kenosha to claim his daughter's body in Highland Mills, Genevieve Augustine's father received a puzzling telegram from Kay Ray. According to an International News Service story, as reported in the *Port Arthur News* on June 4, 1937, this telegram cryptically stated, "Do not contact other people without seeing me first. Have important news." It read like a royal command from a reigning monarch to a paean. Was this any way for Kay to address her dead friend's father? Kay was attempting to seize control of any inquiries Mr. Augustine may have wanted to make about the death, which concerned him more than it ever should have concerned Kay. But why would Kay want to control Genevieve's father's conversations about his own child's suicide? Genevieve was gone. As far as is known, Kay Ray wasn't staying in, or visiting, Gypsy's house on the day the suicide happened. If she wasn't there, and wasn't directly involved with what happened, why would she need to prevent Genevieve's father from speaking to anyone else before he spoke to her? Or is it possible that Kay was in the house? If the entire party plus the two handymen had gone to Monroe that afternoon, might she have slipped into the house unnoticed and been upstairs waiting for Genevieve? This is pure speculation. But the wording of that telegram is enough to make one speculate. It hadn't been enough that Kay had tried to interfere with Genevieve's life. Now Kay was hoping to take control of her death.

Later, after Rose became posthumously famous—rather infamous—owing to the musical *Gypsy*, she would in many people's minds be the likeliest candidate to have caused of all of Genevieve's misery. Rose was even considered by some to have been Genevieve's killer. Such assumptions jibed with the character in the show, but not with the facts of the case. Nobody ever looked into Kay Ray's actions, though she was a far more sinister and much more likely catalyst for Genevieve's death. She may not have fired the gun, but she seems to have expended an enormous amount of energy pushing fragile Genevieve to the limit. To make matters even odder, Charles Augustine would not initially reveal Kay's identity to an International News Service reporter. He revealed the contents of the telegram, but he would not disclose who sent it.

So questions about the death remain. What, for example, might Charles Augustine have known about Kay that prevented him from revealing her name? Was he perhaps afraid of what Kay might do to retaliate if he named her outright? The police would only confirm to the *Port Arthur News* that there had been "the presence of a girl companion of the artist." The phrase "girl companion" was almost certainly a euphemism for lesbian lover, which in 1937 was considered a fact well worth hiding. So the police would not reveal her name. They said only that she was not involved with the case. If it was indeed Kay, this meant that the "girl companion," who was not involved with the case, was telling the dead woman's father that he needed to talk to her before he spoke to anyone else about the case in which she wasn't involved. The situation is convoluted, but it is clear that Kay was up to something. She might have wanted to suppress some personal incident, but she kept trying to draw attention to the suicide. It would have been more prudent to let the matter rest.

For a time, the situation with regard to Genevieve's death, as least as far as Rose was concerned, settled down. The girl's father arrived in Highland Mills. He claimed the body. That should have been the end of the whole miserable matter. The peace and the quiet lasted for almost a week. But on June 10, 1937, wire services began distributing a photograph of Genevieve along with the latest news, which was that Kay Ray, described as a prominent women's clothing designer (where she designed clothing was never revealed), was now asking the police to look into the case. Kay Ray had made it into a news story. She even succeeded in getting mentioned by name this time.

Gypsy, back at the Hollywood studio, was finally working in a Twentieth Century-Fox movie, "You Can't Have Everything," with Alice Faye and Don Ameche. The studio was trying valiantly, though half-heartedly, to legitimize her. They issued a totally fictitious news item claiming she had been the captain of her high school girl's basketball team. Another news story showed her dressed in new fashions. Still another issued a picture of Louise Hovick hanging out on the film set with Ameche and Faye.

Gypsy and Faye had started off on the wrong foot. Gypsy saw Alice's spectacular trailer and innocently had asked how someone could get such a nice thing. Alice took her question the wrong way and thought it meant Gypsy was offering to provide "horizontal services" in order to obtain one! What a leap on Alice's part! She would later apologize, and the papers covered the end of the "feud" between the actresses, but the misunderstanding is an indication of the level of suspicion that greeted Gypsy's move to Hollywood. She was being misapprehended as a prostitute for having had a past in burlesque.

Gypsy Rose Lee already knew that she wasn't really welcome or wanted in Hollywood. Still more letters descended upon the studio, protesting her hiring. The Hollywood in-crowd considered her somehow inferior, and they made many snide remarks to Gypsy about her alleged lack of morals. Devoid of her fabulous trademark name, Gypsy Rose Lee, she lost a lot of the saucy personality she had created, and she wasn't fitting in at the studio. On the other hand, fitting in might not have been a blessing, either. Hollywood was asking Gypsy to annihilate her true self in order to become a blank slate, a bland creature called Louise Hovick. It was an experiment destined to fail. There was truly no reason to stamp out the persona of Gypsy Rose Lee, and the entertainment world would have lost something irreplaceable if this original woman had faded into the homogeneity of just another Hollywood supporting player.

Gypsy's stay in Hollywood during 1937–38 would be one of the most miserable times in the otherwise ebullient woman's life. But while she was still there, in August 1937, the studio came up with another crazy idea: For the sake of her image, Gypsy needed to get married. This turn of events was good news for Rose. She was on the guest list and thrilled to hear she'd be traveling to California.

On the far right, the original wooden Egle Saloon building (1867), which later became the Eagle Hotel. Courtesy of the Dakota County Historical Society.

The Herber family's Luxemburger Hof <House> hotel (1878). The ladies in the upper story windows may either be the Herber daughters, or "professional gals" who worked there. Courtesy of the Dakota County Historical Society.

3RD STREET LOOKING NORTH, FARMINGTON, MINN.

Farmington business district, rebuilt in brick (ca. late 1880s). Mary Louise Egle's new establishment was probably one of those on the right side of the street. Courtesy of the Dakota County Historical Society.

The Egle and Thompson family's nemesis: Clara Day Egle (ca. 1890s), Jordan Egle's impossible wife and Mary Louise's business rival. Courtesy of Nancy Gross and Mary McClure.

Mary and Peter Herber (ca. 1880s), Mary Louise Herber Egle's brother, who temporarily gave Mary Louise and her children a home after "The Great Farmington Fire" destroyed the Eagle Hotel. From the Collection of Kathy Charvet.

Stephen Hurd Thompson, left, and Rose Thompson (ca. 1893) in Wahpeton, North Dakota, where Rose was born in 1891. Courtesy of the Gypsy Rose Lee Archive.

Rose Thompson with a Gibson Girl hairstyle,
1910. Courtesy of the Gypsy Rose Lee Archive.

Four generations of lovely ladies: Anna
Thompson, left, holding Rose Louise
Hovick, Mary Louise Herber Egle Stein in
the middle, and Rose Thompson Hovick
on the right. From the Collection of Chuck
Mosberger.

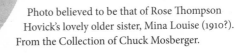

Photo believed to be that of Rose Thompson
Hovick's lovely older sister, Mina Louise (1910?).
From the Collection of Chuck Mosberger.

STATE OF WASHINGTON
County of _King_ } ss.

Nº 41097

𝕸𝖆𝖗𝖗𝖎𝖆𝖌𝖊 𝕮𝖊𝖗𝖙𝖎𝖋𝖎𝖈𝖆𝖙𝖊

𝕿𝖍𝖎𝖘 𝕮𝖊𝖗𝖙𝖎𝖋𝖎𝖊𝖘 *that the undersigned,* _Judge of the Superior Court_
by authority of a License bearing date the _14_ *day of* _Nov_ *A. D. 19__*
and Issued by the County Auditor of the County of King, did on the _14_ *day of* _Nov_
*A. D. 191_2_ *at the* _Court House_
County and State aforesaid, join in 𝕷𝖆𝖜𝖋𝖚𝖑 𝖂𝖊𝖉𝖑𝖔𝖈𝖐 _Harry A Briggs_
of the County of _King_ *and* _Mina L Thompson_
of the County of ____ *with their mutual assent in the presence of*
Mrs J O Hovick *and* _M M Rushing_ *witnesses.*

𝕴𝖓 𝕿𝖊𝖘𝖙𝖎𝖒𝖔𝖓𝖞 𝖂𝖍𝖊𝖗𝖊𝖔𝖋, *witness the signatures of the parties to said ceremony, the witnesses and myself this*
_14_ *day of* _Nov_ *A. D. 191_3_

Witness:	Parties:	Officiating Clergyman or Officer:
Mrs J O Hovick	H A Briggs	Boyd J Tallman
M M Rushing	Miss Mina Thompson	Judge of the Superior
		P. O. Address _____ Washington

FILED
IN CLERKS OFFICE
NOV 14 1913
Filed _____ 191_

W. K. SICKELS
CLERK

This Certificate must be filled out and filed with the County Clerk of the County where the ceremony is performed, within three months after the ceremony.—See Hill's Code, Vol. 1, Sec. 1386.
The County Clerk's Fee for recording this Certificate is One Dollar, to be paid by the party applying for the license at the time each license is issued.—Hill's Code, Vol. 1, Sec. 1387.
Failure to make and deliver Certificate to the County Clerk within three months is punishable by a fine of not less than $25.00 or more than $300.00.

If Rose's daughter June really was born on November 8, 1913, Rose made a speedy recovery. She was the witness to her sister Mina's second marriage a week later on November 14. As an adult, June believed she was born in 1912. Courtesy of Ancestry.com.

A stunning Rose Thompson Hovick (ca. 1910) in a white hat that may have been created by her mother, Anna. Courtesy of the Gypsy Rose Lee Archive.

Rose Hovick, left, her sister Belle Thompson, and Baby June Hovick at what may be a theatrical hotel (ca. 1916). Courtesy of the Gypsy Rose Lee Archive.

THE SEATTLE SUNDAY TIMES, MAY 28, 1916.

DANCING ACADEMY PUPILS WILL APPEAR IN ELABORATE BALLET

June Hovick.

PUPILS of the Douglas Dancing Academy will stage a "Ballet 1916" at The Moore Friday night. The pupils have been very carefully rehearsed and those who have seen dress rehearsal say that the entertainment will be one of the best of its kind.

Little June Hovick, 3 years old, will appear as Pavlova in a solo toe dance.

Fern McLean, 4 years old, has a solo dance, and Margaret Dow and James Craig have Scotch dances.

Twenty-two little ones ranging from 3 to 6 years old will appear in two numbers.

The program is said to be an elaborate one, including a number of solos and ensemble numbers. Russian, Grecian, Scotch, Egyptian, Spanish and Hungarian dances are included.

Thirty high school girls will appear in an ensemble number.

Miss Silvia Metzenbaum, Miss Inez Zimmerman, Miss Margaret Graham and Miss Margaret Pellis have special numbers.

June had something special. While still a toddler she was the main student showcased by Professor Douglas Dancing Academy in this photo from 1916. Courtesy of the *Seattle Times.*

Baby June (seen here ca. 1915) was often billed by Rose as "The Pocket-Sized Pavlova." The tales that she "could dance on her toes at age two and a half" were true. From the author's collection.

Sheet music from the 1919 song "The Vamp," one of the numbers June sang in her vaudeville act.

Rena "Sweetsie" Diehl, Lenora Diehl, Louise, and June as the Diehl & Hovick Sisters (1920). From the collection of Chuck Mosberger.

Reginald Rankin (1947), the first of Rose's sister Belle's three husbands, whose family history intrigued Rose so much that she appropriated it as her own. From the collection of Theresa Rankin.

Reginald Rankin greeting a totem in Canada (1945). He is remembered as having been full of fun. From the collection of Theresa Rankin.

Daisy Shinn Rankin (ca. mid-1880s), Reginald Rankin's elegant mother, who raised her grandson Norman after Reginald and Belle divorced. From the collection of Theresa Rankin.

Norman Rankin, Belle's son, reclines on the mat (1948). Reginald Rankin's new wife and baby, both named Theresa, are on the left. From the collection of Theresa Rankin.

Charlie Thompson, June, and Louise at an amusement park (ca. 1919). Courtesy of the Gypsy Rose Lee Archive.

June and Louise with Murray Gordon Edelston (ca. early 1920s), Rose's salesman boyfriend who joined the act and elevated it onto the Orpheum circuit. Edelston was the only father figure June would remember. Courtesy of the Gypsy Rose Lee Archive.

Baby June, ornately dressed in a Jazz Age performance costume (ca. 1916). Courtesy of the Gypsy Rose Lee Archive.

Louise in costume (ca. early 1920s). While June was the singing and dancing star of the act, Louise was always featured in comedy numbers at which she excelled. Courtesy of the Gypsy Rose Lee Archive.

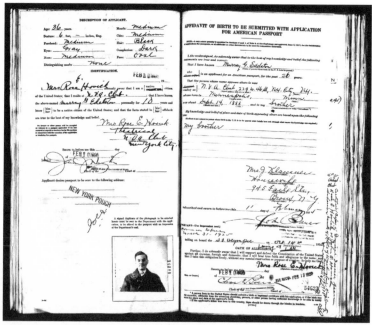

June, Louise, and Rose pose for US passport pictures in 1925 in New York City. The pictures were taken for a European journey they weren't really planning to take. Courtesy of Ancestry.com.

Murray Gordon Edelston's 1925 passport picture for the group's non-trip. Courtesy of Ancestry.com.

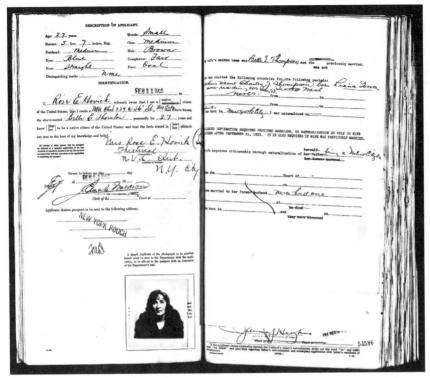

Belle's 1925 passport picture. The entire group's passports were part of a ruse. Courtesy of Ancestry.com.

The Throop Hotel in Topeka, Kansas, the very last town to see the Dainty June act. June and her first husband, Weldon "Buddy" Hyde, ran away from this hotel after eloping in 1928. From the author's collection.

May Sherwood, shown here performing with a partner (ca. 1926–27), bore a resemblance to June. Rose hired May to join the new act she built around Louise. From the collection of Rob Brandreth-Gibbs.

Joe Dealy presents his Big Summer Special
Mme. Rose Debutantes
Direct from Hollywood

The new act was initially called Madam Rose's Debutantes. The girls looked a little too young for such a designation. Louise created the costumes. From the collection of Rob Brandreth-Gibbs.

Gypsy Rose Lee with her half-siblings, Betty and Jack Hovick, on their trip to New York City in the 1930s. From the collection of Bette Solomon.

Rose and Gypsy, backstage at a theater (ca. late 1930s), where they also dined. From the collection of Robert Strom.

Glamor shot of Gypsy Rose Lee wearing lace (ca. 1937). From the author's collection.

Rose Thompson Hovick and a friend
(ca. mid-1930s). Courtesy of the
Gypsy Rose Lee Archive.

Genevieve Augustine, top row left, and
her siblings (ca. 1920), whose home life
left a lot to be desired. From the collection of Margaret Craft.

The Genevieve Augustine crime scene, with investigators (1937). The gun is lying at a strange angle, since the crime scene was compromised when the body was discovered. Courtesy of Barry Yellen.

Gypsy Rose Lee, Rose, and Bob Mizzy, shortly after Gypsy's marriage to Bob in California (1937). From the author's collection.

Back in business: June as Gladys Bumps in *Pal Joey* on Broadway (1940). The show was destined to be a hit. From the author's collection.

A very happy June in her dressing room during *Pal Joey* (ca. 1941). From the author's collection.

Rose, after falling over in a faint, is carried out of the courtroom where she testified in her lover Patricia Donovan's reckless endangerment trial (1943). Patricia is on the right. From the collection of Chuck Mosberger.

Jack Hovick (seen here in 1962) had a great marriage with his second wife, Elizabeth. June avoided them, but Gypsy got on beautifully with her father and stepmother. From the collection of Bette Solomon.

Gypsy Rose Lee and Randolph Scott in the movie *Belle of the Yukon* (1944). Gypsy dated Otto Preminger while filming and soon gave birth to his son, Erik. From the author's collection.

Gypsy Rose Lee, baby Erik, and Anna Thompson (1946). Gypsy made sure to play an engagement in Seattle so that Big Lady Anna could meet her son. From the collection of Chuck Mosberger.

Gypsy Rose Lee feeding Erik at a lunch counter as her aunt Hilma Braid, Jack Hovick's sister, looks on (1946). From the collection of Chuck Mosberger.

The approach to Copalis Beach, Washington, where Rose's sister Belle opened a souvenir shop. Courtesy of the Museum of the North Beach, Moclips, Washington.

Archway at Copalis Crossing, Washington. Courtesy of the Museum of the North Beach, Moclips, Washington.

June Havoc and Gypsy Rose Lee (1958). From the author's collecti◆

A Merry Christmas for Rose at last! Louis, Ginny, and Judy Polhemus with Rose, Christmas 1952. From the collection of Judith Polhemus Leiner.

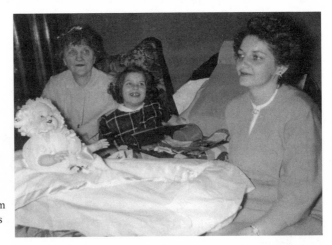

Rose with Judy and Ginny Polhemus (1952). Rose gave Judy the large doll for Christmas. From the collection of Judith Polhemus Leiner.

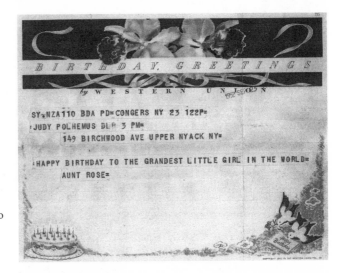

BIRTHDAY GREETINGS
by WESTERN UNION

SY⹀NZA110 BDA PD=CONGERS NY 23 122P=
:JUDY POLHEMUS DLR 3 PM=
    149 BIRCHWOOD AVE UPPER NYACK NY=

:HAPPY BIRTHDAY TO THE GRANDEST LITTLE GIRL IN THE WORLD=
    AUNT ROSE=

Birthday Telegram from Rose to Judy Polhemus, 1952. From the collection of Judith Polhemus Leiner.

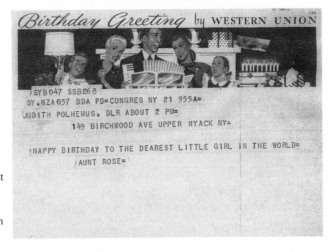

Birthday Greeting by WESTERN UNION

:SYB047 SSB268
SY⹀NZA037 BDA PD=CONGRES NY 21 955A=
:JUDITH POLHEMUS⹀ DLR ABOUT 2 PM=
    149 BIRCHWOOD AVE UPPER NYACK NY=

:HAPPY BIRTHDAY TO THE DEAREST LITTLE GIRL IN THE WORLD=
    :AUNT ROSE=

"Aunt Rose" sent birthday telegrams to Judy Polhemus, her best friends' daughter, in 1952 and even in 1953, when Rose was dying. From the collection of Judith Polhemus Leiner.

Photo showing Rose's sister Belle's motel, Thornton's Modern Cabins and Betty Thornton Souvenirs, Copalis Beach, Washington (ca. 1950s). Belle went by the nickname Betty. Courtesy of the Museum of the North Beach, Moclips, Washington.

Rose and children believed to be her Camp Rose Ridge campers (ca. early 1950s). Courtesy of the Gypsy Rose Lee Archive.

Photo of Rose with three of her beloved pets, including one of her Great Danes, probably taken in the summer of 1953. She was gravely ill, and her hair had gone gray, but she was still well enough to reopen her children's camp. From the collection of Judith Polhemus Leiner.

Erik Kirkland Preminger, Gypsy Rose Lee, and Gypsy's dog Fu Manchu in Holiday Isles, Florida (1959). Gypsy wrote most of her memoir a few years earlier in another Florida motel. From the author's collection.

Opening Night of *Gypsy* on Broadway (1959). Gypsy Rose Lee, Ethel Merman, who starred as Broadway's first Rose, and actress Polly Bergen. From the author's collection.

Actress Rosalind Russell, in costume as Rose, and director Mervyn LeRoy on the *Gypsy* movie set, visited by former First Lady Mamie Eisenhower (1962). From the author's collection.

Lisa Peluso as Baby Louise, Angela Lansbury as Rose, and Bonnie Langford as Baby June in the first Broadway revival of *Gypsy* (1974). From the author's collection.

Jonathan Hadary as Herbie, the character based on Murray Gordon Edelston, and Tyne Daly as Rose in the second Broadway revival of *Gypsy* (1989). From the author's collection.

Ed Asner as Charlie Thompson and Bette Midler as Rose in the 1994 TV movie of *Gypsy*. Photo by Tony Esparza; from the author's collection.

Patti LuPone as Rose Hovick singing "Rose's Turn," pictured on the cover of the playbill for the fifth Broadway revival of *Gypsy* (2008). From the author's collection.

Alayna and Lauren Brandreth-Gibbs, great-granddaughters of May Sherwood of the Hollywood Blondes, continue the family tradition of performing into the twenty-first century (2011). As Rose Hovick would have said, "Always ahead and onward!" Courtesy of Rob Brandreth-Gibbs.

CHAPTER 13

DR. JEKYLL AND MRS. HOVICK

TWENTIETH CENTURY-FOX BELIEVED THAT MARRYING GYPSY ROSE LEE off to somebody—anybody, really—would enhance her image with the public. Making her over into a wholesome package was already an uphill battle, given the public's inability to get over her past. Letting her remain single, in the eyes of the publicity mavens anyway, would only make matters worse. The studio did not really care whether or not getting married at this point in her life would be the best thing for Gypsy the woman. But marriage was a great plan for Gypsy the studio property.

She had been dating a dental salesman named Arnold Robert "Bob" Mizzy, whom she adored. The studio was pushing her into matrimony with a higher degree of unconcern for her welfare than had ever come from her mother Rose, later called "the stage mother from hell." The two young people agreed to tie the knot.

The wedding took place with Rose's blessing but practically over Bob Mizzy's mother's dead body. When she heard that her precious son was about to wed "that stripper," she sent an emissary, Morton Minsky's wife Ruth's Aunt Mae, who was one of her friends, to interrogate Morton in the office area of Minsky's Republic Theater. Aunt Mae grilled him about Gypsy's character, probably secretly hoping to hear all manner of dirt.

To his eternal credit, Morton Minsky kept quiet about the mildly unorthodox happenstances he'd noticed taking place around Gypsy over the years: that she was friendly with gangster Waxey Gordon; that she had shown blue movies in her dressing room; that she had a raucous time encouraging her pet monkeys to mate in their cage. Instead Mort opted to praise Gypsy's intelligence and leave it at that. The wedding was on.

It was the middle of August 1937. Rainy weather had been plaguing the Highland Mills area for several dark and miserable weeks. Rose was due to go west to California to attend the unique little wedding that Gypsy had planned, but her chronic asthma got in the way again. Rose coughed so much and so badly that she couldn't sleep at night and wasn't much relieved during the daytime, either. Gypsy had mentioned to her mother that Los Angeles was going through a foggy spell. That clinched it; fog made Rose's asthma worse. Having someone drive her out to California and directly into the fog struck her as out of the question. Going by train, Rose thought, was too expensive. Rose admitted to feeling lonely and rather useless. She no longer had Gypsy's career to manage and was resisting letting June too far back into her life. She hadn't been allowed to adopt April. She didn't have a boyfriend or, for that matter, a girlfriend. Finding poor Genevieve's dead body hadn't helped. Yet in the spirit of the Egle family's tradition of emotional regeneration, she'd manage to rise above it all in fairly short order.

It is revealing that Gypsy had no qualms about inviting her mother out to California for her wedding. Only two months after Genevieve Augustine had committed suicide at the house, Gypsy did not believe her mother had any complicity in the chauffeur's death. She didn't bring the matter up in her correspondence with her mother and was clearly not concerned about it. She wanted her mother at her wedding.

Gypsy had a wedding to plan, and in typical Gypsy style, she wasn't going to have a traditional one. She wasn't even going to have just one. Instead, she planned two wedding ceremonies, something that definitely got the attention of the press. On Friday the thirteenth, a date she'd chosen for fun, Gypsy and Bob applied for a marriage license in Santa Ana. Then they proceeded to Long Beach. Once there, they hired a water taxi. The first ceremony was, literally, a "marriage at sea." The captain of the water taxi married the couple as they sailed around on the little boat in the midst of the Pacific. Gypsy's father, Jack Hovick, was overjoyed to have been selected as one of the witnesses to his daughter' wedding. The other witness was a friend of Gypsy and Bob, David Albers.

Jack Hovick had probably inspired the nautical nature of this wedding. He told his daughter that generations of Hovicks had been Vikings and that it was a Hovick family tradition to be married at sea.

After the first ceremony, to make certain there would be no additional scandals attached to her name or accusations of impropriety thrown in her direction, Gypsy and Bob made sure they married a second time, in Santa Ana and in more staid surroundings. They made a big show of not spending the night together until after this second Santa Ana ceremony.

Rose was devastated to have missed all of the excitement and fun. By August 16 she finally felt better and was ready to start planning her trip to Hollywood. She wired Gypsy to say she would be leaving in a matter of days. The prospect of the trip may not have cured her asthma, but it certainly put Rose into a sunnier frame of mind. She soon arrived in Los Angeles. On August 26· there was a pictorial display in the *Los Angeles Times* showing Rose—devoid of makeup but wearing a jaunty little hat—with Bob Mizzy and a gorgeous Gypsy, all with their arms around each other. Rose's aversion to using makeup may have stemmed from a lifetime of wanting to help her daughters. Gypsy looks spectacular in this photo, as Rose herself probably would have looked had she also put on a little Max Factor. But she didn't, and the contrast between the two women helps to make Gypsy the undisputed standout.

The picture of Rose, Gypsy, and Bob appeared between a photo of Mussolini exploring a sulfur mine, and a photo of the Belgian royal children. The same two-page photo spread included a photo of Japanese and Chinese nationals fraternizing in Fengtai, China. It is a fascinating photo collage because it showcased the peaceful world that was about to disappear. War was coming, though nobody fully realized it. Mussolini would soon side with Adolf Hitler against most of humanity, Belgium was three years away from being invaded by Hitler's goose-stepping Nazis, and China and Japan would become enemies during the same worldwide conflict. Yet at that particular moment, there still was peace on most of the earth.

Another photo of Rose taken during that trip shows her happier than she ever had appeared before, ensconced in a wicker chair with a palm tree in the background. She was clearly having a wonderful time.

The Twentieth Century-Fox publicity department went to work right after the wedding. They hastily arranged several stories for public consumption about Gypsy's newfound domesticity, accompanied by photos of her fixing meals in a kitchen. Gypsy finally bought a silver chrome trailer of her own to use as a portable hotel room during long distance trips. She and Bob drove it across the country and back to Highland Mills. They brought Rose along for the ride. It was to be like the old days, when she and Rose and the Hollywood Blondes had camped out around the country in their tent. But Mother Nature intervened, spoiling their fun. The heat in Texas was so intense that in El Centro Gypsy had to cool down her Dachshunds by pouring soda pop on them after the trailer ran out of water. Several miles later, a wilting, overheated Rose had to be temporarily deposited in an apartment in Dallas to escape the sweltering vehicle. She may have returned to

Highland Mills separately, rather than continuing on with Gypsy and Bob. However she got there, she was in place at Witchwood Manor for a photo opportunity, welcoming her daughter and son-in-law when they arrived. That trip would provide Gypsy with a wealth of outrageous material a few years hence, when she penned a mystery entitled *Mother Finds a Body* and set it in a Texas trailer camp.

But if the trio were hoping for a bit of peace and quiet in Highland Mills, it wasn't to be. Kay Ray was back in the picture. Her desire for an investigation into the circumstances of Genevieve Augustine's death had surfaced yet again. This time it seems probable that she'd approached Genevieve's mother, Lillian, to push for a more formal inquest. Genevieve's father had immediately accepted the idea that his emotionally troubled daughter had killed herself, but Genevieve's mother did not. She wasn't too stable a woman so it was easier for a Machiavellian schemer like Kay to manipulate her. The grieving mother wrote to Chief Inspector A. B. Moore of the New York State Police to say that she was not satisfied with Coroner Garrison's suicide verdict. She wanted a full investigation of her daughter's death and the events leading up to it. In other words, Mrs. Augustine was suggesting to the police that Genevieve had possibly been the victim of foul play. In addition to all of the revived *sturm und drang* surrounding Genevieve's suicide and the possibility of a new investigation, a personality clash erupted between Rose and Bob Mizzy. All were relieved when Gypsy and Bob returned to the West Coast in the trailer.

A grand jury was convened in the Augustine case in the nearby town of Newburgh on October 25. Three "showgirl friends" of Gypsy Rose Lee were photographed on the steps of the Newburgh courthouse, two of them smiling nervously, the third looking away from the camera. They were Pearl Brooks, Juanita Lopez, and Anna Matt, who were all identified as having been at Witchwood Manor with Rose when Genevieve shot herself, and had returned to testify. The Helen Leudhardt who was reportedly there when Genevieve died may also have returned, but this time the press gave her name as Helene Lambert. A few additional girls who had stayed at Rose's house prior to the day of the shooting, had known Genevieve, and had information to share regarding her emotional state, also arrived to provide testimony. They included Alice Whitehead, Marcia Miller, and Rose Hart.

Rose was supposed to appear on the first day of the proceedings but wasn't feeling well enough to do so. Her asthma, which could be set off whenever she was in an unfavorable emotional state, was probably the culprit. The idea of reliving the events of June 1 on a witness stand may very well have been enough to set off a major attack. The grand jury listened to four hours of testimony that first day, then adjourned for about a month, possibly in deference to Rose's illness and inability to appear. They reconvened on November 24. Rose showed up, sufficiently recovered, and was photographed on her way to court, this time wearing a cute hat with a brim and a few pom-poms on top. Rose is not smiling in this photograph. She appears to be quietly dignified.

This time, Kay Ray was among those who took her place on the witness stand. Testifying should have been problematic for her, but chances are it wasn't. Witnesses have to swear an oath to tell the truth, but conscienceless Kay wasn't concerned about such minor technicalities. She would get on the witness stand and tell it the way she wanted, which was not the same as telling what really happened. The entire grand jury, along with Michael A. Hoey from the district attorney's office, concluded their investigation two days later by paying a site visit to Witchwood Manor to see exactly where the suicide had occurred. Rose met the large contingent at the door and showed the whole group through the house. They were able to see firsthand how far she and the guests who had been sitting outside the house had been from Genevieve's bedroom. That concluded the investigation. The findings of the court were released on November 29. The verdict was suicide. There would be no further trials or investigations into the matter.

Gypsy Rose Lee and Rose were no doubt relieved. Kay Ray, wherever she was, probably threw a monumental tantrum. But the matter was legally ended, once and for all, and Kay Ray would not be able to agitate against Genevieve, dead or alive, any longer. At this point Kay finally faded out of the picture. She would not surface again.

Yet the troubles for Rose that would stem from these incidents were not over. They were about to be renewed, causing a breach between her and her beloved eldest daughter. Rose went back to living in New York City for a little while, to get a change of scenery and recover from the strain of the events of the summer and autumn. This move was almost certainly made at Gypsy's behest. It was no longer feasible for her mother to be acting as the chatelaine of her country house, while simultaneously taking in the kinds of guests or helpers that could include a young woman troubled enough to commit suicide on the property. And Gypsy had not needed any additional questionable publicity like the kind she got from the investigation into Genevieve's death. Changes had to be made. Rose's paying guests were all shown the door. Gypsy decided she no longer wanted to remain in touch with many of her New York friends who had been at the house party back in May. And Rose would no longer be allowed to run the house. Gypsy asked Rose to live elsewhere and continued to support her financially.

Rose was not as devastated by being asked to leave the house as she had been when June ran off in 1928, but her removal was another betrayal, this time coming from her most loyal daughter, and she didn't handle the news of having to move all that well. Rose had loved Witchwood Manor. It was a stunning place and she had wanted to stay there for the rest of her life.

Ultimately Rose and Gypsy had a gigantic row. It was such an altercation that Gypsy did not wish to see her mother for a long while afterwards. Rose would later beg her forgiveness, claiming she was "sick and terribly disappointed about so many things" when the big blow-up took place. But Gypsy's forgiveness was a long time coming.

Once "exiled" to New York City, Rose had a tough time paying the rent and bills on the allowance that Gypsy provided for her, or so she claimed. She felt there wasn't enough left over for the quality-of-life extras that she considered essential, like nice clothes and Broadway show tickets. Rose was not having a good time in New York. She had never had a bad time in New York City until her daughter requested that she vacate Witchwood Manor. After that, New York City wouldn't do. Rose wanted to get back to Highland Mills. She had friends there and missed them. This move had not been her choice, and she wasn't ready for it.

Back in Hollywood, Gypsy was described in an April, 1938, *Los Angeles Times* article as having "won acclaim" in films as "a portrayer of unsympathetic characters," the only roles the studio had dared allow the burlesque veteran to play. Things were still not going well for her in Tinsel Town.

By May 1938, Rose had rented a little two-hundred-year-old farmhouse in Highland Mills about a mile away from Witchwood Manor. It wasn't fully furnished, but Rose thought she knew a creative way around that little problem. Gypsy was still out in Hollywood, and a new caretaker, Lester Smith, was staying in one of the cottages on the Witchwood Manor property. Smith had taken over responsibility for the house and all of Gypsy's animals, including her monkey, Dachshunds, and a large Great Dane named Jerry. Rose went for a stroll over to Gypsy's empty house and decided to borrow some needed items. As her daughter was not there to use them, Rose did not see any harm in what she planned. But Rose didn't realize that what she was about to do was going to cause a gigantic rift between herself and her faithful daughter.

Never a bastion of restraint, Rose went overboard in her furniture expedition. According to Lester Smith, Rose helped herself to so many items that it took a ten-page handwritten letter for him to account for everything. Rose helped herself to enough furniture to fill a moving van, if not two. The diverted items included a wicker furniture set, a full dining room set, an oil stove, a cooking pot, a day bed, a brass bed "from the living quarters" (which seems to mean from Smith's own cottage), end tables, lamps, lawn chairs, indoor chairs, flower pots, flower baskets, fruit jars, a gardening hoe, a rake, a bookcase complete with books, a garden swing, a rocking chair, quilts, more wicker chairs, chair cushions, chicken wire, a kerosene can, and a radio. Rose also took many of Gypsy's animals. She grabbed Jerry the Great Dane, who had attacked a local child, broken her arm, and was considered dangerous. He may have been in danger of being destroyed if she hadn't taken him. She also grabbed quite a few chickens and several of Louise's Dachshunds. Lester Smith had to fight to retrieve the Dachshunds from Rose.

It was hard to imagine how Rose managed to get all of these items out of her daughter's vacant house and carried a mile away to her own new quarters. Taking the garden hoe or a lamp down the sweeping driveway and ambling with them for a mile was one thing, but how did a petite asthmatic like Rose move items like a dining room set, a bookcase, and two beds? She must have had an accomplice—with a truck.

The poor caretaker was frantic. Rose had told him that she had her daughter's permission to liberate everything. Lester Smith had been manipulated, knew it, and was disturbed to the point he spoke to a local justice of the peace, fearing he'd lose his job or somehow get implicated in property theft. The justice of the peace counseled him to wait the situation out; there was no point in panicking about it until they found out what Gypsy had to say.

Normally unflappable Gypsy was furious. The misappropriation of the furniture was bad enough, but Rose had also helped herself to some of the animals, which except for the chickens were Gypsy's pets. This was going too far. At first it did not dawn on Rose how much she had unintentionally enraged her daughter. She had set out to borrow the furnishings, had reasons for taking the animals, and didn't realize that what she had done was to set herself up for a major no-holds-barred battle.

Gypsy's relationship with Rose seems to have been on congenial enough terms until the grand jury investigation in October of 1937. Everything between the two women seems to have changed for the worse afterward. Gypsy even began to keep a file of her mother's correspondence after the furniture incident. She also kept copies of her responses, just in case she needed them as legal evidence later. It was a miserable turn of events in the relationship of this mother and daughter who had once been so close.

As sophisticated as Gypsy's humor was onstage and as elegant a lady as she had become, she was still only twenty-six years old—and believed herself to be twenty-four. She was supporting her mother, her grandmother, Anna Thompson, and also her Aunt Belle Thompson Rankin Thornton McKenzie, whose most recent marriage hadn't lasted any longer than the other two had. Belle was an alcoholic. She would later temporarily overcome the condition, only to relapse. Her addiction added to her overall physical woes, which were great, and rendered Belle less employable than a lady with the crippled leg would have been without them. On the other hand, since Anna had reached the point of needing around-the-clock assistance, Belle could not easily go out to work, either. Gypsy was thus supporting three adult family members dispersed on two coasts. She was also paying for the Highland Mills house and grounds and her Pacific Palisades house in California, not to mention providing a salary for her staff at each. She had far too much financial responsibility and more dependents than any young woman her age needed. And none of her dependents were children of her own.

To Gypsy's credit, she consistently met the responsibilities that had been foisted on her. The trouble was that these responsibilities were going to last what must have felt like an infinite amount of time to Gypsy. Gypsy did not cut off her support of Rose, Anna and Belle, yet the pressure of having to pay for them was stifling her. She was also a newlywed whose marriage was already in trouble. The idea of Rose taking so many items and animals from her Highland Mills house without asking, on top of everything else, was the last straw. Gypsy informed Rose in a telegram that what she had done was illegal.

From her Spanish-style California beach house, which she had hoped would become a peaceful Pacific refuge, Gypsy also told her mother that unless she returned each of the stolen items, she would not be getting her allowance. This threat was the one that made Rose take notice. She did not relish the idea of being without an allowance. Nobody stopped to think about the topsy-turvy plight of an adult child doling an allowance out to her mother. Gypsy supported Rose, Rose wanted the money, and Gypsy had no qualms about withholding it in order to get her property back.

Rose sent a telegram back a day later. She sent it not directly to Gypsy, but to Gypsy's African American maid, Eva Moncur, whom she knew was reliable and would deliver it straight to her daughter. Rose's response was red-hot. She informed Gypsy that she had never even entered "the house," a relative term in this case, since she went on to admit she had taken things from the garage and the basement, adding that everything she had taken really belonged to her anyway. She did not explain why she had removed items from the living quarters Lester Smith shared with his wife and two babies. Rose presumably didn't know that Gypsy already had found out about that part of her mother's furniture collection. Rose said that Jerry the Great Dane belonged to her. She claimed Gypsy had given her a little Dachshund dog named Wilhelmina (one of the dogs Gypsy had had with her when she had made her entrance at the station on her 1937 arrival in Hollywood), along with Wilhelmina's pups so that she could start a breeding kennel with them.

Then Rose's reply took a bizarre turn. She claimed Bob Mizzy's parents had access to Gypsy, but she didn't. She told Gypsy she and Bob should be ashamed of themselves, added they'd one day be punished for their actions, and threatened that they shouldn't push her too far. The great furniture fight of 1938 was off to a flying start.

Rose must have had second thoughts after sending such a furiously worded telegram. She also must have been furious at herself for the expense of doing so, because it was much longer than cheaper telegrams, limited to ten words, were. Her remorse probably gave Rose a sleepless night. The threat of the loss of her allowance was real. The next day she sat down and wrote a much calmer and more reasonable letter to her daughter. The letter was such a switch from the volatile telegram that preceded it that it almost seemed to have been written by a different person. In the letter she explained that she had wanted to go to California and visit Gypsy and then go on to Seattle, but had decided not to proceed with that plan after getting Gypsy's telegram. She casually mentioned that she was going through the change of life and having rather wild symptoms, which were setting her nerves on edge and making her feel anxious. She was almost continuously sick, seemingly a euphemism for bleeding, which was weakening her. Rose described the two-hundred-year-old farmhouse she had rented and its gorgeous grounds, praised Gypsy's caretaker Lester by calling him "a nice little fellow," expressed worries about the health of his babies, but then got a little dig in by suggesting that a single man would be better to have as a caretaker—and cheaper.

She talked of her plans to breed the dachshund, Wilhelmina, and her puppies, and mentioned that she had cared for Joseph Bush, the former Witchwood Manor caretaker, when he was in New York City because he had been sick, hospitalized, and his wife had thrown him out. She told her daughter that she had wanted to cozy her new place up and that was why she had taken items from Gypsy's house, adding that when Gypsy came back to Highland Mills she could see what had been borrowed and take back whatever she needed.

Rose told her daughter that her latest Hollywood picture had held her "spellbound" and was hoping it would prove to be the break Gypsy had been awaiting. She asked her to write her back and urged her to try to be kinder. She continued by providing a shrewdly edited list of what she claimed were all of the items she had taken from Witchwood Manor. Conspicuously absent were the day bed, the brass bed, the rocking chair, the radio, all of the lamps, and many smaller items.

Still, the tone of the letter is warm and reasonable, not confrontational and warlike as her telegram of just the day before had been. If her reported mood swings truly stemmed from the hormonal fluctuations of menopause, and not abject rage against her daughter, Rose was suffering terribly. She claimed she'd only borrowed items from her absent daughter's vacant house, which to her mind it wasn't a criminal offense.

This furniture fight may have been the first time Gypsy had gotten tough and absolutely put her foot down where her mother was concerned. Rose was blind-sided, caught completely unprepared. The unhappy woman's life might have moved in a more positive direction if she had been able to get involved with a small enterprise like a Dachshund breeding kennel. Her asthma may have prevented her from holding down a regular job, but it wouldn't have stopped her from feeding dogs and selectively breeding them. This woman, who had managed troupes of kids all over the vaudeville and burlesque circuits, was someone who needed, and would have excelled at, a little project like running a kennel. Rose desperately needed to be running *something*; she was practically stagnating out in the countryside.

Gypsy may have responded to this letter negatively, because four days later, Rose fired off another missive, and this one was like a literary brickbat. Resentment pours out of it like molten lava from an out-of-control volcano. Rose must have been having hormonal mood swings or may even have suffered from bipolar disorder, a mental condition marked by alternating euphoria and depression. Either way, she was flaming mad.

Gypsy Rose Lee was dealing with Dr. Jekyll and Mrs. Hovick.

Never mind that four days earlier Rose had expressed concern about caretaker Lester Smith's sick babies. Now she called him an untrustworthy liar, said his wife was "a half wit," declared that the babies are ill and the man was a drinker who brought fellow inebriates to his cottage on Gypsy's property. The last bit of information was something she had learned from people who knew Lester. Obviously, she found out in the intervening days that Lester Smith had relayed to Gypsy the full list of what Rose had taken from Witchwood Manor, and may have also heard he'd been discussing her with the local justice of the peace.

Rose was madder than hell. The letter did not start off nicely and then became ferocious. Rose proceeded to attack Gypsy. "I was your colored slave and maid for years and years," reads one accusation, "I was a house-keeper for you." Aside from the reference to skin pigmentation, there was a lot of truth to that claim. Rose had been taking care of Gypsy's house. Everything just went out of control the moment the poor Augustine girl had seen and used the rifle. "The few pennies I scraped together after expenses were taken care of I put back into *your house*, never dreaming I would some day be turned out," Rose went on. "Louise please remember you brought anything unpleasant into our lives before I ever even knew about it. Drink, night club [sic], bad camping; reifers [sic], French moving pictures. Fags, and all those people you hate so today; *you brought them into our home.* They were all your friends."

This last was a reference to Louise shunning many of her old friends after Genevieve's suicide. On raged the letter:

How can you feel so perfect? What have I ever done that you haven't done twenty fold worse. You still entertain those people that you shun. Whitehouse and Marsha what are they? My God they live with you and Bob. Drink with you eat with you. Dozens of your letters tell how you like those people and you even advised the last fatal party that took place. You wrote me then and told me to ask them to the house. I mention all this because I want to know why I am so unwanted all of a sudden. It's a pretty tough time to let me down Louise.

Two of the girls mentioned had been witnesses before the grand jury. Apparently they had not been written off and were now included in Gypsy's inner sanctum. Rose's misery is clear: Other people have access to her child, and she doesn't. She can't even borrow the furniture. Yet she completely misses the point that taking it was an invasion of Gypsy's space. Rose concludes the letter by airing her unhappiness about her eviction from Witchwood Manor: "I always understood that the house on the hill was mine. To live in, in my old age. Now it appears that others will live their old age in it. *Please wire me at once.* Your Mother."

This was a direct order, but Gypsy chose to disregard it. Perhaps owing to Bob Mizzy's influence in her life Gypsy held firm. She now had a husband who was on her side, buoying her up. Gypsy's reply was a study in cool detachment. She would not engage in a battle of words with her mother, but she made succinct points: "Months ago I told you that your friends are *your* friends. When your association with them involved me in unpleasantries—which is putting it mildly—I complained—You can't hurt me any more in any way." The last line reads like a declaration of independence. Gypsy goes on to include a postscript that addresses Rose's allowance and calmly states, "Return my things—you receive your check."

Another erratic missive from Rose to Gypsy followed. Written in a maddeningly calm tone, it again raised the question of whether Rose had bipolar disorder. At least there was some logic to Rose's more unpleasant missives: They were usually sent in response to situations that she found untenable, like this one. Her displeasure could be enormous, but actual events were always the catalysts. She didn't rail in a paranoid manner about non-events; she addressed real ones. Unfortunately for Gypsy, the actual events that set Rose off were usually ones involving trying to con more out of her daughter than her daughter was willing to give.

There were letters where Rose described her isolation, loneliness, and depressed feelings that seem consistent with bipolar disorder. So does Rose's alcohol consumption, which added to her unstable moods. Whether she was actually bipolar or not, Rose nevertheless made her own bathtub gin, kept plenty of it available and loved to imbibe. She might have been self-medicating and turning into something of a Jekyll and Hyde just from over-indulgence.

Whatever the reason for the roller-coaster mood shifts expressed in the letters, the image of Rose, fountain pen in hand, bent over her writing paper creating letter after letter addressed to Louise and endlessly trying to get back in her daughter's good graces, is a sad one. Over the years, beginning with the furniture fight, there would be scores of these missives. The next calm letter claimed that Gypsy did not really understand what had happened with the furniture, which by now Rose may very well have considered cursed. Rose said she'd found the dining room set in the leaky, water-filled basement, covered with mildew, and felt she could take better care of it at her new place. She also said she had borrowed the bookcase full of books so she could read them. The garden furniture and the wicker set were pieces she, Rose, had bought at auctions. Everything could always be returned to Louise. Rose had already returned the animals. Rose asks her daughter if she should move closer to her in California, adding, "I will live *like* you want me to or where you want me to."

It was a desperate and revealing line, illustrating that Rose was far too enmeshed, at least in her own mind, with this daughter. She could not bear to be apart from Gypsy. So great was her anxiety about their separation, she put this sadly cloying, deferential statement in writing. Rose couldn't get past the empty nest syndrome. As a young divorcee, Rose had chosen to create a life centered on her two daughters. But Gypsy hadn't chosen to spend her adult life with her mother.

Then the only direct reference to the Genevieve Augustine suicide that Rose was ever known to commit to writing appears in this same calm letter: "I will regret for as long as I live the unfortunate, unhappiness I caused you through the Ginny affair that I was helpless to avoid." If she was outside with the others on the lawn when Genevieve shot herself, she had been quite literally helpless to prevent it. The ensuing media attention and then the grand jury hearing could be blamed more on Kay Ray than it ever could or should have been blamed on Rose, but that truth got lost in the mad shuffle.

Rose threw in the line that there wasn't anything left for her to live for. If this was a bid for attention, it failed. No reply came. No check came immediately, either. And Rose was not the sort of woman who could withstand being ignored without taking some kind of action. Rose waited a couple of months, which must have seemed to her like decades. Then she decided that she'd existed in "Louise limbo" long enough. So she sent Louise and Bob yet another letter, and in this one, she, a menopausal woman with asthma, announced that she was about to hitchhike across the continental United States: "I can last here for another week then I am hitting the highway. I am hitchhiking to Hollywood. I will see your father, Bob and you before I leave there." Rose was on her way to Hollywood to continue the battle in person.

CHAPTER 14

HOT SOUP

ROSE'S TRIP WAS A MISTAKE, OF COURSE. GOING TO CALIFORNIA UNIN-
vited did not help mend the frayed relationship with Gypsy. Confrontation
made matters worse.

Nevertheless, Gypsy was worried about her mother. Rose was bringing a
woman along to California with whom she had recently taken up romantically. During the 1930s it was always possible that Rose could be arrested
for her romantic inclinations. Gypsy confided her concerns to her grandmother in a letter. Big Lady responded that she didn't like the idea of Rose's
woman, either. If Rose was hoping for acceptance, it wasn't forthcoming
from her family. Yet Big Lady also knew better than to fight Rose. Rose was
going to do whatever Rose felt like doing, and at this point she felt like having a woman. Big Lady told Gypsy she hoped the woman would be "a nice
girl." A nice female companion for Rose could prove tolerable. Rose was
headed for Los Angeles first and Seattle second, and the infirm Big Lady
was delighted to hear that her daughter was coming home for a visit, no
matter who she brought along as a companion.

Gypsy was not so thrilled about the prospect of seeing her mother. She
had been having a fine time at her beach house with her husband Bob and
their circle of friends, though she still wasn't doing as well as she'd hoped
professionally in Hollywood. She had a feeling that Rose was going to upset
the delicate balance of her little Hollywood world. Gypsy's intuition, this
time, was on target.

Days later Big Lady, with a little help from fate, found an excuse to get
Rose up to Seattle: Rose's sister Belle, forever in frail health, needed to have
a kidney removed immediately. She was already in the hospital. Big Lady
was a wreck and wanted Rose to get there as soon as possible. She genuinely
needed Rose's help; she also knew Louise would be thrilled to have Rose

head as far away from Hollywood as they could get her. But Rose did not go directly to Seattle, despite Belle's hospitalization. It was Gypsy she had gone west to see. She remained in Hollywood for two months before proceeding north, staying with Gypsy, for a miserable portion of that time.

It went terribly. Gypsy made it clear that she emphatically didn't want Rose to be there. Gypsy's two maids, Dell and Eva, also made it obvious that they didn't want Rose there, either, no doubt doing so at Gypsy's urging. More than anyone, Bob Mizzy didn't want Rose on the premises. At one point Rose jokingly chased him around the house while wielding a gun. Bob didn't realize the gun wasn't loaded. After that, Bob considered Rose his mortal enemy.

For her part, Rose was increasingly ill. Her asthma was always made worse by stress, and she had aggravation in abundance during this visit to Gypsy's place, where she so clearly was not wanted. Her menopause complications, with their savage mood swings, hadn't abated yet and didn't help. The state of her overall health was made all the more unbearable because the one place Rose most wanted to be was near this beloved daughter who wanted her to pack up and leave.

Anna wrote and urged Rose to proceed to Seattle, to stay with her, someone she could always count on. If she wasn't wanted and wasn't needed in Hollywood, okay, then. Rose would leave, but on her own terms, not her daughter's. Rose came up with an idea so spectacular that it gave her health a boost. Rose put on ragged garments and the same kind of deathly-white powder she had once used to get bookings out of lodge moguls, back before June's old act was booked on the Orpheum circuit. Surely Rose knew how horrified Gypsy would be when she found out about the bizarre display her mother was about to make of herself. Dressed in raggedy duds, Rose invaded the office of Gypsy's ultimate boss, Darryl F. Zanuck, the head of Twentieth Century-Fox. She went right into the same routine that had worked so well so long ago, but threw in a few new twists. She was not playing the role of the deserted wife of a lodge brother this time around. She introduced herself, instead, as Gypsy Rose Lee's neglected and hungry mother. Rose put on a stellar performance, claiming she was weak, broke, and needed—what else—some hot soup.

The ploy had worked magnificently before, so Rose thought it would be an effective strategy again. What she hadn't bargained for was that Daryl Zanuck wasn't a small-town lodge brother. He was not moved by the spectacle Rose made of herself in his office. He was appalled. Gypsy was not just furious, but utterly mortified. As if she didn't already have enough trouble in Hollywood, with so many people mindlessly treating her like a pariah for having once worked in burlesque, now her out-of-control mother had invaded the studio's executive office. Zanuck's impression of Gypsy was now worse than it had been, and he'd been disdainful of her for quite some time. Gypsy Rose Lee came with far too many problems. He now had reason to wonder about her entire family.

Rose's asthma was so severe that she was undoubtedly not getting enough oxygen when she breathed, and this problem, combined with the hormonal fluctuations of menopause, the effects of years of drinking her own bathtub gin, and a need for attention from her eldest daughter that was becoming almost pathological, contributed to a compromised mental state. Gypsy's need for some space from her mother was only making matters worse. Gypsy needed space but Rose needed closeness. Her daughter had been the primary person in Rose's life from the day June ran off with Weldon Hyde back in 1928, ten years earlier, and Rose was having a hard time trying to live without her.

They'd been like companions, best buddies, Rose and Gypsy, for years. But now, a husband had entered the picture, married her daughter, and basically usurped her authority over her child. But it was 1938. The child was fully twenty-seven years old and entitled to her own separate life.

Once back in Highland Mills after visiting Anna and Belle in Seattle, Rose tried another tactic, perhaps her most desperate appeal of them all. Rose had heard that Gypsy was looking for another new caretaker for Witchwood Manor. She wrote a letter suggesting that she and her companion Connie take the job. She was willing to become her own daughter's employee in order to have access to her once again. Rose made quite a good case for her and her partner to take on the job. She said that Connie could do the work of a man and was competent in both carpentry and electrical work. They would leave the farm whenever Gypsy and Bob were going to be in residence and go off to "work their racket," Rose added intriguingly. It's almost a shame that Louise didn't take Rose up on her offer. And it's also unfortunate that Rose, with her asthma, wasn't able to work at a job that wasn't physically taxing. She mentions wanting to study Christian Science, an activity that was possible for her. While Rose embraced Christian Science and its teaching that medical conditions weren't real, she never stopped going to doctors in search of an asthma cure.

Rose found herself totally adrift, and with nothing much in her life to think about except Gypsy, who still was not communicating with her regularly. She had yet to learn that sometimes, if a situation was untenable to her, it was best to simply try to wait it out.

In November, 1938, during the same week Kristallnacht took place in Germany, beginning the countdown to World War II, Gypsy filed for divorce from Bob Mizzy, whom she had married primarily to appease the studio. Her stint in the movies hadn't worked out and neither had the marriage, so Gypsy was going to cut her losses, go home to New York, and resume her old stage name. Bob had been a contributing factor in Gypsy's estrangement from her mother, because after Bob was out of the picture, Rose was at last allowed back in. Rose was even permitted back into the Highland Mills house. She was living there again during the summer of 1939, along with Jerry, the Great Dane who had been restored to her, when a friend of Gypsy's needed a place to hide from the authorities.

Her name was Hope Dare, and she was a showgirl with titian hair who was the girlfriend of mobster Dutch Schultz's lawyer, J. Richard "Dixie" Davis. Dutch himself had been murdered. Dixie Davis had been jailed over his involvement with Schultz and, once out of the pen, went into seclusion. This was a good move on Dixie's part. He knew the police figured he knew all manner of details about the Schultz gang's operation, so he wanted to get out of town. The cops were in the process of trying to put an end to several New York and New Jersey mobs, and it followed that they wanted to force Dixie to start talking. They hoped that Hope Dare had the same information her boyfriend had, so they wanted to find and question her, too.

Gypsy took pity on her. Hope was having a tough time getting a dancing job owing to all the negative publicity about her association with Dixie and his association with Dutch—not to mention the fact that the cops kept following her. Gypsy agreed with Hope's suggestion that Gypsy stash her up in Highland Mills with Rose for a little while, hoping the cops' interest in her would level off.

Rose had a nice dinner of leg of lamb and mashed potatoes prepared for Gypsy and Hope when they arrived. She was thrilled to be in the thick of this particular caper. She made plans to barricade the place and also to create a cellar hideout in case either the cops or members of the Schultz gang showed up, but of course they didn't. Rose was the first to jump at the noise of the wind blowing down from the Catskills. She told the women to bolt their bedroom doors and put chairs under the doorknobs when they went up to their rooms to sleep that night. She was having an absolute ball, and had been delivered back into her daughter's good graces besides.

Of course, after Gypsy returned to New York the next morning, Rose and Hope remained in the house, but they soon began to tire of living life "in hiding." When Gypsy returned four days later she discovered Rose and Hope had gone into the village so that Hope could go house hunting. For this outing Hope wore a conspicuous disguise consisting of a black wig, sunglasses, high heels, and a silver fox cape. The dancer easily could have passed for a high-class hooker, and the populace of tiny Highland Mills took of notice of her. Hope began to think she'd been spotted by the mob, the police, or both, so Gypsy put her in her car and spirited her back to New York City. Gypsy later denied knowledge of Hope's ever having stayed on her home in a story that was sent out over the Associated Press wire, so somebody in Highland Mills must have identified Hope, disguise and all. A month later, Hope and her man Dixie were married. They moved to California and ran a fruit stand, Dixie having tired of being a lawyer.

Rose didn't stay put in Highland Mills. She didn't stay put anywhere for quite some time. In January 1940, she went with a friend to Tucson, Arizona. By May, she was living on Greenwich Avenue in Manhattan. By October, she was still in Manhattan but staying on Hudson Street, where she reverted to her maiden name, while calling herself Mrs. R. Thompson. From this point on, she was to use the surnames Hovick and Thompson interchangeably, signing one or the other with no apparent rhyme or reason.

It isn't clear who, if anyone, Rose was living with, but she was increasingly miserable and doing a lot of drinking. Her grandfather Lorenze was said to have died after having drunk too much of his own booze back in Farmington. Perhaps this genetic legacy was affecting Rose. It had certainly afflicted Belle.

June, meanwhile, had introduced Gypsy to producer Mike Todd, and Gypsy and Mike opened a successful revue on the grounds of the New York World's Fair, a futuristic exhibition built on a former garbage dump in Flushing Meadow, Queens. The revue was called "The Streets of Paris." Gypsy and Mike got along well. He was married but did not wish to divorce his wife for the sake of his son, or so he said. Gypsy nevertheless hoped Mike Todd would become her second husband. This situation did not bode well.

While she was appearing in the revue, Gypsy sent Rose her old mink coat as a present. The gift prompted Rose to write her daughter a heartfelt thank-you note, and to beg Gypsy to see her. The estrangement between the two was on again. Gypsy had sent her mother the gorgeous, elegant coat, but she apparently did not wish to get together with Rose. Gypsy was giving her mother strangely mixed signals. It was as if she didn't want Rose around but couldn't bear to fully let go of her, either.

June didn't stop trying to get resituated in show business. She got another break, and it was big this time: she landed the role of Gladys Bumps in the Broadway musical *Pal Joey*. For the rest of her life, June would be proud of the way she ensured that her role in the show was developed. She had been cast to appear in the second act only. She had also been initially engaged to sing just two songs. Yet she wound up with her role expanded, appearing in both acts and performing five songs. June found a way to stand out. She would stand behind the chorus girls while they were being taught their routines by the choreographer and practice their dances with them. Ostensibly, she did it "just for fun," but her behavior constituted a subtle strategy intended to get her noticed by the show's creative team. It worked. Choreographer Robert Alton certainly noticed her, her role was expanded, and producer-director George Abbott considered June the "find of the year."

Nobody in New York City seemed to realize that June had been the find of the year decades earlier, when she started working in Seattle in 1916. June, of course, had a long history of professionalism in the theater, and she knew that simply getting noticed was a primary requirement. Now, it was New York's turn to discover her, and the theatergoing public took to the newcomer, not realizing she wasn't really new at all.

The show was publicized, of course, so Rose found out about June's participation. Rose gleefully pronounced photos of June in the paper awful, still unable to forgive the child who'd run away back a dozen years earlier.

Rose was invited to a New Year's party given by Marian and Lou Parrish to usher in 1941. Gypsy was also invited. Rose went in the hope of seeing her daughter. She waited for hours, until about five o'clock in the morning, but Gypsy never arrived.

Rose was even more estranged from June than she was from Gypsy and, since she was living in Manhattan, she decided to pop over to George Abbott's office and try the same outlandish attention-getting routine on George Abbott she had tried to use on Darryl Zanuck out in Hollywood. Rose may have been drinking so much at this point that any internal brake she might have possessed, no matter how faulty, was incapable of activation. So once again, Rose arrived at her daughter's boss's office fully costumed in a shabby old coat and worn-out shoes, with sickly white powder on her otherwise lovely face. Then she made her favorite point of asking for hot soup, in addition making a plea to be allowed to watch her daughter's performance from the standing room only section of the theater.

If Rose's new goal in life was to drive her grown children crazy, she was achieving it. Gypsy had been upset by Rose's routine when it was presented in Hollywood. June, who was not as emotionally strong as her sister, was mortified, embarrassed, furious, and floored as Rose reprised her act in New York. Fortunately for June, the kindly George Abbott did not react badly. He even made June feel better about her mother by telling her Rose's act was a common routine and had been tried by every stage mother in the business.

Both girls were in over their heads where their mother was concerned at that point, not knowing how best to handle the situation except by avoiding her. They were beginning to think of their mother as an unexploded time bomb, primed to detonate without warning. Rose knew that her shenanigans could impact her daughters' careers, but she was bent on creating maximum damage. June and Gypsy had both taken to communicating with Rose through lawyers by that point, and they tried to have their attorneys deal with her about one thing only: money. It was a plan doomed to backfire. Rose saw it as an invitation to trump up reasons for requesting more money from her children. If they were willing to pay her bills and not otherwise bother with her, then Rose would run up more bills. No matter how much they gave her— and Gypsy, in particular, had made a point of providing for her handsomely—Rose always needed more.

Next Rose started pestering June, who was finally making a good salary in *Pal Joey*. June checked in with Gypsy prior to making any offers of support. She shrewdly asked her sister how much she was giving their mother and asked if Gypsy knew what Rose was worth before moving ahead. June ultimately arranged for fifty dollars a month to be sent to her mother, providing that Rose stayed out of her life. Getting those fifty additional dollars a month from June was to hurt Rose more than it helped her. If she had wanted to find a way back into her younger daughter's good graces, she was now being paid to stay away.

Rose wasn't finished with June and *Pal Joey* yet, though. George Abbott had arranged for show tickets for Rose after she had begged him for them when she had gone to his office pretending to be neglected and indigent. She arrived drunk and with a companion in tow to get her tickets, but June had already alerted the box office not to hand them over to her mother. Someone from the show got word to June that Rose was there. June went out to the box office and stood right in front of her mother, but Rose was reeling, slurring her words, and so stupefied she didn't know who June was. Fortunately June's husband, Donald Gibbs, was on hand that evening to take control of the situation. After sending Rose's companion on her way, he took his mother-in-law to a nearby bar. There he endured a three-hour-long diatribe in which Rose claimed her girls behaved like "heels" to her. It was the alcohol talking, but alcohol was beginning to affect Rose's view of reality.

Her actions were starting to alter June's sensibilities. June was so furious about this latest stunt that she was pushed nearly beyond reason. In the letter June wrote to her sister describing the embarrassing incident, she called the friend who had accompanied Rose to the theater a "lesbo," suggested that their mother should go to work digging ditches, and even called petite Rose "an Amazon." She also admitted to her sister that she wished "something" would happen to Rose, the clear implication being that she hoped their mother would drop dead. June's resentment was raw, and she was incapable of comprehending her mother's emotional situation. The break between Rose and June was now beyond irreparable.

In Seattle, Belle and Big Lady Anna were still living in genuine dire financial straits, and they too constantly mentioned money in letters to Gypsy, hoping for more. Gypsy was still sending monthly checks to them. In one memorable letter Belle wrote the spring of 1941, she informed Gypsy that she was trying to collect on a debt her first husband and the father of her son Norman, Reginald Rankin, had once owed Charlie Thompson. The debt probably was incurred around 1917, when Belle and Reg were married. Belle wanted Reg to repay the money by giving it to her mother, Anna. Charlie had passed away in the 1930s, so Belle had waited a long time to collect on it.

Reg did not send Belle money. He replied that he was not in a great financial place himself, which at that moment in time was a staggering understatement. Reg, who had a knack for thinking outside legal and societal boundaries, had realized that there were individuals making enormous amounts of money trading in illegal abortions. Reg approached the illegal abortion trade in much the same way that bootleggers had approached the sale of alcoholic beverages during Prohibition: as a legitimate enterprise that filled a need. He proceeded to recruit medical doctors, and even had the foresight to set up a loan organization to finance the illegal procedures. Reg became the business mastermind behind the largest abortion enterprise in the West, with practitioners providing services in several states. His net worth was estimated at one million dollars when the law finally caught up with him. At the moment that Belle contacted him, her ex was on trial. Reginald Rankin would be sent back to prison, and Belle gave up on getting any money out of him. She continued, though, to write letters to Gypsy filled with interminable tales of medical and financial woe. As she brazenly once told Rose, Belle thought that Gypsy would never miss the money that she threw her aunt's way.

Gypsy had been hard at work on her first book, *The G-String Murders*, and fans and friends could hardly wait to read it. June wanted an advance copy. The book came out in the autumn of 1941 and promptly became a bestseller. Gypsy did a wonderful job of writing about the world she knew best: the backstage goings-on at a burlesque theater. Out in California, Jack Hovick, who by then was the publisher of the periodical *Hiram's Masonic Journal*, was so thrilled for her that he included a note about Gypsy's book in his publication: "We just have to boast a little as our daughter got into the 'Best Seller Class' with her first book, *The G-String Murders*. . . . Maybe we can think of something to make Hiram sell like that." Gypsy loved the blurb so much that she cut it out and put it in her scrapbook. Her otherwise un-productive Hollywood stay a few years earlier had accomplished something great after all: It solidified her place within her father's second family.

The book enhanced Gypsy's reputation and led to additional assign-ments with magazines. She wrote an article for *Harper's Bazaar* in Decem-ber of 1941 about one of the magical Christmases Rose had created for her and the children in the Dainty June troupe when they were kids. Then Gyp-sy's first mystery was made into a movie, *Lady of Burlesque*, which would be released in 1943 with Barbara Stanwyck in the leading role.

Meanwhile Rose became involved with a much younger woman named Patricia Donovan in 1941. Donovan was a woman in her twenties, younger than both Gypsy and June. She was the niece of General William J. "Wild Bill" Donovan. A few months before the Japanese attacked Pearl Harbor, Wild Bill had been appointed by President Franklin Roosevelt as the di-rector of the newly formed Office of Strategic Services. This put Wild Bill in charge of all American espionage efforts during World War II, includ-ing the coordination of the Allies' attempts to assist resistance fighters in Nazi-occupied Europe. Rose Thompson Hovick found herself living with the niece of the preeminent spymaster of the free world.

All wasn't sweetness and light between Rose and Patricia. By January 1942, they had already broken up for the first time and were fighting over their communal property. Patricia must have given Gypsy a few presents that she later wanted to take back, because Rose sent Gypsy a telegram that seemed to be written as a means of getting their stories straight: "Pat gave you nothing. Avoid Miss Sanchez." Miss Sanchez was Pat's well-connected high society mother. The telegram also stated that Pat's family was "raising heel." Perhaps the phrase "raising hell" would have offended the telegraph operator in Nyack, New York, where Rose had taken a house on the estate of a gentleman named Fred A. Dibble. Gypsy, who kept her copy of the telegram, seemed amused by it.

Gypsy had begun work on another mystery. Walter Winchell reported in his syndicated Broadway column that the book would be called *Mother Finds a Body*. He explained that the author's mother once had found a body "when a pal committed suicide in their shack . . . . Cozy, isn't it?" This was not the optimal way to have a book project announced, but it was the start of the buzz about her second book. Within a few short months Hedda Hopper, in Hollywood, announced in her syndicated column that Mike Todd wanted Pola Negri to play a part in *Mother Finds a Body*. Todd was already thinking ahead, casting the film version although the book wasn't even finished yet. This was another positive development.

Gypsy's divorce from Bob Mizzy had at last been finalized in 1941, and for her, the divorce came just in the nick of time. She was in love with Mike Todd, with whom she collaborated on the show *Star and Garter*, a burlesque revue created to cheer up the American troops as they passed through New York City. The show appeared on Broadway disguised as a play, thus getting around the anti-burlesque restrictions that had gone into effect back in 1937. *Star and Garter* opened at the Music Box Theater in June 1942, and it was a hit.

Gypsy's love life was not going as well. She had chosen another inaccessible man. She continued to want to marry Mike Todd, and he continued putting her off. Gypsy's lack of romantic sophistication came to the fore when she decided to pair up with a congenial actor, Alexander "Bill" Kirkland, who adored her. She did not adore him, but she was sick of trying to convince Mike Todd to leave his wife. She and Mike had fights backstage at the Music Box Theater that were to go down in theatrical history for their ferocity and decibel levels, yet the fights didn't help. Threats didn't work. Nothing worked. Poor Gypsy. With everything to gain and nothing to lose she came up with a desperate backhanded maneuver. She staged an elaborate a wedding to Bill Kirkland at her Highland Mills house, hoping that it would push Mike far enough to come to his senses and rescue her from the marriage. She was still awaiting rescue as her wedding guests arrived. Bill Kirkland may not have cared if Gypsy went through with this strange wedding. He had recently been spurned by another woman but was secretly bisexual, so it wasn't a genuine love match on his end, either. This was to be a marriage of convenience for both Bill and Gypsy—and a mistake. They both knew as much from the start, but let the wedding take place.

Because she hadn't been banished from the wedding festivities, Rose may have been the only truly happy participant in the charade. Perhaps to milk the wedding for as much publicity as she could get from it—in addition to using it as a bargaining chip with Mike Todd—Gypsy had a grand time planning the quirky festivities. She chose August 31, 1942, Rose's fifty-first birthday, as the wedding date, selected midnight as the hour for the nuptial ceremony to begin, and pressed her pet monkey into service as the ring bearer. Gypsy sported a headpiece made from a bunch of grapes, which looked a lot more dazzling than it sounds. Somehow she also managed to rope in an Episcopal minister to preside over the whole extravaganza.

Gypsy's joy in the preparations evaporated as she dressed for the wedding in black, as if she were attending a funeral. Gypsy posted herself at her upstairs bedroom window, waiting for Todd's car to ride up the sweeping driveway of Witchwood Manor like Lochinvar in Sir Walter Scott's poem, in which the hero rides to rescue the fair maiden Ellen before she marries "a laggard in love and a dastard in war." But Mike didn't show.

Gypsy's guests knew nothing about any of this. She waited for Mike as long as she dared, then she emerged from her room and went downstairs for the ceremony and the party that followed. The affair was, after all, being covered by the press. *Life* magazine was in attendance, and so was *Spot*, along with Gypsy's friends Georgia Sothern, Max Ernst, Peggy Guggenheim, and the artist Pavel Tcheltichew, among others. Rose enjoyed the wedding ceremony more than her unhappy daughter, who in all probability had not confided the real reason behind it to her mother. A few press photographers took photos of Rose with Bill Kirkland's mother, Mrs. Gurlow Kirkland. Rose gaily called out, "Catch us quick, boys, because we'll only be radiant for a minute." The line wound up in Leonard Lyons's syndicated entertainment column. The marriage was doomed and, no surprise, lasted only four months. Gypsy's association with Mike Todd in *Star and Garter* would last longer. It continued until December 1943, over a year.

A more positive development came in October 1942, when Gypsy's second mystery was published. Called *Mother Finds a Body*, it was set in a trailer camp in Texas that was based on ones Gypsy had visited on her honeymoon with Bob Mizzy. She wrote it in the first person, used herself as a character called Gypsy Rose Lee, called Rose Evangie (a shortened form of Aunt Belle's middle name), and made her one of the main characters. Gypsy added, as other characters, various fictitious burlesque friends based on people she knew, such as Rags Ragland and Georgia Sothern. While Rose had definitely been the inspiration for the Evangie character, the book was still a work of fiction. The body Evangie finds in the story was the best man at the fictitious Gypsy's wedding, described as having taken place in a water taxi, just like Gypsy's real wedding to Mizzy. Evangie takes the body, which is found in the trailer, outside and buries it, and then the fun begins. The character of Evangie does a lot of strange things, but her bizarre actions turn out to be part of the plotline. A logical explanation ultimately is revealed when it becomes clear that Evangie's behavior was caused by an accidental dose of dope that had been hidden in her asthma powder.

Gypsy's blending of her own persona with fictitious characters worked in her mysteries yet caused boundless confusion in the minds of the public. Some readers believed that when Rose found Genevieve Augustine's dead body in the bedroom in Highland Mills, she took it outside and buried it, then had it dug back up. The presence of this new book on the market confused a lot of issues surrounding Rose. Rose did not like a lot of the stories that Gypsy was to write about her over the years, but she liked the character of Evangie. She wanted Gypsy to write a dramatic version of *Mother Finds a Body*—and wanted to star in it!

Mike Todd got along wonderfully with Rose. He was her conduit to Gypsy during the run of *Star and Garter*, especially when, once again, Gypsy temporarily stopped speaking to Rose. Mike was the only one who would take Rose's calls or speak with her when she came to the theater. He told Rose that Gypsy was so exhausted she was "ready for a breakdown," so Rose could not see her. Mike did not realize this line would only make a mother's concern for her daughter more intense. In a letter dated Christmas Eve, 1942, Rose begged Gypsy for the two of them not to "go another five years like strangers," telling her daughter that she could not go through that sort of exile again. "I need your love and attention more every day. Now I want to feel Xmas in my heart, but I just can't unless I hear from you dear."

Gypsy apparently was not planning on getting together with Rose any time soon—not even for Christmas. A year earlier she had written the article for *Harper's Bazaar* about the talent Rose had for creating marvelous Christmases for children, but this year Rose and Gypsy were on the outs again. Rose was heartbroken not to be spending the holiday with her daughter. Rose's letter sang the virtues of a new house she wanted to buy in the little town of Valley Cottage, New York. She gave details about the house's features, then concluding by joking, "A pipeless heater burns anything wood, coal (or bodies). Don't please use that last statement for the press." Gypsy had already gotten into the habit of telling the press amusing stories about Rose.

Rose included a mimeographed poem for her daughter. It was the inspirational "Don't Quit" by Edgar A. Guest. The poem concluded with this verse:

Success is failure turned inside out,
The silver tint of the clouds of doubt,
And you never can tell how close you are,
It may be near when it seems so far,
So stick to the fight when you're hardest hit,
It's when things seem worse,
That you must not quit.

Gypsy came through again, as she always would for her family members, and gave Rose $3,900 toward the purchase of the new house, located on a rural street called Ridge Road. The sum was enough to make a sizable down payment and get the house set up, but there was still a mortgage that Rose, who had an annuity, was supposed to pay off. The house was a cozy, two-story Cape Cod built in 1924, with a "praying hands" roof, two chimneys, three dormer windows, four bedrooms, a fully equipped indoor bathroom, and even a little wood house in which to store fuel for the spacious fireplace. It was situated on a four-acre plot of land, prettily landscaped with fruit trees, berries, flowers, shrubs and trees—all in all a lovely property. There were additional cottages, one containing four rooms and the other five, and both equipped with electricity, though not indoor plumbing. Each had its own outhouse covered with vines. The cottages were located in back of the main house, and Rose could merrily rent them out to boarders to bring in cash. There was plenty of land around this house, so Rose set up a new flock of chickens, bringing in still more cash from eggs. Adopting a new lot of animals, she was happy to begin to fill the place up.

Patricia Donovan was back on the scene and this time was destined to stick around for a few years. She was a tall, plain-faced brunette with shoulder-length hair who was absolutely crazy about Rose, to the point that she wanted to get a job and support her. Rose may not have mentioned to Pat that Gypsy was already supporting her and so was June. Pat moved with Rose into the Ridge Road house.

Then Gypsy Rose Lee's first piece for the *New Yorker* appeared on newsstands on April 10, 1943. It was a fabulously written story that she would later incorporate into her memoir, *Gypsy*. The story was entitled "Mother and the Knights of Pythias." It detailed how Rose would pretend to be stranded in a town with the girls, back before they went into vaudeville on the Pantages and Orpheum circuits. Rose would go into her favorite routine, faking hunger, telling the lodge mogul she was alone in the world with the children to support. The girls were supposed to fuss and cry as back up to this minor con job. Next Rose would request some hot soup from the lodge mogul, who would comply—and also get whatever lodge brother owned a theater to book Rose's act that night. The children would perform, and Rose would go home with a pretty profit in her purse.

Gypsy left out of the article the fact that Rose was still playing a variation on the same routine, except now she was the deserted stage mother rather than the deserted wife. Gypsy left out how Rose had tried the routine on Darryl Zanuck in Hollywood in 1938, and had recently tried it again on June's producer George Abbott. The terrible incident in Hollywood may have been what prompted Gypsy to select this episode from her childhood as the first she wrote about. As a means of trying to prevent further occurrences of Rose's starving stage mother gambit, writing about Rose and the mogul was nothing short of a masterstroke on Gypsy's part. Rose would be hard pressed to pull this kind of stunt on anyone again who employed Gypsy or June. Rose was not just embarrassed. She was mortified. There was nothing a mild-level rogue like Rose feared more than having the light of truth and reason shone onto her games. And there the article was on the newsstands, revealing so many of her most treasured techniques. Rose's new friends in Valley Cottage were able to buy the magazine and read all about her. On the plus side for Gypsy Rose Lee, Rose staged no more incidents posing as a poor, neglected and hungry stage mother visiting the offices of her daughters' employers and begging for soup. Rose would, however, soon make plans to put a few other, different stunts into action. It was about this time that Rose told her mother that she was considering writing a book about her life in the theater with June and Louise. The *New Yorker* article may have been what prompted this idea. She also hadn't seen her once-devoted daughter Louise in far too long, and she decided it was time for a new stunt. Rose settled on a strategy that would allow her to see her daughter—in court.

CHAPTER 15

THE LEGAL DEBACLE FOLLIES

ON MAY 12, 1943, ROSE HAULED GYPSY BEFORE DOMESTIC RELATIONS court in Manhattan for trumped-up "non-support proceedings."

If there was ever a daughter who did not deserve to have such an action brought against her, it was Gypsy Rose Lee. She had just handed Rose $3,900 toward her new house in the town of Valley Cottage. She also gave her mother a sizable allowance, supporting her in fine style, especially at a time when the majority of Americans were still just beginning to recover from the Great Depression. Rose's new house stood amidst four vast acres with fruit orchards and even featured two cottages in the enormous back yard. Rose, of course, lost no time renting them and pocketing the payments.

Gypsy hadn't exactly elevated Rose to the level of the Vanderbilts, Rockefellers, and Astors, but she made sure her jobless mother was comfortably ensconced within the Rockland County upper middle class. Nevertheless, Gypsy found herself brought before a judge, with Rose charging that she had "stopped financing her." Even more outlandishly, Rose, a woman who had raised her children in vaudeville surrounded by costumes and props and knew the value of each in setting a mood or a scene, came to court in a limousine that Gypsy had paid for. The vehicle was probably driven by her lover Patricia Donovan. And Rose dressed in the most inappropriate manner possible for a woman who was asking the court to obtain more support money from her daughter. Rose entered the court conspicuously displaying jewels and wearing a luxurious mink coat. And it was the middle of May in New York City. She chose to make a grand entrance, exiting the car in full view of the press. They shook their heads at the limo, the coat, the jewels, and Rose's audacity, then took delight in reporting to the world the incongruities surrounding her arrival.

It was one of those times when Rose's actions raised a host of questions that could never be satisfactorily answered because she never revealed her true motivation. If Rose wanted to win this case, the prosperous image she presented as she sailed into the courthouse defeated her purpose before she ever stood upon the witness stand. On the other hand, Rose may have been staging this whole insane sham just to get her name in the papers, while simultaneously stirring up maximum aggravation for Gypsy. Looking rich while crying poor could well have been her idea of a hilarious ploy to blackmail Gypsy. This fake case was certainly an unprecedented method for a mother to use in an attempt to demand attention from her grown daughter. Then again, going against societal norms never bothered Rose.

Rose might have been over-indulging in alcohol again, and that might have fueled the illogical nature of her lawsuit. More than any other possible reason for the court case, though, Rose's unhappiness with Gypsy's mockery of her in the "Mother and the Knights of Pythias" was in all probability what had inspired her. What better way than to humiliate her daughter than with a bogus charge that could be played out in full view of the press?

Once sworn, Gypsy denied the charge that she had ceased to give her mother an allowance. She gave the court details regarding her financial support of not just Rose, but also Big Lady Anna Thompson and Aunt Belle back in Seattle. She went on to explain that Rose was less than pleased with her for not handing over still more money to pay the income tax on the allowance that she gave her. Rose simply didn't want to pay it, despite having income from boarders that surely was more than enough to cover the amount. But paying income tax was simply not a part of Rose's belief system. She'd even thrown a pesky tax collector off her property years earlier when she had been living in Queens. Letting Gypsy pay her income tax, on the other hand, was Rose's idea of a wholly acceptable arrangement. Gypsy went on to tell the court that her mother wanted her to provide even more money so that she could finish paying off the rest of her mortgage and get a chicken farm up and running on her four new acres.

This legal brouhaha was the sort of hassle that most daughters would probably find too mortifying to want to recall, but Gypsy, who kept detailed records of how many times her name appeared in print every year, decided she wanted reminders of this odd event. The press had sided with her completely and hadn't fallen for Rose's stunts. She went home, cut articles about the court proceeding out of the newspaper, and pasted them in her scrapbook, preserving them for posterity. In contrast, she had not put any articles in her scrapbooks about the Genevieve Augustine case, where both her name and her mother's were mentioned in every article written about the case, which had been too unpleasant to warrant mementoes. This court debacle was worse, in a way, as it was directed at her by her own mother, but the articles also contained the first public mention of Gypsy's support of Big Lady and Belle. That alone would have made the clippings worth saving.

The case did not get Rose the financing for her chicken farm, but she wasn't finished seeking a new and easy way to obtain cash yet. This was only round one. On July 3, 1943, Gypsy Rose Lee's second article about her childhood in vaudeville appeared in the *New Yorker*. This one was called "Just Like Children Leading Normal Lives" and detailed the days when tutor Olive Thompson had taught Gypsy, June, and the boys in the act. The big finish to the story came when Rose berated the tutor for making June and Louise return a host of small items they had expertly shoplifted from Woolworth's. As the article made clear, the shoplifting hadn't been what infuriated Rose; she was mad as hell because the children had been forced to give the stolen articles back. This punishment had upset both of her sticky-fingered girls, particularly June, the star of the show, and immediately before a performance. No one was permitted to get temperamental June into an emotional uproar before a show, since when upset, June could go so far as to bang her head on the dressing room table. Rose had told off the tutor. Then she threatened to fire her. June's propensity for grand-scale hysteria had been left out of the story, so Rose's fury at the tutor was not adequately explained.

Rose almost certainly was infuriated once again over the new article. Her fury was not unleashed in a letter, so it may have been vented to Gypsy either in person or over a phone line.

Only a month after this second article appeared, two months after the hearing in family court, Gypsy did an about-face. She paid off Rose's mortgage, writing a check for over two thousand dollars. Rose now owned the Valley Cottage house, almost free and clear. There was still the matter of a second mortgage that Rose had on the property, but Gypsy may not have known about that one. Two weeks later, Big Lady sent a telegram to Gypsy from Seattle, asking for five hundred dollars for an operation. Gypsy, of course, arranged for her ailing grandmother to receive the money. "Everything possible being done thanks to you," Belle wired gratefully after the surgery.

With so many family members to support, it is a wonder Gypsy had so much as two nickels left to rub together. Fortunately she had just purchased a Manhattan townhouse on East 63rd Street at a bargain price. The basement was flooded, but she was having it repaired, then renovated. It was an investment in something she could keep for herself. She had also been working on a creative venture for more than a year. It was a semi-autobiographical play that went through a few title changes before Gypsy settled on *The Naked Genius*. The plotline concerned a bright stripper who wrote a book. During one of the times when Rose and Gypsy were getting along relatively well, Gypsy told her mother that there would be a character called the stripper's mother in the show. Rose mulled that over for a while, then wrote Gypsy with an inspired idea: *She* wanted to play the role of the stripper's mother in *The Naked Genius* when Gypsy, along with producer Mike Todd, brought the show to Broadway. The plan made perfect sense to Rose. She was the inspiration for the character, and she knew and understood the world of the theater and acting, so she believed she'd be the perfect choice to play the role that was based on her. Never mind that her ever-worsening asthma wasn't exactly conducive to appearing in live performances. She also offered her daughter an alternative. If Gypsy didn't want Rose to play the mother, Rose volunteered to be a part of the new play in any other capacity, even backstage. These were ideas that Gypsy, unfortunately, didn't seriously consider. Given the turn that circumstances would take, perhaps she should have.

⁂

Rose and Patricia Donovan's on-again, off-again relationship was tempestuous. Regular verbal battles energized them both. On September 27, 1943, Patricia was driving Rose in the car that Gypsy had bought for her. She drove it directly into a concrete pillar on West and Barclay Streets in Manhattan. The accident was horrific. It had apparently also been quite avoidable, because Patricia Donovan was immediately charged with felonious driving. She was going to get hauled into court.

Perhaps the two women had been fighting again in the car. Rose and Patricia were both heavy drinkers, so maybe Patricia had had one too many before manning the wheel. Whatever had transpired while Patricia was in the driver's seat that night, the brunt of the whole reckless situation was borne by Rose, who was riding in the front seat when Pat crashed the car. The impact of the accident sent Rose into the windshield, hitting it with great force. She was injured severely and in need of several sophisticated and intricate medical procedures. Her nose was broken and would have to be surgically reconstructed. Her whole face was a pathetically disfigured mess. She suffered a mangled, badly broken arm, which would require a separate surgery and cause her pain for years to come. Perhaps worst of all, Rose's delicate beauty was altered. She would never be the same again.

There was a degree of confusion about the car and the insurance papers for it. Patricia had also been hurt, but she had been protected from severe injuries by the steering wheel. Two weeks later, she had recovered enough to send a telegram to Anna Thompson requesting that any papers pertaining to the car be forwarded to Rose at Downtown Hospital in Manhattan. The papers were in Anna's name. Patricia wisely didn't include the information that she was the one who had been driving the car that injured Anna's daughter. Anna already disliked Patricia. Watching Patricia and Rose's verbal exchanges drove the entire Thompson family mad.

Patricia and Rose remained a romantic item for only a short while longer. Rose didn't ban Pat from her life immediately, and she didn't appear to think Pat had deliberately tried to murder her by crashing into that pillar. But Patricia's days with Rose were numbered, as the crash hastened the volatile relationship's end.

Gypsy Rose Lee rushed to her mother's hospital bed and offered emotional support. The nurses were all crazy about the still-charming Rose. Gypsy found the hospital staff dancing attendance on her mother. Everyone who dealt with Rose at the medical facility enjoyed having her around and pulled for her to get better. She was still a source of a great deal of fun.

Around the same time, Gypsy was heartsick over the downward spiral of the show she had been writing for a year and a half, The Naked Genius. Mike Todd was not gone from Gypsy's life yet, but was producing her show. The storyline of the comedy concerned a striptease artist, Honeybee Carroll, played by the Hollywood film star Joan Blondell. Honeybee was trying to earn respectability by writing a book, though it was actually penned by a ghostwriter who would try to blackmail her for hush money. Honeybee has a crooked mother who fences stolen underwear with a friend. The nefarious endeavors of the ghostwriter, the mother, and the mother's friend all have to be stopped. Honeybee also loves one man who cheated on her and agrees to wed another, hoping for her true love to come to her rescue. In the happy ending that Gypsy didn't get in real life, Honeybee's wedding is stopped in the nick of time when her true love arrives before she and the wrong man exchange vows.

Mike Todd had made changes to Gypsy's original draft, yet the storyline remained intriguing owing to what it suggested about Rose. Rose and her former companion Connie had been working a racket several months out of the year, as Rose mentioned in letters without giving specifics. Rose had

ingenious moments when it came to letter writing, knowing where to elimi-
nate specific details that might incriminate her. What scam had the two of
them actually been perpetrating with their unspecified racket? Were they
into something illegal? If they were, Gypsy surely cleaned the story up a bit
for public consumption by making "underwear fences" out of her two characters. Prohibition had been repealed by 1935, when Rose had met Connie,
so they hadn't engaged in bootlegging. The secret of the racket remains, but
the possibilities are deliciously endless.

It is astonishing that Gypsy would allow Mike Todd to produce this show
after everything that happened between the two of them, but she did. She
was still deeply in love with him and wanted him near her. For the show,
their partnership was a mistake. Todd's usual theatrical genius didn't extend
to being able to fix this production. He was up to something else entirely,
though Gypsy was not yet aware of it. Joan Blondell was being misdirected
in the part that had should have been played by Gypsy, and Mike didn't do
anything about that, either. Blondell wasn't hitting all of her laugh lines. The
story, despite a plot with several potential comic elements, just did not gel
on stage. George S. Kaufman, a multi-talented writer, performer, and director, was brought in to assist with rewriting the script. But Gypsy could see
he was making it worse, not better. She watched as the play she had labored
over was altered beyond repair.

As Rose lay in her hospital bed, Gypsy vented to her about every calamitous new development that was sabotaging the play. The two were as close
as they'd been before Gypsy became famous.

Rose remained hospitalized a month after the accident. Gypsy wanted
to stay close by her mother's side but could not get out of a scheduled trip
she had to make to Baltimore. She instructed her assistant, Josephine Healy,
to get Rose anything she might need. Once in Baltimore, Gypsy wrote
mother a letter full of endearments that began, "Joe Healy wrote me that
you were feeling better. I'm so glad, Honey. Keep it up! I was going to say
keep your chin up, but I guess they won't let you do that just yet." She was
right. On doctor's orders, Rose wasn't supposed to try moving her head yet.
Another line from Gypsy's letter reads, "I'm not going to throw my worries at you when you have so many of your own, nice thing." Honey and
nice thing— these are not terms used by a woman to address a mother she
doesn't love. They seem, instead, to belong to a devoted daughter, perhaps
one even slightly enchanted with her mom. Rose had that effect on a lot
of people. Gypsy also refers to her mother as darling and teases her about
flirting with the hospital interns. Rose may have been romantically involved

with women, but she never stopped batting her eyes at men, covering all potential bases. Gypsy's letter to her was warm and loving. It was also filled with additional details about her disastrously imploding play.

The Naked Genius opened on October 21, 1943, at the Plymouth Theatre on Broadway to atrocious reviews, just as Gypsy had predicted. This reception was a terrible blow to her, but not the only one the hardworking woman would live through on that horrible opening night. Even worse was the emotional punch Mike Todd dealt her when he admitted he would finally be divorcing his wife, news she had long awaited. But he would not be marrying Gypsy. He was dumping his wife *and* Gypsy. Instead, he was marrying the star of the show Gypsy had written, Joan Blondell, their Honeybee Carroll.

Todd kept the play open for thirty-six performances because he would not be able to get his share of the movie rights to the script if the production didn't run for at least that long. He was to get $187,000 for film rights. Fortunately Gypsy also got her share, $100,000, which was probably the welcomest sum she had ever received.

On November 20, 1943, the morning before *The Naked Genius* closed, a third Gypsy Rose Lee article appeared in the *New Yorker*. This one, "Mother and a Man Named Gordon," again put Rose in an uproar. She felt it was the worst one yet. It revealed Rose's deliberate bewitching of Murray Gordon Edelston, whom she charmed into becoming the manager of June's vaudeville act. Rose lowered the boom on Gypsy within a week. She found out that the character of Honeybee Carroll's mother in *The Naked Genius* carried a chicken around in her arms and had a racket as an underwear fence. Had she been given a part in the production, Rose might have laughed this characterization off, but she hadn't been included. She did not like being the punch line of her daughter's amusing stories. She had opened a small chicken farm, similar to the one she'd had in Highland Mills, on her new Valley Cottage property, so the chicken prop was a definite reference to her. It was clear that the character up there on the stage was not a work of fiction.

Rose was too upset to appreciate that Gypsy Rose Lee had a talent for taking people she had known in her life, changing a few identifying details, then tweaking actual events to make them funnier. But Rose didn't enjoy being used as a subject and found these creative edits to be profoundly humiliating, since they altered the facts of actual scenarios and made her look worse. To her daughter, Rose was a source of material that was too funny to keep to herself. Yet Gypsy should have thought twice about publishing amusing tales about Rose while the woman was still living. Her writing was unintentionally harmful to Rose, upsetting her greatly and leading her to write a torrent of unhappy letters to Gypsy. Rose was embarrassed by the stories, especially this latest one, around her lesbian friends, since the whole world now knew the details of the seductive techniques Rose had used on Murray Gordon Edelston. This was, without a doubt, the last sort of information the late-blooming lesbian wanted to see circulated about herself before the entire nation. Rose had put up with Gypsy's embarrassing compositions long enough. She would turn her misery around and give it the force of a boomerang thrown at her literary daughter. Never afraid of a fight, Rose vowed to get even.

Rose instructed her attorneys to focus primarily on the play, probably because "Mother and a Man Named Gordon" contained more truth than she wanted to admit, but her lawyers' battle plan included taking on the magazine, too. Rose's attorneys proceeded to send letters threatening lawsuits to everybody involved with her mortification: Gypsy, Michael Todd, F-R Publishing Corporation, the play's publishers, Twentieth Century-Fox Film Corporation, which was slated to film the movie, and then, last but certainly not least, the publisher of the *New Yorker*. All found themselves threatened with legal proceedings for injunctive relief and substantial damages. The notice served on the *New Yorker*, in particular, must have given Rose satisfaction.

This time Rose's legal complaints had a degree of validity. They worked. An agreement was drawn up between Rose and Gypsy. Rose basically sold Gypsy the rights to use her as a character in the movie version of *The Naked Genius*, which would be filmed under the title *Doll Face*, for $33,000, a whopping sum in 1943 and the equivalent in 2011 of approximately $412,000. The movie studio slated to film *Doll Face* was Twentieth Century-Fox, where Gypsy had toiled in 1937–38 and where Rose had invaded Darryl Zanuck's office in rags. This studio already knew about Rose. Twentieth Century-Fox wrote the character of the mother completely out of the script. The word was out: Twentieth Century-Fox didn't want to contend with Rose.

For her $33,000, all Rose had to do was agree not to sue the group involved with the movie. She agreed quite happily. This was the easiest money she had ever made. But Rose led the whole team on a merry chase by not signing the agreement for two long weeks, letting them wait and wonder just how she might proceed. Rose worked fast once she obtained the money. In less than a week she repaid Gypsy for nearly three thousand dollars in hospital bills that her daughter had covered after Rose's accident. She also repaid the couple that held her second mortgage. The rest went straight to the Equitable Life Assurance Society, underwriters of an annuity that provided Rose with additional.

Sadly for Gypsy, Mike Todd would now no longer consider casting Pola Negri, as Hedda Hopper had reported he had wanted to do when he first heard about *Mother Finds a Body*. He would not be casting any other actress, either, in a film version of Gypsy's second mystery book. Not after Rose's lawsuit. The book would be published a year later, but it was never made into a film. No Hollywood film studio head in his right mind wanted to take on Rose and her attorneys.

ა

It was Christmastime again. June was in Boston for the out-of-town tryout of a new musical, *Mexican Hayride*. This time she had landed a starring role. She was handed a costume that was ready to burst at the seams and create an inappropriate display before a live audience. June contacted Gypsy, who had been sewing and altering costumes since childhood, with a request to pay her a visit and help with emergency alterations.

The theater had become a substitute for a home when June was a child. She loved it still, possibly more than she had ever loved anything or anyone else. There was nothing like the warm feeling she got from the audience. On opening night in Boston, they once again embraced her, and June felt she was home at last.

For her part, Rose got to make yet another court appearance during the holiday season, this time to testify in Patricia Donovan's reckless endangerment trial. Clad in furs, Rose fainted, or perhaps feigned a faint, while waiting to take the stand. A policeman carried her away from the courtroom, and that got Rose, who was misidentified as Anne Thompson, into the newspapers on Christmas Eve. Aside from the excitement of the news item, Rose spent a lonely Christmas without her children. Her string of debacles during the spring, summer, and autumn had made it pretty much inevitable that her girls would avoid her now. Even so, her daughters' lack of contact with her hurt her and made her ache inside.

Fortunately she received a piece of welcome good news after the New Year. Rose's sister Belle was planning to come from Seattle to New York to stay with her for a time, since Rose was still in considerable pain after her accident and very much alone. Her broken arm remained in a cast, rendering it useless and not conducive to running a chicken farm. Rose was downhearted, and the more ebullient Belle could not wait to stay with her sister and nurse her back to health. Besides, Belle was a survivor. She wrote to Rose, "I know you have gone through a terrible experience with your accident and of course you are discouraged being left with your face and arm as they are—But Honey time is a great healer and I am sure I can help you pull out of all that—I have had nothing but sickness and accidents all my life so I can realize fully just how you feel."

It was almost incredible, but Belle, who had not been exaggerating about her lifelong physical complaints, nevertheless retained a positive attitude, and she wanted to share it with her injured sister.

It's also an indication of Belle's character that she did not hesitate to leave her bedridden mother's bedside to go care for Rose. It could not have amounted to much of a holiday for Belle to go from caring for one ailing family member to the other, yet she still proposed to make the trip. Belle and Big Lady Anna continued to live a hand-to-mouth existence. There was an allowance from the ever-generous Gypsy, plus Charlie Thompson's pension from the Great Northern Railroad, but for two women with no other means of support it all added up to a pittance. Belle's mobility was forever affected by her stiff leg and limp. By this point Anna was seventy-five years old and almost entirely bedridden.

It amounted to Belle remaining pretty much stuck. The two ladies had been having a tough winter. There had been plenty of the usual Northwestern rain, and quite a number of Seattle residents, including Belle, had suffered from colds or flu. Belle confided to her sister that she could not even afford a new winter coat, because the little house where she and Anna lived needed so many repairs. Yet she did not hesitate to pay for train fare to head in Rose's direction.

It was arranged for Belle to take care of Rose while a friend came to stay with Anna. From this point onward, Belle was to become a steady and mostly stabilizing influence on Rose's life. She was also the one person who truly seemed to love Rose unconditionally. Sometimes, when the two would argue, hanging on to her loving feelings for Rose was all but impossible for Belle. Yet Belle could never resist forgiving Rose, and she would always try to reach out to her.

On the other hand, Belle didn't want to deal with Patricia Donovan or any of Rose's female lovers. There had been friction between Belle and Rose's companions before. It irked Belle to see her one remaining sister so close to other women when she felt Rose should have been close to her. Anna loved Rose, too, but didn't love or approve of Rose's lesbianism. Rose, of course, was not about to change anything at the behest of anybody, including her mother. Anna found the whole situation untenable. She wanted Rose to give up living with women, telling her in a letter that she was "born normal" and should live in her nice Valley Cottage house alone. It was still possible, she counseled, for Rose to find a husband to ensure she'd be well provided for in old age. Anna assured Rose that "everyone makes mistakes" and added, "I love you as always and want to see you try to put a little happiness in your life."

Of the remaining collection of letters exchanged between Rose and her family members, the majority of those commenting negatively on Rose's choice of female companions were date-stamped immediately after she was nearly killed by Pat Donovan in the automobile accident. Belle didn't want to stay in Rose's house with Pat, Anna didn't want Rose to be involved with Pat, and June had quite a few unflattering things to say about Pat in a letter she sent to Gypsy. Pat didn't seem to have a single friend among Rose's relations. They were probably none too pleased when Pat was finally hauled before the magistrate on February 8, 1944, to hear the verdict on the reckless endangerment charge: She was pronounced innocent. When she and Rose finally broke up shortly thereafter, Rose's family was delighted to see Pat go.

Pat returned to her New York City apartment on West 58th Street. Belle made haste to New York. A highly creative woman despite her constrained circumstances, Belle had several enterprising propositions that she wanted to discuss with her sister. Primary among them was the very plan that she, Rose and Anna all live together in either Valley Cottage or Seattle, and that she and Rose perhaps open a restaurant or shop. They could share the burden of caring for Anna, thus lessening it for Belle, and Rose would no longer have to feel so isolated, especially since she was still effectively exiled from her children and newly without Pat.

June, meanwhile, had opened in *Mexican Hayride* on Broadway and was making a lot more money. Maybe in order to put a move to Seattle into action, Rose planned to relieve her youngest daughter of some of her salary. She obtained the services of another attorney, Charles Finkelstein of Manhattan. Rose's hope was to bring June into family court this time. Rose's attorney offered June the option of contacting him, or having her lawyer do so, to settle the matter quietly and amicably. June had moved in with Gypsy and was sharing her townhouse on East 63rd Street. Rose knew about this arrangement, because that was where Finkelstein sent his letter. It hurt Rose deeply that her daughters were now residing together in such a spacious house, while she was still, in effect, banned from joining them. Threatening them with more legal action was the last move that would ever have resolved this estrangement problem, but Rose often seemed to feel that doing something, no matter how outrageous, was better than doing nothing.

Gypsy soon returned to Hollywood to star as Belle De Valle in the movie *Belle of the Yukon*, a title that must have amused both her grandmother, who had sold clothing creations to prostitutes in the Yukon, and her Aunt Belle. Anna was more concerned about Rose than ever; she felt her daughter would be left completely alone and devoid of family members in New York when Gypsy headed back to Hollywood again, particularly if she were to stay. Belle and Rose, with Anna chiming in via letter, continued mulling over the idea of living together rather than being split between two coasts. By the end of April, Rose had contacted a broker with regard to selling her Valley Cottage property, which now included a chicken house large enough to hold a total of one thousand chickens.

Then Pat Donovan resurfaced. Rose heard once again from Pat's mother, Mrs. Frederico Guillerno Sanchez. At one point Pat had impulsively gifted Rose with some of the Donovan family's heirloom china. Now, Pat wanted it returned, so she got her mother into the fray. Mrs. Sanchez wanted the china back immediately; she was threatening to see Rose in court otherwise.

Rose, as usual, did not take well to being ordered by anybody to do anything. So Mrs. Sanchez wanted the china back, did she? Well, Rose had given Pat a watch, and if Mrs. Sanchez wanted the china back, then Rose decided that she wanted the watch back. Rose's attorney Charles Finkelstein had to get involved in the latest fracas, intervening on Rose's behalf. It apparently took him a sizable amount of time, not to mention considerable use of every persuasive technique in his arsenal, before the two prima donnas agreed to bring the watch back.

Urgent news came from Anna Thompson in Seattle: She was unsteady, kept tripping and falling, and needed Belle, who was still in Valley Cottage, to return home post haste. The situation was bad, worse than anyone knew. Anna didn't realize it, but she was one month away from suffering a stroke. Belle went back to Seattle.

Rose was served with a summons thanks to the continuing machinations of Patricia Donovan and her mother. Other items were now in dispute, ones that Rose was "holding hostage," such Pat's clothing. Pat had left a diary and other personal writings in Rose's house. She desperately wanted them back. There was also the matter of an unsettled one hundred dollar IOU. At that point, Rose re-evaluated her feelings about another court appearance. She was slated to be the defendant, for a change, rather than serving her preferred role as plaintiff. She and Pat were fighting over what amounted to communal property after the break-up of their relationship, and if their relationship came to light, it might cause yet another problem, since lesbianism was still illegal and under the domain of the vice squad. A hearing might also lead to bad press for June and Gypsy, which would not help Rose to reconcile with either daughter or gain residence privileges at Gypsy's mansion. For perhaps the first time in years, the prospect of a courtroom appearance did not fill Rose with glee. She wanted to get out of this one.

Charles Finkelstein knew how worried and scared Rose was. In a kind letter written on June 6, 1944, Finkelstein promised that she would be released from all liability if she would only return the clothes, china, diary, etc. to Patricia. He suggested that Rose bring these things to him so that he could arrange their transfer to Patricia and her mother, thus putting an end to the whole mess. It was a decent plan, but by June 9, Finkelstein was surprised to find he had still not received a reply.

There was long-distance trouble brewing between Rose, Belle and Anna now. Belle and Anna had sent Rose a wire, urging her to proceed with a move to Seattle, and Rose sent back a reply that was strongly and unpleasantly worded. Rose's house hadn't sold, her arm was still in a cast, and the summons remained hanging over her head, so she had reason to be more on edge than usual, but the letter only served to create more distress, this time with her mother and sister.

A full month later, Charles Finkelstein wrote to Rose again, trying to discover why she had not responded to his letters. He had gone to a lot of trouble to straighten out the matter between Rose, Patricia, and Mrs. Sanchez, and could not fathom why Rose was ignoring him. Rose may never have responded to the devoted Mr. Finkelstein. She simply found another attorney. This was a fortunate development for June; with Finkelstein out of the picture, Rose's plan to bring June before a judge evaporated, at least for the moment. Frederick R. Engels of Nyack became Rose's new lawyer. He an affable man and would be Rose's best friend for the rest of her life. It was Frederick Engels who untangled the last messy remnants of the Donovan break-up for her.

Maybe Rose initially held the Donovan property back as long as she could because in returning them she would lose her connection with Patricia and probably never see her again. Rose couldn't bear to be alone, and she was alone now. Belle could have used her help in Seattle. All of the falls Anna had been suffering resulted in a diagnosis. She had had a stroke, and Belle was having a harder time caring for her than ever. Yet Belle and Anna were not the housemates Rose truly wished for. While she did like the idea of joining them, she vacillated about leaving Valley Cottage permanently. Her hesitation stemmed from not wanting to pack up and move to the West Coast while her daughters were together in Gypsy's Manhattan. If Rose relocated to Seattle, she'd be too far away to get the chance to live with June and Gypsy again. Rose didn't yet know that Gypsy, out in Hollywood, was expecting a child of her own and would soon become a mother herself.

CHAPTER 16

WEST COAST WHIRLWIND

ROSE HAD NO IDEA THAT WHILE SHE HAD BEEN CAUGHT IN THE QUAGMIRE of a minor war over Patricia Donovan's clothing, diary, and personal papers, out in Hollywood Gypsy had been seeing Otto Preminger, a cultured Austro-Hungarian movie director. He was the father of Gypsy's unborn child. Otto was a Viennese Jew who had already been extremely lucky. He had moved to the United States in 1935 to accept a job working for Darryl Zanuck at Twentieth Century-Fox, arriving in plenty of time to escape the encroaching Nazi stranglehold on Europe.

The identity of her baby's father was to be Gypsy's best-kept secret. She was still officially married to Alexander Bill Kirkland. Though the marriage was dissolved by divorce in October 1944, Gypsy would, with Bill's consent, give the child her ex-husband's surname in order to make her baby look legitimate. It was the same strategy June used when she gave birth to April and gave her Weldon Hyde's surname. Gypsy did not want her baby to have to bear the taboo of illegitimacy any more than June had wished to inflict it on April.

Rose wrote a missive to Gypsy, claiming that she was about to lose the Valley Cottage house and pleading to live with her daughter. This letter was almost certainly another of Rose's ploys. The property wasn't in foreclosure; Rose already owned the house outright. She wasn't in any danger of losing it. In fact, Rose retained the house until the day she died. So she rented the place out in order to make a profit from it and settled temporarily in a Greenwich Village apartment. Part of the strategy behind this Manhattan move might have been to find a significant other to replace Patricia Donovan. Rose was miserable living alone.

A stroke of rare good fortune soon came Rose's way in the form of a job as the hospitality desk manager at the Hotel Plymouth on 49th Street and

Broadway, next door to Radio City. Once again, she was headed towards the type of venue where her family always felt most comfortable, a hotel. Rose's job had started out as June and Gypsy's lawyer's idea. He told Rose that June was not going to help support her financially and suggested that if she wanted additional money, she needed to get a job. It had taken until 1944 for someone to state the obvious. The job was a godsend, not because Rose—who had few genuine financial worries—really needed the money, but because she craved social interaction. Living in Valley Cottage on four acres of property, away from the activity of a big city, had been stultifying for Rose, as was the situation in Highland Mills. No matter how much better Rose's asthma improved in the Catskills Mountains area, her social isolation there had become unhealthy.

Rose's main job responsibility was to help hotel guests find places to go for entertainment. She wrote to her daughter, "I love it, Louise, and for the first time in years I am terribly happy." This was what Rose had needed all along. Rose kept writing to her daughters, but her letters often went unanswered, and that silence remained devastating to her. She was happy at work but still rather miserable about the estrangement. Spending ten dollars on a bender with friends didn't help. Rose's problem with booze was becoming worse, but she noted in her diary that she did not wish to repeat that particular performance, a step in the right direction.

Then Gypsy made a few more embarrassing statements about her upbringing to the press, and they infuriated Rose to the point that she wrote to tell both daughters. Gypsy had claimed she and June had had "no home" and hadn't attended school for "one day." The children's early lives had definitely been chaotic, what with Rose's marriages and divorces and the family's various moves, but they'd had homes, the most permanent one at their grandfather Charlie Thompson's house. Gypsy had also gone to school. "Public schools. Private school. A tutor on the road who saw you through grammar school," Rose furiously reminded her. She added that Louise had graduated with "a point of 95" in Minneapolis, along with Newsboy songster Georgie Triano. Louise may also have briefly attended a private boarding school, though the details are sketchy. She was to mention having spent a few weeks at one to the press, but the school she said she attended apparently never existed. Rose conveniently forgot that she herself had once bought June a giant-sized doll, and then had gone along with Murray Gordon Edelston when he told the press that General Neville had sent it to June from France as thanks for June's help selling Liberty Bonds for his campaign, an event that never happened. Fabricating tall tales for the press to enhance publicity for their old act had been one thing, but Rose wasn't at all happy when this tradition of twisting the truth was focused on *her*. Rose admitted that putting the children's act together had been her "brain child idea," but added that she "gave up the best years of my life to see you where you are." She charged that she "gave you my heart, soul and life all through your baby days up until you both got too great for me. Until you left me for some one else."

That searing last line reveals Rose's sorrow about her children having outgrown her, and sheds light on how she viewed June and Gypsy's relationships with men. These outside relationships clearly constituted a personal rejection rather than a normal progression. But Rose was the one who had given the children a central position in her life. She could just as easily have chosen to have them all remain in Seattle, living with her father, while Rose went to work to help support her girls rather than "giving up the best years" of her life by putting the children on the stage. Still, she had given them the theatrical background that allowed them to become as successful as they were.

Rose ranted on, threatening to write a book about her life with June and Louise. She added that her life with them had been "anything but a bed of roses." The letter included a dire warning: "Your [*sic*] big today, but you can be little tomorrow and when you do what you two girls are doing to your mother sometimes you have bad luck. God sometimes takes a hand in a case like ours." She continued by professing that both of her daughters were too much like their father, "The Jack Hovick blood shows up too much at times," thus putting her daughters' unhappiness with their unstructured early life squarely in Jack's lap. Rose still wasn't done. After her incongruous signature line, "Love, Mother," she added, "It doesn't do you girls any good to hurt me. Some day the public will know the truth about your mother and they I am sure will not condemn me like you girls have done. I have a clear conscience thank God for the way I raised you both and I know I did all I could for you with what I had to do with."

Perhaps this letter left a bad enough taste Gypsy's mouth, as she did not contact her mother when she went into labor a month later. The contretemps with Rose might even have sparked Gypsy's choice of her child's name. Rose's second grandchild, initially called Erik Lee Kirkland, made his entrance on December 11, 1944. Gypsy gave her baby a Scandinavian first name, a nod in the direction of "the Jack Hovick blood." Erik's proud Norwegian American grandpa was thrilled. For the rest of his life, no matter what Louise did, her father never failed to be happy with her. Jack's pride in her never abated. He was the antithesis of her mother. Rose did not get to see her grandson until a week after he was born. She never did gain access to the Gypsy's hospital room. When Rose paid a visit to the hospital, a nurse held Erik up for her to see through the glass window of the room where the newborns were kept. The new grandmother was hoping to spend Christmas with Gypsy, Erik, June, and April, but once again, that wasn't to be.

Rose may have only a teen when she'd married and given birth to her children, but she had been the nominal adult in their little troika, and she was the one who had chosen their vagabond lifestyle. All through Louise and June's childhood, Rose had seen herself as part of a close-knit three-some. The enforced closeness that she had with her two daughters during their vaudeville period may have been an unhealthy arrangement for all of them, but the girls had moved on, as most children do. Rose was left with the hardest battle letting go.

Otto Preminger came to see baby Erik while he was still in the hospital. He had not known why Gypsy Rose Lee left Hollywood as abruptly as she had after *Belle of the Yukon* finished shooting, but when he found out she was pregnant and realized it was with his child, Preminger didn't hesitate. He went immediately to see Gypsy and told her that he wanted to start supporting his baby son. Gypsy felt she had enough strikes against her after the whole brouhaha her burlesque background had caused. If the fact that she wasn't legally wed to her baby's father ever went public, Gypsy could bid her career farewell. It was better for her to support the baby herself, which she could certainly do, since she was already also supporting her mother, Big, Lady and Aunt Belle. She appreciated Otto's offer but declined it. In 1944, this was an astute move.

Within a few months, Rose, who still owned the Valley Cottage house, also began to manage 116 West 69th Street, a small apartment building in Manhattan. The owner was Felice Bryant Hull, a singer residing in Norwalk, Connecticut, who had inherited the property from a relative. Felice remained in Norwalk, putting Rose in charge of the property, and Rose split her time between the quiet of Valley Cottage and the action in New York City. She was, once again, participating in the family tradition of renting out spaces. It would only be natural for Rose to hope to see her grandson regularly, but she could settle for irregularly, if need be, by remaining in New York. Central Park and a few avenues were all that separated Rose's new residence from the house where June, April, Gypsy, and Erik were living on East 63rd.

Rose proceeded to rent out the various apartments. She was ahead of her time as a building manager. One of her first tenants was an Asian man, and Rose rented to him in the immediate wake of the Japanese attack on Pearl Harbor. She didn't stop at managing the building. She wanted to help her mother and sister in Seattle. Anna was on the verge of being sent to a county-run nursing home. Rose had an idea about a new use for her Valley Cottage property: She decided the two cottages in the back of the house could be utilized to house children in a little summer camp. That would bring in additional cash that could be shared with Belle and Anna. Belle thought the plan was fabulous. She suggested that since Rose had a huge Great Dane named Louiga, a small fluffy white dog called Little Mama, a cat named Fritzie, and even a parrot, Rose could even boast to the parents that she had her own little on-site zoo. Belle wanted to travel to New York and help Rose get everything ready, though leaving their mother was not a possibility. Belle's hope was that eventually all three of them could live together, this time in Valley Cottage. Rose was felled by an attack of asthma, causing the summer camp plans to get put on hold, but she still sent funds to her mother and sister. She was determined to go forward as soon as she felt up to the task.

Gypsy was going to be performing in Seattle and planned a visit with her aunt and grandmother. She especially wanted Erik to get a chance to meet Big Lady. Belle took on a special intelligence mission for her sister. While Gypsy was there, Belle was going to try to get her niece talking. She wanted to find out exactly why Gypsy was so estranged from Rose. Chances are, Rose hadn't told her sister about the hot soup stunts or the legal cases she'd brought against her daughter. Belle wasn't sure she would be successful in getting the information from Gypsy, but she was determined to try. She and Rose exchanged letters about the plan like two spies plotting a coup.

Gypsy, Erik, and Eva Moncur, Gypsy's maid, took an apartment in downtown Seattle because there wasn't room for the three of them in Belle and Anna's tiny three-room house. Seattle welcomed the whirlwind that followed in Gypsy's wake. Anna found herself being photographed with Erik and written up in the local newspapers. Belle attended Gypsy's show every night, then hung out in her dressing room afterwards, socializing. Even the neighbors on Rutan Place had a ball with Gypsy's visit, watching her comings and going in her Rolls Royce and seeing all the exciting press activity at Belle and Anna's place. Only Rose was left out. Belle wrote a profound line to her sister that could have applied to the situation with June, Gypsy, and Rose just as easily as to the one with Belle, Anna and Rose: "I wish you were here Rose—That is as it should be—Too bad our family has to be so divided—Either on or completely off each other—something surely wrong some where." Rose, meanwhile, opened her little camp for the first summer. She sent her mother and sister a happy photograph of herself surrounded by children.

Belle had also found a way to begin making extra money, despite her confinement. She was too creative to remain idle. She started crocheting bedroom slippers that she sold for five dollars a pair; she would eventually make and sell 650 pairs. The industriousness of the Egle and Herber ancestors may have been all but asleep within both sisters, but it coming to the fore now. A nice financial break came for Belle and Anna in 1947 when a new Seattle street was planned to run through the rear portion of their property. They were offered five thousand much-needed dollars for an easement.

Belle came to visit Rose in Valley Cottage again in the spring of 1947, on doctor's orders. The drudgery of her life caring for her mother had pushed her to the point of nervous collapse. Anna hoped Rose would take Belle shopping for new clothes and take her to see a few shows on Broadway. But this wasn't destined to be the two sisters' happiest visit. It started off with Belle escorting yet another sick person on the train from Seattle to Trenton, New Jersey, for which she got paid with a round-trip ticket and extra spending money. It may have been on this visit, which started out amicably, that Rose and Belle came up with the idea of running a chili parlor, popular food outlets at the time. They got in a car and drove around scouting for locations. A name was all picked out for this enterprise, echoing the name The Cherry Sisters, an infamous vaudeville acts: Rose and Belle would call their establishment The Chili Sisters. But the visit did not stay friendly, possibly because, as Benjamin Franklin observed, "Fish and visitors smell in three days." Belle stayed for five weeks. The sisters began to get on one another's nerves.

Rose had a new companion, coincidentally also named Pat. The new Pat was a nice lady and wasn't doing anything to endanger Rose as Pat Donovan had done, but Belle felt like a proverbial third wheel. Worse, Pat and Rose liked to argue. Fighting was a part of their relationship, verbal sparring constituting their idea of sport, and their battles drove Belle half mad. By her own admission, Belle never enjoyed sharing her only living sister with another woman. The lowest point for Belle—and possibly the highest point for Rose—came when Rose bought a sizable number of the clothes Belle had at a price Belle later described as "so damn cheap it was sinful." Belle went along with the deal in order to bring some cash home to Anna, but she resented the doing so. The two sisters spent the last portion of Belle's visit in open warfare.

Belle finally sent a letter to Gypsy, describing the situation with Rose as "impossible" and asking if she could stay in her niece's house for a few days, then go to some Broadway shows from there. She knew that Gypsy was out of town, and Belle wanted Gypsy to either call her at Rose's or respond to her there by letter. However, Belle instructed Gypsy not to put her return address on any response she might send, so that Rose wouldn't know they were in communication with one another. It was another tactic worthy of a spy. Since Gypsy wasn't in town she probably didn't get a chance to answer Belle's entreaty in time to let her aunt stay at her townhouse. Belle returned to Seattle, yet Rose continued the fight with her by deliberately not contacting either her sister or mother or sending them any money. Anna Thompson sent Rose a rather threatening letter two months later, since Rose had promised to help them and had not come through.

But Rose continued to ignore her mother and sister completely, her icy silence upsetting them more than a long-distance phone call that blasted everything out into the open might have. Rose unfortunately never seemed to realize that there were parallels between her situation with Anna and Belle and her relationship with Gypsy and June. All of these women tended to give one another the silent treatment, sometimes carrying the tactic on for years. It wasn't until four months later that Rose finally deigned to get back in touch with Anna and Belle, but she did so just to lambaste them. She was furious because Belle had promised to send her some rosebushes and raspberry plants when she got home to Seattle. These items had never arrived. Rose mentioned the woman who had been living with her, the second Pat, had to be sent away because she "got worse." The reference isn't clear. Rose signs off on this letter, "Love to you both."

Two months went by before Belle sent a reply. She had sent the rose bushes and raspberry plants to her sister, but they had been returned to her "as not acceptable," possibly by the post office. She explained the situation, then breezily continued the fight that had begun six months earlier, bringing up how Rose bought her clothes cheaply and accusing her of being unable to love anyone except herself and her pet dogs. That was the end of Rose and Belle's correspondence for quite some time.

June was out in Hollywood, appearing in a movie. On a double date with her agent, Barron Polan, and English actress Angela Lansbury, June met radio writer William Spier, who was Lansbury's escort. June was immediately enamored with Bill Spier. By the end of the evening, Spier found himself so charmed by June that he forgot all about Angela Lansbury. At the end of January 1948, June married Bill Spier, and she would remain with him until

Spier passed away in 1973. The third time was the charm: June had found the love of her life.

Rose tried to reach June by letter, begging her to forget the past. She received no reply. Of course, since her recent past with June included the drunken "hot soup" stunt in Mr. Abbott's office, June wasn't about to extend an olive branch.

Rose was still suffering complications from Pat Donovan's reckless endangerment stunt. Rose's arm was back in a cast. She had to make numerous hospital visits. A few of her teeth were pulled in an attempt to lessen the pain she still felt in her face. If she was becoming ever more mercurial and argumentative, her mods were aggravated by continuous pain. Gypsy, on the road, had sent Rose Christmas money, and she used it to get her eyes examined and to purchase reading glasses. Gypsy, at least, was making overtures toward her mother.

Gypsy also embarked on a third marriage. She tied the knot with Spanish artist Julio de Diego, becoming Rose de Diego in a civil ceremony held in the Bronx. Some delighted fans recognized her, cheered the couple, and even threw rice in their path. Rose now had two new highly creative sons-in-law in her family, one a writer, the other an artist. She finally decided to forgive Belle for the needless arguments the sisters had waged during Belle's last visit with her. Rose contacted Belle, who was the one person she could count on, asking her to visit again. She was sick, and she wanted her sister. This time Belle didn't bite. She contacted another resident of Valley Cottage, whom she called "Aunt Jennie," in an attempt to find out the truth of Rose's situation before boarding any trains. Belle gloried in playing at clandestine operations. It was a pity she was not very skilled at it. Aunt Jennie, whoever she was, handed Belle's letter over to Rose, and it would be preserved in Rose's voluminous correspondence collection. The letter surely led to a resumption of their fight, with the result that Belle didn't pay Rose a visit.

Belle came to the bitter decision that she would be infinitely better off if she pretended that Rose, like her other two siblings, Mina and Hurd, had already passed. Rose was too aggravating. Belle was going to have to simply take care of their mother without Rose's assistance, and that was that. Anna also had been missing Rose. Anna was eighty years old by then and convinced she would never see Rose again before she died. Two of Rose's closest relatives were both mourning Rose, and Rose was still very much alive.

Rose ignored Belle again and simply returned to the apartment house she managed in Manhattan, where she signed up new tenants and settled in for a New York City summer. When she finally called it was six months later, in the middle of October. Rose's nerves were shot this time, and her asthma was plaguing her. It was harder and harder simply to breathe. Rose would cough horrifically, unable to catch her breath. It was difficult to sleep or eat. She was desperately ill and, with medical science still decades away from finding an effective treatment, she longed for someone to give her a bit of loving care. Naturally, she thought of Belle. Despite their blow-up, Rose knew that Belle was, and would always be, the one and only relative who truly and unconditionally loved her. So, once again, Rose wanted to sell the Valley Cottage house, hoping to move back to the Seattle area to be with her mother and sister.

Or so she claimed.

Belle was jubilant over this encouraging news. If Rose came to live with them, Belle would have back up caring for their mother. Belle's only initial concern was Rose's collection of pets. She adored Rose's Great Dane, Louiga, but the gigantic dog was far too big for the tiny house where she and Anna lived. Anna was practically having a case of the vapors over the whole idea of Louiga's visit, and as Belle declared, "The neighbors too would probably faint at the sight of him." Rose's smaller white dog, Little Mama, would not be a problem to have in the house, nor would Happy Fritz the cat, but Louiga was a whole other gargantuan matter entirely. Anna suggested that Rose *board* him somewhere on the East Coast.

Belle had two money-making ideas for herself and Rose. She already started a sizable lending library of nine hundred books to bring in extra cash, so she asked Rose to bring or mail any additional books she had so that they could be merged into her collection. She also had an idea that involved all three of the women getting a summer home near one of Washington's Pacific beaches and operating a souvenir shop together.

By November, Rose had extricated herself from the apartment management job working for Felice Hull Bryant and was prepared to move, but naturally, given her respiratory condition, ongoing accident injuries, and fate, there were delays. The house hadn't sold yet. Some of her cottage tenants were moving to Connecticut at the worst possible moment; they might have been able to look after the property for her until it was sold, had they stayed. And it was proving impossible to find anyone to take charge of Louiga, even temporarily. Belle couldn't wait for Rose to arrive. Rose was set to leave in mid-November, 1948, before winter hit and made driving cross-country hazardous, and had still not been able to find anyone to take the dogs. So she told Belle she would be bringing five dogs along with her.

This was actually an underestimation on Rose's part, but she didn't wish to tell Belle that part of the story yet. Belle and Anna's tiny ranch house was not large enough to accommodate the Great Dane. Now they were going to have to accommodate the Great Dane, plus, they believed, four more animals.

Belle was not happy about the prospect of five animals—one of which was Louiga—coming to stay, but on the other hand, she was relieved to know that Rose and the woman who was driving her across the country wouldn't have to worry about any robbers overtaking them when they had such a dog as Louiga in the car. Anna advised her sister to place "asthma guns" all over the car, not to mention plenty of dog food, and proceed.

The new woman named Pat drove Rose to Seattle. It was amazing that she got Rose and her retinue there in one piece, because Pat was an active alcoholic. But Pat and Rose arrived in one piece—and with not five animals, but nine, six dogs, and three cats. All of these animals, Rose, and the ever-inebriated Pat descended upon Anna and Belle's one-story, three-room home. The tiny, well-kept, fir-shingled house didn't even have an attic or a basement to utilize for a little additional space, and suddenly they had to accommodate a menagerie. There was also Belle's little resident cocker spaniel. So that made ten animals, only one of which actually belonged there.

Initially Rose didn't last there more than a week. Belle loved the idea of having Rose all to herself, and Rose and Pat were an item, even though as pairs go they were an embattled duo that loved to argue and fight. Belle had been jealous of Rose's other girlfriends, and she was jealous again now. The situation didn't take long to blow up. Pat's mother lived in Los Angeles, and after only one week with Belle and Anna, Rose and Pat left. Rose took off for Southern California to "go with Pat to see her mother," or so she said. There was actually a whole other reason to head south. The real point of Rose's trip to the west involved a doctor in Fontana, California, who had developed an asthma treatment that Rose had heard about. So Rose went to California. Her contingent of nine animals didn't. They remained with Belle and Anna.

Rose went on to Fontana and stayed in a motel cabin. All went relatively well until the day someone robbed the car, where Rose had left her wallet. The proof of ownership papers for the car was lifted along with the billfold. She was now without money and without proof that the car was hers. Her ex-husband Jack, his wife, Elizabeth, and June were all living in Southern California, but Rose opted not to ask any of them for assistance. Instead, she appealed to Gypsy for money, promising to pay her daughter back once she returned home and could rent out the cottages behind her house again. Either the plan to stay in Seattle with Belle and Anna was called off due to some kind of a nearly-immediate blow-out that had happened shortly after Rose's arrival on Belle's doorstep, or it had never been her intention to stay there in the first place. Her letter to Gypsy asking for replacement cash after the robbery was sent in December of 1949, and she had only arrived in Seattle in late November.

For the next few months Rose changed her plans continuously, or so it seemed to Belle. Chances are that Rose had decided in advance exactly how she was going to play it. She bounced all over the Northwest but seemed to be having fun, despite driving her mother and sister nuts with her inability to reliably report in to them. Belle had tried to be a good sister to Rose. She tried to find a place in Seattle for Rose and her menagerie to live, believing Rose still wanted to relocate. But Rose kept her sister and mother up in the air about when she'd return to Seattle.

She was keeping June up in the air, too, or at least some of her past actions were. June was attempting to obtain what, for her, was almost unobtainable: a passport. She probably did not remember the passport for the phony trip to England that the family had applied for and received back in 1925, because she tried to start from scratch and get a birth certificate in order to apply for for a new one. Had she recalled the 1925 passport, she might have been able to ask officials to use the information it contained. June's attorney arranged for a contact in Seattle to search for her birth certificate, and the contact ultimately found one issued in June's full name, Ellen June Hovick, but with Gypsy's birth date in 1911. June noticed another error when she got her hands on a copy of her birth certificate, which proclaimed she was the "one child living of this mother." That was not a factual statement. Gypsy had been born first. To make matters more confusing, the certificate recording this birth in 1911 was not filed until the late 1920s. Rose was an unreliable witness, and she wasn't easily locatable at the moment anyway, as she was all over the West Coast. June decided to contact her father's second wife, Elizabeth Hovick, to see if she could shed any light on the whole murky subject. June explained that she was trying to paddle her way through an informational swamp.

Elizabeth set June straight about her own birth. Elizabeth was a fundamentally honest person and had heard about the girls' births. She told June that the certificate simply had to belong to Gypsy, who'd been born in 1911 in Seattle. June had not been born in Seattle at all, but in Vancouver, British Columbia, a fact June had heard vague rumblings about when she was a child, but which she had never really given much credence. June was actually a Canadian citizen, not an American. The battle to obtain June's passport was going to be fought a bit longer and now was involving officials in America's neighbor to the north.

Still somewhere in California, Rose knew that Belle wanted to open a Washington gift shop, so she found, and appropriated, 1,500 miniature telescopes, provenance unknown. She sent one up to Belle, who liked it and thought it would be a good item to give away on punch boards, where for the price of a chance a customer could punch out a tiny rolled scroll of paper, unroll it and see if he'd won a prize. As she waited for Rose to return, Belle was also working on creating striking ceramics she hoped to sell in the shop she longed to open.

Pat, meanwhile, decided to address Belle's jealousy over her relationship with Rose and sent Belle a lovely letter, hoping to smooth over the trouble between them. Pat was afraid Belle's jealousy had reared its head again, but Belle assured Rose that wasn't the case. She understood that her sister needed to live with another. She also knew that she personally couldn't love Rose in quite the way that Pat could.

Belle hoped that Rose and Pat would return to Seattle and they could all go forward with the gift shop. Rose and Pat finally returned to Seattle. They also stayed with Belle and Anna again, but only for two more months. After that, Rose and Pat headed back to Valley Cottage. Whatever else transpired at Belle's place, the plan for Rose to relocate to Seattle was scuttled once and for all. She had had it with Seattle. She was going home.

Belle's dreams of making money had been awakened by this visit from her sister. Rose may have gone home to Valley Cottage, but Belle's ideas weren't going to evaporate into thin air with Rose's departure. Not this time. Belle was more determined than ever to make them happen. Maybe Rose's disastrous visit was the catalyst for doing so. Shortly after Rose's departure for New York, Belle wrote Gypsy a letter that may very well have been more of a work of fiction than an actual recounting of recent events. Belle may have loved Rose more than just about anyone else, but she wasn't above using her to better her own situation. Despite all of Belle's recent loving letters to Rose—one of which had ended "Lots of love to Pat as well"— she told Gypsy about the Rose, Pat, and pets invasion, then called Pat "a lousy person" and a drunk. There was more. Belle said the doctor who lived across the street from her had pronounced Rose dangerously crazy. Then Belle moved in for the kill. She claimed that Rose had somehow managed to "steal her blind" and also had run up bills that she had charged back to Belle. No documentation of these bills was included with the letter. No itemized list of how much Rose had allegedly taken Belle for was included, either. Belle proceeded to ask Gypsy for $750 to help her open the gift shop. To Belle's credit, she also suggested that Gypsy not send her any additional support money until Belle repaid this loan.

Gypsy, of course, didn't hesitate. She wrote Belle a check and even sent her new awnings to use at the shop. Belle was now set up in business. Rose's visit turned out to be profitable after all.

CHAPTER 17

BED REST AND BLACKMAIL

IT WAS AS IF BELLE HAD BEEN LET OUT OF JAIL. SHE OPENED HER LITTLE souvenir shop at picturesque Copalis Beach, Washington, and began making a go of it. She called the store Betty Thornton Souvenirs, since Betty was her preferred nickname. Only the immediate family still called her Belle.

Belle was also finally out of the miniscule house where she'd cared for her mother, and was residing instead beside the Pacific Ocean. The fishing was grand, people could drive their cars on seventeen miles of beaches, and digging for clams was one of the major attractions. Clams, game, and salmon were so plentiful that the area attracted a lot of poor people who were down on their luck.

Belle, described by a child of Copalis Beach resident Louis Stewart as "kind of a little rough around the edges, but a sweet person with a heart of gold," quickly endeared herself to the local children by buying the shells and glass floats they found on the beach. According to Eileen Owens, another of the children who grew up knowing her, Belle was one of the nicest shopkeepers at the beach. Belle was still attractive, despite her crippled leg, and she would become the self-appointed grand dame of Copalis Beach, a beloved and rather glamorous character in the small community. Eileen Owens recalled Belle wearing scarves around her head in a style that would soon be popularized by Lucille Ball. The tone of Belle's letters improved. Rather than minutely recounting both her mother's medical symptoms and her own, she started writing about beach rides and clam digs.

The little shop was Belle's first step in the right direction, carrying on the family's tradition of owning and operating hospitality outlets.

Gypsy soon found herself in the midst of a rather dangerous imbroglio, given that the Red Scare was in full gear. An irrational but prevailing fear during that era was that communists had infiltrated the entertainment industry and that the Hollywood reds would be using shows and films to indoctrinate the masses. In June 1950, a publication with the alarmist title *Red Channels: The Report of Communist Influence in Radio and Television* appeared. This little volume accused 150 performers, writers, and directors of having communist affiliations. Most of the accusations leveled by the unnamed authors were invalid and inaccurate. The same organization that published *Red Channels* also financed a weekly tome called *Counterattack: The Newsletter of Facts to Combat Communism*, which even accused First Lady Eleanor Roosevelt of being a communist sympathizer. Gypsy Rose Lee was included in *Red Channels* mainly because she had performed at events allegedly held on behalf of communist front organizations. One such group was the New York Council for the Arts, Sciences, and Professions. The weekly also accused her of having spoken at the Hollywood Anti-Nazi League. Gypsy said she was never at the event in the first place.

Gypsy was listed a total of five times in the publication.

This was a major blow that would cost her two good jobs she had emceeing quiz shows on ABC Radio. Gypsy hotly denied all of the charges that had been listed in *Red Channels*, but she was luckier than some despite losing two jobs. Quite a few other people in entertainment wound up blacklisted owing to alleged Communist affiliations, but she wasn't one of them. The brouhaha eventually died down.

Rose was under a microscope, too. Belle had heard from her sister that Rose was in trouble with the IRS. She had listed Anna and Belle as her dependents, and someone at the IRS uncovered the discrepancy. The situation was dire enough and Belle, despite the horrid winter she'd just experienced with Rose and her retinue, was worried about her unpredictable sister. She was terrified that Rose would have to serve time. Rose asked Belle to back up her version of the story in the event an investigation was launched, and Belle loved her enough to agree. She told Gypsy she "wouldn't see her in the pen or such like." Fortunately, the matter was straightened out.

Rose wasn't able to enjoy herself for long. She was having medical problems and, predictably, used them to try to obtain additional money from Gypsy. "Two daughters living in mansions, with everything and I can't get decent medical care from either one," she starts a letter written to Gypsy in October of 1950. "What an awful thing you are both going to answer for," she rages on. "I do feel sorry for you both. Just God pity you. I wonder if you really are a Communist Louise? God alone will surely punish you for your treatment of me." Rose couldn't resist. She just *had* to toss that communist line in there like a grenade. Rose was not indigent; far from it. She not only had an allowance from Gypsy, but enjoyed additional income from her annuity, the eggs from her thousand chickens, cottage rentals, and camp fees. Before she became dangerously ill, Rose sent another letter to Gypsy, on a day when she was in a more pleasant mood and hoping to get together with her to straighten out their relationship: "I am still the funny mama I always was to you, and you will always be the grandest thing in the world to me." But then her condition worsened. So did her bills.

By the spring of 1951, Rose was in severe pain and hospitalized at Good Samaritan Hospital in Suffern, New York. Her situation was already dire. She was suffering from cancer of the rectum, and little could be done. Rose needed to have her colon completely removed. Her prognosis was not good. If she were released from the hospital, for the rest of her life she would have to wear a colostomy bag. Her latest companion was another lesbian with a drinking problem. She was helping Rose, who was receiving transfusions in her hospital bed in preparation for the life-threatening surgery, cook up new trouble for Gypsy. Rose deputized her pal to contact the *New York Daily Mirror* with a sob story about Gypsy and June's "neglect of their mother." The friend was instructed to tell the *Daily Mirror* that Gypsy refused to see her mother and that June had flown off to Paris to avoid Rose. The *Daily Mirror* people contacted Gypsy, tipped her off about Rose's friend's statements, and chose not embarrass her by printing the story.

Rose required surgery, a long hospitalization, two private nurses, and another home nurse after she was released. The medical bills would be major. Gypsy took on the expenses, naturally. She also asked her sister if she could kick in and help pay a part of the costs. She hadn't wanted to ask June earlier for money for Rose, due to the fact that June had April to support, but now Rose's condition was going to prove costly.

Rose's companion didn't just call the *Daily Mirror*. She called Anna and Belle in Seattle, too—at the astonishing hour of two o'clock in the morning Pacific Time, terrifying Anna, who picked up the phone. The caller was inebriated and was incomprehensible in her description of what was going on with Rose in New York. Belle could barely decipher the lady's speech, either, when she took the phone from Anna. But she managed to comprehend that Rose was sick, hospitalized, in pain, and uncharacteristically frightened. Rose apparently knew that she might not survive, so she wanted Belle by her side. Drop everything, the caller slushed and slurred to Belle, and fly across the country to your sister. Belle was not in a position to pack up and leave. Handing over the cash for an airline ticket wasn't an option. Besides, how far should she believe this, coming as it was from a wild-talking, drunken stranger on the telephone in the middle of the night?

Belle called Rose directly at the hospital the next day. She was able to confirm how alarmed Rose was about the upcoming surgery, and she learned how much Rose wanted Belle by her side.

Then Rose changed the subject to one she considered much more pleasant and Belle got treated to an earful of juicy gossip. Rose told Belle all about how she and her friend had been contacting the newspapers about Gypsy's and June's "deliberate" neglect of her, telling her that June had gone off to Paris and Gypsy hadn't been answering her phone. The newspapers, according to Rose, would soon break the story. This was the exact same tale that reporters at the *Daily Mirror* had stopped.

No record exists of June's alleged trip to Paris under any of her surnames. And it is inconceivable that Gypsy Rose Lee, who had lost the two radio jobs and was always on the lookout for a way to make as much money as possible, would deliberately not have answered her telephone. Gypsy had traveled to Rose's bedside and was horrified at her mother's situation, so she hadn't neglected to visit Rose in the hospital. There had, however, been times that both June and Gypsy had not replied to Rose's summons, and Rose was probably using such occasions as inspiration for telling the media a tall tale now. Belle was not taken in by this story. Instead she was furious. She had gone to Rose when her sister had been hurt in the car accident, but Rose had never gone to Belle whenever either she or their mother had been hospitalized. Rose's self-centeredness had annoyed Belle beyond all recognition for years, and her longstanding but unexpressed anger came to the fore now. Besides, she didn't like Rose's latest plans to embarrass Gypsy and Gypsy in particular had been the financial savior of them.

So Belle told Rose off via long-distance telephone. She shouted out a few choice sentiments she had never dared utter before. Belle told Rose, "for God's sake take it [the surgery] on the chin like we have all had to do." Belle did not stop there. She added that Rose should not try to cause her daughters any more grief with the newspapers and to concentrate on anything other than vengeance. Later, Belle felt badly about her conversation with Rose. She also felt terrible that she could not go straight to her sister. Rose had driven quite a few people away from her by then, and Belle felt sorry for her. She actually didn't want to leave her sister to face the surgery alone, but it just wasn't possible to make the trip.

Rose had a colostomy and then remained in the hospital for quite awhile. She was still there two weeks following the operation. Somehow she had gotten fed up, by then, with her drunken female companion. Rose used her solitude as her latest excuse to contact Gypsy, which she did in a letter that she dictated to a nurse at Good Samaritan Hospital. Rose asked for her daughter's help in removing her companion from her life and from her property. Rose wrote in her inimitable style, "This unfortunate maniac who is holding fort at my home is nothing more than an ordinary drunk who I have had with me so I would not be alone while been [*sic*] sick." She wanted the woman tossed out of her house as quickly as possible.

Five days later, the woman, who had yet to be evicted from Rose's home, sent a scathing letter in Rose's name to Gypsy Rose Lee. In all probability, Rose dictated it since it was, in effect, a blackmail letter, with Rose—or whoever wrote it—threatening to make public certain unsavory facts about Gypsy if she didn't sent money posthaste. Rose had sent a few letters like this latest to Gypsy before. She would always delight in threatening to make "certain things" about her daughter known to the public, but she usually didn't elaborate as to what those salacious bits were.

Gypsy was performing in Toronto, Ontario, Canada, so it took about a week for the letter to reach her. She was unnerved by it. "There is nothing about my life which cannot be made entirely public," she wrote to her mother, after reminding Rose of her assets (which included her house, the two cottages she rented out, and her one hundred dollar-per-month annuity) which were more than enough to cover Rose's bills. She told her mother that after having received such a threatening and vile letter, she was also no longer amenable to helping Rose with her hospital bills. That was Gypsy's way of replying to her mother's letter, knowing that any financial cut-off threat would always get Rose's attention. But it wasn't entirely true that she would not help her mother pay her medical bills. Gypsy would assist her mother with her bills until the end of Rose's life. Within a week, Gypsy offered to send her mother to a nice convalescent home where she could recover from the surgery—provided, of course, that there were no more blackmail letters. Rose turned that idea down, returning to her home in Valley Cottage, where the friend had finally gone. Gypsy had taken care of the removal of the "unfortunate maniac."

Rose's mental state was in a downward spiral, and she was also gravely ill from having the surgery that had removed her colon. It is possible that Rose was also taking medication that made her mental state worse than it might have been had she been healthier. She might even have been combining heavy-duty pain medication with alcohol some of her friends might have smuggled into the hospital. In any event, she threatened to bring Gypsy up on charges of "criminal negligence" over "non-support," a threat that came right after Gypsy offered to pay her mother's way at the convalescent home.

Given Rose's frame of mind, Gypsy could not even trust Rose to help her obtain a passport,. Gypsy was booked to perform in London the summer of 1951 and was having a terrible time trying to prove the details of her birth. She did not have a birth certificate; the only one on file for her was the fake filed in the 1920 in Ellen June's name. At least Gypsy had been born in Washington and she didn't have to deal with citizenship status, but still, there was no proof to show that Gypsy had ever been born. There was also the question of her real name. She found no record of herself as Rose or Louise or Rose Louise. Remembering her great-grandmother, Mary Louise Herber Egle Stein, she even tried to find herself listed under Mary Louise, wondering if that might have been her actual name, but there was no certificate under that name, either. She had been born in the house in Everett that Jack Hovick built and delivered in the middle of a snowstorm by a midwife. So how was she supposed to get a passport and get to England? Anna Thompson came through for Gypsy and filed affidavits on her granddaughter's behalf, stating she had been born in Fauntleroy, West Seattle in 1914. That last detail was incorrect, but Gypsy got her passport.

Rose's hospital bill was exorbitant and the state of her health was deplorable, but still, her wiles were intact. She used her charm on her doctor until he lowered her bill to $900. Then she took another mortgage out on her house and paid him the full amount. Rose then closed her Valley Cottage house, thinking she was doing so permanently, yet she was destined to return there in a few more months. She went off to Manhattan, though the effort of getting there must have been too much for her. Although she summoned the chutzpah to get to friend's apartment, once there Rose collapsed. She truly should have been in the convalescent home Gypsy had offered to her. Instead, she was in Manhattan having a physical meltdown. Eventually Rose and her white fluffy dog, Little Mama, found their way to the Belvedere Hotel and checked in there, probably for sentimental reasons. The hotel was located directly across the street from the Henri Court Apartments, where she'd lived with June, Louise, and a few of the Newsboys towards the end of June's vaudeville act, and then with Louise and the Hollywood Blondes later. Rose was back in her old neighborhood.

In Gypsy's absence, June spoke to Bill Fitelson, the lawyer she shared with Gypsy, who handled the finances. June increased her mother's allowance to cover the cost of the hotel and also to repay the new mortgage loan. She had avoided Rose for years, but now June came to see her mother regularly at the Belvedere, bringing a television set with her on one memorable visit. Rose, despite the vitriol she had poured onto June after the girl fled the act, had always secretly been enthralled with her talented daughter. Now, Rose was simply thrilled to have June back in her life. "Every call or visit from her," she wrote to Gypsy, "is just new life for me." Perhaps it was, literally.

June believed her mother could not live very much longer. The prognosis was not good. Rose, by rights, should probably not have lasted this long, considering the type of cancer she had and the complications it created. But 1951 became 1952, and live on she did. June was very good to her mother. She obtained tickets for Rose to see a dozen plays, bought her two pairs of new glasses, and handed her money as needed. Rose responded positively, expressing her gratitude to her daughter four times in writing. Yet the enforced contact with her ailing mother was starting to get to June, who was performing in the Broadway comedy *Affairs of State* eight shows a week. She longed to join Gypsy in London when her show closed—or better yet, simply keep going, "next stop Mars." Rose started submitting lists of medical items that she "needed" to June, who supplied her with all of them, but started to wonder. Those lists were almost as long as the Mississippi River. Rose's daughters checked in with each other about Rose's requests for medical supplies. Gypsy told June that their mother had arranged for a kickback from the medical supplier. She may have been down, but Rose wasn't out. So what if she was practically on her deathbed? That wasn't enough of a reason for Rose to pass up the chance for a new scam.

Rose moved from the Belvedere Hotel to the Holland Hotel, a few blocks away on West 42nd Street, where she captivated the staff and soon had them dancing attendance on her. Amazingly, Rose could still enchant just about anyone, save for her own relatives. Gypsy may have been in England, working, but somehow she still tried, long-distance, to arrange for a nursing home for Rose. The home notified June that it was entirely booked and didn't have an opening, so it was decided that Rose would remain for a while longer at the Holland Hotel.

She wasn't doing well. She wrote Gypsy letters full of love and concern, but apologized because her pencil shook, owing to the amount of pain she was in as she wrote. Winter of 1952 turned into Spring, Spring became Summer, and Rose was still among the living. Fantastically, she seemed to genuinely improve physically. She found a gentleman to rent her house in Valley Cottage and drew up a lease that gave him first option to buy it, hoping with her whole heart that he would. Then she wrote to her mother and sister, telling them that if the house got sold she wanted to travel! Unfortunately the tenant did not opt to buy the house, and Rose stayed put. She ultimately returned to the Valley Cottage house.

June took off for London that September to join Gypsy. It wasn't as if her daughters were leaving Rose behind, since neither lived with her, and both had to earn a living. Besides, Rose was better than anyone had ever expected. But her two children were in the United Kingdom, while her mother and sister remained in Washington. Rose was on her own at a time when she truly would have been a lot happier with a few caring people around her, though none were present. But that was about to change.

CHAPTER 18

ONE LAST LAUGH

ROSE WANTED TO REOPEN HER VALLEY COTTAGE PROPERTY AS A CHIL-dren's camp again, as unbelievable as that may seem. But Rose was Rose. Money was her thing, and reopening the camp would bring in additional income. Or at least, that's what Rose led everyone to believe. It may have been closer to the truth to say that she certainly did love money, but she loved being active, too. Opening another little camp session would allow her to be in the thick of it again, and she could even get paid. She would not be running the camp entirely on her own. She would hire someone to help her when the time was right to reopen.

Meanwhile, there were improvements that needed to be made. It may have been in the course of upgrading the two cottages on her property that Rose contacted a local plumber by the name of Louis Polhemus, whose family was so well regarded in the area that Polhemus Street in Nyack was named for a relative. Louis was a kind-hearted, decent man who attended the Old Stone Church in Upper Nyack. He had a sweet young wife, Virginia, called Ginny, and an adorable little girl named Judy. When he first visited Rose's house he was shocked at what he found: an elderly woman who was not in the best of health, who was living alone, and who seemed to have no one to help her. Louis Polhemus was appalled. He was also enchanted by Rose, just as scores of people had been before him. She was such a lovely, well-spoken woman. There was something about her that drew him in. But the house! It was in a state of disarray, since Rose was not quite strong enough to do all of the housekeeping chores. He was probably even more shocked at the whole scenario if Rose mentioned that she had two celebrity daughters who weren't there because they were in London. But she may not have done so at the time. It's probable that she didn't mention her *Daily Mirror* blackmail plot to them either, which might have explained a lot.

Louis left the house after taking care of the plumbing problem, yet he could not get the older woman out of his mind. The entire situation was untenable. The lady didn't have anyone to help her, and to Louis, that simply would not do. When he got home to Ginny, he sat her down and explained what he'd found at the house, telling her what he knew about Rose. There were plenty of people who would have simply shrugged the whole matter off, but these two were not among them. The young couple agreed that something needed to be done to assist Rose, and in the absence of anyone else, they would help her themselves. Ginny was willing to help Rose with the housework, and the whole Polhemus family got involved helping their neighbor. This was the best possible outcome for Rose. She had been isolated from her children and almost never got to see April and Erik, her grandchildren. Here was a whole intact family that would become like her own, and at the best possible moment. The family came complete with two nice young parents and even a little girl for Rose to love.

And love the child she did. Judy called her Aunt Rose. Aunt Rose went out of her way to send the child birthday telegrams addressed to "the grandest little girl in the world," and bought presents for her on the holidays. Judy loved going over to Rose's home and playing with her dogs. Little Mama, Rose's fluffy white dog, was still with her, and there was also another Great Dane. Judy remembers Rose confiding in her parents that the lack of visits from her children and grandchildren was "making her life Hell." They were astounded when they found out that her daughters were the famous Gypsy Rose Lee and June Havoc.

Christmas of 1952 was the last one Rose would be well enough to enjoy. She had spent years missing her children and grandchildren at Christmastime and was jubilant to throw her energies, limited as they were, into creating a memorable Christmas for Judy Polhemus. Judy would remember that sparkling Christmas for the rest of her life. The woman who had so loved to turn drab hotel rooms into warm holiday chambers when she had once run the Dainty June act on the Orpheum circuit managed to find the biggest, fattest tree that Judy had ever seen. Rose placed it in the middle of a large downstairs room and decorated it with her collection of toy ornaments, the same ones her daughters had once enjoyed, and also plenty of lights. She situated the huge tree so that it was possible to walk all the way around it, allowing it to be viewed from all sides. Judy could hardly believe the magical effect.

Rose went all out that year. She had the Polhemus family over for Christmas dinner, putting cute Christmas tree favors at every place setting. She managed to find a large, lifelike doll, as big as the one with she'd once delighted June with, as a surprise for Judy. Rose served shrimp because she knew it was the child's favorite thing to eat. Rose even decorated herself for the holiday. She had never liked lipstick, but now she put a bit on to give herself a splash of color. She put a ribbon in her hair. It was a Merry Christmas for Rose at last, only flawed by her failure to see April, Erik, and her daughters on the holiday. But fortunately even that thought didn't manage to mar this bright Christmas evening for Rose.

It is worth noting that the Polhemus family did not see any evidence of the wild and crazy behavior that would be attributed to Rose later, after she was dead and the musical based loosely on her life played on Broadway, with Ethel Merman giving her brash, larger-than-life portrayal of this captivating, quiet woman. Judy described Rose as "intelligent, lucid and loving." Later, as an adult with children and grandchildren of her own, Judy even questioned the state of mind of any people who said otherwise. Evelyn Krakower also did not believe there was anything mentally amiss with Rose. "She was very nice but rather eccentric," she recounted, since by then Rose owned a grand total of "about ten cats and a Great Dane." Early in the winter of 1953, Evelyn and her husband, Larry, moved to a Valley Cottage home that was half a mile from Rose's. An ice storm hit the area a week after they arrived and knocked out their plumbing, a minor disaster since they had a baby whose cloth diapers needed to be washed. A friend of Larry's suggested that the couple approach Rose, since she had a well on the property. Rose was happy to comply. She not only let the couple help themselves to as much well water as they needed, but showed them her collection of dolls, some of which had belonged to June and Louise. Rose even showed Evelyn around her new town, suggesting that she shop at the Grand Union Supermarket and pointing out other small stores where she liked to do business. Rose was to inspire the Krakowers to adopt a Great Dane, a breed they came to love. Evelyn confirmed that when she saw Rose's house, it was in a state of extreme disarray, but she had no idea that Rose was ailing when she met her. Rose behaved as though she felt fine.

Perhaps it was the love of the decent Polhemus family that helped Rose to rally, to the point that by spring 1953 she was moving full-speed ahead with her Rose Ridge Camp project. Rose hired Mrs. Charles Hunter to be the camp counselor and appointed herself camp director. She had renovated the property, making the privy on the playing field "fly tight" and ensuring that the well water was safe, which was proven. The New York State Department of Health sent a district sanitary engineer over to Rose's property to perform an inspection, which she passed with flying colors. Rose's camp was given a permit to operate in the year 1953.

She charged less than twenty dollars a week for children to board with her and attend the camp. At those reasonable rates, she secured customers. For the first two weeks of camp, everything went beautifully, though Rose may have pushed herself too hard. And then she had a relapse. Rose returned to the hospital at the end of July 1953. She was still there in the middle of August, and this time, the situation was not looking optimistic for her. Syndicated Broadway columnist Dorothy Kilgallen reported to her readers, with a tinge of regret, that Rose, who had been the subject of Gypsy's "most amusing *New Yorker* pieces," was critically ill. Hopefully Rose did not see this particular article, well meaning though it had been. It was not just that being called "critically ill" in print would have been rather disheartening, but she had been *really* unhappy when she had found herself the subject of those *New Yorker* articles.

This time, after Rose finally managed to get released from the hospital, she summoned her sister to come east and stay with her. On this occasion, understanding the gravity of her sister's condition, Belle came. Among the benefits of Gypsy's having given Belle the money to start her shop in Copalis Beach was the friendship Belle and Anna made with a big-hearted woman named Helen Tallman and her family from Puyallup, Washington, who had taken Anna in, given her a place to stay, and made her a part of their family. Mrs. Tallman, who considered Anna to be "a darling," even wrote letters to Rose that Anna dictated to her. Anna's stay with the Tallmans made life far easier for Belle. She could now easily travel from Seattle to stay with Rose for a few weeks during the autumn of 1953.

Right after Belle's arrival, she and Rose cooked up a plan that was going to alter quite a few scenarios for quite a few people, but they managed to keep what they were up to quiet for awhile—no easy feat for either one of them. While Rose knew how to keep mum when she absolutely had to, Belle was usually a blabbermouth. Not this time. Their plot was top secret. And it was only one of two major plans. The second involved swapping houses. Anna still hoped Rose would relocate to Seattle. Rose was planning to sign her property over to Belle, and when they got to Seattle, Belle was going to sign the Rutan Place house where she lived with Anna over to Rose. This would keep the deeds to both properties securely among the three of them. But the plan stalled because Rose began to feel worse. Despite her undiminished desire to head west, she realized that she wasn't up to traveling anywhere, let alone all the way across the country to Seattle. She was then left in the position of having to stay behind in New York while her sister traveled back home, carrying with her the deed to Rose's house, even though Rose didn't yet have the deed to the Rutan Place property.

Gypsy Rose Lee, back from London, arranged for Rose to go to the elegant Under Elms rest home for ten days in hopes that with around-the-clock care Rose's condition could improve. Rose was initially amenable to the idea, but that only lasted for a few days. She had to be moved from the rest home to the hospital, where she underwent yet another surgery that lasted for two and a half hours. Gypsy visited her mother a few times in the hospital, and then arranged to return Rose to Under Elms once she was released. But something went horribly wrong. Rose no sooner got back at Under Elms on November 21, 1953, than she went on a wild rampage. It must have been an absolutely spectacular one, because it got her kicked out of the nursing home. The convalescent home was not prepared to put up with any patient prone to creating such an uproar. They made haste to call Gypsy. They demanded Rose be removed from the premises within twenty-four hours.

It was an extraordinary development. Rose had been hospitalized many times before and had never previously thrown any tantrums—let alone one so magnificent that her professional caretakers refused to let her stay in their facility. So even though Rose was in severe pain by this time, and probably loaded with medications that may have included narcotic painkillers, which could cause mood swings in even the most temperate of patients, it was out of character for Rose to become enraged and out of control in a medical setting. In any event, it raises the question of what happened at that nursing home—if anything—that could have provoked Rose.

Gypsy and June spent the next frustrating day attempting to find a home that would take the now-notorious Rose, but to no avail. At this point, Rose's situation was a tragedy in the making, since the woman urgently needed around-the-clock medical care. In desperation it was decided that a friend of Rose's would take her back to the house in Valley Cottage. Gypsy hoped for the best but was anticipating additional melodrama. It came. A day later Gypsy had to play referee during a phone call from Seattle. Belle was perhaps trying to have Rose moved out there. Later that week, Gypsy dealt over the phone with another problem concerning Rose's new nurse. The situation became even crazier for Rose when two burglars, Lucille Campbell and Frank Soroka, somehow got into her home and made off with cash and jewelry. Possibly word had gotten out amongst the undesirables of the Nyack area that the woman living alone at the quaint Rose Ridge house was ailing and therefore an easy target. Rose could also have inadvertently have brought the situation on herself. More than once, her neighbor, Larry Krakower, had been called after a woman Rose had met in a bar came back to the house and robbed her. Perhaps a group of thieves were deliberately trolling the local gay and lesbian hangouts, posing as those seeking roman-tic liaisons. However it was that Campbell and Soroka robbed Rose, they picked the wrong victim. Rose, sick though she was, didn't let the duo get away with their crime. She had never remained quiet whenever anyone had the gall to violate her rights, and this time wasn't an exception. She had the couple summarily arrested. The Rose managed to hit them with charges of grand larceny. They had to pay a hefty 1953 bail of $5,000 apiece.

Rose wasn't able to go all-out for Christmas of 1953, which must have upset her terribly since she so loved the holiday. The Polhemus family con-tinued to visit her, though little Judy, who was nine years old by then, began hanging back, distressed with her Aunt Rose's worsening condition. At one point a nurse who was staying with Rose contacted Larry Krakower. She asked him to pick up Rose's favorite cuisine, Chinese food. The nurse said it was "the only thing that Rose could keep down." Larry got it for her.

Gypsy and June made a few trips to see their mother. June would later report that Rose issued a deathbed curse to Gypsy during their final visit. However, Gypsy's son Erik, who as a child was his mother's constant com-panion and traveled with her all over world, never heard his mother speak of this curse. He did not, therefore, believe it had actually issued from Rose's lips. He was no stranger to the fact that June welcomed chances to misrep-resent the truth.

In the end it wasn't the cancer that ended Rose's varied and colorful life. Rose took a final turn for the worse on the afternoon of January 28, 1954. Her doctor was called, probably by Ginny and Louis Polhemus, who were sticking close by her side at this point, aware the end was near. The doctor ordered Rose to return to the hospital. An ambulance was sent to the house to pick her up. Not one family member was there to ride with her. Rose was placed on a gurney and put into the ambulance. She had once so loved riding in the paddy wagon with Gypsy back in the good old days whenever Minsky's got raided. But this time, the ambulance lights flashed and the sirens wailed in vain. They were the last sights and sounds Rose would ever see and hear. Like her grandmother Mary Louise before her, Rose experi-enced a cerebral embolism while riding in the ambulance. She was dead on arrival at Nyack Hospital.

Gypsy Rose Lee had been planning to meet with astrologer Hugh Mc-Craig that evening, but when she got the phone call about Rose's death she cancelled her appointment. Gypsy called the Hugh E. White Funeral Home in Nyack to plan her mother's funeral. Then her phone rang again. The caller was John Galucci, lawyer for the Rose Thompson estate. Galucci apprised Gypsy that her Aunt Belle in Seattle had been appointed executrix of Rose's will. Gypsy had assumed, as Rose's eldest daughter, that she would be given that honor. It came as a mild shock to Gypsy that she was not. Galucci let Gypsy know that Rose had also left strict instructions with Belle about what kind of funeral she wanted. He had a copy of these instructions and offered to begin implementing them. Gypsy got off the phone with the lawyer. Then she immediately sent a telegram to the funeral home to cancel every one of the arrangements she had just asked them to set up. Rose may have had a lifelong interest in Christian Science, but in the tradition of "once a Catholic, always a Catholic," in the end she wanted, and got, a Catholic wake, funeral Mass, and burial.

Little Judy Polhemus, who had been uncomfortable going to Rose's house or visiting her sickroom towards the end of her life, was very upset that her Aunt Rose had passed away. She wanted a chance to say goodbye to the woman she loved. She had never been to a wake before, and her parents were naturally concerned that the experience would upset their nine-year-old. They approached the director of the funeral home, Hugh White. He told Ginny and Louis to bring Judy over to the home before the wake officially opened, so that the child could see her friend one last time without other people around. The man took the time to explain everything that the child was about to see and in such a positive way that Judy was not afraid to view the body at all. The family that had loved Rose towards the end of her life was all present at her wake to see her off.

It isn't clear when Galucci told Gypsy about the secret plan Rose and Belle had set into motion the previous October. Rose wasn't going to let all those years of her daughters' avoidance of her go. Gypsy and June almost never wanted to see Rose until she became sick, no matter how many times she had pleaded with them to get together. The only one who'd ever come running to Rose on a consistent basis when she was in any sort of trouble or misery had been Belle, her nearly impoverished little sister. Fortune finally smiled brightly on Belle Thompson Rankin Thornton McKenzie. Rose had quietly and deliberately designed her last will and testament to contain a few surprises, which she could only have arranged with sheer glee. She may have had to leave the earth a lot sooner than she had wished, dying at the age of sixty-two, but she planned to go out with quite a bang. Save for a small bequest to one of her favorite people, her attorney, Frederick Engels, Rose left her sister Belle everything: the house, its contents, all of her property, and her bank account. If Belle had predeceased her, the will specified that everything was to be split equally between Erik and April. But Belle hadn't died before Rose, so she got everything, all of it, the bulk of this sizable estate in one magnificent fell swoop.

Gypsy and June were cut out of the will. Rose inserted an explanation in the will itself. She said that owing to the fact that her daughters were "amply provided for . . . it is not of necessity that they should participate as beneficiaries in the distribution of my estate." At least, that was the official reason printed in black and white in the will. Unofficially, though, their exclusion surely was motivated by revenge. Rose was probably trying to get even with her daughters for all those years when she had repeatedly begged them to visit her and they had rarely complied. Conveniently left out of the will was the fact that the magnanimous Gypsy had been the one who had paid for Rose's Valley Cottage house in the first place. Now it was all being handed to Belle, when in fairness, that house should have been returned to Gypsy Rose Lee. But Rose was beyond caring about fairness. She finally had the last word, and it gave her the last laugh. Belle would get the house and the money.

Gypsy and June were furious. Gypsy went to St. Ann's Church in Nyack for Rose's funeral mass on Monday, February 1, 1954. June did not attend. Rose's grandchildren, who had hardly known her, were also absent. April was about to go to work as a Copa Girl, a showgirl at the Copacabana night club, and Erik was still in grade school, attending classes that morning at the Professional Children's School in Manhattan. Gypsy paid for Rose's grave on a hillside at Highview Cemetery in Nyack, overlooking the Tappan Zee section of the Hudson River, including the graceful Tappan Zee Bridge. Gypsy also paid for Rose's funeral expenses; Belle would later reimburse her from the estate. But that was as far as Gypsy was able to take it. She paid for the grave but opted to forego paying for a headstone, which technically was also Belle's responsibility as executrix. Belle didn't opt to pay for one, either, and the grave remained unmarked.

Because Rose's daughters did not believe the will should be entered into probate, Gypsy, June, and Belle were summoned to appear in surrogate's court in Rockland County, New York. Apparently Judge Herbert E. Henion saw nothing out of order, and he let the will stand. The estate went to Belle, just as Rose had planned that it would. Belle had most of the contents of Rose's house auctioned off before she sold it; she couldn't bring everything back with her to the three-room Rutan Place house in Seattle. The Polhemus family bid for, and won, Rose's large collection of Christmas ornaments for

Judy, ensuring that they landed with someone who would love and preserve them. Back home in Washington, Belle put her inheritance to good use. At long last, she had the wherewithal to realize two of her fondest dreams. Within a few years she expanded her little shop in Copalis Beach by opening a small motel next door. She called the new establishment Thornton's Cabins. And before long, Belle added a little restaurant.

Rose's story might have ended there, on a positive note, with her legacy to her sister bringing the family's tradition of hospitality full circle and with Belle, at last, landing where she belonged. But Gypsy Rose Lee had another idea.

PART THREE

ROSE: THE LEGEND

"Here she is, boys.
Here she is, world!
Here's Rose!"

—THE CHARACTER ROSE IN

GYPSY: A MUSICAL FABLE

CHAPTER 19

GYPSY, A MUSICAL FABLE

BY 1957, THE STORY OF ROSE, LOUISE, AND JUNE WAS ON THE NEW YORK Times bestseller list. Gypsy did not need to concern herself with her mother's angst at being portrayed in print or on the stage any longer. And if, as June reported, Rose really had issued a deathbed curse on Gypsy, it didn't worry her oldest daughter enough to prevent her from writing a book about their life together. Rose was gone, and Gypsy was free at last to write about her mother without having to wonder whether Rose would hit her with yet another lawsuit. She began work on her autobiography in 1956, two years after Rose's death.

June was also working on an autobiography that she had started in 1954. It was turning out to be much easier for Gypsy to put her story together. She had, after all, been on the bestseller list back in the 1940s with *The G-String Murders*, and she had even written those three articles in the *New Yorker* that had caused Rose such grief in 1943. Now, these well-written pieces could easily be incorporated into Gypsy's autobiography. Gypsy also drew on many of the scenes in her unpublished play about her rise to burlesque fame, "The World on a String."

Gypsy's first audience was her son, Erik. For months, she worked on the book during the day, then read her newly-written pages to her son when he came home from school. The same routine held when they went to Florida during the summer and she continued to write while Erik went fishing. By 1956, newspapers reported that autobiographies by both Gypsy and June were in the works, giving their fans cause for anticipation. Gypsy told reporter Leonard Lyons that she wasn't exactly going to restrain her book to the facts. She said facts were the domain of reporters, not individuals like her. It was to her credit that Gypsy had said as much from the start, but she actually did not stray all that far from reality. She stuck to the basic facts, although she did tweak them a bit for laughs. Her mother had been a positive force in her life, if not necessarily the most scrupulous of individuals on the vaudeville circuit. Rose was portrayed less like her mother and more like her best friend, though one whose favor she had to win while June was getting most of Rose's attention. The act was the family's preferred way of making a living. It was never presented in the book as a substitute for Rose's own thwarted dreams, as it later is in the musical.

Gypsy ended the book in the early spring of 1937, when she left the stage behind for the first time in her life and boarded a train to Hollywood, California, to begin appearing in movies. She did not cover her subsequent unhappy experiences. The book ends before she made an appearance at an event that was associated, however indirectly, with the Communist Party. Early Spring 1937 came before scores of people sent the movie studio protest letters regarding her hiring, and before Genevieve Augustine had picked up the rifle in Gypsy's Highland Mills house. Ending it there was a masterstroke. Gypsy didn't have to address any of the more unpleasant or controversial events in her life.

A few legal issues had to be ironed out before Harper & Bros could publish the book. The law firm representing the publishing company compiled a list of over a dozen people depicted in the book who might sue. One of them was Anna "Big Lady" Thompson, who was still alive in Seattle at the age of almost ninety, which she'd manage to reach before passing away that August. The firm was concerned since at the time it was considered scandalous to have Big Lady portrayed as someone who had once sold clothing and accessories to ladies of the evening. Most of the other problematic people were dead. Two, the New York con artist who had set Rose up to be robbed at the Langwell Hotel, and the self-proclaimed lesbian chauffeur for the Hollywood Blondes act, might both have still been alive and they were considered legal threats. Gypsy was advised to alter their real names in her manuscript before the book went to press.

The book was scheduled for release in April of 1957. Months earlier, in the summer of 1956, before Gypsy ever came up with the idea of having the book turned into a Broadway musical, the savvy author was already talking to agents about turning her book into a movie. Agent Mark Hanna came up with a brilliant suggestion: to have the genteel, classy actress, Spring Byington, rather than a more "pedestrian type," play the part of Rose. Rose Thompson Hovick might have been remembered in an entirely different and more true-to-life manner if this casting choice had been acted upon. Four different offers were pending with regard to the book. There were film offers from MGM and Warner Bros. There were also two Broadway offers, one from Lerner & Loewe, the team that had written the hit musical *My Fair Lady*, and one from producer David Merrick.

Then Gypsy hit upon a brilliant idea, opting to have the book adapted as a Broadway musical rather than a film, at least initially. It was always possible to turn a Broadway show into a film later, after the play opened. She would be able to make money on her book not once, but twice. Gypsy decided to accept David Merrick's offer. David Merrick and his partner, Leland Hayward, began to assemble the creative team that would turn Gypsy's winsome book into a musical. They wanted award-winning gay playwright Arthur Laurents to write the book for the musical, but the project about the life of a burlesque stripper didn't really interest him—until the day Selma Lynch, a guest at his beach house on Long Island, mentioned that Gypsy Rose Lee's mother just happened to have been her first lover.

At Arthur's urging, Selma began to describe the Rose she had known: a woman who had been miserly with a buck, yet bewitching and irresistible. She regaled him with tales of Rose's alleged killer instinct. She claimed that Rose was rumored to have thrown a hotel manager out of a window when he found she had more kids in a room than she'd initially said would be staying there. Selma herself called the story a rumor, and no evidence has ever been found to support it. She also related that Rose had loaded a group of lesbians into her car one night, deliberately crashed into another car, and conned the driver into paying for damages that she'd purposely caused herself. Selma told Laurents that Rose's friends were all smitten with her, to the point they backed up her story. The trouble with that last funny little anecdote, of course, was that Rose had never learned to drive!

Selma's Rose tales were all unsubstantiated and grossly exaggerated, and Laurents knew it, but the playwright was finally becoming interested—not in the character of Gypsy Rose Lee, burlesque star, but in the story of her switch-hitting mother, Rose. Based primarily on Selma's recollections, he developed an idea for a main story character who was unstoppable. Then he took the original idea quite a bit further. He morphed his Rose into a star-struck monster with tunnel vision who was hell-bent on living out her own unfulfilled dreams of fame and onstage glory through her children. It made for a riveting script, but one that didn't reflect what had really happened.

Carefully edited out of the Broadway production were Rose's alcohol problem and all of its attendant upheavals, not to mention her attraction to both men and women. But then, Gypsy had not alluded to any of these matters in her book, either. Still, Rose's interest in the ladies turned was the

242 GYPSY, A MUSICAL FABLE

catalyst that had first interested Laurents. But mainstream Broadway audiences in 1959 were definitely not ready to see a musical comedy with a main character based on a woman who had had husbands, boyfriends, and then a series of female lovers—with several unfortunate drunken incidents thrown in. Rose's "hot soup" routines were gone from the script, too, though they might have provided inspiration for a set of hilarious song lyrics. Laurents left in her penchant for shoplifting, her way of charming people into doing whatever she wanted them to do, and her optimistic way of convincing the children they could succeed.

Actress Ethel Merman, a brassy native New Yorker with a staggeringly powerful voice, was selected to star as Rose. Ethel's real full name was Ethel Zimmermann, and she coincidentally shared Rose's German and Scottish family background, but the similarities ended there. If the two women had met, they would have been considered polar opposites, at least in terms of their approaches to those around them. Ethel was outspoken and direct and loud. Rose had been a much quieter type of seductress. Yet they both usually managed to obtain what they wanted from the world. This show was written with Merman's strengths in mind, not Rose's. The creative team had their star in place before they ever wrote the book and the score. Ethel's vocal range was phenomenal. She was known as a star who never needed a microphone to be heard all they way up in the last row of a theater balcony, so a nice, loud, shrill part was specially created for Ethel. If another actress had been selected to play Rose, say Mary Martin, who had a much softer and sweeter style, the character might have been written so as to resemble the real Rose.

Gypsy Rose Lee didn't particularly care which character the focus was placed on, or whether or not the show was historically accurate. Her main concern was that it retain a title that included own name, *Gypsy*. She even told her sister that she wanted the show to be her "monument." Laurents went over to Gypsy's townhouse to meet with her about his script. While there he noticed that she rented out rooms to tenants, just as Rose had done. Laurents could not get a straight answer to any of his questions about her story, not even concerning how she had come to be called Gypsy Rose Lee. Gypsy breezily told Laurents to make up any explanation he wanted and granted him permission to change all kinds of details with impunity. The truth didn't matter so much to her; the profits she hoped to make did.

June, meanwhile, cared enormously about the way this show was portraying *her*. It was at that point that she got into the fray and began to cause the creative team an enormous amount of grief. June had not liked the project from the start, but she became absolutely horrified after seeing a preview of the show in Philadelphia. Rose's gun may have been confiscated by the police before she could ever use it to blow Buddy Hyde away back in Kansas when he and June eloped, but thanks to the hyperbole of her first husband, June believed it to have been pulled on him. It was no wonder that when she first saw the preview production, June strode out of the theater at intermission, shocked by what she took to be the grotesque misrepresentation taking place on the stage. Intermission came right after the Rose character sang "Everything's Coming Up Roses" to Louise in reaction to June's elopement. "Everything's Coming Up Roses" is about turning Louise into the new star of the act. That song was placed in the action at exactly the moment when June *thought* Rose had tried to shoot her young husband. June was never to see the newspaper article from Topeka that recounted what had really happened. She might also have been offended for a second reason: Rose had rather quickly put another act together starring Louise, sweeping June's accomplishments aside in the process. The song at the end of the first act of *Gypsy* brought home the point that, even though June broke her mother's heart, Rose had marched on, ultimately creating a stellar career for Louise.

There was more. The facts concerning June and her show-stopping, toe-dancing vaudeville act were cut from the show's script. Laurents came up with a rather shrill caricature of a character called Baby June. Her act was shown as hilariously bad and over-the-top. It was meant to be too much, an outward manifestation of the fictional Rose's grandiose dreams of stardom. The child actors and actresses who sang the "Baby June and Her Newsboys" introduction to the abominable (in June's estimation) misrepresentation of her old act all but punched out the lyrics for excess comic effect. The musical's June did not perform any ballet dances *en pointe*, either. The child on the stage was tap dancing, doing cartwheels and the splits, and even twirling vulgar batons, coming across more like a cheerleader than a toe dancer.

To adult June, this representation was jarring. The act came across as a hideous parody, when it had actually been acclaimed wherever it played, as borne out by the countless glowing reviews left in its wake. June wanted the storyline changed to show, at the very least, how her audiences had loved her. This proposed alteration to the script made sense, since it would have ensured that the plot was more accurate. But then she started demanding that the script be altered to show that her age when she had run off and gotten married, had been eleven. June was about to have a time of it demanding that the creative team rewrite her personal history.

By the 1940s, when she needed a passport, June knew that she had been fifteen years old, and had believed herself to be thirteen, when she ran off and wed. Her demand that the creative team lower her age to eleven in the script was not only outrageously inaccurate but also pointless. Why she wanted to change her own personal history to such a degree defies explanation. This demand was also the first indication that June would take as many creative liberties with her version of her story as Gypsy had with hers, the difference being that Gypsy the comedienne had remained true to the basic facts and tweaked hers for laughs, while June wanted to shade her version with false melodrama. Rose had had fun creating scary tales that presented some of her relatives in horrid imaginary scenarios. History repeated itself when June began to do the same, but she seemed to want to present herself not as the accomplished child trouper that she had been, but as a colossal victim.

June's first memoir, *Early Havoc*, would not be released until a year after *Gypsy* premiered on Broadway. The two sisters' books are like the two masks of drama, comedy and tragedy, and their perspectives on the family and the act are as different as the sun from the moon. An unfortunate consequence of publication of June's book was that the public believed her more horrific tales about her family were the true story, and that Gypsy's lighter ones were whitewashed. The real facts would remain buried in countless official documents, facts vastly different from June's twist on them. Two of June's strangest tales concern Aunt Mina's and Charlie Thompson's deaths. June claimed to have been at her Aunt Mina's bedside when the woman died of an overdose. Actually, June had been performing onstage on the other side of the country at the time. Even if it were possible to believe that June, while a child, could have been at someone's bedside as they died and had become genuinely confused about the person's identity, Rose surely knew June hadn't been there when Mina died, and it's almost impossible to believe this subject had never come up with June in the years since. June was almost exclusively in the company of her mother, sister, and the boys in their act until she was fifteen years old. Rose had adored Mina and missed her, so it's probable that Rose would have verbalized quite a bit about Mina's untimely death, and done so in front of her children.

June's tome went on to misreport that her grandfather Charlie had "a neighbor woman with whom he was having an affair" in his car when he had his fatal accident, and that both were killed. It was actually Charlie's wife, Anna, who was beside him in that car. Both were taken to the hospital, severely injured but still alive. Charlie lasted only a few more days, while

Anna lived on. Anna had been present both at Mina's death and at Charlie's accident, but luckily for June she died two years prior to publication of *Early Havoc*. June was already long gone from Rose, Louise, and her old act when Charlie's accident took place. She did not remain in close touch with Anna. But it's hard to believe that June would never have heard the full details about this situation in the intervening years.

The reason for June's fictionalizing to of these two deaths remains a mystery. She creates the false impression that her family members were more dysfunctional than they actually were, so as prevarications go, these were far from harmless. It's possible that June felt the creatively enhanced, melodramatic versions of her family story were better suited to a book titled *Early Havoc* than ordinary truth. Drug overdoses and infidelities are more outlandish than influenza and a grandpa who was injured while riding alongside his wife. On the other hand, June may not have been the actual author of *Early Havoc*. Her lack of a formal education resulted in awkwardness with the written word. Dozens of letters in the family's archive provide evidence of her lack of English language proficiency. The ghostwriter, or perhaps an editor at her publishing house, might have been the one who invented many of her spicier tall tales, thinking that no one would ever bother to check the facts. But this scenario still does not explain why June would sanction falsities by signing off on the book. Naturally these discrepancies in her account raise questions about the veracity of other family vignettes, including those about Rose. Charlie and Anna's accident was well documented in the Seattle newspapers when it took place, but Rose's alleged fights with June backstage at theaters, for example, were not.

Early Havoc had yet to be published when June, in the winter and spring of 1959, insisted she wanted to be falsely portrayed in the musical as having been eleven years old when she eloped. June's behavior around *Gypsy* was illogical in the extreme. She complained vociferously that portions of the show were inaccurate, while insisting on introducing another inaccuracy—and the one she wanted to add was the weirdest lie of all. Possibly she believed that as long as the creative team had altered the family story in one direction, she could control the situation by pushing it in another. June may have simply been harassing the creative team as a bargaining gambit. But as gambits go, this one backfired; the team regarded June as a strangely unreasonable diva. June had not been eleven when she was married, so there was no reason for them to give in to this script change demand. Besides, featuring an eleven-year-old running off to get married would have been a terrible move for the storyline of *Gypsy*. Arthur Laurents proclaimed that it would have made the character of Rose "beyond horror." No audience would willingly accept such a plotline.

June nevertheless refused to sign a release so that the show could use her name. She even threatened the team with a legal injunction if they didn't make the age change. As Rose had protested her portrayal in *The Naked Genius* by threatening a lawsuit, so June protested her portrait in *Gypsy*. David Merrick finally stopped her cold by threatening to write her out of the script completely. That did it. June capitulated. Incredibly, after all of these script change demands and legal threats, June would later claim to the *New York Times* that she'd never done anything to stop the musical *Gypsy*!

The show then gained momentum without anyone realizing or much caring that it would create lasting distortions about Rose Thompson Hovick. Inevitably, the over-the-top, ludicrous, almost evil character that Laurents had based on Rose led to rumors about the real Rose and her family. One of the more ridiculous speculations involved the relationship between June and Louise. The two sisters had been friends their entire adult lives. Gypsy tried her best to protect June's rights when the show was being formulated, yet because of June's insistence that *Gypsy* be called, rightly, "A Musical Fable," people believed that the two women had been feuding their entire lives. Then there was the story that Rose, who had rented out rooms, probably for less than a year, in her Manhattan apartment to ladies who quite possibly had been lesbians, had run "a lesbian boarding house." No one who knew of Rose's love for the almighty buck could have ever bought into the idea that Rose would have turned away paying customers based on their sexual orientation. Paying customers of *every* orientation made Rose's heart sing. She'd even rented to Asians during World War II. She also had no problem later renting her cottages to men or to married couples in Highland Mills or Valley Cottage. All customers, to Rose, were welcome. In *The Naked Genius* Gypsy Rose Lee had even chosen to include one of Rose's favorite lines, spoken whenever Gypsy was writing yet another check for her mother: "Just make it out to Cash."

Easily the most sinister rumors of all were those claiming Rose had committed three murders. The first and most persistent one held that Rose had shot her lover in a lesbian boarding house, a story that was given additional twists because the public confused Genevieve Augustine's suicide with the plotline of Gypsy's second mystery, *Mother Finds a Body*. The details of that book didn't jibe at all with what happened when Genevieve died at Gypsy's country home, yet the fictional plot of this mystery became confused with the real story. Gypsy's mysteries were written in the first person, which didn't help. Gypsy was said to have been at the scene of Genevieve's death, when all evidence points to her having been in California at the time. Further speculation held that Genevieve's death was covered up after a payoff from Gypsy's Hollywood studio (which did not wish to retain her) to New York authorities (over which the studio had no control). The grand jury returned a verdict of failure to indict, and it's quite a stretch to think that the Hollywood moguls bought off an entire grand jury.

The next rumor involved Rose throwing a hotel manager out of a window during the days of June's vaudeville act. That tale was first told by Rose's ex-lover Selma, who said it was a rumor when she related it to Arthur Laurents. But Selma had not been present when the supposed events occurred. She had not even met Rose yet. And no evidence substantiates the tale.

The third rumor was perhaps the zaniest: It was said that when Rose heard an interloper approaching the tent where she, Louise, and the Hollywood Blondes were camping, she didn't shoot a cow, but a person. This last story was refuted by May Sherwood. Rob Brandreth-Gibbs, grandson of May, one of the Hollywood Blondes, recalled that his grandmother often told the amusing story of the night Rose heard a what she thought was a human prowler outside the tent where the girls were camping and fired a gun at him—before realizing the "prowler" was a poor lost cow. May and the girls sat on top of a tarpaulin that hid the cow when the farmer came looking for the animal the next day.

No evidence ever supported the idea that Rose murdered anybody. The story that the cow might have really been a man was absurd. If Rose had sent a man flying out the window of a theatrical hotel, where was the rest of the troupe? The latter alleged event could well have transpired in front of up to nine people: Gordon, June, Louise, and at least six Newsboys. And when Genevieve died, at least fourteen adults were at the house. That's a total of twenty-three potential eyewitnesses.

Rose, it was said, was so charming that everyone who knew anything about any of these episodes stayed mum out of sheer adoration for her. Is it really conceivable that twenty-three people would have loved Rose so much, and so long, that they would have *all* remained silent about crimes they had witnessed for the rest of their lives, taking the details all the way to their graves? Children and teenagers, in particular, do not traditionally know how to keep silent, particularly about events like these. They'd have talked—and talked a lot. What about when people were starving during the Great Depression? Wouldn't someone have sold the story to the press when Louise went to Hollywood, if not sooner? And when every potential witness was questioned about Genevieve's death individually before cops and a grand jury, wouldn't at least one have tripped up or told the truth, even if she were trying valiantly to shield Rose from prosecution?

Surely someone—Murray Gordon Edelston, at the very least—had a reason not to cover for Rose if she were guilty. After Rose had spurned all of his marriage proposals and he got fed up with her and left, Edelston would have had a surefire way of getting even if he had but talked to the nearest cop about Rose having supposedly tossed a man out a window. And the same holds true for any of the kids in the act who may have held a grudge, and for any of the adults at the party in Highland Mills. Yet no one ever talked, almost certainly because nothing had ever transpired for them to reveal.

❧

On the opening night of the show, May 21, 1959, Gypsy Rose Lee sent flowers backstage to the legendary actress who was playing Rose. The bouquet was accompanied by a note that read, "Dear Ethel, How mother would have loved seeing you tonight. Love, Gypsy."

Had she been there, Rose might actually have blown a few gaskets at the thought of being portrayed on stage that evening. Then, in the next breath, she probably would have wanted to sue somebody to get a piece of the profits. She had been nearly apoplectic about the way Gypsy had written about her in the *New Yorker* articles, and she wasn't one bit happy to have found herself fictionalized in *The Naked Genius*, either, so it's possible that she may not exactly have loved what was about to happen on the stage of the Broadway Theater.

Or maybe not. Maybe the idea of having a beloved star like Ethel Merman play her would have thrilled Rose. And she might have loved this powerful and enchanting show, since its plot centered on vaudeville and burlesque, both of which were already, by 1959, becoming forgotten art forms. *Gypsy: A Musical Fable* would allow people a reason to remember. Many a child born after those theatrical eras had ended, and who had never been lucky enough to see a vaudeville act on the Orpheum circuit or a burlesque extravaganza at insouciant Minsky's, would find out about them for the very first time through this show about the intrepid mother from Seattle who had big dreams for her two daughters and their act. In any event, it had been Gypsy who knew Rose best, and if Gypsy thought her mother would have loved seeing herself portrayed by Ethel Merman, chances are good she would have.

The show opened that evening with Jule Styne's astonishing overture, followed by the scene with Baby June and Baby Louise auditioning onstage for a fixed amateur contest, with only one of them, Baby June, singing properly. Ethel Merman's Rose made her unique and unforgettable entrance by barreling up the aisle of the Broadway Theater and straight into theatrical history, calling out, in her clarion voice, "Sing out, Louise!" She hastened to threaten the man she overheard fixing the contest with exposure, thus unfixing it.

Rose is referred to as Mama in the show by June and Louise and as Madam Rose by the rest of the kids in her acts, but most of the public forgot that distinction after they left the theater. Rose was popularly referred to forevermore as Mama Rose. Many of the songs that debuted that night became American popular standards, including "Let Me Entertain You," sung by June and later Louise in their respective acts; "Everything's Coming Up Roses," Rose's song to Louise after June runs away to get married; and "Together Wherever We Go," a song sung by Rose, Louise, and a character called Herbie based on Murray Gordon Edelston. The world that was burlesque is riotously encapsulated in the number "You've Got to Get a Gimmick," as three hilariously bumping and grinding strippers show Louise—who is on the brink of making her first appearance as Gypsy Rose Lee—just how easy it is to create an act in this theatrical art form. This was easily the most beloved showstopper of the evening. But the most memorable moment of the night turned out to be the song called "Rose's Turn," which came at the end of the production. Gypsy Rose Lee had been concerned about the number in rehearsals. She had thought it "too vulgar" and believed it wouldn't work. Perhaps her objections and input resulted in improvement. The number was spectacular by opening night, a meltdown set to music, a song about how the fictional Rose misspent her whole life by attempting to live through her children. The character performs the song as—what else, in a musical that culminates in Louise becoming a burlesque star?—a strip. Mama Rose gets her chance to bump, grind, shake her booty, and "strip"—or at least toss off her little jacket. A far too brief yet mesmerizing film clip in the documentary movie *Broadway: The Golden Age*, shows Ethel Merman performing the number. The clip survives because Ethel Merman had the presence of mind to make a home movie of her performance. The footage shows Merman doing a few frantic burlesque moves. There's no audio, but there doesn't need to be; for anyone who has not seen her performance on Broadway, those few seconds of film illustrate just how electrifying it was.

The brilliant lines preceding and cueing the song are, "With what I've been holding down inside of me, if I ever let it out, there wouldn't be signs big enough. There wouldn't be lights bright enough. Here she is, boys. Here she is, *world!* Here's *Rose!*" No wonder this show, about two theatrical art forms that for the most part died out by the end of the 1930s, still holds up. The character Laurents created touches a universal nerve that transcends the show's time period. Those lines appeal to a broad spectrum of audience: adolescent kids who were not yet able to come into their own and had to hide parts of themselves to survive in a world of peer pressure; closeted gays; self-sacrificing housewives who presumably had the most in common with a character in a play about a mother and her daughters; and anyone, anywhere who has ever wanted to throw back her head and shout, "Hey, world—look at me—*I'm here!*"

As theater, the show is spectacular and possesses a nearly flawless script. Yet the script leaves out so many of the real Rose's better qualities: her positive belief in her children's ability to succeed on the stage; her pride in June's talent; her kindness in buying shoes for Henry Elias when she noticed that his were full of holes; the extravagant Christmas presents she had bestowed on all of the children in the troupe; the spectacular sight of Rose, draped in a bed sheet, making scary noises in the hallway of a theatrical hotel to the amusement of the children in her vaudeville act, one long-ago Halloween. This woman had taken scores of children and turned them into competent performers, had managed an act that made $1,500 a week, and was adored by just about everyone who met her. Rose had also gone forward with her little children's camp in the summer of 1953, just a few months before she passed away. In terms of sheer guts and audacity, this lady was unsurpassed.

Many a child entranced by the world of the theater and fed up with the boredom of attending school and with staying put in one dull locale would adore the show and long for the vanished world of traveling vaudeville troupes, heartily wishing for a mother who would give them the chance to travel, avoid classrooms, and shine on the stage.

After *Gypsy* opened, syndicated journalist Dorothy Kilgallen wrote an article in her Voice of Broadway column entitled "Ethel Merman Reaffirms Her Right to Musical Throne." The column opens, "In case anyone had any doubt about who was queen of the Broadway musical stage, bets were settled convincingly when Ethel Merman opened in *Gypsy* and kept a gigantic audience of pros alternating between guffaws and goose-bumps with her funny, poignant, gutsy and quite incomparable performance." *Gypsy* didn't win Broadway theater's highest prize, the Tony Award, for Best Musical in

1959; the prize was split between *Fiorello!*, a musical about New York mayor Fiorello LaGuardia and *The Sound of Music*. Unfortunately for *Gypsy*, there were too many wonderful shows in the running that year. *The Sound of Music* may well have garnered some sympathy votes, as Oscar Hammerstein II was ailing at that point with the cancer that would end his life a few months later. Jerome Robbins didn't win for Best Director and Ethel Merman didn't win for Best Actress. She lost to Mary Martin, who played Maria in *The Sound of Music*, prompting Ethel to shrug off the loss with the quip, "How can you buck a nun?"

Every actress who was to play Rose on Broadway between 1959 and 2008—Angela Lansbury, Tyne Daly, Bernadette Peters, and Patti LuPone—would be nominated for the Tony Award.

Gypsy opened on the London stage in 1973 starring Angela Lansbury, to the delight of English audiences, who had waited fifteen years since the Broadway opening for the chance to see the show on their shores. Lansbury had been an evacuated child sent to the United States during the Second World War and was also the granddaughter of beloved English politician George Lansbury. The London audiences embraced her wholeheartedly. The production played on the West End for a year before coming to the United States for a tour that ended with a Broadway run in 1974. Lansbury played Rose with the same sense of fun May Sherwood reported to her grandson that the real Rose had possessed. She was the first actress to win the Tony for the role.

The show came back to Broadway again with Tyne Daly appearing as a brash Rose from 1989 until 1991. Her mad-eyed, angry rendition of "Everything's Coming Up Roses" was terrifyingly delicious. The musical classic reopened again in 2003 with Bernadette Peters as a softer-spoken, gentler Rose, playing the part closer to the way the real Rose had been, an interpretation that didn't really work since it was too far removed from the way the role had been scripted. Arthur Laurents was not happy with this production. He was in his nineties by then, but he decided directing another production of *Gypsy* was in the cards.

Then the show returned once again in 2008, with Patti LuPone playing the part of Rose. She did so with a voice as incredible, or so it's been said, as Ethel Merman had when she played the part. Patti added a sense of fun and joy back into the part. This time not only did Patti win the Tony Award for Best Actress, but the rest of the "family" won as well. Boyd Gaines won Best Actor for his portrayal of Herbie, and Laura Benanti became the first Gypsy nominated for Best Supporting Actress to ever win the award. This production also won Best Revival of a Musical. As Gypsy Rose Lee had predicted, there were also film versions of *Gypsy*: a motion picture release in 1962 starring Rosalind Russell as Rose, and a television movie in 1993, in which Rose was played by Bette Midler. A new film version is currently in the works and will star the legendary Barbra Streisand.

The real Rose would have been amazed to see any one of these fabulous stars working in productions of a show that was about her, however loosely based it may have been on her real story. She would have been especially shocked to know that Arthur Laurents would call the show about her life "The *King Lear* of musicals." Her dreams had been for her children, not herself, and the show certainly immortalized them, too. Whatever else may have come to pass, Rose's belief in her daughters had been right on target. Every time a new actress in a new production of *Gypsy* plows down the aisle of a theater shouting, "Sing out, Louise," somehow, somewhere, Rose can only be smiling.

Smiling at first, that is—and then wishing she could be back on earth just long enough to hit the members of the production team with a nice, hefty lawsuit.

EPILOGUE

THE FOLLOWING ARE UPDATES ON ROSE'S FAMILY MEMBERS AND FRIENDS:
Descendants of the Thompson, Egle, and Herber families live all over
the United States. Many of them strayed over the years from their original
home bases in Luana, Iowa, or Farmington, Minnesota. Quite a few of the
Thompsons now live in Oregon.

A few of the buildings that were reconstructed after the Great Farmington Fire of 1879 still stand on Oak and Third Streets, where once stood the
first Egle Tavern, and, later, the Eagle Hotel, and where Mary Louise Herber
Egle Stein had her candy store and restaurant.

Jack Hovick had a total of four children, first Louise and June with Rose,
then a son, Jack, who became a doctor, and a daughter, Betty, with his second wife Elizabeth. To date, Jack has twenty-five grandchildren and great-
grandchildren. Jack and Elizabeth lived happily together to a ripe old age,
in Pasadena, California. They were in contact with Louise until she died,
but were sadly estranged from June, who had no interest in getting to know
them.

In the 1940s, Rose's last known male beaux, Murray Gordon Edelston,
opened a personnel agency in Chicago. Unfortunately that's the final fact
known about him. His experience promoting the Dainty June act stood him
in good stead at his agency, where he promoted job applicants to potential
employers. His daughter Cecille's fate is unknown.

Weldon "Buddy" Hyde, contrary to the rumor that June heard about his
early death, didn't die during the Great Depression. He lived until the age of
sixty in Cascade Locks, Oregon, and passed away in 1969.

Belle happily operated the motel and restaurant she purchased in Copalis Beach, Washington, with her inheritance from Rose, and lived to see
her 80s. She passed away in Aberdeen, Washington, in 1979, and is still remembered fondly by her old neighbors on Rutan Place in West Seattle and
by the children who adored her in Copalis Beach. She is especially remembered for her kindness to the kids.

Norman Rankin, the son Belle had with Reginald Rankin, lived until 1987 in Carlsbad, California.

Two decades after Norman's father, Reginald Rankin, died in prison after being sentenced to jail for running abortion clinics, abortion was declared legal in the United States. Reginald was never given credit during his lifetime for having had the good sense to recruit qualified medical doctors to work in his enterprise, an innovation at the time and currently considered standard procedure. His daughter from a subsequent marriage, Theresa Rankin, is an award-winning artist living in Missouri. Reginald has over twenty-five living descendants as of this writing.

Witchwood Manor was partially damaged in a fire in September of 2010. It's undergoing renovation.

Rose's next house, bought with Gypsy's money, still stands on Ridge Road in Valley Cottage, New York.

Samuel "Roxy" Rothafel, the man who had wanted to finance June's singing and acting lessons, died in 1936. Or did he? One charming New York City legend has it that ghostly but benevolent apparitions of Roxy can be seen at his most famous theater, Radio City Music Hall, which is still in operation. On opening nights, he's been spotted in the theater, accompanied by a beautiful female escort.

Ginny and Louis Polhemus's daughter, Judy Polhemus Leiner, who had been enchanted as a child by Rose's Christmas tree, continues to love the holiday season. She decorates eight Christmas trees every year, one of which still proudly displays all of Rose's old Christmas ornaments that her parents won for her at Rose's estate auction back in 1955. Along with her husband, Jim, she has three children, plus nine grandchildren. Judy has never forgotten her beloved Aunt Rose.

After the Hollywood Blondes act ended, May Sherwood, the petite girl who reminded Rose so much of June, was to continue with a singing career as a solo performer. She went on to own a hotel in a Canadian resort area, where she would regularly entertain the guests using the name Maizie Foulds, Maizie being her nickname and Foulds the name of her second husband. Her performances were well received, and she even entertained in Las Vegas. Until the day she died, May loved to show people photographs of her happy days spent with Rose, Louise, and the Hollywood Blondes. May's great-grandchildren, Alayna and Lauren, are hoping to follow in the same tradition that Rose first taught May back when she came under the older woman's tutelage in 1929. Their father, Rob Brandreth-Gibbs, even built a stage in their home, where the two sisters love to rehearse and perform. A new generation will carry on Rose's legacy.

As a teen, June's daughter, April Rose Hyde, tried her hand at movie acting, using the professional name April Kent. She married a French artist and lived for most of her life in Paris, working as a French-English translator and dubber of films. She passed away in 1998, estranged from June. She didn't have any children.

Erik Lee Preminger is alive and well and living in California. He worked in his father's film company and held other positions in the entertainment industry. Erik has one son, Christopher, and a little grandson named Ian.

June worked successfully as an actress, director, and author, published two books, as well as a play about her experiences, *Marathon '33* (which brought her a best director Tony Award nomination), and lived until her late nineties. In 1978, she purchased and restored a tiny historical Connecticut village called Cannon Crossing, which featured several shops and a restaurant in a one-room schoolhouse. The child who had grown up without a hometown adored having a village of her very own. Naturally she also continued her family's tradition by renting out the apartments above the shops, not to mention the cottage behind her farm. June worked tirelessly saving homeless animals. She died at home in 2010 of natural causes, surrounded by friends who had become her adopted family—but without any relatives present, as she had managed to become estranged from all of them. She believed herself to be ninety-seven years old when she died, but her exact age was still a mystery.

Gypsy Rose Lee lived well, mainly off the royalties from her book and the musical *Gypsy*. She also continued working in films and even had her own television talk show in the 1960s. Gypsy relocated to California and delighted in fixing up a large new house in Beverly Hills. Her love of animals never lessened; the new house even featured an aviary. Gypsy reprised her devotion to America's armed forces during the Vietnam War. She volunteered as a performer with the USO and traveled to Vietnam to entertain the troops, just as she had during World War II. They considered her to be like a sexy older grandmother, and she cheerfully didn't mind that comparison. She passed away far too young, in 1970, although her legend has continued by way of the musical. It may go on forever. She certainly wouldn't have minded that legacy, either.

And for anyone who visits Seattle, Washington, it's simply impossible to miss the site of Rose's childhood home. The Space Needle and Seattle Center now stand on the site of the property where Rose grew up, and where, for a time after her first divorce, little Louise and June lived, too, on the old 321–323 4th Avenue North lot Charlie Thompson purchased in 1900. Warren Avenue School, from which Rose as a child masterminded a non-appearance stunt with her two friends, was located on the site of the present-day Key Arena in the same complex. Built in a style to invoke the mid-twentieth century hope of space exploration and rising 605 feet in the air, the Space Needle is as bold and fearless as the child called Rose, who'd grown up long ago on the exact same spot.

ACKNOWLEDGMENTS

THIS IS GOING TO SOUND ASTOUNDING: I AM THRILLED TO REPORT that almost without exception, every person I contacted for assistance with Rose's story came through with flying colors. Most even went beyond the call of duty. Thank you for not only assisting me with this book, but also for illustrating how phenomenal people can be. *Bravo!*

The first kudos go to my agent, Eric Myers of the Spieler Agency, who didn't hesitate to take a chance on a first-time author, and my publisher, Leila Salisbury at University Press of Mississippi. I landed with the best!

An extra-special warm shout-out goes to four of Rose's relatives who were amazing sources of information: Erik Lee Preminger, Gypsy Rose Lee's son and Rose's grandson; Bette Solomon, daughter of Gypsy's sister Betty and Jack Hovick's granddaughter; Evelyn Dolbow, historian of the Thompson family; and Theresa Rankin, half-sister of Rose's nephew Norman Rankin— all of whom were beyond fabulous! Every member of each of your respective branches of Rose's family has a heritage to be proud of. You four are living proof.

The same holds true for Judith Polhemus Leiner, Rose's best friends' daughter and "adopted niece," and her husband James Leiner, who immediately contacted me when they heard I was looking for information. They filled in a lot of the blanks about Rose's time in Valley Cottage and lived the story of her last days. Judy, I'm so glad Rose had you in her life, and Jim, thanks for teaching me that reporter's trick about how to get a reluctant eyewitness to talk, which worked.

Additional Members of Rose's Family: Nick Hovick, Gypsy's nephew; Ken Gray; Kathy Charvet, Herber family historian; and the late, great Tana Sibilio, loyal assistant to June Havoc, who continued to be in touch even when, unbeknownst to me, she was fighting for her life.

Broadway: Actress Joy Franz, whose name opened so many doors for me; the late Arthur Laurents; Stephen Sondheim; Actors Equity Association; Deborah Jean Templin; Alan Mandell, who introduced me to June

Havoc's assistant; actor Thomas Toner; and Jan Buttram of the Abingdon Theatre.

New York City: Jeremy Megraw, Roderick Bladel, and the staff at the Billy Rose Theater Division of the New York Public Library; Patricia Nixon and Howard and Laurelee Passey, Family History Center, LDS Church, Manhattan; Joseph Ditta, New York Historical Society; Andrew J. Kostka, who looked up April's birth certificate; Steve Bohlen, Bellevue Hospital Press Office; Joseph Baranello, New York City Public Schools; and Annette Lloyd, Harold Lloyd historian.

Farmington, Minnesota: Rebecca J. Snyder, Dakota County Historical Society, who provided me with hundreds of articles on the history of the Egle and Herber families; Nancy Gross and Mary McClure, great-granddaughters of Clara Day Egle and Fred Griebie; Michelle Leonard of the *Farmington Independent*; George Veith; John Powers, Tony Wippler, Sue Miller, and Tim Pietsch of the Farmington Fire Department; and Judy Chown, Church of St. Michael, who sent me the church history, gratis.

Hopkins, Minnesota: Mary Raabe, historian.

Wahpeton, North Dakota: Bonnie McIver, Leach Public Library director; and Jill Nordland, North Dakota Department of Health.

Connecticut: Janet Lindstrom, New Canaan Historical Society, and Edward Goodrich of the Stratford Theatre.

Seattle, Washington: Phil Stairs from the archives at Bremerton, Washington, who found so many records; Carolyn Marr and staff, Seattle Historical Society; Greg Lange, Puget Sound Regional Archives; Eleanor Toews, Seattle Public Schools; Lee Pierce, archival assistant, Washington State Archives; Julie Lundquist, Lakeview Cemetery Association; Sr. Dorothy Dees, Holy Names School, Seattle; and Barbara Greenlee and Karen White, both of Belle and Anna's old stomping grounds at Rutan Place.

Copalis Beach, Washington: The fabulous Kelly Calhoun, executive director/curator, Museum of the North Beach, Moclips; Jane Bennett, research assistant; Eileen Thompson Owens and Louis Stewart, children of Copalis Beach, who grew up knowing Belle Thornton.

North Vancouver, British Columbia, Canada: Rob Brandreth-Gibbs, grandson of May Sherwood of the Hollywood Blondes.

Highland Mills, New York: George Kane, whose mother knew Gypsy; Ben Schwall, Lois Schwall, and Barry Yellen, who provided me with the Genevieve Augustine crime scene photograph; Orange County district attorney Francis D. Phillips; Orange County historian James Nelson; Ralph Ristenbatt, senior instructor of forensic science, the Pennsylvania State

University; Desiree Potvin, Town of Woodbury; John Caher, State of New York; Leslie Rose, historian; Gail Bates.

Valley Cottage, NY: Kato Hetch, Linda Krakower Greene, Evelyn Krakower, Larry Krakower, and Barry Furey.

Topeka, Kansas: Gregory Romer, Topeka Public Library, who found one of the most valuable pieces of information about Rose Hovick for me; Walt Wywadis, Ronald Brown, Ronald Miller; Don Chubb, historian; Larry Tenopir, Jayhawk Theatre Society

Wisconsin: Sister Lois Hoh, archivist at St. Clara's Academy, Sinsinawa, and fabulous researchers Margaret Craft and Kathy Wagner, nieces of Genevieve Augustine.

My fellow authors and researchers: Thom Peterson, researcher of the Dainty June act, generously provided many of the missing elements in the act's itinerary; Noralee Frankel, author of *Stripping Gypsy*; Karen Abbott, author of *American Rose*, my terrific research buddy at the New York Public Library of the Performing Arts; Rachel Shteir, *Gypsy: The Art of the Tease*; Trav S. D., vaudeville historian and author of *No Applause, Just Throw Money: The Book That Made Vaudeville Famous*; Robert Strom, *Lady of Burlesque*; Doug Waller, *Wild Bill Donovan*; Tony Velella, *Character Studies/"Rose"*, DeeJae Cox, LA Women's Theatre, *A Tuesday in June* playwright; Ethan Rarick, *Desperate Passage*; Keith Garebian, *The Making of Gypsy*; Jane Briggeman, *Burlesque: A Living History*; and last but most certainly not least, the one, the only Chuck Mosberger, unofficial Gypsy Rose Lee historian and collector, who has been the biggest help of all, and who became one of the best friends I've ever had. Chuck, you need to write a book next!

Family: My parents, Frank and Mary Quinn, who took me to see *Gypsy* in 1974, unintentionally inspired this project and have been a steady source of help and moral support throughout; godmother Pat McGann; Pat Davis; Rita Quinn, who had a friend on the Denver police force look at the crime scene photo; Theresa Quinn Delahunt; Joe Quinn; and my parents' best friends, Arno and Carol Lehmann.

Friends: Dr. Jian Zhang, who had never sneaked onto rich people's private property for a closer look before I taught her how to get away with it in Highland Mills; Arlynn Lieber Presser, Esq., who helped with copyright issues; photographer Alexis Pierro, who resized several photographs; Mary Kelly, Claudia Bell, Karen Green Thomas, Maija Delands, Elga Mitchell and Catherine Ard, friends for life; authors Karen and Edward Underwood, Johanna Reiss, and Ordin and Malana Ashlie; Shirley Krtek, Jeremey-Stuart

De Fishberg, Richard Skipper, Jen Lau, Chenleng Cai, Yong Zhao, Sheri-Lynn Fujimoto, Denise Kostka, Rev. Kathie Davis Thomas, Gloria Loring, Dr. Bruce Gelb, Dr. Gila Leiter, Beccy Josowitz, Leah Honor, Ilan Riess, Dhandapany Perundurai, Cheryl Tan, Sonia Mulero-Navarro, Cindy Ko, Sherly Pardo, Lenny Babus, Chuck Kahler, Max Gipson, Nancy Matz, Barbara Grundeman, Joy Gleason, and my whole "Facebook Family" cheering squad.

Last but not least, I'd like to give a long overdue shout-out to my most inspirational teachers: Tina Padas Mavroudis, Michael Cohn, Edward Warshow, George Kurek, and especially Norma Heyman, who created a positive learning environment and proved there's no better place for kids to thrive and bloom than a good public school. *See what you started?*

NOTES

PROLOGUE

Laurents' script: Arthur Laurents, *Original Story By*, New York, Alfred A. Knopf, 2000, 375–78.

Selma Lynch description: email to the author from Arthur Laurents, March 9, 2010.

Styne included with Sondheim at Merman's insistence: Laurents, 380.

Styne, burlesque piano: Garebian, *The Making of Gypsy*, Toronto, ECW Press: 1994, 68.

Jule Styne's bookie enforcers: Laurents, 380.

Julie threatens to throw Robbins in the pit: Garebian, 105.

June won't sign release/tin cans: Laurents, 388.

David Merrick/3rd daughter named Beth: Laurents, 389; Jack Hovick's third daughter Betty: Letter, Elizabeth Hovick to Gypsy Rose Lee, May 31, 1966, Gypsy Rose Lee Papers, New York Public Library.

David Merrick/"Baby Claire": Laurents, 389–90.

Gypsy's concern they were "not coming in as a hit": 1959 Datebook of Gypsy Rose Lee, 21 April 1959, GRL Papers, NYPL.

Mastodon of all stage mothers: Garebian, 109.

Boiler room in full operation: Garebian, 111.

Royalties largely supporting Gypsy the rest of her life: Erik Preminger, *Gypsy & Me*, Boston, Little, Brown & Company, 1984, 99.

CHAPTER 1

Egle Family Immigration information: boarded *Emblem* with all fares fully paid; names, professions, and ages of family members: Ship Record for the *Emblem*, arriving July 1, 1851, in New York from Antwerp, the Battery Park Conservancy, www.castlegarden.org.

Egles from Baden-Wurtemburg, Germany: US Bureau of the Census, Year: 1870, Census Place: Empire, Dakota, Minnesota; Roll: T132_2; Page 78; Image 438.

Within next decade they were in Farmington, MN: Farmington Billiard Room ad, *Farmington Telegraph*, June 1, 1868.

Growth rate of Dakota County from 1850 to 1870: email to author from Rebecca Snyder, Dakota County Historical Society, June 19, 2010.

L. Egle & Bro. sold ice in summertime: "Keep Cool," *Farmington Telegraph*, August 6, 1868.

L. Egle & Bro sold hydraulic pumps: *Farmington Telegraph*, September 3, 1868.

Lorenze Anglicized to Lawrence: "A Hook and Ladder Company," *Farmington Press*, January 15, 1873.

Lorenze marries Mary Louise Herber: Minnesota Historical Society, State and Territorial Census, 1875, Farmington, Dakota County, Minnesota.

Herbers owned Luxembourger Hof/Rumors about ladies in hotel photograph: email to author from Rebecca Snyder, Dakota County Historical Society, South St. Paul, Minnesota, July 3, 2010.

Mary Louise called "Louisa"/sister also named Mary: "Back from Germany," *Dakota County Tribune*, Farmington, Minnesota, October 7, 1897.

In Seattle Mary Louise resumed using her full name: Seattle City Directory, Seattle, Washington, 1897.

Anna Egle born July 21, 1868: Minnesota Territorial & State Census, 1875, Dakota County, Farmington; Letter to Anna Thompson from Eugene Casserly, July 25, 1938, GRL Papers, NYPL.

Rose Egle born in 1871: Minnesota Historical Society, State and Territorial Census, 1875, Farmington, Dakota County, Minnesota.

Birth years of Lula, Charles and George Egle: John Dalby, *Minnesota Cemetery Inscription Index, Select Counties*, The Generations Network, Inc., 2003, database on Ancestry.com.

Lula's headstone description: photograph, Friends of the Highland Cemetery, Rootsweb. com, http://freepages.history.rootsweb.ancestry.com/~friendsofthehighlandcemetery/.

Lorenze officer of volunteer Farmington Hook & Ladder Company: *Farmington Press*, January 15, 1873.

First murder in Dakota County in a saloon in 1871: "John Emery & The Truth," Website of the City of Farmington, Minnesota, http://www.ci.farmington.mn.us/AboutFarmington/ FarmingtonHistory/John_Emery_Truth.html.

Temperance Movement led by John Emery, *Farmington Press* editor: May 23, 1877, *Farmington Press*.

Temperance crusaders praying Egle would give them lemonade: *Farmington Press*, July 9, 1874.

Simon buys second building and moves it: *Farmington Press*, April 22, 1875.

Griebie's brick General Store: "The Great Farmington Fire, in Farmington," *Farmington Press*, November 26, 1879.

Saloon corner infamous for noise: *Farmington Press*, May 23, 1877.

Lorenze caught selling liquor to minors: "Justice Court," *Farmington Press*, September 16, 1875.

Rosina Egle's death, October 26, 1875: *Farmington Press*, October 28, 1875; and John Dalby, *Minnesota Cemetery Inscription Index, Select Counties*.

Lorenze fined for disorderly conduct: "Justice Court," *Farmington Press*, September 16, 1875.

John Emery printing comment that Lorenze drank too much: *Farmington Press*, Wednesday, October 15, 1879.

Simon Egle's wife's death in March 1876: *Hastings Gazette*, Saturday, March 18, 1876, and *Farmington Press*, Thursday, March 16, 1876.

L. Egle & Bro. is dissolved, Mary Louise's ad to settle all accounts: "Notice," *Farmington Press*, October 19, 1876.

Egle Saloon closed, building to become hotel: *Farmington Press*, August 25, 1877.
"The old saloon corner looks a little lonesome now": *Farmington Press*, May 23, 1877.

Anna comfortable with prostitutes: email to the author from Erik Lee Preminger, July 9, 2010.

Taverns—"entertainment centers" of their day: S. D., Trav, *No Applause—Just Throw Money: The Book That Made Vaudeville Famous*, New York, Faber and Faber, 2005.

1877, Lula Egle dies of scarlet fever: *Farmington Press*, Wednesday, August 22, 1877; John Dalby, *Minnesota Cemetery Inscription Index, Select Counties*.

Headstone, pony, "Our little Lula": photo, Friends of the Highland Cemetery, Rootsweb, http://freepages.history.rootsweb.ancestry.com/~friendsofthehighlandcemetery/.

Former slave Ben Richardson: email to author from Rebecca Snyder, Dakota County Historical Society, July 3, 2010.

Eagle Hotel, "Rise o posterio": "A Fall and a Rise," *Farmington Press*, May 22, 1878.

Oculist, August 20, 1879: "At the Eagle House," *Farmington Press*, August 20, 1879.

Description of Clara Day Egle: photograph from the collection of Nancy Gross and Mary McClure, great-granddaughters of Clara Day Egle.

Clara Day marries Jordan Egle: *Farmington Press*, May 28, 1879.

Clara's former husband William Alonzo Moor, daughter Grace living with grandparents: 1880 United States Federal Census, Empire, Dakota, Minnesota; and email to author from Nancy Gross (great-granddaughter of Clara Day Egle) on April 12, 2012; also email to the author from Nancy Gross on June 24, 2012.

Hot weather: *Farmington Press*, October 15, 1879.

Lorenze Egle almost died: *Farmington Press*, October 8, 1879.

Lorenze's death on October 8, 1879: *Farmington Press*, October 15, 1879.

John Emery's line about Lorenze's "excessive drink": *Farmington Press*, Wednesday, October 15, 1879.

John Emery's hate mail: "John Emery & The Truth," Website of the City of Farmington, Minnesota, http://www.ci.farmington.mn.us/AboutFarmington/FarmingtonHistory/John_Emery_Truth.html.

Heat wave breaks a few days after Lorenze dies: "'Minnesota weather' graded sadly below par the first nine days of October," *Farmington Press*, Wednesday, October 15, 1879.

The Great Farmington Fire details: "The Great Farmington Fire, In Farmington," John Emery, *Farmington Press*, November 26, 1879.

Wind described as "very violent" on night of the fire: George B. Young, reporter, *Minnesota Reports, Cases Argued and Determined in the Supreme Court of Minnesota, Volume 31, July 1883, March 1884*, St. Paul, West Publishing Company, 1884, 58.

Niskern once witnessed an Indian massacre: *History of Dakota County and the City of Hastings, including the Explorers and Pioneers of Minnesota, and Outlines of the History of Minnesota*, Neill, Rev. Edward D. and Williams, J. Fletcher, Minneapolis, North Star Publishing Company, 1881, 368.

Lorenze's brothers, the Egle Brothers Bucket Brigade began that night of the fire: "Big Fire of 1879 Was Spur to Fire Department; Egle Company Bucket Brigade Was First Fire Department Here in Early 70's—Two Modern Trucks Used Now," *Dakota County Tribune*, June 27, 1996.

Ben's Barbershop run by former slave Ben Richardson: email to the author from Rebecca Snyder, July 3, 2010, Dakota County Historical Society, copy of inscription on photo of Farmington.

Fire ignites elevator/Jordan Egle secured his barley: *Farmington Press*, December 3, 1879.

Mary Louise and children move in with brother Peter Herber: US Bureau of the Census, Year: 1880; Census Place: Castle Rock, Dakota, Minnesota; Roll: 618; Family History Film: 1254618; Page: 245D; Enumeration District: 202; Image: 0174.

People gagging from fire fumes: *Farmington Press*, December 3, 1879.

"On the burnt spot," John Emery comment: *Farmington Press*, December 3, 1879.

Georgie Egle dies June, 1880: John Dalby, *Minnesota Cemetery Inscription Index, Select Counties*.

Carl Egle dies February 12, 1881: John Dalby, *Minnesota Cemetery Inscription Index, Select Counties*.

Jordan Egle's "Condition Powders," November 8, 1882: *Farmington Press*.

Jordan Egle in Justice Court over the Masonic Ball, under bonds to keep the peace: "A Family Breeze," *Farmington Press*, June 29, 1881.

Jordan Egle refusing to pay Clara's debts: no masthead, "Town Notices, Caution," August 10, 1881, from the collection of the Dakota County Historical Society.

Charlie Thompson from Monona Township, Iowa, in Farmington to run train depot about 1882, "Egle-Thompson," October 8, 1885: *Dakota County Tribune*.

Charlie's family background information: email to author from Evelyn Dolbrow, wife of Charlie's sister Emma's descendant, July 10, 2010.

Charlie's parents born in United States: US Bureau of the Census, Year: 1900, Census Place: Seattle Ward 8, King, Washington; Roll: 1745; Page: 7A; Enumeration District: 114.

Thompson Family's lives built around Presbyterian Church: "Eight Children and a 4th Generation Survives Mrs. Thompson," obituary for Elizabeth R. Thompson, undated clipping, scrapbook of Charles J. Thompson, private collection of Erik Lee Preminger; also obituary for Stephen H. Thompson, Wednesday, March 19, 1879, no masthead, private collection of Erik Lee Preminger.

Charlie's father's interests, home filled with flowers and music: Stephen H. Thompson, obituary, March 19, 1879, "The News," unspecified paper, clipping in the scrapbook of Charles J. Thompson, private collection of Erik Lee Preminger.

Charlie played music by ear: Gypsy Rose Lee, *Gypsy: A Memoir*, New York, Harper & Brothers, 1957, 10.

Charlie in the Farmington Band: "In Justice Court," *Dakota County Tribune*, July 12, 1888.

Priest marries Charlie Thompson and Anna Egle, October 6, 1885: marriage certificate, Dakota County, Minnesota, GRL Papers, NYPL.

Six-hour long wedding reception at Mary Louise's place, wedding gifts: "Egle-Thompson," *Dakota County Tribune*, October 8, 1885.

Iowa honeymoon: "Egle-Thompson," *Dakota County Tribune*, October 8, 1885.

Mina Louise Thompson's birth date: email to the author from Dave Lilja, Dakota County Minnesota, April 13, 2010; unsigned note in the GRL Papers, postmarked Seattle, dated October 16, 1933.

Rosie Egle's death on August 7, 1886: Irving Todd, "DIED. EGLE— In this village, on Saturday, August 7, 1886, of rheumatism of the heart, MISS ROSE EGLE, daughter of Mrs. M.L. Egle, aged 15 years," *Dakota County Tribune*, August 12, 1886.

Mary Louise and Peter Herber opening Clearwater, Wisconsin hotel: *Dakota County Tribune*, December 2, 1886.

Mary Louise marries Carl Stein: *Dakota County Tribune*, July 28, 1887.

Mary Louise returns to Farmington to assist Anna with Mina: *Dakota County Tribune*, August 18, 1887.

Charlie Thompson in court over Clara Day Egle's unnamed unpleasantness: "In Justice Court," *Dakota County Tribune*, July 12, 1888.

Stephen Hurd Thompson born July 16, 1889: unsigned note, postmarked Seattle, October 16, 1933, NYPL.

Charlie Thompson transferred to North Dakota: email to the author from Rebecca Snyder, Dakota County Historical Society, March 19, 2010.

Rose Thompson born in Wahpeton August 31, 1891: "Born," Richland County Gazette, September 4, 1891.

CHAPTER 2

Rose Elizabeth: unsigned Letter, Seattle October 16, 1933, GRL Papers, NYPL; and name is listed as Rose Elizabeth Hovick on US passport application, "Divorcee Rose E. Hovick," dated February 4, 1925: National Archives and Records Administration (NARA); Washington DC; passport applications, January 2, 1906–March 31, 1925; Collection Number: ARC Identifier 583830/MLR Number A1 534; NARA Series: M1490; Roll #: 2708.

Rose's birth notice: "Born," *Richland County Gazette*, September 4, 1891.

Photo of Rose and Hurd in Wahpeton: GRL Papers.

Lilacs in Wahpeton: June Havoc, *More Havoc*, New York, Harper & Row, 1980, 129.

Charlie Thompson day operator at depot: *Dakota County Tribune*, November 8, 1894.

Candy Store fire details: "Fire," *Dakota County Tribune*, Farmington, Minnesota, February 1, 1894.

Mrs. Stein will rebuild: "The Local News," *Dakota County Tribune*, February 8, 1894.

Charlie transferred to Seattle: *Dakota County Tribune*, Farmington, Minnesota, November 8, 1894.

Mary Louise would move to Seattle within the year: 1895–96 Seattle Polk Directory.

Mary Louise retains ownership of Farmington building: *Dakota County Tribune*, Farmington, Minnesota, March 21, 1895.

Seattle was the train line's western terminus: Murray Morgan, *Skid Road: An Informal Portrait of Seattle*, Seattle, University of Washington Press, 1951, 105.

City engineer took steps to level the inclines: Murray Morgan, *Skid Road: An Informal Portrait of Seattle*, University of Washington Press, 1951, 168.

Belle Thompson born in Minnesota in 1895: US Bureau of the Census, Year: 1900, Census Place: Seattle Ward 8, King, Washington; Roll: 1745; Page: 7A; Enumeration District: 114.

Belle Evangeline: unsigned Letter, October 16, 1933, GRL Archive, NYPL.

Thompsons moved to 10th Avenue North: "Dream Comes True," *Seattle Post-Intelligencer*, Wednesday, August 25, 1897.

Mary Louise Stein's trip to Germany: "Back from Germany," *Dakota County Tribune*, Farmington, Minnesota, October 7, 1897.

Anna Thompson's premonition and Hurd Thompson's death: "Dream Comes True: Dreaming Mother Witnesses the Drowning of Her Child," *Seattle Post-Intelligencer*, Wednesday, August 25, 1897.

"Accidental drowning": King County Death Register, Washington State Digital Archives, Reference #: HRPKNG_breg13810, Page 248, Record 2907.

Charlie and Anna thought other kids were present at Hurd's death: "Boy Took a Cramp: Hurd Thompson Drowned in Lake Union Yesterday," article without newspaper masthead, August 27, 1897, scrapbook of Charles J. Thompson, collection of Erik Lee Preminger.

Body brought to undertaker: "Dream Comes True: Dreaming Mother Witnesses the Drowning of Her Child," *Seattle Post-Intelligencer*, Wednesday, August 25, 1897.

Neighbor apprises Anna of Hurd's death: "Boy Took A Cramp: Hurd Thompson Drowned in Lake Union Yesterday," no masthead, scrapbook of Charles J. Thompson, Collection of Erik Lee Preminger.

Neighborhood kids too frightened to give information: "Dream Comes True: Dreaming Mother Witnesses the Drowning of Her Child," *Seattle Post-Intelligencer*, Wednesday, August 25, 1897.

Wake in the house: "Deaths and Funerals," *Seattle Post-Intelligencer*, Thursday, August 26, 1897.

CHAPTER 3

Mary Louise Stein visits Farmington following Europe: "Back from Germany," *Dakota County Tribune*, Farmington, Minnesota, October 7, 1897.

Mary Louise/Convent school idea: *Gypsy*, Gypsy Rose Lee, 84.

R. Thompson/Holy Names School: email to the author from Sr. Dorothy Dees, Holy Names School, Seattle, October 7, 2009, re: 1898 Attendance Book.

Rose and Jack did not elope: Washington State Digital Archives, King County Marriage Records, Reference Number: kingcoarcmr_18414.

Mary Louise sells building to tenants: *Dakota County Tribune*, September 2, 1904.

Family moves to 323 4th Avenue North, Seattle, Washington, June 11, 1900/Charlie bought the lot on 4th Avenue North for $1300: *Seattle Daily Times*, Saturday Evening, June 16, 1900.

Charlie builds second house in 1905 on the lot with 323 4th Avenue North: King County Assessor's Record, Seattle, Washington.

Hilda Troast and Rita Kuppe, servants on 4th Avenue North: US Bureau of the Census, Year: 1900, Census Place: Seattle Ward 8, King, Washington; Roll: 1745; Page: 7A; Enumeration District: 114.

Mary Louise temporarily returns to Farmington, Minnesota, coinciding with servants' arrival: "New Store," *Dakota County Tribune*, Farmington, Minnesota, August 18, 1899.

Rose at Warren Avenue School in 1907 and probably earlier: "Dad Not So Slow" by Rose Thompson, *Seattle Sunday Times*, May 19, 1907.

Rose stifled at school: "Three Runaway Girls Enjoy Brief Liberty," *Seattle Times*, Wednesday, February 14, 1906.

Rose was pretty, wholesome-looking girl: GRL Papers, Photographs, NYPL.

Rose gifted in music, Mandolin: June Havoc, *Early Havoc*, 14–15.

Zither: Gypsy Rose Lee, unpublished draft of *Gypsy*, GRL Papers, NYPL.

Saxophone: Gypsy Rose Lee, unpublished draft of *Gypsy*, GRL Papers, NYPL.

Charlie not allowing Rose to be an actress: June Havoc, *Early Havoc*, 14–15.

John Considine/Pimp: Trav S. D., *No Applause—Just Throw Money*, New York, Faber and Faber, 2005, 153–54.

Juvenile Bostonians reviews: article in the *Port Townsend Washington Leader*, January 6, 1906.

Juvenile Bostonians: Ernest A. Wolff and Mrs. Lang, *Victoria Daily Colonist*, Sunday, September 9, 1906.

Charlie Thompson forces Rose to return home: June Havoc, *Early Havoc*, 14–15.

Anna working in Everett millinery shop: "Three Runaway Girls Enjoy Brief Liberty," *Seattle Times*, Wednesday, February 14, 1906.

Charlie's claim that Anna "abandoned" him in 1905: divorce papers, Charles J. Thompson v. Anna Thompson, filed August 29, 1929, County Clerk's Office, King County, Washington, No. 222617.

Anna with Charlie the rest of her life, even after he divorced her: "Traffic Claims Life of Seventh Victim in 1934," *Seattle Daily Times*, January 9, 1934.

Rental fees, 323 4th Avenue North, Seattle: *Seattle Sunday Times*, March 17, 1912.

Rental fees, 321 4th Avenue North, Seattle: *Seattle Daily Times*, Friday Evening, April 27, 1917.

Mina Thompson's marriage to Stetson Harlan: Washington State Digital Archives, King County Marriage Records, September 24, 1907, Reference No. kingcoarchmc22757.

Stetson Harlan physical description: US WW I Draft Registration Cards, 1917–1918, Registration State: Washington, Registration County: King, Roll: 1991926, Draft Board: 9.

Stetson's family and birthplace: US Bureau of the Census, Year: 1900; Census Place: Seattle Ward 8; King, Washington, Roll: 1745; Page: 7A; Enumeration District 114.

Valentines Day 1906/Runaway escapade details: "Three Runaway Girls Enjoy Brief Liberty," *Seattle Times*, Wednesday, February 14, 1906.

Parents of runaways frantic: "Three Runaway Girls Enjoy Brief Liberty," *Seattle Times*, Wednesday, February 14, 1906.

Train station apprehension, Ballard, Washington: "Three Runaway Girls Enjoy Brief Liberty," *Seattle Times*, Wednesday, February 14, 1906.

Running away to join the chorus: "Gypsy and June—Mother's Girls: Hovick Sisters in Chips Now, Can Grin at Frantic Youth," *New York Sunday News*, June 22, 1941.

The Children's Times writing contest rules: *Seattle Times*, July 7, 1907.

Frog Story, "Frogs Haunted Him" by Rose Thompson: *Seattle Sunday Times*, May 5, 1907.

The Children's Times, Rose's winning entry, "Dad Not So Slow" by Rose Thompson: *Seattle Sunday Times*, May 19, 1907.

1907 Mina marries Stetson Gerdon Harlan: Washington State Digital Archives, King County Marriage Records, September 24, 1907, Reference No.: kingcoarchmc22757.

Stetson born in Indiana/living on 4th Avenue North: US Bureau of the Census, Year: 1900; Census Place: Seattle Ward 8; King, Washington, Roll: 1745; Page: 7A; Enumeration District 114.

Mary Louise Stein is marriage witness: Washington State Digital Archives, King Marriage Records, Reference Number: kingcoarchmc22757.

September 24, 1907, wedding date was also Stetson's birthday: World War I Draft Registration Cards, 1917–1918, State of Washington, County of King, City of Seattle, Draft Board 9, Roll Number: 1991926.

Red light district: Murray Morgan, *Skid Road: An Informal Portrait of Seattle*, Seattle, University of Washington Press, , 1951, 59–61 and 65–66.

Anna charging up to fifty dollars a hat: Gypsy Rose Lee, "Mother and the Rising Generation," unpublished draft of *Gypsy*, GRL Papers, NYPL.

Anna selling in Tonopah, Nevada: Gypsy Rose Lee, *Gypsy: A Memoir*, 11.

Anna selling in Juneau, Alaska: Gypsy Rose Lee, *Gypsy: A Memoir*, 11.

Photo of Anna in Juneau, with plumed hat: Photo File, Gypsy Rose Lee Papers, NYPL.

CHAPTER 4

Jack Hovick born August 6, 1886, Crookston, Minnesota: US Bureau of the Census, Year: 1920; Census Location: Los Angeles, California; Roll: T625_106; Page 33A, Enumeration District 152; and email to author from Bette Solomon, Jack's granddaughter, May 30, 2012.

Jack's family situation unhappy: email to author from Bette Solomon, Jack's granddaughter, August 23, 2012.

Ole J Hovick: email to author from Bette Solomon, July 17, 2010.

Marit Hovick homesick in America: email to author from Bette Solomon, August 23, 2012.

Sven Hovick made a living in Norway from the sea and wanted to live near it again: email to author from Bette Solomon, July 18, 2010.

Jack seven years Rose's senior: US Bureau of the Census, Year: 1900, Census Place: Seattle Ward 8, King, Washington; Roll: 1745; Page 14B; Enumeration District 115.

Jack an adman for a Seattle newspaper: divorce papers, July 3, 1914, Superior Court of the State of Washington for King County, 162195, Rose E. Hovick, Plaintiff, v. John O. Hovick, Defendant, Affidavit of Plaintiff.

Jack and Rose married May 28, 1910; Anna Thompson and Mary Louise Stein were witnesses: Washington State Digital Archives, King County Marriage Records, John Hovick and Rose Thompson, May 28, 1910, Reference Number: kingcoarchmc31387.

Jack was a decent man: email to the author from Bette Solomon, August 23, 2012.

Rose Louise born January 9, 1911: January 9, 1914 was her official birthdate of record, but she was listed as three years old in the 1914 divorce papers, putting her actual birth date in 1911.

Gypsy born in Fauntleroy neighborhood: "Gypsy Rose Takes Plenty of Time to Put On Dress," *Seattle Times*, June 20, 1946.

Snowstorm details on January 9, 1911; Great Northern Railroad train forced to return from Whitefish, Montana: *Seattle Times*, Wednesday Evening, January 11, 1911.

Storm conditions on January 8–11, 1911; Port Townsend ships: *Seattle Times*, Tuesday Evening, January 10, 1911.

Louise was a gigantic baby: June Havoc, *More Havoc*, 2.

Snow coming through exposed portions of the roof, Louise was born on dining room table: June Havoc, *More Havoc*, 92.

Black midwife: "Gypsy and June—Mother's Girls: Hovick Sisters, in Chips Now, Can Grin at Frantic Youth," Florabel Muir and Robert Sullivan, *New York Sunday News*, June 22, 1941.

Born with two veils: Gypsy Rose Lee, *Gypsy: A Memoir*, 44—45.

Louise's childhood nickname of "Gypsy": Gypsy Rose Lee, *Gypsy*, 238.

Jack and Rose Hovick didn't get Rose Louise a birth certificate: letter from Gypsy Rose Lee to Anna Thompson, May 24, 1951, GRL Papers, NYPL.

Rose torn to shreds during Gypsy's birth: June Havoc, *Early Havoc*, 121–22; also June Havoc, *More Havoc*, 2 and 92.

Rose did not want more children: June Havoc, *Early Havoc*, 123–24.

Louise won a healthy baby contest: Erik Preminger, *Gypsy & Me*, 26.

1913 as the educated guess for year of Ellen June Hovick's birth: Social Security Death Index record for June Havoc, born 8 November 1913.

June believed she was born in 1912, had five birth certificates during vaudeville: Anita Gates, "June Havoc, Actress Who Outgrew Tyranny of Her 'Momma Rose,' Dies," *New York Times*, March 29, 2010.

Article Rose wrote in 1940 stated June was "19 months younger" than Louise: Mrs. Rose Hovick, "Gypsy's Growing Pains," *Independent Record*, Helena, Montana, July 16, 1944.

Registering a fake birth certificate in 1920s: letter from June Havoc (calling herself Julia) to Gypsy Rose Lee, April 25, 1949, GRL Papers, NYPL; Gypsy Rose Lee, *Gypsy*, 77–80.

Baby was to be named "Olaf John": June Havoc, *More Havoc*, 92.

Rose attempting to miscarry June: June Havoc, *More Havoc*, 92; also June Havoc, *Early Havoc*, 14.

June born in Vancouver, BC: June Havoc, *Early Havoc*, 14.

June's head in teacup: June Havoc, *Early Havoc*, 14.

Rose's hunger strike during pregnancy with June: June Havoc, *Early Havoc*, 14.

Rose a witness at Mina and Harry Briggs's marriage, November 4, 1913: Washington State Digital Archives, King County Marriage Records, Reference Number: kingcoarchmr_30850.

"Ellen June" listed on divorce papers, Jack lost job 1913, Jack borrowed money, Rose blames "grippe" on Rainier Beach house, separated last 2 months of 1913, West Apartments, 1914, Jack employed by *Seattle Sun*, 1914, Orinoco Apartments, 1914, Jack arranges move to Zindorf Apartments, Rose doesn't want to live in the Zindorf: Superior Court of the State of Washington for King County, No. 102,195, Rose E. Hovick, Plaintiff, v. John O. Hovick, Defendant, 8 July 1914.

Rose allegedly kills kitten: email to the author from Bette Solomon, Jack Hovick's grand-daughter, May 31, 2009; also email to author from Bette Solomon on May 18, 2012; also email to the author May 19, 2012.

Rose and Jack have violent fight on June 20, 1914, Jack allegedly beats Louise and puts her in closet, Rose spirits daughters away and won't reveal location, Jack calls Rose with option to follow to new apartment if she wants, Rose knew Zindorf by reputation only, Jack speaks to Rose but doesn't succeed in removing furniture, Rose bars doors and windows and meets with attorney P. V. Davis, Jack sees her leave and climbs in the window, Rose claims Jack became destructive in apartment, even taking bedrails, Rose files restraining order against Jack: Complaint No. 102195, Superior Court of the State of Washington for King County, Rose E. Hovick, Plaintiff, v. John O. Hovick, Defendant, July 8, 1914.

Jack's character witness J. Fred Braid: Superior Court of the State of Washington for King County, Affidavit of Fred Braid in Order to Show Cause, Rose E. Hovick v. John O. Hovick, Restraining Order, July 7, 1914.

Jack's character witness Owen Rowe: Superior Court of the State of Washington for King County, Affidavit of Owen A. Rowe in Order to Show Cause, Rose E. Hovick, Plaintiff, v. John O. Hovick, Defendant, July 7, 1914.

Jack's character witness A. J. Copeland: Superior Court of the State of Washington for King County, Affidavit of A. J. Copeland in Order to Show Cause, Rose E. Hovick, Plaintiff, v. John O. Hovick, Defendant, July 7, 1914.

Judge's preliminary ruling: Superior Court of the State of Washington for King County, Order, No. 102195, Rose E. Hovick, Plaintiff, v. John O. Hovick, Defendant, July 10, 1914.

Judge's Findings of Fact and Conclusion of Law re: Hovick v. Hovick: Superior Court of the State of Washington and for King County, Findings of Fact and Conclusions of Law, Rose E. Hovick, Plaintiff v. John O. Hovick, Defendant, August 19, 1914.

Jack inconsolable losing custody of girls: letter, Elizabeth Hovick to Louise, May 31, 1966, GRL Papers, NYPL.

Jack delighted to have freed himself of Rose: email to the author from Bette Solomon, May 31, 2009.

Jack, hobo: email to author from Bette Solomon, August 23, 2012.

Jack meets Elizabeth in Santa Monica: email to author from Bette Solomon, August 22, 2012.

Jack missed Louise and June until Betty was born: Elizabeth Hovick's letter to Gypsy, Series I, Subseries I, Personal, Box I, Folder 6, Mrs. John H. Hovick, 2516 Cliff Drive, Newport Beach, California, May 31, 1966, GRL Papers, NYPL.

Kitten: email to the author from Bette Solomon, Jack Hovick's granddaughter, May 31, 2009; also email to author from Bette Solomon on May 18, 2012.

Background of Judge Boyd J. Tallman: Boswell, H. James, *American Blue Book Western Washington*, Seattle, Lowman and Hanford, 1922, 29.

Dream dictionary: Gypsy Rose Lee, *Gypsy: A Memoir*, 44–45.

CHAPTER 5

Professor Harold Douglas, class at Oddfellows Hall: advertisement, *Seattle Sunday Times*, September 8, 1918.

June dances in class/allegedly tries to stand on her toes: June Havoc, *Early Havoc*, 15.

Rose approaches Professor Douglas for private lessons for June: June Havoc, *Early Havoc*, 15.

Charlie disapproves of theatrical people: Gypsy Rose Lee, *Gypsy*, 9.

Baby June debuts at Charlie's lodge hall: June Havoc, *Early Havoc*, 16.

Anna called "Big Lady" by granddaughters: Gypsy Rose Lee, *Gypsy*, 10–11.

Louise's song in act: Gypsy Rose Lee, *Gypsy*, 12.

Charlie believes theatrical career all right for June not Louise: Gypsy Rose Lee, *Gypsy*, 11.

"Mother was never stage-struck": Alex Witchel, "This Vaudeville Baby Keeps on Working," *New York Times*, August 2, 1992.

Rose's severe asthma: Gypsy Rose Lee, *Gypsy*, 22.

Photo of Louise and June in leafy glen: GRL Papers, NYPL.

Rose and Judson Brenneman's marriage: Washington State Digital Archives, King County Marriage Records, May 26, 1916, Reference No.: kingcoarchmr_35675.

Judson Brenneman's birth in Indiana: US Bureau of the Census, Year: 1900; Place: Columbia, Whitley, Indiana; Roll: 414; Page: 29B; Enumeration District 113.

June's *Seattle Times* write-up: "Ballet 1916," *Seattle Times*, May 28, 1916.

June's appearances at Seattle benefits: June Havoc, *Early Havoc*, 16.

June appears with Anna Pavlova: June Havoc, *Early Havoc*, 16–17.

June appears at Ad Show: "Baby's Twinkling Little Feet Delight Big Crowd at Ad Show," *Seattle Times*, September 9, 1916.

Judson/Sunday School: Gypsy Rose Lee, *Gypsy: A Memoir*, 13.

Judson wanted more children with Rose: June Havoc, *Early Havoc*, 123.

Charlie finances Rose's forays to Hollywood: Gypsy Rose Lee, *Gypsy*, 18.

Louise may have stayed with a Christian Scientist: Gypsy Rose Lee, unpublished draft of *Gypsy*, GRL Papers, NYPL.

Jack Hovick never had custody of Louise: email to author from Bette Solomon, August 23, 2012.

June's claim that Louise lived with Jack: June Havoc, *More Havoc*, 29.

June's other claim Louise lived with Rose's friend "Aunt Rita": June Havoc, *Early Havoc*, 18.

Elizabeth Hovick's letter to Gypsy stating Jack had missed her and June: letter, Mrs. John H. Hovick to Gypsy Rose Lee, May 31, 1966, GRL Papers, NYPL.

Seattle School District No. I: enumeration record for J. O. Hovick re: Rose Louise Hovick, May 15, 1916, Seattle Public Schools.

Gypsy attended Kindergarten at John Hay School: July 7, 1946, *Seattle Sunday Times Rotogravure*.

Louise predominantly self-taught: Gypsy Rose Lee, *Gypsy*, 94.

It's not known if Louise was enrolled in other schools: letter, Rose Thompson to June Havoc and Gypsy Rose Lee, November 2, 1944, GRL Papers, NYPL.

June's attendance at Ernest Belcher's Dancing School: "Local Girl Is Hit," *Los Angeles Times*, June 19, 1924.

June selected as Queen of the Allied Carnival: "Tot to Rule Frolic," *Los Angeles Times*, February 12, 1917.

Numbered posies: "Posies to Flood Allied Carnival," *Los Angeles Times*, February 11, 1917.

Allied Carnival event details: "Will Use Joy to Ease Pain," *Los Angeles Times*, February 16, 1918.

June going on film auditions: June Havoc, *Early Havoc*, 18–19.

June could pick up dancing routines by watching them: "Gypsy and June—Mother's Girls: Hovick Sisters, in Chips Now, Can Grin at Frantic Youth," Florabel Muir and Robert Sullivan, *New York Sunday News*, June 22, 1941.

Louise was a detached observer: June Havoc, *More Havoc*, 29–30.

June didn't speak until she was three: June Havoc, *More Havoc*, 28.

Rose gets June to sing: June Havoc, *Early Havoc*, 19.

Rose returned to Seattle several times for more money: June Havoc, *Early Havoc*, 18.

A single coin in Rose's purse, down to their last 25 cents: June Havoc interview, *Vaudeville, An American Masters Production*, Thirteen/WNET, KCTS/9 Television and Palmer/Fenster, Inc., 1997.

June working with Chicken Pox: June Havoc, *Early Havoc*, 59–62.

Hot soup, Rose's routine at the lodges/Louise not comfortable with them but proud of Rose's acting ability: Gypsy Rose Lee, *Gypsy: A Memoir*, New York, Harper & Brothers, 1957, 14–16.

Rose and children return to Seattle for Judson Brenneman divorce: Superior Court of the State of Washington for King County, No. 124577, Judson Brenneman, Plaintiff v. Rose E. Brenneman, Defendant, September 5, 1917.

Peak of Olympic Mountains named after Judge Walkinshaw: Olympic Mountain Rescue, *Olympic Mountains: A Climbing Guide*, Mountaineers Books, Seattle, 2006.

Brenneman divorce becomes final October 19, 1917: Superior Court for the County of King, No. 124577, Judson Brenneman, Plaintiff v. Rose E. Brenneman, Defendant.

Judson makes same claim when he divorces second wife: Superior Court for the County of King, No. 168472, Judson Brenneman, Plaintiff v. Mildred Brenneman, Defendant, August 15, 1923.

Back to California: US Navy Training Base Show on Thanksgiving, 1917, Souvenir Program, US Navy Training Base, November 28, 1917.

Charlie joins Rose and children for vacations: Venice Beach photo at the pier, GRL Papers, NYPL.

Belle Thompson marries Reginald Rankin: Portland, Oregon City, Directory, 1916.

Rankin an astonishingly entrepreneurial man: "Abortoria," *Time*, October 19, 1936.

Norman Rankin's Birth in January 1917: scrapbook of Charles J. Thompson, collection of Erik Lee Preminger; Social Security Death Index, Record for Norman K. Rankin, No. 537-03-1361, Issue State: Washington, Issue Date: Before 1951.

Belle's stiff leg injury: letter, Seattle Welfare Department to Gypsy Rose Lee, November 14, 1938, Gypsy Rose Lee Papers, NYPL.

Children beautifully dressed: Photographs, GRL Papers, NYPL.

Rose's alleged third marriage to "Daddy Jay," garage and fish pond: June Havoc, *Early Havoc*, 123–24.

"On the Jump" and "Hey There!" overlapping film schedules: email to the author from Annette Lloyd, Harold Lloyd biographer, August 11, 2009.

Angels/Mary Pickford Movie: Gypsy Rose Lee, *Gypsy: A Memoir*, New York, Harper & Brothers, 1957, 18–19.

Casting couch: Gypsy Rose Lee, draft of *Gypsy*, unpublished chapter, Series IV, Writings, Boxes 43 and 44, GRL Papers, NYPL.

June selected to play urchin: June Havoc, *Early Havoc*, 18–19.

Mary Stein dies/Catholics don't cremate: Western Union Telegram, Anna to Charlie, scrapbook of Charles J. Thompson, collection of Erik Lee Preminger, January 9, 1919.

June's engagement at the Hotel Alexandria: "Baby June, Toe Dancer," *Seattle Times*, October 12, 1919.

CHAPTER 6

June Hovic/"The Net": Wilkes Theater Programme, Wilkes Theater, Seattle, WA, October 19, 1919, GRL Papers, NYPL.

Lenore Diehl and Her Three Clever Kiddies Featuring Baby June Hovich/Palace Hip Theater, continuous 1 to 11: *Seattle Times*, Sept. 8, 1920.

Diehl Family information: US Bureau of the Census, Year: 1920; Census Place: San Francisco, California; Roll: T625_134; Page: 105B; Enumeration District 68; the Diehl address is also on Sweetsie Diehl's sheet music found in Gypsy Rose Lee's Archive, GRL Papers, NYPL.

Pedophiles: June Havoc, *More Havoc*, 174.

June's dirty looks: Gypsy Rose Lee, unpublished draft of *Gypsy*, GRL Papers, NYPL.

Pavlova's dying swan dance and June: Gypsy Rose Lee, unpublished draft of *Gypsy*, GRL Papers, NYPL.

Mrs. Diehl jealous of June: Gypsy Rose Lee, unpublished draft of *Gypsy*, GRL Papers, NYPL.

June honored by Maccabbees: *Seattle Daily Times*, Friday Evening, September 10, 1920.

Laddie Kenneth from Long Beach, CA: "Sophisticated Little Miss Is Wee Actress, Baby June, And She Has Right to Be" by First Nighter, *Wisconsin State Journal*, Madison, Wisconsin, October 22, 1922.

Pericles name changed to Alexander Pantages: *Skid Road*, Morgan, 151.

Pantages's first theater in Nome, Alaska/actors get investment back: *Skid Road*, Morgan, 154.

Pantages's genius for choosing acts/ran away from Greece, worked as cabin boy: *Skid Road*, Morgan, 155.

Letter arrives telling Rose act is booked on Pantages circuit: Gypsy Rose Lee, *Gypsy*, 17.

Charlie Thompson provides money for costumes: Gypsy Rose Lee, *Gypsy*, 19–20.

"The Pan Time": Fred Allen, *Much Ado About Me*, Wildside Press, 2008, 195.

Dogs dressed in baby clothes on trains: Gypsy Rose Lee, unpublished draft of *Gypsy*, GRL Papers, NYPL.

Louise sewing clothes for her pet monkey: Gypsy Rose Lee, *Gypsy*, 90–91.

Seven Little Foys act content: "Stars of Vaudeville #130: Eddie Foy, The Seven Little Foys, and The Youngest Foy of All," *Travalanche* Blog by vaudeville historian Trav S. D., March 9, 2010, http://travsd.wordpress.com/2010/03/09/stars-of-vaudeville-130-eddie-foy-the-seven-little-foys-and-the-youngest-foy-of-all/.

Seven Little Foys—Most were talented but not all: email to the author from Trav S. D., May 21, 2012.

Cherry Sisters act: *No Applause, Just Throw Money*, Trav S. D., Faber & Faber, 2005, 100.

Oscar Hammerstein encouraging audience members to throw vegetables at Cherry Sisters Act: *No Applause, Just Throw Money*, Trav S. D., Faber & Faber, 2006, 101.

Performers stole anything not nailed down: Trav S. D., *No Applause, Just Throw Money*, 24–25.

Backstage culture, every man for himself: Trav S. D., *No Applause, Just Throw Money*, 145.

Vaudeville's a jungle, Rose a "jungle mother": Gypsy Rose Lee, *Gypsy*, 6.

Backstage Rules, No Profanity, etc.: Gypsy Rose Lee Article, *Variety Anniversary Issue*, 1942, GRL Papers, NYPL.

Rose reportedly had sticky fingers: Gypsy Rose Lee, *Gypsy*, 89–90; Havoc, *More Havoc*, 4.

Louise and June with Victrola records hidden in bloomers: "Gypsy and June—Mother's Girls: Hovick Sisters, in Chips Now, Can Grin at Frantic Youth," Florabel Muir and Robert Sullivan, *New York Sunday News*, June 22, 1941; also Gypsy Rose Lee, unpublished draft of *Gypsy*, GRL Papers, NYPL.

Store manager storms the theater/Rose threatens a lawsuit: "Gypsy and June—Mother's Girls: Hovick Sisters, in Chips Now, Can Grin at Frantic Youth," Florabel Muir and Robert Sullivan, *New York Sunday News*, June 22, 1941.

Vaudeville "crime" of stealing another's act: "I, Said the Fly: Nuts for the Underman" by June Havoc, article in "I, Said the Fly" the Guthrie Theater program, 1973–74, Minneapolis, 13.

Milton Berle notorious for stealing other performers' material: *When Television Was Young: The Inside Story with Memories by Legends of the Small Screen*, Ed McMahon and David Fisher, Thomas Nelson, 2007, 103.

Rose lifted other kids' acts for June to perform: Gypsy Rose Lee, *Gypsy*, 12.

Sweetsie Diehl's Sheet Music in the archive: "Won't You Be My Husband?" sheet music by George Arthurs and C. W. Murphy, GRL Papers, NYPL.

June a quick study for learning other kids' acts: "Gypsy and June—Mother's Girls: Hovick Sisters, in Chips Now, Can Grin at Frantic Youth," Florabel Muir and Robert Sullivan, *New York Sunday News*, June 22, 1941.

Francis Renault's rhinestone dress: "I, Said the Fly" program, article by June Havoc, the Guthrie Theater Program, 1973–74, Minneapolis, 13–14.

"While all three performers possess a great degree of talent": "At the Capitol," undated article, no newspaper heading, scrapbook of Charles J. Thompson, collection of Erik Lee Preminger.

June in seven numbers out of nine in act: "I, Said the Fly: Nuts for the Underman" by June Havoc, article in "I, Said the Fly," the Guthrie Theater Program, 1973–74, Minneapolis, 14.

Seven scenery changes: "I, Said the Fly: Nuts for the Underman" by June Havoc, article in "I, Said the Fly" the Guthrie Theater Program, 1973–74, Minneapolis, 14.

Additional children, Freddie Richards: photographs, GRL Papers, NYPL.

Dainty June and Company, 1922: "Dainty June Hovick Here in Person at Ideal Theater," *Wisconsin Rapids Daily Tribune*, Tuesday, June 6, 1922.

Dainty June and Her Newsboy Songsters, 1924: "By Long Odds the Biggest and Best Vodvil Show of the Season," *Bradford Era*, Bradford, Pennsylvania, Thursday, January 10, 1924, 3.

Act opened with "The Bowery": Gypsy Rose Lee, *Gypsy*, 123.

Act closed with military gun drill finale: Gypsy Rose Lee, *Gypsy*, 63, 188.

Adagio dance: "I, Said the Fly: Nuts for the Underman" by June Havoc, *I, Said the Fly* Guthrie Theater Program, 1973–74, Minneapolis, 15.

Pet dog ballad: Gypsy Rose Lee, *Gypsy*, 123.

Cow number; papier-mâché head, Rose's cow dream: Gypsy Rose Lee, *Gypsy*, 32–35.

Orpheum Time; "Stopped show 8 curtain calls": handwritten notation on article, scrapbook of Charles J. Thompson, collection of Erik Lee Preminger.

June's numbers, *Won't You Be My Husband; I'm Nobody's Darling*: "'Dainty June's' Act is Curbed," Tuesday, January 23, 1923, *Evening Tribune-Times*, Hornell, NY.

June's numbers, "Mary," "Oh! You Bowery Gal", and "Powder Puff Vamp": "I, Said the Fly: Nuts for the Underman" by June Havoc, article in "I, Said the Fly" the Guthrie Theater Program, 1973–74, Minneapolis, 14.

Song number, "I Want To Be A Janitor's Child": "'Dainty June's' Act is Curbed," Tuesday, January 23, 1923, *Evening Tribune-Times*, Hornell, NY.

Not upsetting June, present handed to her by child in act: Gypsy Rose Lee, unpublished draft of *Gypsy*, GRL Papers, NYPL.

Crying could swell June's face: June Havoc, *Early Havoc*, 133.

June insisting kids wait for her in wings at Christmas: Gypsy Rose Lee, unpublished draft of *Gypsy*, GRL Papers, NYPL.

Louise thought adults encouraged June to be "highly strung": Gypsy Rose Lee, unpublished draft of *Gypsy*, GRL Papers, NYPL.

June and Louise found homes for stray animals: June Havoc, *Early Havoc*, 130–31.

Louise originally disdained vaudeville: June Havoc, *More Havoc*, 30.

Louise was in the Opening and Finale: June Havoc, *More Havoc*, 30.

Louise singing "I'm A Hard-Boiled Rose": Gypsy Rose Lee, *Gypsy*, 12.

Holy Yumping Yiminy, Louise's comic routine, October 22, 1922: Wisconsin State Journal, Madison, Wisconsin, "Sophisticated Little Miss Is Wee Actress, Baby June, And She Has Right to Be," by First Nighter, October 22, 1922.

Backstage Pantages Rules/June busted for stockings, Louise for Yiminy: *Variety Issue*, 1942, by Gypsy Rose Lee.

Won't You Be My Husband song vetoed; "Holy Yumping Yiminy" vetoed: article by Gypsy Rose Lee, *Variety Anniversary Issue*, 1942, GRL Papers, NYPL.

Billing of Acts, billing spots, chaser act, order of spots on the bill: Trav S. D., 87–88.

Sophie Tucker moving June's act on bill, June and Sophie Tucker: June Havoc, *Early Havoc*, 136–38.

Other act's props disappearing courtesy of Rose: Gypsy Rose Lee, *Gypsy*, 12–13.

Rose liberating the Mae Murray wig: June Havoc, *Early Havoc*, 78–80.

Rose leading other performers: June Havoc, *Early Havoc*, 69.

Prohibition leading to the rise of Italian and Chinese restaurants, wine at Italian restaurants, Italian and Chinese food containing ingredients for Americans: Kathleen Morgan Drowne and Patrick Huber, *The 1920's, American Popular Culture Through History*, Greenwood Press, Westport, CT, 2004.

June's recollections of restaurants being cheap and close to theater: June Havoc, *Early Havoc*, 69.

Chinese Food, largest quantities the lowest prices: Barbara Gimla Shortridge and James R. Shortridge, editors, *The Taste of American Place: A Reader on Regional and Ethnic Foods*, Rowan & Littlefield, 1999, 173.

Men attracted to Rose in droves, Rose refreshingly unpainted: June Havoc, *Early Havoc*, 58–59.

Murray Gordon Edelston, physical description from passport: National Archives and Records Administration (NARA); Washington DC; Passport Applications, January 2, 1906–March 31, 1925; Collection Number: ARC Identifier 583830/MLR Number A1 534; NARA Series: M1490; Roll #: 2708.

Murray's birth in 1888 in Minnesota to Romanian Jewish parents and spouse and daughter and employer information: US Bureau of the Census, Year: 1920; Census Place: Detroit, Ward 1, Wayne, Michigan; Roll: T625_803; Page: 11B; Enumeration District 11; Image: 46; World War I Draft Registration Card, Registration State: Ohio, Registration County: Franklin; Roll: 1832026; Draft Board: 2; World War II Draft Registration Card, National Archives and Records Administration (NARA); Washington, D.C.; State Headquarters: Illinois; Microfilm Series: M2097; Microfilm Roll: 75.

No registration for the act at US Patent Office/"US Patt. Off": author's investigation at the Library of Congress, November 2009.

Gordon's promotional strategies, new clothes for everybody: Gypsy Rose Lee, *Gypsy*, 25–26.

June, Tam O'Shanter and diamond rings: Gypsy Rose Lee, *Gypsy*, 25–26.

Beaver coats: Gypsy Rose Lee, *Gypsy*, 25–26.

Gypsy dressing as a boy: Gypsy Rose Lee, *Gypsy*, 25.

Note on back of photo of Louise dressed as boy: photographs, GRL Papers, NYPL.

Staying in hotel suites: Gypsy Rose Lee, first draft of *Gypsy*, GRL Papers, NYPL.

Louise missed staying with Rose and June once Gordon arrived: Gypsy Rose Lee, *Gypsy*, 21.

Louise fasting on Jewish holiday: Gypsy Rose Lee, *Gypsy*, 83–84.

Gordon's claims June's doll was gift from "General Neville": First Nighter, "Sophisticated Little Miss Is Wee Actress, Baby June, And She Has Right to Be," *Wisconsin State Journal*, October 22, 1922.

Georgie and Tommy Triano: Gypsy Rose Lee, unpublished draft of *Gypsy*, GRL Papers, NYPL.

Johnny: Gypsy Rose Lee, unpublished draft of *Gypsy*, GRL Papers, NYPL.

Mildred LaSalle, Delorre St. Paul, Charles Favis: First Nighter, "Sophisticated Little Miss Is Wee Actress, Baby June, And She Has Right to Be," *Wisconsin State Journal*, Madison, Wisconsin, October 22, 1922.

Olive Thompson's teaching qualifications: GRL Papers, NYPL.

Olive Thompson: First Nighter, "Sophisticated Little Miss is Wee Actress, Baby June, And She Has Right to Be," *Wisconsin State Journal*, October 22, 1922.

Staged photo of Rose as teacher: Gypsy Rose Lee, *Gypsy*, photo section following page 56.

Dentist/Doctor for Rose's injuries: June Havoc, *Early Havoc*, 121 –22.

Gordon calls June "tender-hearted," "Madam Hovick, The Developer of Children": First Nighter, "Sophisticated Little Miss Is Wee Actress, Baby June, And She Has Right to Be," *Wisconsin State Journal*, October 22, 1922.

Dancing cow with papier-mâché head, June's barnyard number, Orpheum circuit bookers took notice: Gypsy Rose Lee, *Gypsy*, 32–35.

CHAPTER 7

Mina's second and third marriages: to Harry Briggs, Washington State Digital Archives, King County Marriage Records, 14 November 1913, Reference No.: kingcoarchmr_30850; to George Foster, Washington State Digital Archives, King County Marriage Records, 10 May 1918, Reference No.: kingcoarchmc62803.

Mina's death: telegram, Anna Thompson to Charles Thompson, January 13, 1923, personal scrapbook of Charles J. Thompson, collection of Erik Lee Preminger.

Mina "drug overdose" tall tale: June Havoc, Early Havoc, 24–25.

Melba: June Havoc, *Early Havoc*, p. 20–21.

Bradford, PA, engagement: "Dainty June will Receive at the Grand," *Bradford Era*, Bradford, PA, January 6, 1923.

June at Rochester Children's Shelter: June Havoc, *Early Havoc*, New York, Simon and Schuster, 1959, 177–79.

Telegrams re: Rochester authorities: Rose to Charles Thompson, January 20, 1923, GRL Papers, NYPL.

"Dainty June's" Act is Curbed: *Evening Tribune-Times*, Hornell, NY, Tuesday, January 23, 1923.

"Managing a troupe of talented, temperamental kids was more work than fun": "Gypsy's Growing Pains" by Mrs. Rose Hovick, *Independent Record*, Helena, Montana (King Features Syndicate article), Sunday, July 16, 1944.

Easter and Halloween, Rose Scaring Sonny: Gypsy Rose Lee, unpublished draft of *Gypsy*, GRL Papers, NYPL.

Rose in "M-O-T-H-E-R" Tableau: June Havoc, *More Havoc*, 165.

"You have a bright star on your head, dear": "World on a String," unpublished play by Gypsy Rose Lee, Series 6, Writings, GRL Papers, NYPL.

Samba's death: June Havoc, *Early Havoc*, 132–35.

Halloween story: Gypsy Rose Lee, unpublished draft of *Gypsy*, GRL Papers, NYPL.

Riveting storyteller/Donner party reference: email to the author from Ethan Rarick, Donner Party scholar and author of *Desperate Passage*, December 8, 2008.

Reginald Rankin's family in Donner Party: "Donner Party Member's Kin Dies at Arcadia," obituary of Daisy Shinn Rankin, *Los Angeles Times*, January 12, 1950; emails to author from Theresa Rankin, February 2, 2011, and February 3, 2011.

Ghost floating through room: June Havoc, *Early Havoc*, 125.

Omen dreams featuring "Doddie" (Mary Louise Stein): Gypsy Rose Lee, *Gypsy*, 33.

Louise reading fortunes; nicknamed Gypsy: Gypsy Rose Lee, unpublished raft of *Gypsy*, GRL Papers, NYPL.

Graduation; Louise and Trianos: Gypsy Rose Lee, unpublished draft of *Gypsy*, GRL Papers, NYPL; also letter, Rose Thompson to June Havoc and Gypsy Rose Lee, November 2, 1944, GRL Papers, NYPL.

Shoplifting at Woolworth's: Gypsy Rose Lee, *Gypsy*, 50–51.

Christian Science Statement as punishment assignment: Gypsy Rose Lee's Scrapbook, GRL Papers, NYPL; also Gypsy Rose Lee, "World on a String," unpublished play, GRL Papers, NYPL.

"Merry Christmas to my little stars": Gypsy Rose Lee, "World on a String," unpublished play, GRL Papers, NYPL.

United States Passport Application, "Divorcee Rose E. Hovick," dated February 4, 1925: National Archives and Records Administration (NARA); Washington DC; passport applications, January 2, 1906: March 31, 1925; Collection Number: ARC Identifier 583830/ MLR Number A1 534; NARA Series: M1490; Roll # 2708.

Never boarded the SS *Olympic*, No records of a 1925 departure on any ship were found for Rose, Louise, June, Belle, or Murray: Gordon Edelston in the immigration and travel records on www.ancestry.com.

Seattle bogus birth certificate: affidavit of Dr. Daniel Buckley, State of Washington, County of King, dated 6 June 1923, GRL Papers, NYPL.

June's act, stopping the show four times: June Havoc, *Early Havoc*, 128–29.

Gordon's fights with Rose over marriage: Gypsy Rose Lee, *Gypsy*, 95–98.

Fanny Brice scene with Louise: Gypsy Rose Lee, *Gypsy*, 69–76.

June's nervous breakdown: June Havoc, *More Havoc*, 27.

Rose and Gordon's fights: writings, Series VI, Gypsy Rose Lee, unpublished draft of *Gypsy*, GRL Papers, NYPL.

CHAPTER 8

Rose's $4,000 ring: "Her Stage Kick Pulls Curtain on Gunplay," undated article, no masthead, in a New York City paper, the scrapbook of Charles J. Thompson, collection of Erik Lee Preminger.

"F. E. Gorham," real name "B. G. Graham": letter, January 4, 1957, Barry Lee Cohen of Greenbaum, Wolff & Ernst to Mr. Robert Appleton, Harper & Bros., GRL Papers, NYPL.

"F. E. Gorham's" cockroach scam: Gypsy Rose Lee, *Gypsy*, 104–5.

"F. E. Gorham's" building site scam: Gypsy Rose Lee, *Gypsy*, 116–18.

Robbery details: "Her Stage Kick Pulls Curtain on Gunplay," undated article in a New York City paper, no masthead, the scrapbook of Charles J. Thompson, collection of Erik Lee Preminger.

Roxy Rothafel: June Havoc, *Early Havoc*, 140–45.

Henry Court; vegetables, pawning diamonds: Gypsy Rose Lee, *Gypsy*, 130–32.

June stuttering and dropping props: June Havoc, *More Havoc*, 35.

June meets "Bobby Reed"/Buddy Hyde: June Havoc, *Early Havoc*, 190–94.

Rose Find the June and Buddy in Traveler: June Havoc, *Early Havoc*, 195–97.

Louise and Stanley: Gypsy Rose Lee, *Gypsy*, 138–41.

June's wedding: marriage license, Ellen Hovick and Weldon Hyde, North Platte, Nebraska, November 30, 1928.

Photos of Last Dainty June Tour in 1928: photographs, GRL Papers, NYPL.

Police Complaint Information, June & Buddy Run for It: "Court Notes and Police Gossip," *Topeka State Journal*, December 31, 1928.

Rose tries to allegedly murder Weldon: June Havoc, *Early Havoc*, 200–5.

Louise awaiting Stanley in parking lot: Gypsy Rose Lee, *Gypsy*, 142.

June stashed away: June Havoc, *Early Havoc*, 200–5.

Boys skipped out: "Strip to Fame," *Collier's*, December, 1936.

CHAPTER 9

Henry down at heel: "Strip to Fame," *Collier's*, December 1936.

Rose betrayed by June, June statement to Louise that Rose has never forgiven her: Gypsy Rose Lee, unpublished draft of *Gypsy*, GRL Papers, NYPL.

Louise creates costumes: Gypsy Rose Lee, *Gypsy*, 153–57.

Los Angeles: Gypsy Rose Lee, *Gypsy*, 158–60.

Little Mary, Rose's Favorite, June replacement: Gypsy Rose Lee, unpublished draft of *Gypsy*, GRL Papers, NYPL.

May Sherwood, time of her life, showing photographs of the act until she died: email to author from May's grandson Rob Brandreth-Gibbs, March 12, 2011.

May Sherwood's description of Rose: *Weekend Magazine*, "On the Road with Gypsy Rose Lee," Bruce Moss, undated, collection of Rob Brandreth-Gibbs.

Photo of Louise and June: "Madame Rose and Her Ten Dancing Daughters at the Yuma R. & N.," *Yuma Morning Sun*, 3 March 1929.

May Sherwood on Rose using June's photo in Yuma: *Weekend Magazine*, "On the Road with Gypsy Rose Lee," Bruce Moss, Undated, collection of Rob Brandreth-Gibbs.

Rose singing "Mother Machree" in Yuma: Karen Abbott, *American Rose*, Random House, 2010, 168.

Cooking School Revue: Tuesday, April 2, 1929, *El Paso Times*.

Teatro Colon ads: *El Paso Times*, April 4, 1929.

Rose calling herself Jane: "Gypsy and June—Mother's Girls: Hovick Sisters in Chips Now, Can Grin at Frantic Youth," Florabel Muir and Robert Sullivan, *New York Sunday News*, June 22, 1941.

Yo soy una gancha: Gypsy Rose Lee, *Gypsy*, 166.

Hair dye initial disaster: *Weekend Magazine*, "On the Road with Gypsy Rose Lee," Bruce Moss, undated, collection of Rob Brandreth-Gibbs.

Charlie Thompson's divorce: Charles J. Thompson, Plaintiff v. Anna Thompson, Defendant, August 14, 1929, Superior Court of the State of Washington for King County, No.: 222617.

June believed Charlie wanted to marry neighbor: June Havoc, *Early Havoc*, 181–83.

"Do Men Prefer Blondes? Test": *Sandusky Star-Journal*, Saturday October 19, 1929.

"Wall Street Lays an Egg" headline in *Variety*: Gypsy Rose Lee, *Gypsy*, 170–71.

June on the census: US Bureau of the Census, Year: 1930; Census Place: Portland, Multnomah, Oregon; Roll: 1951; Page: 2B; Enumeration District: 215; Image: 653.0; FHL microfilm: 2341685.

Sam Middleton/Burlesque debut: "If I'd Said No in Kansas City," by Gypsy Rose Lee, *Twenty-Sixth Variety Anniversary Issue*, undated article, GRL Papers, NYPL.

Tessie, theater is raided, monkey fur pants: Gypsy Rose Lee, *Gypsy*, 205.

Club Bagdad contract: contract between D. A. Davis, Club Bagdad, Hialeah, FL and Rose Louiss [*sic*] Company of New York City, NY, November 20, 1930, GRL Papers, NYPL.

Club Bagdad; "Club Oasis"; papaya grove story: Gypsy Rose Lee, *Gypsy*, 208–13.

CHAPTER 10

Tent: Gypsy Rose Lee, *Gypsy*, 215—18.

Rose shoots cow: Gypsy Rose Lee, *Gypsy*, 220–22.

May Sherwood's memories of cow shooting: email to the author from Erik Preminger quoting Rob Brandreth-Gibbs, February 22, 2011.

Gladys "Youth" Clark: "Girls From Follies" has Gladys Clark, *Pittsburgh Post-Gazette*, March 4, 1930.

Lombard in suit: Joe Morella and Edward Z. Epstein, *Gable & Lombard & Powell & Harlow*, New York, Dell, 1976, 29.

Ed Ryan/wife Gladys in jail: Gypsy Rose Lee, Gypsy, 225–26.

Burlesque Wheels: *A History of the Musical: Burlesque, Misunderstood Genre* by John Kendrick, 1996—2003, http://www.musicals101.com/burlesque.htm#Genre1996—2003.

Gypsy's debut as star: Gypsy Rose Lee, *Gypsy*, 226—31.

Contract for the tour; flowers over footlights from "An Admirer": Gypsy Rose Lee, *Gypsy*, 231—32.

Gypsy boots Mary Noel: Gypsy Rose Lee, *Gypsy*, 234—37.

Frog story: Gypsy Rose Lee, *Gypsy*, 234—37.

Booing boys: Gypsy Rose Lee, *Gypsy*, 246—47.

Mike leaves: Gypsy Rose Lee, *Gypsy*, 242–44.

The girls leave: Gypsy Rose Lee, *Gypsy*, 245.

Marathons/June: Gypsy Rose Lee, *Gypsy*, 247.

Marathon Set-up: Calabria, Frank, *Dance of the Sleepwalkers*, Popular Press, 1983, 70.

June believed she was not Jack Hovick's daughter: author's telephone interview with June Havoc's assistant Tana Sibilio, January 19, 2009.

Nothing could put a smile on Rose's face like pulling off a scam: June Havoc, *More Havoc*, 212.

CHAPTER 11

Yetta Lostit/Ada Onion: Gypsy Rose Lee, *Gypsy*, 255.

ASPCA/Angel wings: Gypsy Rose Lee, unpublished draft of *Gypsy*, GRL Papers, NYPL.

June, Marathon kidnap situation: June Havoc, *More Havoc*, 85–88.

Minsky's red light system against Sumner: Karen Abbott, *American Rose*, 80.

Sumner raids: "Burlesque Show Raided," *New York Times*, April 11, 1931.

Minsky's raid, blue spotlight: Fiona Matthias, "How to Strip for Your Husband," *London Telegraph*, August 10, 2004.

June visits Rose and Gypsy in 1931: June Havoc, *Early Havoc*, 252–56.

Rego Park "Ave Maria" doorbell: June Havoc, *More Havoc*, 64.

December 1931, Anna, Buddy, and June stay with Rose and Gypsy: *Greater Show World*, December 15, 1931.

Rosebushes in Rego Park: June Havoc, *More Havoc*, 98-101.

Charlie's accident: "Traffic Claims Life of Seventh Victim in 1934," *Seattle Daily Times*, January 9, 1934.

Anna Thompson in car during accident: "Traffic Claims Life of Seventh Victim in 1934," *Seattle Daily Times*, January 5, 1934.

Minskys pay for Charlie's grave: Gypsy Rose Lee, unpublished draft of *Gypsy*, GRL Papers, NYPL.

Bathtub gin recipe: Joseph Nicholson, "Making Bathtub Gin," ehow.com, http://www.ehow.com/how-does_4779424_making-bathtub-gin.html.

House in Rego Park, Queens: *New York American*, 1931, GRL Papers, NYPL.

Mafia gay bars: George De Stefano, *An Offer We Can't Refuse: The Mafia in the Mind of America*, New York, Faber and Faber, 2006, 222.

June touring the Tetons as guide with Jaime: June Havoc, *More Havoc*, 73–77.

Beating Jamie to a pulp: June Havoc, *More Havoc*, 81—83.

June arrives at Rose's apartment, Rose thinks she wants an abortion: June Havoc, *More Havoc*, 98—101.

No known lesbian traditions involving grapefruit: email to the author from DeeJae Cox, October 24, 2009.

Lesbian grapefruit fight info: June Havoc, *More Havoc*, 107—10.

Rose, Gypsy, and two friends on vacation: photographs, GRL Papers, NYPL.

Banned from hospital: June Havoc, *More Havoc*, 125—26.

CHAPTER 12

Rose's offer to adopt April: June Havoc, *More Havoc*, 144–47.

Betty Hovick's trip to New York City via South: email to the author from Bette Solomon, October 3, 2010.

David Merrick remembers Beth Hovick: email to the author from Arthur Laurents, March 8, 2010.

Rose sells ticket to *Forbidden Melody*: undated letter, June Havoc to Gypsy Rose Lee, possibly ca. 1959–60, maybe even 1957, is in regard to a draft of *Early Havoc*, Series I, Family Correspondence, Letters from June Havoc, Undated, Box 2, Folder 12, GRL Papers, NYPL.

Guest rate at Witchwood Manor, beer guzzling: Gypsy Rose Lee, *Gypsy*, 284.

April stays with Rose: June Havoc, *More Havoc*, 165–66.

Gypsy, legitimate at last in *The Ziegfeld Follies*: "Gypsy Rose Lee Remembers Burlesque," sound recording, Fort Lauderdale, FL, Stereoddities, c. 1962, Performing Arts Research Recordings, NYPL.

June says Rose hates her: Gypsy Rose Lee, unpublished draft of *Gypsy*, GRL Papers, NYPL.

Cow's head used for kindling: Gypsy Rose Lee, unpublished draft of *Gypsy*, GRL Papers, NYPL.

Article: "Gypsy Rose Lee Ready for her Celluloid Debut," *Albuquerque Journal*, April 18, 1937.

Gypsy not allowed to show even one knee: *Los Angeles Times*, "Ready to Invade New Field," April 19, 1937, photo caption.

"Gypsy Rose Lee, Strip tease Artist, Arrives for Films"/English accent: *Los Angeles Times*, April 19, 1937.

Gypsy's act was all in fun: Grace Kingsley, "Gypsy's Strip Act All in Fun," *Los Angeles Times*, April 25, 1937.

Rose's girlfriend Connie: undated letter, Rose Thompson to Gypsy Rose Lee, maybe 1937–38, mentions Gypsy's then-husband Bob Mizzy, Series I, Personal Correspondence, Family, Rose Thompson, Undated Letters, Box 1, Folder 14, GRL Papers, NYPL.

Genevieve's sister Frances remembered her as a clown: email to author from Kathy Wagner, Genevieve's niece, June 28, 2012.

Genevieve Augustine's home life, father's rages and roving hands, mother's mental illness, brother beaten: author's telephone interview with Margaret Craft, Genevieve's niece, March 16, 2011.

Family member recounting Genevieve was interested in West Point cadet: email to author from Kathy Wagner, Genevieve's niece, May 21, 2012.

Kay Ray obsessed with Genevieve: "Art Student Shoots Self: Mystery Surrounds Death at Dancer's Home," *Port Arthur News*, Friday, June 4, 1937; also Series I, Subseries I, Personal, Box 1, Folder 1, Personal Correspondence-Family, 1937–42, From Jean Augustin, February 21, 1937, GRL Papers, NYPL.

June's story of Rose's alleged "description" of Genevieve's suicide: June Havoc, *More Havoc*, 175–76.

Trip to Monroe, Genevieve a problem child, Genevieve's suicide: "Art Teacher Shoots Self Near Monroe: Home of Gypsy Rose Lee's Mother Scene of Suicide, Attempted Previously," *Middletown Times Herald*, June 2, 1937.

Genevieve attended St. Clara's Academy in Sinsinawa: yearbook photo of Genevieve Augustine, Kenosha High School, from the collection of Margaret Craft.

Genevieve's grades at St. Clara's Academy: email to author from Sr. Lois Hoh, Archivist, St. Clara's Academy, Sinsinawa, WI, February 15, 2011.

Twentieth Century-Fox convention: "Film Salesmen Visiting City," *Los Angeles Times*, May 31, 1937.

Gypsy's screen name announced at convention: "Walter Winchell— On Broadway New York and Hollywood Heartbeat," *San Antonio Light*, June 5, 1937.

Georgia Sothern's story to Erik Preminger: email from Erik Preminger to the author, September 20, 2009.

Georgia Sothern's autobiography where she admits to several lies: *Georgia: My Life in Burlesque*, New York, Signet Books, 1972, lied to uncle about nonexistent "great" bookings, 13; lied about being from St. Louis, 18; lied about name, 19.

Ruled a suicide: "Art Teacher Takes Own Life in Home of Gypsy Rose Lee," Wednesday Evening, June 2, 1937, *Observer-Dispatch*, Utica, NY, June 2, 1937.

Whitehead, Miller, Hart, Lambert, and Lopez: "Death Inquiry Will Continue," *Middletown Times Herald*, October 26, 1937.

Telegram to Genevieve's Father: "Art Student Shoots Self: Mystery Surrounds Death at Dancer's Home," *Port Arthur News*, Port Arthur, TX, June 4, 1937.

Gypsy wearing a suit: *Enquirer*, Cincinnati, June 6, 1937.

Gypsy, Don Ameche, and Alice Faye photo: "Candid Camera," *Denver Post*, June 13, 1937.

Feud with Alice Fay: "Actresses Settle Feud; Others Carry Right On," Harold Heffernan, June 16, 1937, *Los Angeles Times*.

CHAPTER 13

Morton Minsky questioned on Gypsy's character: Morton Minsky and Milt Machlin, *Minsky's Burlesque*, Arbor House, 1986, New York, 237–38.

Rose's asthma prevents attendance at wedding: undated letter, Rose Thompson to Gypsy Rose Lee, GRL Papers, NYPL.

Wedding at sea: "Strip Dancer Married at Sea," August 15, 1937, *Los Angeles Times*, and Morton Minsky and Milt Machlin, *Minsky's Burlesque*, 239.

Rose devastated to have missed fun: telegram, Rose Thompson to Gypsy Rose Lee, August 16, 1937, GRL Papers, NYPL.

Rose leaving the 25th: telegram, Rose Thompson to Gypsy Rose Lee, August 16, 1937, GRL Papers, NYPL.

Honeymoon trailer trip across country, overheated dachshunds, Rose in Dallas apartment: "Honeymoon in a Trailer Appeals to 'Gypsy Rose,'" *Lowell Sun*, November 23, 1937.

Rose in Highland Mills on Gypsy and Bob's trailer arrival: photo, *Life*, September 17, 1937.

Gypsy no longer in touch with friends who'd been there: letter, Rose Thompson to Gypsy Rose Lee, May 10, 1938, GRL Papers, NYPL.

A portrayer of unsympathetic characters: "Louise Hovick," *Los Angeles Times*, April 3, 1938.

Ten-page letter from caretaker: letter, Lester Smith to Gypsy Rose Lee, May 7, 1938, GRL Papers, NYPL.

Threatening to stop Rose's allowance: copy of letter or telegram, Gypsy Rose Lee to Rose Thompson, May 4, 1938, GRL Papers, NYPL.

Your friends are your friends: copy of undated letter, Gypsy Rose Lee to Rose Thompson, Rose Thompson correspondence, May 10–26, 1938, GRL Papers, NYPL.

Return my things, you receive your check: undated letter, Gypsy Rose Lee to Rose Thompson, Rose Thompson Correspondence, May 10–26, 1938, GRL Papers, NYPL.

Rose found dining room set in water-filled basement, Rose regretting the unhappiness caused Louise: letter, Rose Thompson to Gypsy Rose Lee, May 26, 1938, GRL Papers, NYPL.

Louise not wanting to repeat last year's scenes: undated copy of telegram text, Gypsy Rose Lee to Rose Thompson, Rose Thompson correspondence, May 10–26, 1938, GRL Papers, NYPL.

"Please forgive any unpleasantness; disappointed": letter, Rose Thompson to Gypsy Rose Lee, May 26, 1938, GRL Papers, NYPL.

Hitchhiking to Hollywood: undated letter, Rose Thompson to Gypsy Rose Lee, Rose Thompson correspondence, May 10–26, 1938, GRL Papers, NYPL.

CHAPTER 14

Gypsy worried about Rose: letter, Anna Thompson to Gypsy Rose Lee, September 3, 1938, GRL Papers, NYPL.

Days later, with a little help from fate: telegram, Anna Thompson to Gypsy Rose Lee, September 5, 1938, GRL Papers, NYPL.

Rose and Connie as Gypsy's caretakers: undated Letter, Rose Thompson to Gypsy Rose Lee, GRL Papers, NYPL.

Connie needs a home and friends: undated Letter, Rose Thompson to Gypsy Rose Lee, GRL Papers, NYPL.

Bob was a factor in Gypsy's estrangement from Rose: "Gypsy Rose Lee Weds Actor Alexander Kirkland," *Racine Journal-Times*, August 31, 1942.

Gypsy hides Hope Dare at Witchwood Manor: "Dixie Davis in Seclusion," *Citizen Advertiser*, Auburn, NY, July 30, 1939.

Dutch Schultz murdered: Gypsy Rose Lee, unpublished draft of *Gypsy*, GRL Papers, NYPL.

Rose served dinner, barricade the house: Gypsy Rose Lee, unpublished draft of *Gypsy*, GRL Papers, NYPL.

Tucson: letter, Rose Thompson to Gypsy Rose Lee, January 27, 1940, GRL Papers, NYPL.

Greenwich Avenue: letter, Rose Thompson to Gypsy Rose Lee, May 24, 1940, GRL Papers, NYPL.

Hudson Street: letter, Rose Thompson to Gypsy Rose Lee, October 23, 1940, GRL Papers, NYPL.

Disguise: Gypsy Rose Lee, unpublished draft of *Gypsy*, GRL Papers, NYPL.

For the rest of her life June would be proud, June in both acts: interview, June Havoc, *Broadway: The Golden Age, by the Legends Who Were There*, A Rick McKay Film, 2004.

June's photos in the paper: undated letter, Rose Thompson to Gypsy Rose Lee, GRL Papers, NYPL.

Both girls were dealing with Rose through lawyers: author's telephone interview with Tana Sibilio, June Havoc's assistant, January 19, 2009.

Belle appeals to Reginald Rankin for funds owed to Charlie: letter, Belle Thornton to Gypsy Rose Lee, May 20, 1941, GRL Papers, NYPL.

Norman Rankin seeking evidence to help his father: undated letter, Norman G. Rankin to "Dear Sir," from the collection of Theresa Rankin.

Reginald Rankin awaiting trial: "Appeal Argued in High Court," *Reno Evening Gazette*, February 18, 1941.

June checking with Gypsy on Rose's allowance: letter, June Havoc to Gypsy Rose Lee, GRL Papers, NYPL.

Tickets, beer joint, heels: undated letter, June Havoc to Gypsy Rose Lee, GRL Papers, NYPL.

Gypsy's *Harper's Bazaar* article on Christmas in Chicago: "Gypsy Rose Lee Feels at Home in Chicago Where She Spent Christmas 1924," *Harper's Bazaar*, December, 1941.

Guests at wedding: Noralee Frankel, *Stripping Gypsy*, Oxford University Press, 2009, 122.

Rose saying "We'll only be radiant for a minute": Leonard Lyons, "The Lyons Den," *Miami News*, September 7, 1942.

Christmas Eve letter: Rose Thompson to Gypsy Rose Lee, December 24, 1942, GRL Papers, NYPL.

Description of Ridge Road property: copy of unsigned letter to Miss Mary Maguire, April 26, 1944, GRL Papers, NYPL.

Wild Bill Donovan's niece: article in Gypsy's scrapbook, GRL Papers, NYPL.

Fight about communal property, family raising heel: telegram, Rose Thompson to Gypsy Rose Lee, January 3, 1942, GRL Papers, NYPL.

Mother Finds a Body: Walter Winchell, "On Broadway: New York Heart Beat," *St. Petersburg Times*, April 23, 1942.

Details of *Mother Finds a Body*: Gypsy Rose Lee, *Mother Finds a Body*, New York, Simon and Schuster, 1942.

Rose's positive reaction to *Mother Finds a Body*: undated letter, Rose Thompson to Gypsy Rose Lee, GRL Papers, NYPL.

Mike Todd wanting to cast Pola Negri in *Mother Finds a Body* movie: Hedda Hopper, "Hedda Hopper's Hollywood," *Berkeley Daily Gazette*, July 29, 1943.

Dead bodies letter, Mike Todd in contact with Rose, "Don't Quit" poem: letter, Rose Thompson to Gypsy Rose Lee, December 24, 1942, GRL Papers, NYPL.

Gypsy's first story in the *New Yorker*: "Mother and the Knights of Pythias," *New Yorker*, April 10, 1943.

CHAPTER 15

Court: "Gypsy Rose Lee Says She Takes care of Family," *Nevada State Journal*, May 13, 1943.

Court: "Daughters," *Time*, May 24, 1943.

Tax man/Queens house: Gypsy Rose Lee, *Gypsy*, 267.

Rose wanting to play character based on her in *The Naked Genius*, or be otherwise involved: undated letter, Rose Thompson to Gypsy Rose Lee, GRL Papers, NYPL.

Patricia Donovan felonious driving: "Cleared in Auto Accident," *New York Times*, February 9, 1944.

Confusion about insurance papers: telegram from Patricia Donovan to Anna Thompson, October 19, 1943, GRL Papers, NYPL.

Play Gypsy had worked on writing for a year and a half: letter from Gypsy Rose Lee to Rose Thompson, date unclear, possibly October 30, 1943, GRL Papers, NYPL.

Naked Genius synopsis: Noralee Frankel, *Stripping Gypsy*, 125.

Rose's lawyers sending threat letters to Gypsy, Michael Todd, F-R Publishing Company, the *New Yorker* publisher, and Twentieth Century-Fox Film Corporation: agreement dated November 27, 1943 between Louise Hovick and Rose Hovick, GRL Papers, NYPL.

Rose not signing agreement for two weeks: agreement dated November 27, 1943 between Louise Hovick and Rose Hovick, GRL Papers, NYPL.

Disbursement of the $33,000: letter from Rose E. Thompson to Mr. Reibeisen, 21 December 1943, GRL Papers, NYPL.

Rose faints at Patricia Donovan trial: "Faints," *Milwaukee Sentinel*, December 24, 1943.

Belle to visit, can't afford a coat: letter, Anna Thompson to Rose Thompson, January 13, 1944, GRL Papers, NYPL.

Letter from Anna about Rose's lifestyle: letter, Anna Thompson to Rose Thompson, February 10, 1944, GRL Papers, NYPL.

Letter from Anna suggesting Rose find a husband: January 13, 1944, Anna Thompson to Rose Thompson, GRL Papers, NYPL.

June's unflattering comments about Paddy: undated letter, June Havoc to Gypsy Rose Lee, GRL Papers, NYPL.

Pat exonerated: "Cleared in Auto Accident," *New York Times*, February 9, 1944.

Pat returned to New York apartment: undated note on calling card of Mrs. Frederico Guillerno Sanchez, GRL Papers, NYPL.

Rose taking June to family court: letter, Charles H. Finkelstein to Roney Thompson (Rose Thompson), April 1, 1944, GRL Papers, NYPL.

Letter to June about support of Rose: Charles Finkelstein to Miss June Hovick, c/o Miss Louise Hovick, April 1, 1944, GRL Papers, NYPL.

Don't use me as your tool, remember I am still your mother: letter, Rose Thompson to Gypsy Rose Lee, August 18, 1945, GRL Papers, NYPL.

Gypsy going to Hollywood, Rose alone in New York: letter, Anna Thompson to Rose Thompson and Belle Thornton, April 25, 1944, GRL Papers, NYPL.

Pat's Clothes, $100 IOU, diary and personal writings: letter, Charles H. Finkelstein to Roney (Rose Thompson), June 6, 1944, GRL Papers, NYPL.

Trouble between Rose, Belle, and Anna, wire and reply: letter, Belle Thornton to Rose Thompson, June 25, 1944, GRL Papers, NYPL.

Rose's arm still in a cast: letter, Rose Thompson to Gypsy Rose Lee, July 7, 1944, GRL Papers, NYPL.

CHAPTER 16

Rose possibly losing house: letter, Rose Thompson to Gypsy Rose Lee, July 23, 1944, GRL Papers, NYPL.

Rose on drinking bender: Rose Thompson's diary, September 15, 1944, GRL Papers, NYPL.

Rose's job, I love it Louise: letter, Rose Thompson to Gypsy Rose Lee, November 4, 1944, GRL Papers, NYPL.

Girls not having a home or schooling, the Jack Hovick blood: letter, Rose Thompson to June Havoc and Gypsy Rose Lee, GRL Papers, NYPL.

Louise claiming to attend school that didn't exist: "Gypsy and June—Mother's Girls: Hovick Sisters in Chips Now, Can Grin at Frantic Youth," Florabel Muir and Robert Sullivan, *New York Sunday News*, June 22, 1941.

General Neville tale: First Nighter, "Sophisticated Little Miss is Wee Actress, Baby June, And She Has Right to Be," *Wisconsin State Journal*, October 22, 1922.

Rose seeing baby through hospital window: Noralee Frankel, *Stripping Gypsy*, New York, Oxford University Press, 2009, 150.

Otto Preminger seeing Erik: Erik Lee Preminger, *Gypsy and Me*, Little, Brown, 1984, 258.

116 West 69th Street, New York, NY inherited by Felice Hull Bryant from Minnie Margaret Hillman: mortgage, NYC Assessor's Office, Block 1140, Lot 39-116 West 69th Street, Liber 4765, Page 463, filed September 6, 1945.

Another contretemps ensued, Rose's book: letter, Rose Thompson to Gypsy Rose Lee, August 23, 1945, GRL Papers, NYPL.

Framing the baby pictures: letter, Rose Thompson to Gypsy Rose Lee, September 1945, no exact date, Personal Correspondence-Family–Rose Thompson Correspondence, 1945, GRL Papers, NYPL.

Gypsy's checks not received by Belle and Anna: letter, Anna Thompson to Rose Thompson, February 8, 1946, GRL Papers, NYPL.

Plans for Anna to enter nursing home, Rose's plans for children's camp: letter, Belle Thornton to Rose Thompson, March 13, 1946, GRL Papers, NYPL.

Belle wanting to help Rose: letter, Belle Thornton to Rose Thompson, April 11, 1946, GRL Papers, NYPL.

Belle on special mission for her sister: letter, Belle Thornton to Rose Thompson, June 19, 1946, GRL Papers, NYPL.

Rose opened children's camp: letter, Belle Thornton to Rose Thompson, July 23, 1946, GRL Papers, NYPL.

Belle on verge of breakdown: letter, Anna Thompson to Rose Thompson, March 19, 1947, GRL Papers, NYPL.

Belle escorting sick person to Trenton: letter, Belle Thornton to Gypsy Rose Lee, GRL Papers, NYPL.

Pat Blom: letter, Belle Thornton to Gypsy Rose Lee, May 16, 1949, GRL Papers, NYPL.

The Chili Sisters: letter, Belle Thornton to Rose Thompson, October 15, 1948, GRL Papers, NYPL.

Rose buying Belle's clothes: letter, Belle Thornton to Rose Thompson, October 4, 1947, GRL Papers, NYPL.

Belle's letter asking to stay in Gypsy's house: letter, Belle Thornton to Gypsy Rose Lee, undated, Series I, Sub-series 1, Personal Correspondence-Family, Undated, Box 1, Folder 7, GRL Papers, NYPL.

Anna Thompson's tell-off letter to Rose: letter, Anna Thompson to Rose Thompson, May 20, 1947, GRL Papers, NYPL.

Four months until Rose contacted Belle and Anna, would send Anna money after sale of house: letter, Rose Thompson to Belle Thornton and Annie, August 18, 1947, GRL Papers, NYPL.

Belle sent rose bushes: letter, Belle Thornton to Rose Thompson, October 4, 1947, GRL Papers, NYPL.

June Havoc meets William Spier: Sam Irvin, *Kay Thompson from Funny Face to Eloise* New York, Simon & Schuster, 2010, 145.

Rose wrote June to forget the past, accident ailments: letter, Rose Thompson to Gypsy Rose Lee, January 17, 1948, GRL Papers, NYPL.

Gypsy marries Julio De Diego in Bronx civil ceremony and is recognized by fans: Noralee Frankel, *Stripping Gypsy*, 157.

Belle's letter to "Aunt Jennie" about Rose: letter, Belle to "Aunt Jennie," no full name, undated, Belle Thornton to Rose Thompson File, Series I, Subseries 1, Personal Correspondence-Family, Rose Thompson Correspondence, Letters from Belle Thornton, April 1948–March 1949 and Undated File, GRL Papers, NYPL.

June's passport fiasco: letter, June Havoc to Gypsy Rose Lee, April 25, 1949, Series I, Family Correspondence-Letters from June Havoc, 1941–53, Box 2, Folder 9.

Rose sick from asthma: letter, Rose Thompson to Gypsy Rose Lee, December 11, 1949, GRL Papers, NYPL.

Belle came to the bitter decision: letter, Belle Thornton to Rose Thompson, October 15, 1948, GRL Papers, NYPL.

Anna also "mourned" Rose: letter, Belle Thornton to Rose Thompson, October 15, 1948, GRL Papers, NYPL.

Anna praising Belle for her care: letter, Anna Thompson to Rose Thompson, January 13, [1944], GRL Papers, NYPL.

Concern about Louiga and dogs: letter, Belle Thornton to Rose Thompson, October 15, 1948, GRL Papers, NYPL.

Lending library, summer home: letter, Belle Thornton to Rose Thompson, October 18, 1948, GRL Papers, NYPL.

Opening gift shop: letter, Belle Thornton to Rose Thompson, November 12, 1948, GRL Papers, NYPL.

Showing up with nine animals: letter, Belle Thornton to Gypsy Rose Lee, May 16, 1949, GRL Papers, NYPL.

Details of Belle's three-room house: Office of the Secretary of State, Division of Archives and Records Management, Puget Sound Regional Branch, King County Assessor's Report on 4812 Rutan Place, Seattle.

Asthma treatment, stranded in Fontana, California: letter, Rose Thompson to Gypsy Rose Lee, December 11, 1949, GRL Papers, NYPL.

Rose's plans, Belle's fights with Pat, telescopes: letter, Belle Thornton to Rose Thompson, March 1, 1949, GRL Papers, NYPL.

Belle asks Gypsy for $750, description of Rose's visit: letter, Belle Thornton to Gypsy Rose Lee, May 16, 1949, GRL Papers, NYPL.

CHAPTER 17

Clam Digs and Copalis Beach scene: letter, Belle Thornton to Gypsy Rose Lee, June 2, 1949, Series I, Personal Correspondence–family, Box 1, Folder 5, GRL Papers, NYPL.

Betty Thornton Souvenirs, Copalis Beach, Washington, Buying shells and glass floats: email from Kelly Calhoun, Moclips. Washington, to the author mentioning information from Eileen Thompson Owens, June 9, 2011.

Lucille Ball scarf: Eileen Owens, email to the author, June 16, 2011.

Red Channels publication, Gypsy fired from two quiz show jobs: Noralee Frankel, Stripping Gypsy, 167–69.

Two daughters living in mansions, I wonder if you really are a Communist Louise?: letter, Rose Thompson to Gypsy Rose Lee, October 28, 1950, GRL Papers, NYPL.

Rose in Good Samaritan Hospital, cancer of the rectum, lesbian calling the *Daily Mirror*, Gypsy asking June to contribute money: letter, Gypsy Rose Lee to June Havoc, Undated, Series I, Sub-series 1, Family Correspondence, Letters from June Havoc— Undated, GRL Papers, NYPL.

Rose's friend calls Belle and Anna while drunk, asked Belle to visit New York, Rose's plans to put neglect stories in paper: letter, Belle Thornton to Gypsy Rose Lee, April 16, 1951, GRL Papers, NYPL.

No record exists of June's trip to Paris: author's search of Ancestry.com Immigration and Emigration Records for 1951 revealed nothing under June Havoc or Ellen June Spier.

Belle told Rose to "for god's sake take it on the chin": letter, Belle Thornton to Gypsy Rose Lee, April 16, 1951, GRL Papers, NYLP.

"This unfortunate maniac who is holding fort at my home": letter, Rose's nurse at Good Samaritan Hospital in Suffern, NY, to Gypsy, April 25, 1951, GRL Papers, NYPL.

Gypsy's offer to send Rose to convalescent home: letter, Gypsy to Rose, May 11, 1951, GRL Papers, NYPL.

Gypsy had no birth certificate: letter, Gypsy to Big Lady Anna Thompson, May 24, 1951, GRL Papers, NYPL.

Big Lady's affidavit of Gypsy's birth: letter, Gypsy to Big Lady Anna Thompson, June 6, 1951, GRL Papers, NYPL.

Rose's second mortgage, staying at Belvedere Hotel, June visiting and increasing allowance: letter, June Havoc to Gypsy Rose Lee, November 24, 1951, GRL Papers, NYPL.

June getting Rose theater tickets and glasses, "next stop Mars": letter, June Havoc to Gypsy Rose Lee, February 7, 1952, GRL Papers, NYPL.

Medical items requested for a kickback: June Havoc, *More Havoc*, 1–2.

Rose at the Holland Hotel, Pencil shaking from pain: undated letter, Rose Thompson to Gypsy Rose Lee, Series I, Sub-series 1, Personal Correspondence-Family, Rose Thompson Correspondence, Undated, GRL Papers, NYPL.

Rent house to a gentleman, first option to buy: lease, 1 April 1952, Rose E. Thompson, Landlord, and Frederick P. Dyckman, Tenant, GRL Papers, NYPL.

Rose wants to sell house and travel: undated letter, Rose to Anna Thompson and Belle Thornton, Series I, Sub-series 1, Personal Correspondence-Family, Rose Thompson Correspondence, GRL Papers, NYPL.

CHAPTER 18

Recollections of Polhemus family's involvement with Rose, Rose's daughters' absence made her life hell: author's interview, Judy Polhemus Leiner, December 26, 2009.

"Intelligent, lucid and loving": author's telephone interview, Judy Polhemus Leiner, May 20, 2009.

Evelyn and Larry Krakower's experiences with Rose: author's telephone interview, Evelyn Krakower, November 25, 2012.

Camp inspection, license, Mrs. Charles Hunter as camp counselor, Rose as director, the privy: letter, State of NY Dept. of Health to Mrs. Rose E. Hovick, June 16, 1953, GRL Papers, NYPL.

$19 a week: letter, Leon Appel to Rose Thompson, July 16, 1953, GRL Papers, NYPL.

Rose critically ill, *New Yorker* pieces: Dorothy Kilgallen, "On Broadway," *Pittsburgh Post-Gazette*, September 23, 1953.

Anna staying with Mrs. Helen Tallman: letter, Anna Thompson to Rose Thompson, written for Anna by Mrs. Tallman, January 28, 1953, GRL Papers, NYPL.

Belle and Rose's plot: as evidenced by the last will and testament of Rose E. Hovick, 6 October 1953.

Anna hoping Rose could come to Seattle in summer: letter, Anna Thompson to Rose Thompson and Belle Thornton, October 16, 1953, GRL Papers, NYPL.

Swapping houses: unsigned agreement, November 1953, Box 2, Folder 7, Series I, Family Correspondence, Rose Thompson Correspondence-Legal & Financial Papers, 1953–1954, GRL Papers, NYPL.

Gypsy arranged for Under Elms Nursing Home: Gypsy's appointment calendar, November 8, 1953, GRL Papers, NYPL.

Rose moved to hospital for 2 1/2 hour surgery: Gypsy's appointment calendar, November 13, 1953, GRL Papers, NYPL.

Rose on a rampage: Gypsy's appointment calendar, November 21, 1953, GRL Papers, NYPL.

Rose adored by medical staff during previous hospitalizations: undated letter, Gypsy Rose Lee to Rose Thompson, Series I, Personal Correspondence, Rose Thompson Correspondence-Undated, Box 1, Folder 14, GRL Papers, NYPL.

Rose's friend takes her back to Valley Cottage: Gypsy's appointment calendar, November 23, 1953, GRL Papers, NYPL.

Refereed a call from Seattle: Gypsy's appointment calendar, November 24, 1953, GRL Papers, NYPL.

Larry Krakower's recollections of Rose getting robbed more than once: author's telephone interview, Larry Krakower, November 25, 2012.

Grand larceny charges against Lucille Campbell and Soroka: obituary of Rose Thompson, *Rockland Country Journal News*, 1954, collection of James Leiner.

Larry Krakower gets Rose Chinese food: author telephone interview, Evelyn Krakower, November 25, 2012.

Rose's erratic nurse: Gypsy's appointment calendar, November 29, 1953, GRL Papers, NYPL.

Deathbed Curse: June Havoc, *More Havoc*, 275–76.

Erik not hearing about the deathbed curse: email to the author from Erik Lee Preminger, December 3, 2010.

Funeral: Gypsy's appointment calendar, February 1, 1954, GRL Papers, NYPL.

Intriguing deed swap document: copy of an unsigned agreement, November 1953, Series I, Family Correspondence-Rose Thompson-Correspondence, Legal & Financial Papers, 1953–1954, Box 2, Folder 7, GRL Papers, NYPL.

CHAPTER 19

Both sisters writing books, Gypsy not sticking to the truth: "The Lyons Den" column by Leonard Lyons, *Reading Eagle*, November 27, 1956.

First audience for Gypsy's book was Erik: Erik Lee Preminger, "Afterword," Gypsy Rose Lee, *Gypsy: A Memoir*, (Orig. pub. 1957), Frog, Ltd. Ed., Berkeley, 1986, 347.

Four offers: Erik Preminger, *Gypsy & Me*, 41.

Merrick reminded Gypsy of Mike Todd: Erik Preminger, *Gypsy & Me*, 42.

Eleven, Arthur Laurents proclaimed this would have made the character of Rose beyond horror: Stephen Citron, *Sondheim and Lloyd-Webber*, Chatto & Windsor, London, 2001, 89.

June claimed she didn't do anything to stop the show *Gypsy*: Alvin Klein, "Theater; Charting Personal Territory With June Havoc," *New York Times*, August 30, 1998.

Mina's death, false overdose story: June Havoc, *Early Havoc*, 24–25.

Charlie's death, false neighbor woman story: June Havoc, *Early Havoc*, 182–83.

"Mother's number too vulgar": Gypsy Rose Lee's datebook, Saturday, March 21, 1959, GRL Papers, NYPL.

"Ethel Merman Reaffirms Her Right to Musical Throne": Dorothy Kilgallen, *Daily Reporter*, Dover, Ohio, May 28, 1959.

King Lear of Musicals: Laurents, "In Gypsy, a Rose is a Role is a Killer," *New York Times*, May 13, 1990.

INDEX